The TIMELINE HISTORY *of* ISLAM

The **TIMELINE**
HISTORY *of* **ISLAM**

JUSTIN WINTLE

Series Editor Justin Wintle

BARNES
& NOBLE

NEW YORK

Acknowledgements

Inevitably—and rightly—a book of this sort is a team effort, and the author would like to express his personal indebtedness to, among the many who have assisted in its preparation: Jonathan Buckley, Andy Dickson, Sharon Martins, Matthew Milton, Katie Pringle, Ed Wright, Richard Trillo, Claire Southern and Demelza Dallow. The author would also like to thank his agent, Clare Alexander at Gillon Aitken Associates.

Copyright © 2003, 2005 by Justin Wintle

This edition published by Barnes & Noble Publishing, Inc.

ISBN 0-7607-7977-5

Printed in Thailand

CONTENTS

INTRODUCTION

"ISLAM" IS AN ARABIC WORD MEANING "SUBMISSION" in English, which describes a religious and sociopolitical system founded by the "Prophet" Muhammad in **Arabia** at the beginning of the 7th century. Following Muhammad's death in 632, Islam spread into the Middle East, and then further afield: into central, southern and eastern Asia; into Africa; and into southeastern Europe. Today, Islam has approximately one billion followers—one sixth of the world's population.

In the fourteen hundred years since its inception, Islam has manifested itself as a continuous and continuously evolving civilization that has at times outshone other civilizations—as, for instance, at the glittering court of Suleiman the Magnificent, sultan of the powerful Turkish-Ottoman empire in the 16th century, whom half of Asia and all of Europe held in awe. Earlier, during the 10th and 11th centuries, Islamic scholars did much to preserve the learning of the ancient Greeks, to the benefit of all mankind. In the same period, significant advances in medical science took place within Islam, while throughout its history Islam has promoted an architecture that in its rich diversity is one of the glories of human ingenuity.

In the **Koran**, a scriptural text definitively assembled after Muhammad's death, he claimed that a comprehensive series of truths emanating from God—**Allah**—had been revealed to him through the intermediary of the archangel Gabriel. Yet the monotheistic core of the Koran, that there is one God and one God only, was already well established. Both Judaism and Christianity, which had penetrated Arabia, espoused the same philosophy, and long stretches of the Koran are absorbed with measuring Judaic and Christian history and thought against the "message" proclaimed by Muhammad, who, in common with many other Arabs of his time, acknowledged **Abraham** (Ibrahim) as a founding patriarch.

It is sometimes said that Islam has never undergone, or been prepared to undergo, "reformation." This, though, is simply untrue. In its very nature Islam was and remains quintessentially reformist, sometimes being characterized as a "reformed Judaism," as well as (less convincingly) a rehash of **Arianism**, a Christian "heresy" that insists on the separateness and inferiority of Christ to God. More generally, the Islamic faith strongly emphasizes the concept of renewal, both of the individual and of society, and Islam itself was launched as a political as well as doctrinal revolution.

Muhammad contended that the people of Arabia, a barren, tribal and largely nomadic territory on the fringes of the then "civilized" world, were overdue a "revelation" of their own. But the revelation he provided explicitly superseded existing monotheistic revelations, whether Judaic or Christian, giving rise to a supremacist attitude that rapidly translated into conquest and dominion. For not only was Muhammad the outstanding articulator of Arab culture, he was also a warrior politician, and his example inspired others to spread Islam by the sword.

In Muhammad's wake, the Arabs broke out of Arabia, creating with surprising rapidity an empire that stretched from **Spain** in the west to **Afghanistan** in the east, overrunning the ancient **Persian empire**, a large part of the **Roman Byzantine** empire, and the coastline of **North Africa** in the process. The impetus behind Arab expansionism was the revolutionary dynamism of the Islamic faith: although for a century at least the conversion of others seems not to have been a priority among Arab conquerors, the great majority of those overrun were eventually persuaded or cajoled into becoming Muslims. And in the longer term, Islam spread its tentacles still further: down the eastern coast and other parts of **Africa**; way into **Central Asia** and the **Indian subcontinent**; into pockets of **China**; and into **Southeast**

Asia. Most famously, **Constantinople**, the hub of the Byzantine empire, was seized by Muslim forces in 1453, sealing the fate of Christianity east of the Hellespont. But as Islam spread, it lost much of its Arab character. By the mid-16th century, three discrete Muslim empires existed, none of them Arabic: the Turkish **Ottoman** empire, the Persian **Safavid** empire and the **Mughal** empire in India.

Since then, Islam has sought to come to terms with its fragmentation and diversity. On the one hand, it enshrines the cardinal belief in an Islamic *umma*, or cohesive transnational community, promoted by Muhammad himself. On the other is the bald fact that as Islam has expanded, so it has been affected by contact with different cultures— never more obviously, perhaps, than with the emergence of **Sufism**, the "mystical wing" of Islam, partly shaped by the ideas and practices of older kinds of mysticism in Persia and India. From early in its history, Islam was also riven by internal dissent, part political and part doctrinal, which during the course of the 8th and 9th centuries produced an enduring split between "majority" **Sunni** Muslims and "minority" **Shiite** Muslims—a division that has frequently been the cause of bloodshed.

Furthermore, Islam has had to contend with external enmity. The medieval Christian **crusades** are notorious for a brutality that matched the Arab conquests. But still greater damage was inflicted by the 13th century **Mongol invasions**, and from the 17th century onwards Islam was pressed by European imperial expansion. By 1914, virtually the whole of Islam was subject to non-Islamic influence in one way or another. This influence was predicated on European military and industrial might, and has since been sustained by the West's thirst for **oil**, which by the accidents of geography—Muslims would say by the dispensation of Allah—is concentrated in Islam's Middle Eastern heartlands. Since 1914, access to Middle Eastern oil reserves has been a determining factor in the strategic policy of Europe and the United States, often to the detriment of Islamic interests.

More recently, however, Islam has demonstrated resilience. The story of Islam in modern times has been one of resurgence—a reassertion of Islamic values coupled with a determination among some Muslim leaders to eliminate what are perceived as outsiders' colonial pretensions. The gauntlet was most dramatically thrown down during the Iranian **Islamic Revolution** of 1979, led by **Ayatollah Khomeini**. Although Khomeini was a Shiite, and therefore an advocate of Islam's minority way, his actions—and his strident anti-American rhetoric—provided an example for Sunni Muslims as well, including his arch-rival **Saddam Hussein**, hailed as the "new Saladin" during the Gulf War that followed his seizure of Kuwait in 1991. While Hussein's assault on Kuwait was launched to increase Iraq's share of global oil production, and therefore had little to do with Islam per se, once confronted by an American-led military coalition he swiftly adopted the persona of a defender of the faith.

Yet Hussein was, and remains, the leader of the "secular" Baath Party in Iraq, and is therefore distanced from the "**fundamentalist**" or "**Islamist**" movement that has steadily gathered momentum since the creation of the **Muslim Brotherhood** in Egypt in 1928—a movement which, through its insistence on preserving and promoting Islamic values, and on combating Western influence, has created the conditions in which some extremists have turned to international terrorism as a means of gaining their ends.

Among extremists, the figure of **Osama bin Laden** looms large—the man deemed most responsible for the devastating destruction of the twin towers of the World Trade Center in New York, and part of the Pentagon in Washington, on 11 September 2001, through the use of four civilian aircraft hijacked by a suicide squad of Muslim militants. The attack on New York, which resulted in the deaths of approximately 3000 civilians, brought home to many outside Islam the depth of ill-feeling towards the United States. Its immediate consequence, however,

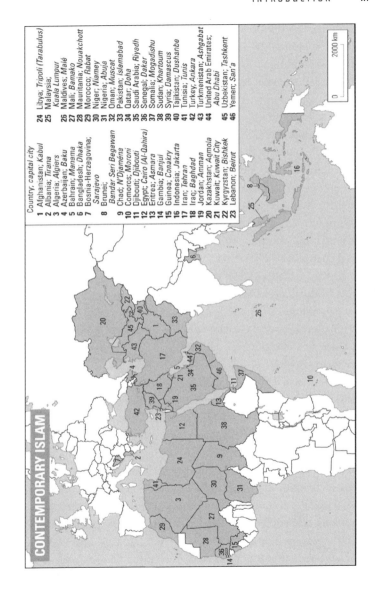

CONTEMPORARY ISLAM

Country; capital city
1 Afghanistan; Kabul
2 Albania; Tirana
3 Algeria; Algiers
4 Azerbaijan; Baku
5 Bahrain; Manama
6 Bangladesh; Dhaka
7 Bosnia-Herzegovina; Sarajevo
8 Brunei; Bandar Seri Begawan
9 Chad; N'Djaména
10 Comoros; Moroni
11 Djibouti; Djibouti
12 Egypt; Cairo (Al-Qahira)
13 Eritrea; Asmara
14 Gambia; Banjul
15 Guinea; Conakry
16 Indonesia; Jakarta
17 Iran; Tehran
18 Iraq; Baghdad
19 Jordan; Amman
20 Kazakstan; Aqmola
21 Kuwait; Kuwait City
22 Kyrgyzstan; Bishkek
23 Lebanon; Beirut

24 Libya; Tripoli (Tarabulus)
25 Malaysia; Kuala Lumpur
26 Maldives; Malé
27 Mali; Bamako
28 Mauritania; Nouakchott
29 Morocco; Rabat
30 Niger; Niamey
31 Nigeria; Abuja
32 Oman; Muscat
33 Pakistan; Islamabad
34 Qatar; Doha
35 Saudi Arabia; Riyadh
36 Senegal; Dakar
37 Somalia; Mogadishu
38 Sudan; Khartoum
39 Syria; Damascus
40 Tajikistan; Dushanbe
41 Tunisia; Tunis
42 Turkey; Ankara
43 Turkmenistan; Ashgabat
44 United Arab Emirates; Abu Dhabi
45 Uzbekistan; Tashkent
46 Yemen; San'a

2000 km

was the declaration of a "war against terrorism" by President George W. Bush, supported by a coalition of other leaders, including some in the Islamic world, and the launch of a military campaign in Afghanistan to capture Bin Laden and members of his **al-Qaeda** "terrorist network," as well as to overthrow their hosts there, the **Taliban** regime. Yet although Bush succeeded in putting the Taliban to flight, Bin Laden has eluded him.

In 2003 another US-led coalition invaded Iraq to remove Saddam Hussein, though this time President George W. Bush acted without the comfort of the international community's undivided approval. Inside Islam the response to these events has been mixed. While many Muslims criticized what Bin Laden had done, a minority openly applauded his actions, while others remained tight-lipped. Many feared that a backlash would inflict far more damage on Islam than Bin Laden had inflicted on America—the more so since Russia and China, both facing Islamic insurgency in their own territories, initially had no interest in opposing US policy. But that Muslims were neither unanimous nor especially vocal in condemning Bin Laden after 9/11 was in some measure due to America's continuing support for the state of Israel.

Yet Muslim feelings about Bin Laden are also divided in a manner than transcends any immediate territorial, racial or religious dispute, and which goes to the core of Islam's identity. Prior to "9/11," as it was rapidly dubbed, Bin Laden had already proclaimed a *jihad*—"holy struggle"—against not just Islam's "foreign oppressors" but also the House of Saud, the present-day and, in Bin Laden's view, irredeemably corrupt rulers of **Arabia**, the Islamic Holy Land. In this there is little that is new: while the Koran itself urges qualified tolerance toward Jews and Christians, as "Peoples of the Book," it makes no bones about the legitimacy of waging war against "hypocrites" as well as "infidels." Indeed, such warfare is urged as the sacred duty of the Muslim male, and the history of Islam provides many examples of individuals and radical groups, often spawned on its peripheries, who have sought through violent means the restoration of a pristine Muslim *umma* at the expense of fellow Muslims—*jihad* waged as a means of reforming self-correction.

With regard to Muslim extremists, it is sometimes difficult, if not impossible, to cleanly separate "mainstream" Islam—the faith as practiced by a majority of its followers—from its more volatile manifestations. One reason for this is precisely the abiding sense of an Islamic *umma*, a single community committed to defending all its fellow members whatever the circumstances. Another is that, within Islam, lines of authority are blurred. A majority of Muslim nations have relatively centralized, secularized, governments, but these share authority with a vast body of clerics who, beholden to no common religious leader other than Muhammad, are as likely to preach *jihad* as urge restraint.

In its ideal form, Islam is a pure **theocracy** in which religious and political authority are literally indistinguishable. In the decades that followed Muhammad's death, Islam was ruled by a caliph who, together with a council of advisers, combined supreme religious and political authority—as indeed Muhammad himself had done. But as Islam expanded territorially, the synthesis crumbled. New provinces and new populations required temporal administrations and amirs to run them, yet no overarching ecclesiastical structure evolved.

Today, religious authority has become diffused among the *ulama*, or clerical scholars, and the imams, each with his own mosque and appointed by the community he serves. As a result, in so far as Islam retains a theocratic character, it does so in a bottom-up rather than top-down way. Muslims may have become reluctantly reconciled to the necessity of temporal power-holders, but the key to Islam's future may still rest in the hands of tens of thousands of clerics delivering potentially idiosyncratic commentaries on current world events from tens of thousands of pulpits during Friday prayers.

AUTHOR'S NOTE

To the Muslim believer, Islam offers an incontestable divine truth and a template for how all human beings should aspire to live—both individually and socially. To the secular historian, however, Islam is but one among many faiths and ideologies that have shaped today's world. The present book has been compiled from the viewpoint of just such a commentator—something that should be acknowledged upfront, in the interests of what the philosopher Bertrand Russell called a writer's "professional ethics."

The core terminology of Islam is Arabic, but there exists no universal system for transliterating Arabic words into the Roman alphabet. Very broadly, I have opted to use the simplest English equivalents, while providing common alternatives in parentheses. I have also opted to retain, on the grounds of familiarity, some transliterations that have gone out of fashion in academic circles: the most obvious example is the retention of "Koran" as opposed to "Quran." (Where I have quoted from the Koran, I have used N.J. Dawood's Penguin Classics translation.) Matters become somewhat more complex when dealing with other Muslim languages—for example Persian, Turkish and Urdu, each of which have absorbed Arabic vocabularies. As a result, a word like "sheikh" sometimes appears as "shaykh." Such apparent inconsistencies are part and parcel of Islamic diversity.

It needs also to be said that I am acutely aware that the history of Islam involves the histories of many different nations and peoples, each of which demands its own detailed appraisal. Here, I have only attempted to provide a framework in which such narratives run parallel. In certain cases—India and Egypt, for instance—companion *Timeline Histories* already exist.

CHAPTER ONE

Muhammad

{570–632 (UP TO 10 AH)}

ISLAM WAS FOUNDED FOURTEEN CENTURIES AGO in Arabia by **Muhammad ibn Abdallah**—a man of exceptional talents and, doubtless, presence. Although Muhammad asserted that he was the bearer of a divine message fit for all mankind, historically he belonged to a specific time and a specific place—coordinates that are fully reflected both in the **Koran**, the primary scripture of the Islamic faith, and in the crucial early development of the Islamic community (**_umma_**). Equally, the heroic stature of Muhammad himself forms an integral strand in Islamic ideology. Strictly speaking, if the doctrines and tenets of Islam are true, then Muhammad, as their involuntary cipher, is almost incidental. Yet Islam is, and always has been, dominated by his colossal, yet curiously elusive figure.

Arabia in the early 7th century was an uninviting land that no great empire had succeeded in fully conquering, although the Romans had claimed a colony in its western parts. The southwestern corner excepted, it was mostly arid. The northern half, known as the **Najd**, was an upland stony wilderness, while the southern half, known as the "**empty quarter**," was an unrelieved desert of sand. Only in mountainous **Yemen**, known to the Romans as **Arabia Felix** (literally "Arabia the happy," meaning "bountiful"), were conditions sufficient to produce an agricultural surplus—the basic requirement for creating cities and the semblance of a state. But everything else was **Arabia Deserta**, interspersed with odd pockets of settlement on its long coast or centered on wells and oases.

Strategically, Arabia's situation was more promising. To its west, across the **Red Sea**, was Africa, the rich Byzantine province of **Egypt** and the relatively fertile kingdom of **Abyssinia**. To its east was the **Persian Gulf**, since ancient times an important waterway connecting the Middle East to the Indian subcontinent and beyond. To the north-east of Arabia lay **Iraq** and the **Fertile Crescent**, the heartlands of the Sassanian Persian empire, while more directly north was the Byzantine province of **Syria**, whose well-developed Mediterranean coastline included present-day Lebanon and Palestine.

Yemen apart, "civilization" had never really taken off in Arabia—there were, for example, no great cities or temple complexes, and the earliest examples of Arabic writing, based on an earlier **Semitic script**, date only from the 4th century. Around Arabia's oases and mountain enclaves were ancient irrigation works, but these could hardly compare with those that tentacled out from the Nile, the Euphrates or the Tigris. Such advancement as there was came mainly from outside: goods, technologies and ideas introduced either by adventurous traders, or by military expeditions from Arabia's more affluent, developed neighbors.

At the time of Muhammad's birth, a majority of Arabs—Arabia's indigenous Semitic inhabitants—were **settled**, living in mainly small communities in the few places that offered a dependable water supply. But a large number of Arabs still subsisted as **pastoral nomads**, grazing their camels, goats and sheep wherever scant vegetation might be found. There was also a third constituency, the **semi-nomads**—people who had animals to graze, but who were also small-time agriculturists, cloth-iers, artisans and merchants.

Binding these different social groups together were the tribes, and a fierce sense of tribal allegiance. Typically, larger tribes had both members who were nomads and members who were settled. When nomads brought their animals and animal products to market at set times during the year, they stayed with their kinsmen in the dwellings that surrounded the watered marketplaces. Likewise, when settled Arabs needed armed escorts to protect their merchant caravans setting off for distant destinations, they turned to their desert cousins.

The tribes were fluid in their composition: if a tribe grew, it subdivided into clans, which might, in time, grow into tribes in their own right. If it failed to grow, it might have to seek the protection of a more successful tribe or risk perishing altogether. Tribes were also highly competitive, sometimes aggressive—forced to fight over the meager resources offered by Arabia's harsh, unforgiving landscape. To the Roman Byzantines and Persians, the dominant powers of the day, Arabia was "barbarian"—a place of pagan beliefs and pagan superstitions, too tribally fragmented to offer a threat to the status quo. Yet desert life had honed a race of formidable warriors, whose military power would redraw the political map of the entire Middle East.

The opportunity to do just that came in the 7th century. The Persian and Roman Byzantine empires had alike suffered from their constant wars against each other, and their influence in the region was beginning to look uncertain. But without Muhammad's **Islamic revolution**—which welded the fractious tribes of Arabia into a single, outward-looking whole—it is unlikely that much would have changed. By any standards, Muhammad was a revolutionary. Born in **Mecca**—the one city in later 6th-century Arabia that could boast a degree of prosperity because of the disruption caused to traditional trading routes by the Persian-Byzantine wars—a great deal of his puritan polemic contrasted the moral desuetude of his fellow urbanites with the traditional tribal virtues. Mecca, he stated, was a place of idol-worship, usury, alcoholism, prostitution and self-satisfaction. But in pressing for a unified Islamic society, he conceived of a system which would transcend tribalism itself.

Such a reformed society needed an ideology, and this was provided by a series of **revelations** Muhammad claimed to have received from **Allah** (God) through the archangel Gabriel, eventually collected together as the Koran. For Muslims, it is an article of faith that the

Koran is indeed a divine message. While non-Muslims may reach for other kinds of explanation, what is beyond dispute is the strong connection between the Koran and both **Judaism** and **Christianity**. Moses, Christ and other Judeo-Christian "prophets" are mentioned throughout the Koran, and the distantly commanding figure of **Abraham** (Ibrahim), whom many Arabs shared with the Jews as a founding patriarch, also appears. This seems to demonstrate that the Koran embodied a revised understanding of **monotheism**, already established as a religious currency in Arabia. But by providing a radical reworking of whatever monotheistic ideas were in circulation, Muhammad became not just the orchestrator of a revolution, but its ordained agent.

There is no evidence to suggest that Muhammad thought of himself as anything other than what he claimed to be: the bearer of a universally valid message emanating from an actual, living and exclusive deity. For the non-Muslim historian, though, there are numerous problems of validation, quite apart from the "authenticity" of the Koranic revelation. No contemporaneous mention of Muhammad is made in sources outside of Arabia, for instance, and the "closest" sources we do have for his life and mission are invariably Islamic. The most important of those sources, other than a handful of biographical details embedded in the Koran itself, are the *Hadith*, or "**traditions**" of the Prophet and his Companions. But these were first transmitted orally, not being written down until several generations after Muhammad's death, leading some to question their reliability—and it is in any case improbable that the *Hadith* as a whole would not have idealized their subject matter.

That said, it is beyond doubt that a revolutionary upheaval, essentially religious in character, occurred in Arabia in the early 7th century. The narrative that immediately follows is, necessarily, mainly an **Islamic narrative**—appropriately enough, perhaps, in the sense that it rapidly became the bedrock of the expanding Islamic faith and empire.

c.570 During a war between the Roman Byzantine and Sassanian Persian empires that has lasted since 527, the Persians succeed in expelling a Byzantine presence from **Yemen**. Byzantine and Persian political influence is also felt along the northern boundaries of Arabia.

The country's interior is inhabited and controlled by nomadic, semi-nomadic and settled **Arabs**, whose primary political allegiances are tribal. There are few cities or towns in Arabia at this period, but the most prosperous of them is **Mecca**, dominated by the Quraysh (Koresh) tribe, and it is here that Muhammad ibn Abdallah is born c.570. Muhammad's father **Abdallah**, a trader, belongs to a clan called the **Banu Hashim**, or Hashimites, a branch of the powerful Quraysh—a noble family who are described as having seen better days. Abdallah's name, which means "Servant of God," suggests that **monotheism** may have taken root among the Quaraysh.

Around the time of Muhammad's birth his father dies, and for the first few years of his life the boy is raised by his mother, **Aminah**.

c.575 When Muhammad's mother Aminah dies he is taken into the care of his grandfather **Abd al-Muttalib**, a prominent figure among Mecca's Qurayshi mercantile aristocracy. At an unknown date Abd al-Muttalib also dies, and Muhammad is taken in by a paternal uncle, **Abu Talib**, also a member of Mecca's ruling oligarchy. His senior paternal uncle, **al-Abbas**, apparently declines responsibility, but nonetheless stands at the head of a lineage that, as the **Abbasids**, will one day rule Islam as its second dynastic caliphate. Prior to the Abbasids, Islam will be ruled by the **Umayyads**, descended from another more distant relative: Muhammad's great grand-uncle **Abd Shams**, again on his father's side.

Under Abu Talib's tutelage, Muhammad spends his youth learning about trade, how to graze animals and how to fight. It is also likely—though it is not recorded—that he spends some of his time acquiring a knowledge of **Jewish history** from Mecca's small Jewish community. As a younger member of Mecca's elite he is also exposed to vigorous debates between the city's elders, and to recitations of Arabic poetry. It is likely that at an early age he takes part in *razzias*, raiding parties sent against hostile tribes. According to tradition, he gains a reputation for trustworthiness; also according to tradition, he develops an early antipathy toward idols and idol-worship, for which Mecca, the site of the Kabah, is renowned.

c.580 The Quraysh of Mecca begin a **five-year war** with the Hawazin to protect their control of trade in Yemeni perfumes. Across the northern boundaries of Arabia there is fierce fighting between two

ARABIA AT THE TIME OF MUHAMMAD

tribes of Arab descent: the **Ghassanis**, Christianized clients of the Byzantines, and the **Lakhmids**, clients of the Persians.

In the south, a great dam at **Marib** collapses, hastening the decline of kingdoms in South Arabia.

589 Amid continuing hostilities between the Byzantine and Sassanian Persian empires to the north of the Arabian peninsula, **Chosroes II** (Khusraw II, or Khusru Parviz) accedes to the Persian throne. During his 39-year reign the Sassanian regime reaches its apogee, but then falls into steep and sudden decline.

c.595 Muhammad takes his first wife, **Khadijah**, a wealthy widow whose business interests he has been managing. Although Khadijah is some fifteen years older than Muhammad, according to tradition the couple are devoted to each other, and Muhammad takes no other wives while she is alive. Muhammad has **six children** by Khadijah: two sons, who die in infancy, and four daughters: **Zaynab**, **Ruqqayah**, **Fatima** and **Kulthum**. Only Fatima—married to Muhammad's cousin Ali ibn Abu Talib—will provide Muhammad with grandchildren, the two boys **al-Hasan** and **al-Husayn**. No other future wife will bear Muhammad's children, although Maryah, a Coptic slave girl in his service, will give birth to a son.

608 In Mecca, the **Kabah is rebuilt** using stone and wood. According to tradition Muhammad resolves a dispute about who will have the privilege of reinstalling the Black Stone by setting it in place himself.

The Sassanian Persians invade the Byzantine provinces of **Syria** and **Mesopotamia** from their strongholds in Iraq.

610 Aged around 40, Muhammad experiences—or claims to experience—the sudden presence of the Archangel Gabriel (Jibreel) on **Mount Hira** outside Mecca during the eighteenth night of Ramadan, an Arab month traditionally set aside for fasting. During this **first visitation**, which occurs in a cave Muhammad has often used as a place of meditation, Gabriel delivers to Muhammad the first of 114 *suras* (chapters), subsequently collected together to form the

MECCA

*M*ecca's origins are obscure, but by 570 it had existed as a trading center for at least a thousand years. Sited forty miles from the Red Sea on a dry riverbed known as the Wadi Ibrahim and surrounded by mountains, its site was advantageous, roughly halfway up the main West Arabian trade route at a point where other trans-Arabian routes converged. It was famed for its production of myrrh and frankincense, used for religious and cosmetic purposes throughout the eastern Mediterranean and beyond, and was also a market town, a place where surrounding nomads could sell or barter their livestock products. By the 2nd century it was known to the Greek geographer Ptolemy as Macorabi, and at the time of Muhammad's birth had emerged as Arabia's richest city, governed by a council of tribal elders known as the *qusayy*, in turn dominated by chieftains of the Quraysh tribe and its various clans.

The city's prosperity and prominence were reliant on two particular circumstances. First, the seemingly endless wars between the Byzantine and Persian empires had disrupted traditional overland trade routes between the Persian Gulf and the Mediterranean, a main conduit for goods originating in India, China and elsewhere in the East. As a consequence—greatly to Mecca's advantage—the same goods tended to be shipped instead to Yemen, the southern terminus of the West Arabian route. Second, Mecca was home to the Kabah, the most venerated of all the shrines in Arabia. Crucially, the Kabah was surrounded by a *haram*, a traditional Arab sanctuary inside whose precincts tribal feuding or any other kind of violence was forbidden. Because the Kabah occupied the center of Mecca, Mecca itself gained a reputation as an unusually safe place to do business, adding further to the city's attraction, and perhaps providing the basis of the Islamic concept of a unified community (*umma*), in which tribal differences are laid aside.

Koran (*Quran*), an Arabic word meaning "recitation(s)." In this first encounter the angel announces himself with the words: "You are God's messenger, and I am Gabriel," before delivering the first *sura* (chapter 96 in the Koran), beginning with the words "Recite in the name of your Lord who created—created man from clots of blood. Recite! Your Lord is the Most Beautiful One, who by the pen taught man what he did not know." As Muhammad is illiterate, he commits what he hears to memory, only later to be set down on parchment by scribes. According to tradition, Muhammad is asleep during the first visitation, and remembers it as a vision when he awakes. At once, as the first paragraphs of the new scripture pour involuntarily from his mouth, he is seized with fear and trembling, but is persuaded by his wife Khadija that he has indeed been singled out as the messenger of Allah (God). For two years, however, as the visitations continue, Muhammad keeps the experiences to himself, confiding only in Khadija, her Christian cousin **Waraqa ibn Nawfal**, and perhaps one or two other close acquaintances.

In Constantinople, **Heraclius** becomes emperor of the Byzantines.

611 As Persia's control over Syria expands with the help of Syrian Arab auxiliaries, Persian forces overrun and sack **Antioch**. A smaller Persian army is defeated by the Arab Bakr tribe, however.

612 Now convinced of the authenticity of the *suras* he is receiving from Gabriel, Muhammad **begins preaching** in Mecca, by tradition on the hill of **Safa** close to the Kabah. Muhammad proclaims that there is only one God, the all-merciful and all-vengeful Allah, that there will be a final Day of Judgment, when the virtuous will enter Paradise and evildoers be consigned to Hell, and that earthly wealth should be more equitably distributed within a new *umma*, or community, based in faith in Allah rather than in tribal allegiance.

Muhammad begins to attract **disciples**, among them his close friend **Abu Bakr**, another merchant named **Uthman ibn Affan** (a member of the powerful and distantly related Ummaya clan), and also his cousin **Ali ibn Abu Talib**, the son of his uncle Abu Talib. The majority of Muhammad's early converts, inspired by his egalitarian-ism, are drawn from the lower levels of Meccan society: artisans, ser-vants and slaves, and women in particular. Because of this, and because of his denunciation of pagan worship (the majority religion of the city), Muhammad soon attracts criticism from Mecca's elders. For a while, however, he is tolerated as one harmless self-proclaimed "prophet" or "warner" among many. Muhammad also continues to enjoy the protection of his "guardian" Abu Talib, although he fails to convert him to Islam.

ALLAH

*A*t the time of Muhammad's birth, the Arabic word *Allah* was sometimes employed to denote a "high god" whose author-ity trumped the authority of any other, but Muhammad elaborated a distinctive understanding of who, or what, Allah is. In the Koran Allah is consistently described as being all-compassionate, all-merciful and omniscient, but also all-powerful and all-vengeful. Allah is not only the creator of everything that is, but it is only through Allah that the entire fabric of the universe is sustained. Similarly, Allah has an inti-mate knowledge of human hearts and thoughts. Allah is also, it would appear, a jealous God. Those who submit to his will and struggle on his behalf shall, at the Last Judgment, be rewarded in Paradise; while those who offend against his will, or refuse to acknowledge his being, are eter-nally confined to Hell.

As such, Allah would appear to be an amalgam of the Lord of Hosts of the Torah and the God of Love of the Christian New Testament; and, histor-ically, there is little question that this largely is the case. But the Islamic understanding of God differs in one key respect: the religion's principal

614 Damascus, the provincial capital of Byzantine Syria, falls to the Persians.

615 The Persians, a majority of whom are followers of the Zoroastrian religion, capture **Jerusalem**, the historic center of both the Judaic and Christian religions.

In Mecca, some of Muhammad's followers emigrate to **Abyssinia** (Ethiopia) to escape growing persecution. The number of Muhammad's followers continues to increase, however.

emphasis is on Allah's otherness. Whatever attributes he may have, he is not to be considered in any human or anthropomorphic terms. Least of all should he be given any pictorial representation other than through the inscription of his name. He may have created Adam, but not in his own image. Rather, he is to be considered as an ultimately impersonal being: not only the maker of nature, but nature itself.

Philosophically, however, such abstractions do not resolve the sort of conundrums familiar to students of Judaism and Christianity. How is it that humans, Allah's creations, are capable of disobedience to His will? Is such disobedience in fact wilful, therefore lying outside Allah, or part of some master-plan? And even if humans have free will, why should Allah be much concerned with them anyway? Can it really be that the Koran, revealed in a human language to a human being, adequately conveys such a supra-human subject matter? Given that the Koran specifically discourages *zannah* (speculative theology), however, many Muslim believers—much like some followers of other faiths—reject such questions. Whatever is, is as Allah wills it—*inshallah*. Obedience to Allah is the only permissible path.

616 As Muhammad preaches openly against the greed of Mecca's merchant aristocracy—assuring the rich that no amount of wealth will spare them punishment at the Day of Judgment—the city authorities finally take action against him. Opposition to Muhammad is led by **Suhayl ibn Amr**, a foremost practitioner of pagan rites, by **Abu al-**

THE KORAN

*T*he Koran (*Quran*) is the holy book of the Islamic religion. It is divided into 114 chapters or *suras*, purportedly revealed to Muhammad as the Word of Allah through the medium of the archangel Gabriel from around 610 until shortly before Muhammad's death in 632. Because Muhammad was illiterate, the *suras* were either memorized by his followers or inscribed on various materials—parchment, leather, bone, wood—by his "secretaries." The Koran as we have it was not finally compiled until the 650s at the command of the third caliph, **Uthman**. Nor are its *suras* presented in the order in which Muhammad received them. Rather they are arranged according to length—the longest towards the beginning of the book, the shortest at its conclusion. Each *sura* is given a name—"The Cow," "The Bee," "The Fig," and so forth—although such titles rarely provide a guide to a *sura*'s content, being merely based on catchwords within the text. Indeed, the longer *suras* especially exhibit a marked tendency to jump from one subject matter to another in a sort of unfurling stream of supra-consciousness.

Despite such idiosyncrasies, the Koran is regarded by orthodox Muslims as being beyond any kind of reproach, textual or otherwise. Nor, although the Koran specifically refers to itself as but a "similitude" of God's Word, can it or should it be translated—a situation that has sometimes provided a vehicle for Arab supremacism in the wider Islamic world. But for the

Hakam, dubbed "Father of Lies" in the Koran, and by **Abu Sufyan**, previously a friend of Muhammad. At first attempts are made to buy Muhammad off, but, according to tradition, Muhammad responds by declaring, "If they put the sun in my right hand and the moon in my left, I would not abjure my message." Threats are made against his life,

Arabic speaker, the Koran is—whether considered as scripture or literature—simply wondrous. While being composed in prose, its inlay of rhythms and cadences is profoundly poetic, and no other work in Arabic comes close to it. Its curiously insistent inter-meshing of varied moods and topics, of exhortations and prescriptive law-giving, has had an enduringly powerful effect.

For the Jewish or Christian reader, too, the Koran can prove surprising. Great stretches of it are concerned with either validating or repudiating Christo-Judaic beliefs and experience, and had Islam not taken wing as a separate religion then it would stand as evidence for the deep penetration of Jewish and Christian ideas into early 7th-century Arabia. Where it diverges most markedly from its scriptural predecessors is in its emphasis on the importance of the God-fearing community or *umma*, to which the individual is subservient just as s/he is subservient to Allah. From this flows a set of precise humanitarian injunctions—particularly with regard to orphans, widows, slaves, the sick, beggars and the needy. Conversely, the whole of the Koran deploys a kind of eschatology familiar from other religions. The pleasures of Paradise and the unpleasant provisions of Hell, both eternal, are made vividly manifest. And the world below is equally divided, between *dar al-Islam* ("abode of Islam/peace") and *dar al-Harb* ("abode of war"); to protect and enlarge the former at the expense of the latter can be an integral part of the believer's salvation.

but because of Muhammad's clan connections and the protection of Abu Talib, his life is spared. In the way of prevailing Arab custom, however, it is decided to put pressure on Muhammad by placing a **collective interdict** on the Hashimites. Following a council of chieftains, the Hashimites are formally ostracized. Other members of the Quraysh tribe, and indeed members of other clans in Mecca, are forbidden to exchange goods with Muhammad's clan and followers, and the Hashimites are **driven from the city**. Under Abu Talib's leadership they resettle, along with another clan, the **Muttalib**, in another part of the valley complex in which Mecca is situated. The Hashimites face financial ruin and starvation, but because of clan solidarity they do not disown Muhammad. Many of Muhammad's lesser followers,

I am the Relenting One, the Merciful. But the infidels who die unbelievers shall incur the curse of God, the angels, and all mankind. Under it they shall remain forever; their punishments shall not be mitigated, nor shall they be reprieved. Sura 2, "The Cow"

Abraham was neither Jew nor Christian. He was an upright man, one who submitted to God. He was no idolater. Surely the men who are nearest to Abraham are those who follow him, this Prophet, and the true believers. God is the guardian of the faithful. Some of the People of the Book wish to mislead you; but they mislead none but themselves, though they may not perceive it. Sura 3, "The Imrans"

Men have authority over women because God has made the one superior to the other, and because they spend their wealth to maintain them. Good women are obedient. They guard their unseen parts because God has guarded them. As for those from whom you fear disobedience, admonish them and forsake them in beds apart, and beat

though, endure more severe persecution: slaves and the low-born who have converted are assaulted, and sometimes bound by ropes to endure the midday sun. While some are murdered, others flee Mecca.

617 The persecution of Muhammad's followers in Mecca continues, and a **second wave** of Muslims crosses the Red Sea to **Abyssinia** to seek sanctuary at the hands of the Negus, Abyssinia's Coptic Christian ruler. While their numbers are probably small, in Islamic tradition their journey takes on the significance of an early *hijra*. The Meccan authorities send their own emissaries to Ethiopia, offering the Negus gifts if he will hand over Muhammad's *muslims* (literally "believers"), but the Negus refuses.

them. Then if they obey you, take no further action. Surely God is high, supreme. Sura 4: "Women"

It is God who splits the seed from the fruit-stone. He brings forth the living from the dead, and the dead from the living. Such is God. How then can you turn away? Sura 6, "Cattle"

Did you not see how God compares a good word to a good tree? Its root is firm and its branches are in the sky; it yields its fruit in every season by God's leave. God speaks in parables to mankind so that they may take heed. But an evil word is like an evil tree torn out of the earth and shorn of all its roots. Sura 14, "Abraham"

We have revealed the Koran in the Arabic tongue that you may understand its meaning. It is a transcript of the eternal book in Our keeping, sublime, and full of wisdom. Sura 43, "Ornaments of Gold"

—from the Koran, trans. N.J. Dawood

An illustrated edition of the Koran

In Mecca itself, according to tradition, Muhammad braves his enemies by periodically **visiting the Kabah**, where he publicly offers prayers to Allah.

618 The **interdict against the Hashimites is lifted**, perhaps because moderates—swayed by Abu Talib's determined defense of his nephew—gain ascendancy in the tribal council. According to tradition, the decision to reinstate the Hashimites coincides with the destruction of a proclamation against Muhammad—previously attached to the Kabah—which is eaten by worms. The Hashimites are permitted to return to Mecca, where their trading rights and properties are restored. Some of the Muslim emigrants to Abyssinia also return to Mecca, but are not treated well. Muhammad himself, encouraged by further messages from Allah through Gabriel, **resumes preaching** his doctrines.

619 Muhammad's safety in Mecca is again jeopardized following the **death of Abu Talib**, his protector. To ensure the continuance of Islam, he begins exploring the possibility of creating a base outside Mecca, and to this end travels to **Taifa** (al-Taif), an oasis township forty miles or so to the southeast of Mecca. But, forewarned by the Meccans, the people there refuse to give Muhammad the hospitality conventionally accorded a stranger. Returning to Mecca, he offers fresh prayers at the Kabah and secures the protection of **al-Mutin ibn Adiy**—a Quraysh, but not a Hashimite.

Muhammad's first wife Khadijah dies aged 65. Before his own death Muhammad will take some fourteen further wives. Some are the daughters and widows of his companions; other marriages are contracted to create bonds between himself and various tribal chieftains. Although Islam prescribes a maximum of four wives, Muhammad is specifically permitted by a Koranic revelation to exceed this number. The first wife he takes after Khadijah is the widow **Sawdah**.

620 Having failed to make headway in Taifa, Muhammad opens discussions with tribal chiefs from **Yathrib**, who are visiting Mecca either to trade or to worship at the Kabah or both. From these contacts Muhammad learns that the eight Arab tribes of Yathrib—a predominantly agricultural oasis settlement 250 miles to the north of Mecca famed for its dates, and where Muhammad has relatives on his mother's side—are at loggerheads with each other, and that the township is gripped by communal violence. He also learns that in Yathrib, partly because of the presence of three groups of Jews, people are receptive to monotheism. According to tradition, Muhammad succeeds in **converting** the visitors from Yathrib to Islam.

Chosroes II of Persia conquers the Byzantine island of **Rhodes**, so making the extent of his Sassanian empire equal to that of his great Archeminid predecessor King Darius I.

THE KABAH

The origins of the Kabah (from the Arabic for "cube") are veiled in obscurity. Although it has often been rebuilt, in the 6th century it consisted – as it does today—of a relatively small raised building with a slightly rhomboid ground-plan, measuring approximately 144 meters squared. It contains three or four sacred stones, including the oval **Black Stone**, sometimes claimed to have fallen from heaven to earth and destined to become an integral aspect of the Islamic pilgrimage (hajj) to Mecca once the Kabah itself had been reconsecrated in the name of Allah.

Such stones were common throughout early Semitic culture, while the Kabah itself has obvious and significant parallels with the **Ark of the Covenant**, the holiest object of the Israelites. At the time of Muhammad's birth, however, the Kabah was used for the worship of a multitude of pagan deities, represented by some 360 idols. There was a persistent legend that the Kabah had originally been erected by no less a figure than **Abraham** (Ibrahim), the common ancestor of Jews and Arabs alike, and had then been

According to Islamic tradition, in this year Muhammad also makes his celebrated "**Night Journey**" (*isra* or *miraj*) to Jerusalem, borne on the back of a flying horse called Busraq provided for him one evening on Mount Hira by Gabriel. In Jerusalem, Muhammad alights on the **Temple Mount**, from where, with Gabriel at his side, he is further transported into the Divine Presence itself.

621 As the inter-Arab conflict in **Yathrib** threatens to get out of hand, Muhammad offers to migrate to there as a peacemaker and religious leader. Close to desperation, envoys from Yathrib respond positively to Muhammad's initiative, and Muhammad begins making plans for the wholesale transfer of his Islamic following.

maintained by his son Ismail (Ishmael) — a gloss that may well have been encouraged by Mecca's handful of resident Jews. Related legends ascribed the Kabah to Adam and to Noah. For Muhammad, anxious to establish Islam as the culminating expression of a monotheism that stretched back to an era well before the Jewish prophet Moses, the association between the Kabah and Abraham was all-important. There was also an obvious advantage in not jettisoning what for most Arabs was already the most sacred site in Arabia.

In 630, re-entering Mecca after an eight-year exile in Medina, he destroyed the idols placed inside and outside the Kabah and ordered its interior walls to be scrubbed clean of everything apart from a representation of Abraham and an image of the Virgin Mary. Thus cleansed, the Kabah and its surrounding haram (sanctuary) became Islam's focal point — in time graced by an imposing Grand Mosque and visited ever since by Muslim pilgrims, who today number over two million annually.

622 In order not to arouse the suspicions of the Meccan authorities, Muhammad's followers begin **leaving for Yathrib** in small groups. Once the majority of Muslims have deserted Mecca, Muhammad himself sets out from the city at the beginning of September, accompanied by Abu Bakr and a handful of others. Learning of his escape, the Meccan authorities attempt to have Muhammad killed, but he evades assassination. This exodus, beginning on July 16, is known as the *Hijra* (*Hegira*) and constitutes in Islamic history the **true beginning of Islam itself**—to the extent that in the Islamic calendar 622 CE/AD is represented as 1AH ("1 *al-Hijra*").

THE "FIVE PILLARS" OF ISLAM

*A*lthough Islam has evolved a complex theology and a great diversity of doctrines, its attraction for many resides in the austere simplicity of its original demands and forms of worship, conventionally summarized from very early on in Islam's history as its "Five Pillars" (*arkan ad-din*), each derived from the Koran. These are: (1) an avowal of Allah and Muhammad in the form "There is no God but Allah and Muhammad is his Messenger," known as the *shahadah*; (2) *salah*, or routinely offering prayers to Allah, originally three times a day, but later five times; (3) giving alms (*zakat*) for the relief of the poor and needy; (4) observing a fast (*sawm*) during the month of Ramadan; and (5) making a pilgrimage (*hajj*) to Mecca and the Kabah at least once during the course of a lifetime.

Each of these has its own specific rules. The *shahadah* is the principal requirement of the Islamic faith—so much so that as long as the believer sincerely affirms Allah and Muhammad and does not repudiate them, s/he may be absolved of neglect of the other four Pillars at the Last Judgment. As regards prayer, this should be accompanied by certain basic rituals,

In Yathrib—renamed by Muslims **Medina**, sometimes al-Medina, meaning simply "the City" (or Medina al-Rasul, "City of the Prophet")—Muhammad is welcomed as a *sayyid* (chieftain), and his people are accorded equal status to the eight other Arab tribes living there. Because of his status Muhammad is expected to maintain a **harem** of wives, among them the daughters of Medina's tribal chiefs, taken as a means of creating bonds between Muhammad and his hosts. Later he will also take older, unprotected women as wives in order to enlarge his household and offer them security.

chiefly the cleansing of the hands and feet beforehand and the act of pros-tration. Prayers should be offered facing towards Mecca, but may be per-formed anywhere. Ideally though, prayers should be offered communally, not individually, and preferably at a mosque. The giving of alms—originally a Jewish custom—likewise strengthens the Islamic community while redressing the individual's propensity to gather wealth for selfish ends. Although it is not specified in the Koran, traditionally 2.5 percent of a per-son's wealth and/or income is regarded as appropriate, and *zakat* has some-times been levied as a non-voluntary tax. Fasting during Ramadan involves eating nothing between sunrise and sunset (though water may be swal-lowed) and other prohibitions—notably, not making war, except in the defense of Islam. Similarly, while the *hajj* confers great spiritual merit on a Muslim, he or she may be excused pilgrimage if health and finances do not permit. Yet again, there is clearly a communal as well as an individual dimension to the *hajj*, since it involves traveling with and meeting many other members of Islam.

According to tradition, upon arriving in Medina Muhammad untethers his camel, and the spot where it pauses to graze becomes the site of the **first Islamic mosque** (*masjid* in Arabic, meaning "place of prostration/prayer"). The mosque itself is simple, barely more than a roof supported by the trunks of palm trees, and contains no altar. An unadorned stone marks the direction (*qiblah*) in which

JEWS AND CHRISTIANS: THE PEOPLE OF THE BOOK

*I*n Islam, Jews and Christians are called "People of the Book" (*ahl al-kitab*)—fellow monotheists who, hypothetically at least, worship the same God as Muslims, whose histories are rehearsed in the Koran, and who are alike descended from Abraham (Ibrahim). Furthermore, according to the Koran and the *Hadith* (the posthumously collected "traditions" of Muhammad), where Islam has spread and established political control, Jews and Christians are entitled to protection from their Islamic rulers—in much the same way that, in pre-Islamic Arabia, stronger tribes often took smaller, weaker tribes under their wing. Islam has sometimes been praised for its tolerance; and historically Christian and Jewish communities have often been left to their own devices within Islamic territories—with the proviso that they pay a special tax, *jizya*, in lieu of military service to the Islamic state.

Yet in certain respects the boundaries of this accommodation have been blurred. Under Islamic rule, Jews and Christians were often prohibited from building new synagogues and churches, and suffered other restrictions. Whereas a Muslim man was permitted to marry a Jewish or Christian woman, no Jewish or Christian man could marry a Muslim woman. In the Koran too there are some inconsistencies between different *suras*, which were received by Muhammad over a period of time in which his relations with Jews

prayers to Allah should be offered—at this stage towards **Jerusalem** in honor of Abraham. A larger complex is quickly built up around the mosque, but a courtyard where Muhammad's *umma* can gather is preserved, also used as a meeting-place for Medina's tribal elders. Placed around the courtyard is separate accommodation for Muhammad and his steadily increasing number of wives. Later an office for scribes and

deteriorated. While Moses is upheld as a valid and important prophet from whom Muslims can learn, the episode of his brother Aaron's idolatrous worship of the Golden Calf is presented as a *prima facie* example of a Jewish tendency to abandon the principles of "true" religion. Likewise, Jesus is acknowledged as an important prophet, but the Koran rejects any notion that he is or could be the son of God and denies the Crucifixion took place. For Muslims, Allah is one and indivisible, so the Christian trinity of Father, Son and Holy Ghost makes a mockery of the principles of monotheism. In one reading, then, the Koran suggests that Jews and Christians are perfectly acceptable provided they behave and think like good Muslims.

There is also a grey area in the Koran on what does and does not constitute a "just war." Some *suras* directly state that hostilities should only be undertaken against non-Muslims where there is clear provocation, while others imply that not to acknowledge Allah and his Prophet may offer just such a provocation, and that to wage war against the "kaffir" (infidel) of whatever creed is not only permissible, but a sacred duty. For their part, some Jews and Christians, irked by the Koran's insistence that Muhammad is the last prophet who supersedes all others, and who, according to tradition, ordered the expulsion of all Jews and Christians from Arabia on his deathbed, have turned the tables on Islam and characterized Muslims themselves as infidels.

other administrative buildings will be added to the complex, so that it becomes a governmental as well as spiritual center.

Once the mosque has been erected, Muhammad institutes **communal prayer meetings** on Friday afternoons, to which all the men of Medina are invited, including members of the three resident Jewish clans—the **Qaynuqah**, the **Nadir** and the **Quarayzah**. Medina's Jews generally resist Muhammad's attempts to incorporate them into Islam, however. Already possessed of their own monotheistic faith, they resent Muhammad's retellings of events in their own scriptures, and the suggestion that the "final" prophet of the Abrahamic succession should not be a Jew. They may also fear that if Muhammad succeeds in binding all the Arabs of Medina into a single community, their own status and influence will suffer. From the Medinan Jews Muhammad adds to his existing knowledge of the tensions between Jews and Christians, as well as of the divisions within Judaism and Christianity.

To seal his companionship with Abu Bakr, Muhammad contracts to marry his 6-year-old daughter, **Aisha**. When Aisha comes of age she will be known as Muhammad's favorite wife.

Emperor Heraclius's forces win their first victories against the armies of Chosroes II.

623 Either in this year or towards the end of the preceding year, Muhammad issues the **Constitution of Medina** (also known as the "Covenant of Yathrib"), a comprehensive legal document designed to promote harmony among the Arabs and Jews of Medina, and to effect an accommodation between Muhammad's Islamic *umma* and existing tribal structures. Towards the beginning of the document its signatories are described as "a single *umma* distinct from other peoples." Its many clauses include clarifications about setting ransoms and blood-money (compensation to a clan whose members have been killed). Significantly, the Constitution also stipulates that disputes between tribes and clans should be referred to Muhammad for settlement and resolution—a clear indication that his authority is already established in Medina.

> Once the pagan surrenders to God, he becomes fully equal to the believer and deserving of equal rights with him. Warring on the unbeliever, therefore, is an act of mercy resulting in a more perfect brotherhood. At no time does the believer question the right of the unbeliever to mercy and brotherhood.
>
> —Abd-al-Rahman Azzam,
> *The Eternal Message of Muhammad* (1946)
> trans. Caesar E. Farrah

By this time it is likely that a majority of Medina's Arabs have **converted to Islam**, and only a small group (led by **Abdallah ibn Ubbay**) oppose Muhammad's ascendancy. Yet the Constitution also furnishes guidelines for developing amicable relations between Muslims and non-Muslims, and it is notable that *suras* of the Koran received by Muhammad around this time are less uncompromising toward "infidels" than others received later. Conversely, from early on in the founding of the Islamic *umma* at Medina, a distinction emerges between the **muhajirun**—those who have come with Muhammad from Mecca, sometimes called the Emigrants—and the *ansar* ("helpers"), Medinan Arabs who become Muhammad's first converts outside Mecca.

Historically, the Constitution becomes an important model for **Islamic diplomacy**, and also as the first exercise in **Islamic jurisprudence**. In immediate terms it embodies the principles of non-aggression and mutual defense between members of a new confederacy.

624 As tensions between Medina's Muslims and Jews deepen, in January Muhammad **alters the *qiblah***, instructing worshippers to place their prayer-mats so that they no longer face towards Jerusalem, but towards **Mecca** and the Kabah instead—a gesture that indicates Muhammad's ambition to spread Islam among all the people of Arabia.

Yet Muhammad and the *muhajirun* are still confronted by problems of economic survival. Unable to trade with Mecca, Muhammad reverts to the *razzia*—the traditional Arab custom of conducting raids against other Arabs. While the allowable purpose of such raids is to acquire livestock, goods, women and slaves, custom also dictates that they be carried out with minimal bloodshed—a shepherd guarding a flock should be chased away rather than killed, so as to avoid unending vendettas. On the pretext of avenging the former maltreatment of his followers, Muhammad targets Meccans. While his first *razzias* appear to be unsuccessful, in March Muhammad plans a **major raid** on a large Meccan caravan as it makes its way to Mecca from the north. Mecca responds by dispatching a sizeable force to crush

This great religion is based not so much on revealed truth, as on an inability to establish links with the outside world. In contrast to the universal kindliness of Buddhism, or the Christian desire for dialogue, Moslem intolerance takes an unconscious form among those who are guilty of it; although they do not always seek to make others share their truth by brutal coercion, they are nevertheless (and this is more serious) incapable of tolerating the existence of others as others. The only means they have of protecting themselves against doubt and humiliation is the "negativisation" of others, considered as witnesses to a different kind of faith and a different way of life. Islamic fraternity is the opposite of an unadmitted rejection of infidels; it cannot acknowledge itself to be such a rejection, since this would be tantamount to recognizing that infidels existed in their own right.

—Claude Lévi-Strauss,
Tristes Tropiques (1955),
trans. John and Doreen Weightman

Muhammad and his raiders. The two forces meet and fight near **Badr**. Against the odds, Muhammad's men **defeat the Meccan forces**. According to tradition, 350 Muslims, of whom only seventy are mounted on camels and two on horseback, overcome a hundred horsemen and 850 foot-soldiers. Also according to tradition, Muhammad's fighters are miraculously reinforced by a **squadron of angels** sent by Allah. After the battle, Abu Bakr orders the enemy dead to be deposited in a dry well to give them the customary right of immediate burial.

Returning to Medina, victory celebrations are short-lived: the Jews and remaining pagans **condemn Muhammad** for actions which can only involve Medina in a full-scale war with Mecca. And indeed news soon arrives that the Meccans, under the leadership of **Abu Sufyan**, have renewed their commitment to **eradicating the Islamic *umma***—not only have the Muslims begun interfering with Mecca's trade, but they threaten to displace Mecca as a religious center in Hijaz.

Muhammad takes **Hafsah**, the daughter of his companion **Umar ibn al-Khattab**, as his third wife.

The Sassanians suffer a **second defeat** at the hands of the Byzantines, and Constantinople begins reimposing its rule on Syria, Egypt and other provinces previously under Persian control.

625 Mecca sends out an army against Medina, and inflicts heavy casualties on Muhammad's forces on the slopes of **Mount Uhud**. According to tradition, Muhammad himself is wounded. The Meccans, sustain heavy losses too, though, and Medina itself is spared.

Soon after the Battle of Uhud, the Jews of Medina revolt against Muhammad's regime, but are crushed. Possibly as a result of the intercession of the pagan leader **Abdallah ibn Ubbay**, two of the three Medinan Jewish communities, the **Qaynuqah** and the **Nadir**, are expelled, rather than being made to endure greater punishment. Medina's third Jewish community, the **Quarayzah**, who have not

Both Judaism and Christianity are religions of profound pathos—
Judaism with its dream of ethnic redemption from present wretchedness,
Christianity with its individual salvation through the sufferings of
a God of love. In each case the pathos is indeed moving; but it is a
pathos which too easily appeals to the emotion of self-pity. Islam,
in contrast, is strikingly free of this temptation. The bleakness which
we saw in its conception of the relationship between God and man is
the authentic, unadulterated bleakness of the universe itself.

—Michael Cook,
Muhammad (1983)

participated in the revolt, are unaffected. Many of those Jews leaving
Medina make their way to a Jewish settlement at **Khaybar**, and there
enter into an alliance with the Meccans against Muhammad.

Around this time, Muhammad **dispatches emissaries** to Arab leaders throughout Arabia, inviting them to join his new confederacy.
Around this time he also arranges for letters to be sent further
afield—to **Abyssinia**, **Constantinople** and the Persian capital
Ctesiphon—outlining God's message. The Abyssinian **Negus**
responds warmly; **Emperor Heraclius** gives Muhammad's entreaties
a more cautious reception; while **Chosroes II**, a devout Zoroastrian,
destroys his letter and expels Muhammad's envoy.

627 Mecca again **attacks Medina**. Warned of the army's approach,
Muhammad orders a deep ditch to be dug around Medina, with the
result that in the ensuing **Battle of the Trench** the Meccan cavalry
is disabled. Victory for the Muslims is ensured by the timely advent
of a great **dust storm**. The Meccans retreat in disorder, and Medina
is again saved.

Because the Meccans had been aided by the Quarayzah Jews,
Muhammad orders the immediate **massacre** of 700 Quarayzah men,

and arranges for their women and children to be sold into slavery. From this date no Jews remain in Medina, except those few who have already converted to Islam.

Following the failure of Mecca's second attempt to destroy Muhammad, his reputation in Arabia grows, and deputations from the chieftains of the tribes that surround Medina make representations to him, expressing their willingness to embrace Islam and **join the Muslim confederacy**. Among those now coming to Medina are dissidents from Mecca itself.

In December, the Persian Sassanians are decisively beaten by the Byzantines at the climactic **Battle of Nineveh**, wrecking Chosroes II's ambitions for a permanently enlarged empire.

628 In an astute political move, Muhammad publicly abandons his *jihad* against Mecca and instead launches a peace offensive. In March, he announces he will join the annual *hajj* (pilgrimage) to the Kabah, and sets off for Mecca with 1000 unarmed followers dressed in white—fully aware that any assault against him would be regarded as sacrilege throughout Arabia. Troops are dispatched to intercept the pilgrims between Medina and Mecca, but Muhammad evades them and enters the city, where he sets up camp at **Hudaybiyyah**, on the perimeter of the *haram* (sanctuary area surrounding the Kabah). Through skilful negotiation Muhammad persuades the Quraysh to enter into the **Treaty of Hudaybiyyah**, which imposes a binding peace between Mecca and Medina. As news of the treaty spreads, Muhammad's standing among Arabs is further increased, particularly among the nomadic Bedouin tribes.

Soon afterwards, Muhammad launches a successful attack against the mainly Jewish oasis town of **Khaybar**. But although Khaybar is home to many of those Jews who have previously turned against him at Medina, he offers Khaybar his protection in return for half its annual agricultural produce.

Chosroes II of Persia dies. Around this time, Islam enters into hostile relations with the recovering Byzantine empire. In the first of a series

WOMEN IN ISLAM

*N*umerous misconceptions surround the relationship between Islam and women. High among them are the notions that the Koran instructs all females to wear the veil, and that women are denied the possibility of entering Paradise. Neither is accurate. Whereas the Koran does stipulate that in the interests of modesty women should cover themselves between the ankle and the neck, the obligatory use of the veil was reserved for Muhammad's wives. And again, *sura* 4 of the Koran specifically guarantees that all those believers who perform good works, "both men and women," may enter Paradise.

Muslim commentators have also drawn attention to other provisions in the Koran that affect women beneficially. They are granted property and inheritance rights, may sue for divorce, and widows should be supported by the *umma* if their families are unable to. Muhammad also decreed that under no circumstances should a woman be separated from her children. All these and other injunctions, it is claimed, show that the Koran and Muhammad were well in advance of their times. While polygamy is condoned, this is because in Arabia it was universally practiced as a means of providing for women whose husbands had died in battle.

The problem is that times have changed. Yes, the Koran grants women the right of inheritance, but it also says women should inherit only half what a man is allowed to. The Koran also declares that women lacking "obedience" may be beaten by their husbands. Controversially, *sura* 66, unusually alluding to details of Muhammad's private life, condones concubinage as well as slavery. In it, Muhammad appears to have had a run-in with two of his senior wives, Aisha and Hafsah, because of his unwillingness to forego his Coptic slave-girl Maryah despite his promises to the contrary. Muhammad retires to his cave to commune with Gabriel, who advises him: "God has given you absolution from such oaths." Armed with this authority, Muhammad returns to his harem and tells his wives that if they do not "turn to God in repentance" he may divorce them, in which case Allah "will give him in your place better wives than yourselves, submissive to God and full of faith, obedient, penitent, devout, and given to fasting."

Such passages and episodes have regularly prompted criticism among non-Muslims. The 18th-century English historian Edward Gibbon suggested that the reason the Koran is so specific about the joys awaiting male entrants into Paradise (it mentions the favors of seventy or so *houri* maidens—the exact number is uncertain), but does not mention equivalent benefits for women, is that Muhammad baulked at suggesting his companions' wives might expect similar pleasures. Many have argued that Islam is especially vulnerable on the "woman question," and that the status accorded women in the Koran and by Shariah Law undermines the whole Islamic project. A more moderate view, however, allows ambiguities. Orthodox Muslims question whether the constant focus on under-clad women as sexual objects in Western culture does not in fact constitute a greater degradation; while a recent survey of Muslim women in Iran, obliged to wear the veil in public, revealed that many felt it was not a constraint on their freedom so much as a protection of their privacy. Some contemporary Islamic feminists have also sought to demonstrate that Islamic law, preserving "pre-Muhammadan" attitudes, is itself at variance with what at least is implied in the Koran.

of events that supply pretexts for Islamic aggression against the Byzantines, **Farwah ibn Umar al-Judhami**, the prefect of Aman (present-day Jordan) and a convert to Islam, is **crucified** at Ufra on the orders of the emperor Heraclius after he refuses to return to the Christian faith. No contemporaneous Latin record of this episode has been discovered, however. From Islamic sources it is clear that Muhammad has already started sending agents to proselytize among Arabs in Byzantine **Syria** and its constituent parts.

629 Exercising their right under the Treaty of Hudabiyyah, Muslims from Medina **make a *hajj* to Mecca**. One of Muhammad's followers, a black Abyssinian convert named **Bilal**, surmounts the Kabah and issues a summons to prayer (*adhan*). In Islamic tradition Bilal thus becomes the first *muezzin*. In the future, special towers, called **minarets**, will be built beside mosques for the benefit of Bilal's successor *muezzins*.

According to Islamic sources, Muhammad sends a delegation of fifteen men to **Aman** to disseminate the doctrine of Islam, and perhaps to gather intelligence about the Byzantines—whom Muhammad suspects of preparing operations against him. The Muslims are attacked at a place called **Tallah**, however, and only one person survives. At around the same time an agent sent into Syria is also killed. In September, Muhammad appoints **Zayd ibn Harithah** commander of a force of 3000, which is dispatched northwards against the Byzantines, but Zayd is killed in battle at **Muta**, near al-Karak. His subordinate **Jafar ibn Abu Talib**, a cousin of Muhammad, assumes command, but he too is soon wounded. According to Islamic heroic tradition, Jafar loses first one arm, then the other, but somehow manages to keep his army's banner aloft between the stumps of his arms, before dying of multiple wounds. When Muhammad learns of his bravery, he says Allah will replace his arms with wings, and so Jafar passes into legend as "**Jafar the Flier.**" In his stead, **Khalid ibn al-Walid**, third in command, disengages with the enemy, and leads the depleted Muslim force safely back to Medina.

As Byzantium endeavors to revive a system of client tribes on the northern boundaries of Arabia to protect its territories, **skirmishes between**

Islamic and Byzantine fighters continue until the end of the year, with neither side being able to establish any strategic advantage. Of greater significance, though, is the conclusion of a **peace treaty** between the Persian and Byzantine empires in the same year. Notwithstanding, the Persians are unable to reimpose their previous authority over the tribes of northern Arabia or in the Persian Gulf.

630 According to Islamic historians, the Quraysh of Mecca violate the Treaty of Hudaybiyyah (628) by attacking the **Khuzaah**, a tribe formerly associated with Medina. Drawing on the resources of the confederacy he has created, Muhammad assembles an army of 10,000 men and **marches on Mecca**. Knowing that many there are sympathetic to

A print depicting Muhammad exiting Earth into the heavens

Islam, the Quraysh leadership—still headed by Abu Sufyan—**surrenders** their city, and the gates "open of their own accord" according to the *Hadith*. Once inside, Muhammad destroys 360 pagan idols placed around the Kabah, and **consecrates the shrine to Allah** (according to tradition, each of the idols falls over and smashes when Muhammad points his rod at them). Many pagans, sensing their own gods are powerless to protect them, embrace Islam—among them Abu Sufyan himself. There are no enforced conversions, however, and Muhammad orders that com-

MUHAMMAD (C.570–632)

*I*n retrospect, it is clear that Muhammad was the foremost religious, political and military leader of his time. The received narrative of his life suggests an individual of rare intuition – he was a visionary who was also unflaggingly pragmatic, both in the provisions he made for the new social order he created, and in the management of the relations between that order and the peoples immediately surrounding it. He could offer peace and diplomacy or turn to vengeance and reprisal.

Yet about Muhammad the man relatively little is known. We are told that he was of medium height and build, and had long, flowing black hair that he plaited into pigtails, and that his face was inordinately handsome. No contemporary or even near-contemporary portrait exists, however – famously, any pictorial representation of Muhammad is forbidden under Islamic law. In the centuries that followed his death a great number of memories, stories and anecdotes about Muhammad were recorded and eventually collated as the *Hadith*, but their authenticity remains questionable.

Even so, it is possible to detect within the different strands of his historic persona distinctive Arab archetypes. As a warrior, he engaged in the time-honored practice of the *razzia*. As a politician, he manipulated tribal

passion be shown towards his former enemies. Although some who remain opposed to Muhammad are executed, victory is accompanied neither by looting nor rape—the customary rites of conquest.

Outside Mecca, a coalition of tribes that have remained resilient to Islam, centered on **Taifa**, assembles a force. Muhammad leads out his own army in response, and defeats his enemies at the **Battle of Hunayn**. Taifa falls into his hands, and with it undisputed mastery of

frameworks with real success, attaching smaller tribes to his cause as "clients" and standing up to anyone that opposed him. Equally, with a Meccan's grasp of financial affairs, Muhammad knew how to make advantageous adjustments to any treaty he entered into. In his dealings with others he habitually combined severity and largesse, in the manner of any tribal potentate. As a religious leader, too, he operated largely within tradition – on one hand he was a "warner," someone "sent" to castigate his own people about their moral shortcomings; on the other he assumed the role of a *mansib*, the head of a cult, and was the provider of a *haram* (sanctuary) where feuding factions could resolve their differences under the *mansib*'s guidance.

In the milieu in which Muhammad grew up, there were several paths to influence and power. Muhammad pursued them all, and with such consummate agility that a majority of his Arab contemporaries were persuaded to recognize him as their supreme leader. Yet Muhammad pushed his victories even further. Not content to be a conciliator between tribes, he forged a super-tribe based on faith, not blood. And in doing this he proclaimed himself, or allowed himself to be proclaimed, not just a prophet, but the "seal of the prophets." For orthodox Muslims, after him there could be no one of comparable status.

all Hijaz. At Hunayn, however, Muhammad is reputedly wounded for a second time.

631 News of Muhammad's latest and most impressive triumphs spreads rapidly, and during this "**Year of Delegations**" emissaries from all parts of Arabia flock to Medina to acknowledge his overlordship. Although some enclaves of non-compliance persist—and although Muhammad uses land grants to encourage conversion to Islam—he becomes the master of the whole of Arabia, not just of Hijaz.

Pagans and other "idolaters" are **forbidden to worship** in Mecca.

632 At the beginning of the year Muhammad launches a program for the systematic **Islamicization of Arabia**, sending his agents out among the tribes who have acknowledged his suzerainty both to inculcate the doctrines of Islam and to collect *zakat* (alms) and other taxes. Some of these agents remain with the tribes they visit as permanent representatives of Muhammad and Medina. For a majority of Arabs, such methods are revolutionary. While in the long term they guarantee the emergence of a new aristocratic elite based in Medina (and to a lesser extent in Mecca), in the short term they also create resentment among some newly "converted" tribes.

After making a last pilgrimage to Mecca, Muhammad contracts a fever, and delivers a "**farewell speech**" to tens of thousands of followers at **Mina**. He then **dies on the night of June 7/8** (in the Islamic calendar, each day begins at sunset), according to tradition in the arms of his beloved wife Aisha. He is quickly buried within the grounds of his mosque in Medina—a site that becomes one of the holiest places in Islam alongside the Kabah in Mecca.

Muhammad is survived by nine wives and his Coptic concubine Maryah. His daughter **Fatima** dies later in the same year, leaving her husband **Ali ibn Abu Talib** (Muhammad's cousin as well as son-in-law) to bring up their two sons, **al-Hassan** and **al-Husayn**. Muhammad also bequeaths an immediate and far-reaching leadership crisis within the politico-religious system he has founded.

CHAPTER TWO

The Rashidun

{632–61 (10–40 AH)}

MUHAMMAD'S DEATH IN 632 plunged his Arabian confederacy into disarray. He left no clear indication of his preferred successor, and there was mounting discontent among some of the tribes that had been brought within the Islamic fold. Bedouin chieftains, used to being masters of the desert, resented the taxes Medina sought to impose, and Muhammad's religion was not without its rivals: other prophets were claiming that they too had had divine revelations. In addition, Medina was rife with tension between the Meccan *muhajirun* and the indigenous *ansar*—both groups were Muslim, but each was wary of the other and wanted to seize control.

In such circumstances it seemed probable that Arabia would revert to what it had been before the advent of Muhammad: a patchwork of bickering tribes and different beliefs confined to the perimeter of the civilized world—a condition defined in the Koran as *jahiliyyah* (barbarism). Islam might very well have gone down in history as an idea and a movement that never properly took off. Yet this didn't happen—within barely twenty years Medina had become the center of an Arab empire that included among its territories Syria, Iraq and Egypt. The **Arab conquests** had begun, and the appetite for a "universal" society that Islam presented formed an integral part of this expansion. But other factors played a role. Conquest also meant a chance to acquire massive amounts of booty (a practice the Koran did not discourage), as well as the opportunity to live in lands far more fertile and pleasant than anywhere in Arabia.

Yet Islam could neither have survived, nor have been involved in conquest, had the vacuum at the center of Islamic politics remained unfilled. One possible solution to the leadership crisis, which would have been in line with conventional tribal practice, was to promote someone from within the Prophet's own Hashimite clan, namely Muhammad's cousin and son-in-law **Ali ibn Abu Talib**—a devout man who had proved himself in battle. Although he had strong support, however, his inexperience counted against him. In the event, the older **Abu Bakr** was chosen to become the first **caliph**, or successor to Muhammad.

Between them Abu Bakr and the Second Caliph, Umar ibn al-Khattib, firmly restored the cohesion and purpose of the new Muslim confederacy. To do this, they resorted to the time-honored political device of overcoming dissent at home by focusing their followers' minds and energies on military adventures abroad. With breathtaking success they attacked Arabia's imperial neighbors, **Byzantium** and **Persia**.

Until they could lay their hands on stockpiles of enemy weapons, the Arabs were poorly armed. Yet this deficit was more than made up for by their fighting spirit, driven by both religious zeal and by a desire for plunder. But there were other factors that account for the Arab Muslims' success. Both the Byzantine and Sassanian Persian empires were weakened by the long wars they had fought against each other, and had also been devastated by a series of famines. Byzantine garrisons along the Arabian border, used to control local nomads, had been largely abandoned. There was, too, widespread discontent among many of Byzantium's more southerly subjects, reinforced by Christian sectarianism. **Monophysite**, **Nestorian** and **Jacobite** Christians greatly resented the attempts of those in Constantinople to impose their "Greek" version of Christianity. Similarly, in Persia, Christians of various denominations bridled at the Zoroastrianism of their overlords.

Evidence suggests that in both empires dissident Christians welcomed the Arab-Muslim invaders, who promised to respect their faith and customs in return for payment of the *jizya* tax. This was a pragmatic offer by Abu Bakr and Umar—as well as being in accordance with the Koran—just as it was pragmatic to keep the administrative structures they encountered intact, since the Arabs had no experience in governing a foreign land. But the Muslims were helped above all by the fact that Arabs were already living in Iraq and Syria—mainly as Bedouin, though some had drifted into cities such as Damascus and Jerusalem in the west and Hira in the east. The Muslims' strategy was to build up strength in the desert first, and then attack urban settlements and citadels. To this end they sought to attach Syrian and Iraqi Arabs to the Islamic confederacy, both as a means of spreading the faith and of building up their manpower. In this sense, the first Arab expansion was a liberation movement—freeing fellow Arabs from the dominance of non-Arab rule.

During the early part of his reign, the Third Caliph, **Uthman ibn Affan**, continued Islam's foreign wars, consolidating Medina's hold over **Egypt** (the most likely springboard for a Byzantine counterattack), making the first big push across North Africa, and advancing into **Khurasan** (the northeastern part of modern Iran). But although Uthman gained eternal credit among Muslims by commissioning the definitive text of the Koran, his rule incited renewed domestic unrest, and in 656 he was murdered by rebellious Arab soldiers.

At last it was Ali's turn to become caliph. But much had changed since 632. While in Medina the old rivalry between the *muhajirun* and the *ansar* rumbled on, the acquisition of an empire had opened up fresh divisions within the Islamic *umma*. While it was recognized that the arts of civil government needed to be honed and a new, more autocratic style of leadership was called for, some began hankering for a return to the values of Muhammad's original community. Ali was unable to satisfy either camp, and the Fourth Caliph surrendered much of his power to the more energetic Umayyad governor of Syria, **Muawiyyah ibn Abu Sufyan**. Yet, despite his failings, after his death Ali acquired central importance in the unfolding story of Islam, as the first Imam of the **Shiite succession**—the basis of the minority but persistently influential Shia Islamic faith.

The first four caliphs, each of whom had a close personal connection to Muhammad, are conventionally known as the **Rashidun**, or "rightly guided ones" (more rarely as the "Four Patriarchal Caliphs"). As such, they form a distinctive chapter in the early history of Islam. Yet many Muslims have attempted to grade the individual Rashidun caliphs: whereas minority Shiites have valued Ali most highly, majority Sunni Muslims have generally set Abu Bakr and Umar over and above their two successors. One reason for this is that Abu Bakr and Umar are perceived to have ruled in frequent consultation with their peers—through the *shura*, or council—in keeping with Arab custom and the spirit of the Koran.

As the Arab empire expanded, however, a different style of government was called for. While the Fifth Caliph, Muawiyyah ibn Abu Sufyan, decisively established the dynastic principle, it was felt that the Third Caliph, Uthman, had begun the process whereby the caliphate became a determinedly autocratic institution, one comparable to the Persian and Byzantine monarchies. For some members of the early Muslim community, this tendency was unacceptable: neither the Koran nor Arab custom legitimated kingship. As a result, towards the end of the Rashidun period, there emerged the first of a succession of dissident sects that have been a dynamic feature in the Islamic landscape ever since. Known as the **Kharajites**, these early rebels sought to recover what they perceived as the true values of Islam. That such a movement should have erupted within thirty years of Muhammad's death reflects how fast the Muslim-Arab world was changing.

632 Muhammad's death in June **exacerbates tensions** already present within the new Islamic nation-community. As the question of who will assume the role of leader becomes more urgent, in the "capital" Medina there is rivalry between the *muhajirun* (the original Muslims who had traveled from Mecca in 622) and the *ansar* (Medinan Arabs converted by Muhammad during and after 622). Each faction presses for a leader to be chosen from among its own ranks. There is also friction from other sources, as **outlying tribes** that have pledged their loyalty to Muhammad threaten to withdraw from the Islamic *umma*. In eastern and southern Arabia there is **outright rebellion**, some chiefs declaring that their allegiance was merely a personal arrangement between themselves and Muhammad—the **Bedouin** showing particular recalcitrance. There is an upsurge in the number of people claiming to be prophets, imitators of Muhammad who wish to create their own theocratic power-bases and who disseminate their own "revelations." Among their number are **Musayliwah** and an individual known variously as the **"veiled prophet"** and **al-Aswad** (lit. "The Black One").

At an enlarged council convened among tribal and clan leaders and their followers later in the year at **Medina**, it is agreed that a single *khalifa*, or "successor" to Muhammad, should be chosen. Among the candidates put forward is **Ali ibn Abu Talib**, Muhammad's cousin and son-in-law by virtue of his marriage to Fatima. At 30, Ali is considered too young for the responsibilities involved, however, and Umar ibn al-Khattab proposes that Muhammad's closest companion, **Abu Bakr**, be appointed instead. The council agrees, and Abu Bakr becomes the **First Caliph**, immediately promising to uphold the *sunna* (practices) of Muhammad. In full, the title he adopts is *Khalifat Rasul Allah*—"Successor of the Prophet of God." Whether Abu Bakr is chosen unanimously is unclear, however; later it will be claimed by some of Ali's followers that the succession should have passed by right to Muhammad's closest surviving male relative. Out of this claim will be born **Shiism**, the largest of the Islamic minorities, named after "the party of Ali."

Abu Bakr's standing and personal qualities are such that his election resolves the immediate tensions between the *muhajirun* and the *ansar*, and he deliberately adopts a consultative style of rule. Muhammad's status as the "seal" of the prophets is confirmed, and Abu Bakr energetically pursues both ideological and military campaigns against "false" prophets. He also moves speedily and effectively against tribes who want to cut their ties with the Islamic confederacy, ordering that no reprisals be taken against those who return to Islam, but ruthlessly punishing those who persist in rebellion. Where fighting occurs, it is known as the **_Ridda_** (more fully *Hurub al-Ridda*, literally "War of apostasy").

Abu Bakr encourages a greater dissemination of Islamic teaching by posting teachers and reciters throughout Arabia, and sets an example to other Muslims by giving all his wealth to the needy and adopting a humble lifestyle. Abu Bakr also echoes Muhammad's militarism by initiating **hostilities against Byzantine and Persian forces** north of the Arabian peninsula, and it is from his reign as caliph that the beginning of the **Arab Conquests** is conventionally dated.

633 The **_Ridda_ wars** reach a successful conclusion following the defeat by Khalid ibn al-Walid of a confederation of rebellious tribes at the **Battle of al-Aqaba**, and of the "false" prophet Musaylamah elsewhere. As a result of these victories **Islamic control over Arabia** is consolidated, and with the support of his fellow leaders Abu Bakr is able to concentrate Islam's forces to the north. Particular efforts are made to convert those Arabs living in Syria and Iraq to the Islamic faith, and to wean their leaders away from "client" dependency on the Byzantine and Persian thrones. As in Arabia itself, such Arabs are both nomadic and settled. Medina's strategy is to gain the allegiance of the desert Arabs first, and then begin encroaching on the towns and cities of the Syrian coastline and the fertile alluvial basin of the Euphrates river. By the end of the year, Islamic forces have penetrated deep into Persian territory in two coordinated thrusts: one into **southern Iraq**, under the command of **al-Muthanna ibn Harithar**, the other,

ABU BAKR (C.573–634)

*A*lthough Abu Bakr's reign as First Caliph lasted barely two years, his contribution to Islam during its formative period was decisive. He was born as Abd Allah into a relatively minor merchant family of the Quraysh, and was Muhammad's right-hand man in Medina—helping to establish a rudimentary Islamic administration and conducting the delicate negotiations needed to bring outlying tribes into the Islamic fold. Tradition asserts that of all the "Companions of the Prophet" he was the closest: not only was he the first man to be converted to Islam outside Muhammad's family, but when Muhammad left Mecca for Medina in 622 with his enemies in pursuit, he traveled with Abu Bakr. Muhammad also took Abu Bakr's daughter Aisha as a wife—indeed Abu Bakr's name, adopted perhaps towards the end of his life, means "Father of the Maiden." During Muhammad's final illness Abu Bakr took over as prayer-leader at the first mosque, and for the support he gave Muhammad he is widely known as *as-Siddiq*, "the Faithful."

But it was after Muhammad's death that Abu Bakr came into his own. Because he had been so close to their leader, the Muslims of Medina were able to accept him as the natural successor and bury the differences between them, temporarily at least. It seems that Abu Bakr's outstanding talent was as a conciliator, but he also recognized that warfare outside the Arabian peninsula was the likeliest means of guaranteeing and extending the *umma*. Having overcome a series of domestic revolts, he not only rejected reprisals in most cases, but instead offered all Arabs the prospect of lucrative campaigns against the Byzantine and Persian empires. Nor was this simply a political solution—the campaigns were to be undertaken in the name of Allah as they had been in Muhammad's own lifetime. In this, Abu Bakr not only confirmed the practical direction Islam was to take, but helped cement its deep fusion of the religious and the political.

under the command of **Khalid ibn al-Walid**, towards **Hira** (once the capital of a powerful pro-Persian Arab dynasty known as the Lakhmids). At the same time Islamic agents and Koranic reciters are sent into the urban communities of Syria, Iraq and Egypt, and even at this early stage it is possible that some **Christian churches** in Jerusalem, Antioch and Alexandria are converted to mosques.

634 Abu Bakr dies aged 61. According to tradition, he nominates **Umar ibn al-Khattab** as his successor, but in any event Umar is acclaimed as the **Second Caliph** in Medina, Ali ibn Abu Talib again being passed over. Like his predecessor, Umar governs Islam in consultation with

UMAR IBN AL-KHATTAB (C.586-644)

*I*n 632 Umar ibn al-Khattab was the first man to swear allegiance to Abu Bakr as Muhammad's successor or *khalifa*; two years later he was rewarded with the caliphate itself. Whereas the first caliph was thoughtful and conciliatory, Umar had a reputation for being outspoken and aggressive, and made his name as a fearless war-leader.

A member of the Meccan Qurayshi elite, he had opposed Muhammad up until 618. Indeed, in that year he had determined to kill him, but—so the legend goes—was dissuaded by his own sister, Fatima, and her husband Said ibn Zayd. Fatima (not to be confused with Muhammad's daughter of the same name) had already converted to Islam, and when Umar tried to make her renounce her new faith, she responded by reciting *suras* from the Koran. Umar immediately underwent conversion himself, and thereafter began to support Muhammad, proving himself an invaluable battle commander during the conflict between Medina and Mecca. Like Abu Bakr, he offered Muhammad one of his daughters in marriage, and so became father-in-law to a man some fifteen or so years older than himself.

his peers and distributes at least half of his wealth to the poor and needy. According to tradition Umar continues to live humbly after becoming caliph, wearing worn-out clothes and repairing his own sandals. He is, however, the first caliph to adopt the title *amir al-Muminin*, "Commander of the Faithful," and it is during his caliphate that the first phase of the Arab Conquests culminates, with the subjugation of **Syria**, **Iraq** and **Egypt**. Because of these triumphs, Umar unambiguously secures the authority and prestige of the caliphate.

While the Islamic creed continues to spread and conquest proves highly profitable, Umar decides against sharing out conquered land among his

As caliph, Umar entrusted the execution of his strategies to his fellow commanders, among them the brilliant "Sword of Islam," **Khalid ibn al-Walid**. Umar did not initiate the wars against the Byzantine and Persian empires, but his purposefulness undoubtedly contributed to the first great wave of Arab conquest. On the political front, he devised the policies that made the conquests possible. Above all he insisted that conquered Jews and Christians be allowed to retain their faiths, and that existing administrative structures, including their personnel, be left largely intact—necessarily so, perhaps, since Arab-Islamic statecraft was still in its infancy. Towards his own people he was somewhat less accommodating, denying Muslim warriors the right to carve out estates for themselves in the conquered territories. Instead he instituted a system of stipendary rewards (the *diwan*) that greatly encouraged the emergence of an elite based on the *muhajirun* and *ansar*. Notwithstanding, within Islam Umar is regarded as the greatest of the Rashidun caliphs and his reign is still vaunted as a golden age.

troops, instead leaving ownership untouched and imposing **taxes**. To reward Islam's warriors, he establishes a register of stipends called the *diwan* (a term later used to describe the Islamic bureaucracy itself), each warrior receiving an annuity. Though the largest stipends are reserved for Muhammad's wives, those deemed "**Companions of the Prophet**" (ie who knew or served alongside Muhammad) receive larger allowances, while those only recently enlisted get less. While this system co-opts the Bedouin more fully into the Islamic *umma*, it reinforces the emergence of a **Medina-based elite**.

During the first year of Umar's caliphate, the war between Islam and the Byzantine empire intensifies as **Emperor Heraclius**, realizing the Arab-Islamic threat to Byzantine rule in Syria, begins dispatching larger armies for its protection. In the **Syrian desert** up to 25,000 Muslim troops, drawn from Hijaz, the Najd and Yemen, raid Byzantine outposts and successfully convert Syrian Arabs to their cause—thereby adding to their numbers. Khalid ibn al-Walid defeats a main Byzantine force at **Ajnadayn**, and is then transferred to the Persian front in Iraq, where he **captures Hira**. When Umar learns that Heraclius has dispatched another army to defend the provincial capital, **Damascus**, he orders Khalid to take his army to the Syrian front. Having advanced further north up the Euphrates, perhaps as far as **Mosul**, Khalid marches westwards across the Syrian desert. According to tradition, his men overcome dehydration by slaughtering some of their camels and drinking the water from their stomachs. At any rate, either at the end of this year or the beginning of the next, Khalid dramatically appears near Damascus.

635 Khalid ibn al-Walid defeats a Byzantine army during a major engagement at **Marj al-Saffar**. Following this victory, **Damascus** itself falls to Islamic forces, and rapidly becomes a center of Islamic faith and power in the Syrian region. The news from Iraq, however, is less heartening: a Muslim army suffers defeat at the hands of the Persians during the **Battle of the Bridge (*al-Jisr*)**, north of Hira. Up to 4000 Muslim warriors die fighting, or drown shortly afterwards.

Umar orders the **expulsion of Jews and Christians** from Arabia—either to rid the Islamic heartland of potential support for the Byzantine or Persian empires or to create an undiluted Islamic *umma* in the same territory. In conquered territories, however, Jews and Christians are permitted to practise their faiths; and in some occupied towns, churches are used alternatively for Christian and Muslim worship.

636 The Battle of the Bridge is avenged when a Persian army is crushed by **al-Muthanna** at **Buwayb**. According to Islamic histories, the Arabs are aided by the **Banu Taghlib**, a tribe of Nestorian Christians; because of their assistance, the Taghlib are absolved from paying *jizya*.

Arab control over **Iraq** is extended by **Sad ibn Abi Waqqas**, who emerges as a front-rank Muslim commander.

In **Syria**, Khalid ibn al-Walid wars against the northern cities of **Aleppo** and **Antioch**. Further south, Arab forces under **Abu Ubayda** set about reducing garrisons and cities in what are now **Lebanon, Jordan** and **Palestine**.

637 In **Iraq**, the Sassanian Persians, led by **Yazdegird III**, attempt a counter-offensive, but are heavily defeated by Sad ibn Abi Waqqas during a three-day battle at **al-Qadisiyya**, and later at **Ulalula**. As a result of these victories Sad is able to march on the Persian capital, **Ctesiphon**, which is hurriedly abandoned by Yazdegird III. With the fall of Ctesiphon, Arab-Islamic control over Iraq is secured. Mustering such forces as remain loyal to him, Yazdegird III retreats eastwards into Khurasan, pursued by Islamic forces.

In the wake of the victories in Iraq, Umar orders the creation of **Islamic garrison-towns** along the Euphrates, leading to the foundation of **Kufa** (al-Kufa) and **Basra** (al-Basra).

Probably in the same year, a Muslim army defeats Byzantine reinforcements on the banks of the **Yarmuk**, a tributary of the river Jordan, enabling Medina to strengthen its hold over Palestine.

Byzantine influence is increasingly confined to Mediterranean garrison ports such as Caesarea, which can be supplied from the sea, but these too come under Muslim siege.

At Umar's behest, the **Islamic calendar**, beginning with the *Hijra* of 622, is formalized. According to this system, 637 CE becomes 15 AH (*al-Hijra*).

638 In southern Syria (Palestine), **Jerusalem falls** to an army led by Abu Ubayda. Caliph Umar travels to Jerusalem, where he prays to Allah on the **Temple Mount** (Al-haram al-Sharif)—formerly the site of the Jews' central place of worship, destroyed by the Romans in 70 AD. Believed by Jews and Muslims alike to be the place where Abraham was prevented from killing his son Isaac by God's direct intervention, Muslims also hold that it is the site where Muhammad is said to have ascended to Allah in 620 on his "Night Journey"—making Jerusalem the third holiest city of Islam after Mecca and Medina.

Islam's power over **Iraq** is consolidated as Yazdegird III is pushed further east. The Persian ruler appeals to Emperor Taizong of China for military assistance, but his entreaties are ignored.

639 While Muslim forces push northwards into **Armenia**, a new front is opened against the Byzantine province of **Egypt**, where **Alexandria** falls into Muslim hands. According to tradition, when Umar is asked what should be done with the great library of Alexandria, he orders it to be destroyed, on the grounds that those books in accordance with the Koran are superfluous, while those that aren't cannot be permitted to survive. The Arab-Muslim conquest of Egypt proceeds rapidly, partly due to the complicity of Egyptian **Coptic Christians**—who are resentful of Constantinople's attempts to impose "Greek" orthodoxy on them. The Copts, whose doctrines are similar to the Syrian Monophysites, are assured the right to continue their own forms of worship.

640 During what becomes known as the "**Year of Ashes**," many of Islam's conquerors in Syria die of the plague, including the commander Abu Ubayda. Umar orders that a **mosque** be built in Jerusalem, and prohibits the building of new churches and synagogues in conquered territories.

The Syrian port cities of **Caesarea** and **Tripoli** continue to hold out against the Muslims.

641 Byzantium attempts to recover Syria, but is repulsed, while Caesarea and Tripoli fall to the Muslims. However, Islamic armies fail to cross the Taurus mountains into **Anatolia** (present-day Turkey).

In **Egypt**, Islamic control is assured after the Byzantine governor unilaterally hands over the whole province to the caliphate. The Arab commander, **Amr ibn al-As**, founds the garrison town of **Fustat**, located in the suburbs of present-day Cairo.

642 The remains of the Sassanian Persian army are defeated at the **Battle of Nehawand**.

In Egypt, work begins on the **Amr Mosque** in **Fustat**. A **canal** between the Nile and the town of Suez, commissioned by the Egyptian Pharoah Necho II in 610 BC, is restored, enabling Arabia—particularly the Hijaz region—to benefit from Egypt's sizeable **grain surplus**.

Khalid ibn al-Walid dies, having been judiciously "retired" by Umar.

644 In November, **Caliph Umar dies** after being stabbed by **Abu Luluah Firoz**, a converted Persian slave belonging to the governor of Basra, as he is shepherding the faithful into the mosque in Medina to offer prayers at daybreak. Before he dies, however, Umar is able to recommend that a *shura* (council) of the surviving senior "Companions of the Prophet" is convened to choose his successor. The council, whose members include Ali ibn Abu Talib, Uthman ibn Affan, Zubayr and Sad ibn Abi Waqqas, determines that **Uthman** should become Third Caliph. Ali is once again passed over.

Uthman, a son-in-law of Muhammad by virtue of successive marriages to two of Muhammad's daughters, Kulthum and Raqqyyah, and a member of the powerful Meccan **Qurayshi Umayya** clan, continues the policies of his predecessors, further expanding Islamic territories during the early years of his reign. He also regularly consults the *shura* that has chosen him as Caliph, partly to ensure the loyalty of Ali, and evidence suggests that he is a capable administrator. However, he is generally regarded as being less able than either Abu Bakr or Umar, and his inflexibility about refusing to allow his commanders and wealthy supporters land grants in newly conquered ter-

ISLAM AND THE ARAB CONQUESTS

*T*he three main monotheistic religions spread and were disseminated in quite different ways. Judaism began as the faith of the Jewish people and has largely remained that way, fanning out across the world with the Jewish diaspora before returning to the Middle East with the creation of the state of Israel after World War II. Christianity—which, like Islam, has frequently been promoted as a universal creed—was first disseminated by missionaries traveling through the Roman Empire; only much later, when European Christian nations began acquiring overseas possessions, were proselytization and conquest combined. Islam, however, was carried out of Arabia by a series of conquests largely motivated by religious faith itself. Indeed, it is often said that Islam was "spread by the sword."

This is not the whole story, however. From the time of Muhammad onwards, Muslim agents worked to promote the "Message of the Prophet"; likewise, recorded instances of conquered peoples being forced to accept Islam are the exception, not the rule. But it is undeniable that conquest—viewed by its perpetrators as a form of *jihad*—enabled the gradual Islamicization of territories taken first by the Muslim Arabs, and later on by non-Arab Muslims such as Persians, Berbers, Afghans and Turks. Initially,

ritories opens up divisions within the Islamic *umma*. As a *muhajirun* he is also generally less conciliatory towards the *ansar* of Medina, and incurs widespread resentment by appointing relatives to high office—among them **Muawiyyah**, the son of Muhammad's great "adversary," Abu Sufyan. Uthman is also accused of displaying "vanity" as caliph, to the annoyance of many Arabs—particularly those of Bedouin descent, resistant to any form of kingship.

too, the Arabs adopted some of the means of imperial rule employed by their Byzantine and Sassanian predecessors: diplomacy among tribes was employed, existing religious and cultural practices were tolerated, and fortified garrisons were constructed. Significantly, though, Islamic garrisons invariably included a mosque as part of their structure, which all those living inside were expected to attend for Friday prayers. Newly commissioned garrisons at Kufa and Basra in Iraq, Fustat in Egypt and Qum in Iran attracted migrants from Arabia keen to exploit new opportunities in new lands, and in time became great cities as well as regional centers of Islam.

While conversion to Islam was not discouraged in the first century of conquest, it wasn't greatly encouraged either—largely because Muslims were exempt from the *jizya* tax. If the newly conquered countries had been converted en masse, the Arab empire would have rapidly been drained of revenue. Tolerance was the norm instead, and Christians, Jews and some Zoroastrians became *ahl-adh-dhimma*—protected peoples. But if there were practical reasons for extending tolerance at first, as time passed and growing numbers of people did convert, a sort of reverse conquest inevitably occurred. Islam ceased to be an exclusively or even mainly Arab enterprise, and became strongly influenced by the cultures and customs it absorbed.

Muslim armies begin to **advance across northern Africa** from Fustat in Egypt. The Byzantine city of **Tripoli** (modern Tarabulus, the capital of Libya) falls to Islam. As a result, a new Islamic province, **Ifriqiya**—an Arabized version of the Roman "Africa," also used as the name of a territory in central North Africa—is declared.

Islamic forces simultaneously take control of **Armenia**, and advance eastwards through **Khurasan** into Afghanistan, seizing the Persian city of **Herat**. Conceptually at least, the **River Oxus** now becomes the target eastern boundary of Islam, while further south Muslim

JIHAD

*A*t its most literal, *jihad*—sometimes called the "sixth pillar of Islam"—is cognate with words such as "struggle," "endeavor" and "effort." As such, it may be applied to almost any kind of striving, individual or collective, that accords with Islamic principle. To qualify as an architect and aim to build a mosque, or to construct a dam where it will benefit members of the Islamic *umma*, are both examples of *jihad*. In this sense it is a sort of selfless social duty.

Yet *jihad* also means, or quickly came to mean, "holy war." In the Koran there are several passages that deal with the relations between *jihad* and combat. The fourth and fifth verses of the ninth *sura* ("Repentance") declare: "Proclaim a woeful punishment to the unbelievers, except to those idolaters who have honored their treaties with you in every detail and aided none against you. With these keep faith, until their treaties have run their term. God loves the righteous. When the sacred months are over slay the idolaters wherever you find them. Arrest them, besiege them, and lie in ambush for them everywhere. If they repent and take to prayer and render

troops make their first forays into **Baluchistan** and **Sind** on the edge of the Indian subcontinent.

645 In Egypt, **Alexandria revolts**, aided by a Byzantine fleet dispatched from Constantinople. Just six years after seizing the city, its Muslim rulers are temporarily driven out.

646 The rebellion in Alexandria collapses. Islam offers Alexandria's Coptic Christians unprecedented **compensation** for having failed to protect them against Byzantine aggression. As control over Egypt is

the alms levy [*zakat*], allow them to go their way. God is forgiving and merciful." Hardly surprisingly, such injunctions have been taken to imply open season against anyone who is not a Muslim—or indeed, since elsewhere the Koran is equally critical of "hypocrites," on Muslims whose faith is thought lacking.

Equally, though, the Koran is specific—if not altogether consistent—about when war or violence is legitimate. Generally speaking, Muslims should not cast the first stone, though what constitutes that is problematic. In theory at least, no war can be justified unless it is in some sense "holy"—one reason, perhaps, why the Arab Conquests were regularly dressed up by their instigators as *jihad*. Yet, in a profound sense, *jihad* considered as holy war was and is secondary. According to tradition Caliph Umar, returning from a visit to the front against Byzantium, famously declared that warfare was the "lesser *jihad*." The "greater *jihad*" was to build a just and equitable society amongst those who already swore obedience to Allah.

re-established, Arab-Muslim warriors resume **campaigning west-wards** along the North African coast.

647 Advancing further westwards into **Tunisia**, the Arab Muslims defeat a Byzantine army at **Subaytilah** (Sheitla).

649 Having built up a navy of its own in Egyptian and Palestinian dockyards, Islam mounts an assault against **Cyprus** in the eastern Mediterranean, currently held by the Byzantines. The island is captured, and becomes a forward base for raids against **Anatolia** and **Greece**, both Byzantine provinces.

650 **Political unrest** spreads in Arabia and among parts of the newly acquired Arab empire. As well as resentment at Uthman's "family" appointments, there is a widespread feeling that the spoils of Islam's conquests are not being fairly distributed, but are finding their way into the hands of the Umayya clan. At garrisons including **Kufa** and **Basra** in Iraq, the "common" soldiery, many of Bedouin stock, voice frustration at being required to serve for long periods so far away from their homelands for inadequate rewards. As dissent grows, a new kind of criticism emerges—namely that Islam is failing to live up to the ideals asserted by Muhammad. Amid these circumstances there is increased support for **Ali ibn Abu Talib**, although for the present Ali himself remains aloof from factional infighting and loyal to Uthman.

Uthman commissions a **standardization of the Koran**, compiled under the supervision of **Zayd ibn Thabit**, previously a close companion of Muhammad as well as his personal scribe and secretary. Zayd collates existing versions of the revelations received by Muhammad. The resultant volume becomes the "authorized" version, accepted by all future Islamic sects as the true text. Once Zayd has completed his work, Uthman orders copies to be made by other scribes, and these are distributed throughout the Arab empire. In retrospect the glory acquired by Uthman as the instigator of this undertaking outweighs his shortcomings as a ruler—though it is probable that his motives in commissioning the project also involve stamping out heterodoxy.

The last Sassanian ruler, **Yazdegird III**, is murdered at Merv in northern Iran. Within a few years the whole of his former empire will have been successfully incorporated within the Arab empire.

In this year **Abu Sufyan**, the acknowledged head of the Qurayshi Umayya clan, dies. Although after 622 Abu Sufyan was one of Muhammad's principal Meccan enemies, following his conversion to Islam in 630 he was rewarded with high office, and at the time of his death he is governor of southwest Arabia (including Yemen). His son, **Muawiyyah ibn Abu Sufyan**, already governor of Damascus, becomes the new Umayyad chief.

651 According to tradition, Uthman **loses the "Ring of the Prophet**," a piece of jewelry formerly belonging to Muhammad, in a well outside Medina. Islam is beset by difficulties for ten years, supposedly as a consequence.

653 Arab-Islamic control of **Armenia** is consolidated.

654 The Arabs plunder the Byzantine island of **Rhodes**.

655 A **Byzantine fleet is defeated** by an Arab fleet off the coast of **Lycia**, marking the end of Byzantine maritime dominance of the eastern Mediterranean.

In both Iraq and Egypt, there is **mutiny** among some elements of the Islamic army in protest at the "corruption" of Uthman's court.

656 As unrest spreads inside the empire, a band of soldiers travels from Fustat in Egypt to Medina and **surrounds Uthman's compound** in an attempt to gain redress. When their demands are refused, they storm Uthman's living quarters and murder him; according to tradition, Uthman is assassinated as he reads the Koran. In the ensuing turmoil **Ali ibn Abu Talib** is proclaimed the **Fourth Caliph** in Medina. As well as being supported by a majority of the chieftains of Medina—who are annoyed at the continuing dominance of the Meccans in general, and of the Umayya clan especially—Ali enjoys the backing of an emergent sect later known as the **Kharajites** (literally "seceders"). It is hoped, especially among the Kharajites, that the elevation of a close relative of Muhammad known for his piety will lead to a restoration of Islamic purity. Ali's elevation is not universally approved,

THE KHARAJITES

A strong feature of Islamic history is the periodic eruption of movements and sects that have as their goal the full implementation of the Koran and the restoration of what they consider to have been the sort of community or *umma* molded by Muhammad himself. Given that the Koran is, in most interpretations, intrinsically puritanical—demanding submission to Allah, and forbidding the consumption of alcohol and other human pleasures—these movements have often been characterized as "fundamentalist."

The first such sect that sought a return to the 'true' values of Islam were the **Kharajites**; and because they were the first, they are of unique importance. During the rule of the third caliph, Uthman, a body of Muslims, angered by the ascendancy of the Umayya clan and by Uthman's drift toward autocracy, attached themselves to Ali, who as Muhammad's closest surviving male relative seemed an altogether more appropriate leader. But among some, attitudes hardened yet further. After the Battle of Siffin and the inconclusive negotiations between Ali and Muawiyyah that followed, this smaller group renounced even Ali, and it is from this disavowal that the Kharajites (literally 'seceders'), derive their name.

The slogan of the Kharajites was *la hukm illa li-llah*—"No decision but Allah's." From this flowed two maxims: first, that only a man of outstanding piety and integrity was fit to lead Islam; and second, that anyone guilty of a "grave sin" should be expelled from the *umma* and

however: it is opposed by **Muawiyyah ibn Abu Sufyan** in Syria and by Muhammad's widow **Aisha**—probably on account of her rivalry with Ali's wife Fatima.

treated as an infidel—among such sins being irregular (let alone non-) attendance at a mosque. What the Kharajites proposed, therefore, was analogous to a community of saints. Significantly, some of the Kharajite leaders are said to have been "reciters," those who had learned the Koranic *suras* directly from Muhammad and then disseminated them.

The Kharajites were prepared to fight and die for their beliefs—even against fellow Muslims. But the fight went against them, and many Kharajites were either killed in battle by Ali's forces or were subsequently eliminated. Yet a sufficient number survived, gathering first in Basra, later in Kufa. In time they abandoned warfare, although they continued to attack the authority of the caliphate.

In the 7th and 8th centuries the Kharajites spawned a number of other reformist sects, among them the Najdaites, Azraqites and Waqiffiya; and in modern times Kharajism is represented by the Ibadites, who make up a majority Islamic following in Oman, as well as by enclaves in North Africa—in all, over half a million souls. But historically their impact has been far greater. They were the precursors of the Wahabis, the Muslim Brotherhood, even the Taliban. Literalistic in their attitudes toward Muhammad and the Koran, the Kharajites advanced an interpretation of Islam as a sort of permanent revolution. For them, no departure from the original master plan was acceptable, however slight. If the pursuit of "truth" meant conflict, then conflict was a sacred duty.

Ali's difficulties are compounded by his reluctance to disown his more outspoken followers (sometimes called the **Alids**) or punish Uthman's murderers, who also support him—even though there is no suspicion that he is implicated in Uthman's death.

Aided by her kinsmen **Talhah** and **Zubayr**, Aisha creates a strong anti-Ali party, and at the same time the garrison in **Basra**, southern Iraq, mutinies against the new caliph.

As battle lines harden, and the Arab-Islamic empire descends into a civil war known as the **first *fitna*** (literally "time of temptation"), Ali abandons Medina and establishes his capital in **Kufa**, which has declared in his favor. Determined to destroy Ali, Aisha and her faction follow him into Iraq, and establish themselves at **Basra**, where they attach the rebels to their cause. Before the end of the year Ali moves to attack his enemies, and the two armies meet outside Basra. In the ensuing **Battle of the Camel**—so named because Aisha watches the fighting seated on a camel—Ali is victorious, while Zubayr and Talhah are slain. Aisha is taken prisoner and returned to Medina under house arrest. Ali remains at Kufa, however, and Medina ceases to be the administrative center of the Arab-Islamic empire.

657 Despite his victory, Ali fails to assert his authority over the empire at large. Discontent in the army continues as, like his predecessors, Ali refuses to allow conquered lands to be distributed as booty among Arab Muslim warriors—though he does permit his close followers to take possession of **Sawad**, a fertile region south of Kufa.

In **Egypt**, the governor (sympathetic to Ali's cause) is overthrown by Arabs loyal to the Meccan establishment. In **Damascus**, Muawiyyah ibn Abu Sufyan, insistent that Uthman's death be avenged, continues to withhold his allegiance and assembles an army, which marches against Ali in Iraq. For the second time in the space of barely a year two Muslim armies confront each other—this time at **Siffin** on the upper Euphrates. Although the battle lasts three days, it is inconclusive and the two sides agree to negotiate instead. **Amr ibn al-As**, the veteran conqueror of Egypt, presides but these discussions are equally indecisive. Without formally giving in to Ali, Muawiyyah retains control of Syria, while Ali retains the title of caliph, his authority crippled.

In the aftermath of Siffin, the Kharajites, dismayed by the Caliph's willingness to compromise, withdraw their allegiance from Ali—the act of "secession" from which their name derives.

658 Having returned to Syria, Muawiyyah expands his power-base and is **proclaimed caliph in Jerusalem**. Ali rejects Muawiyyah's elevation, but lacks the military strength to challenge him.

The **Kharajites**, meanwhile, establish themselves as an armed **resistance movement** in Iraq and Arabia. Opting to reimpose his authority by eliminating the Kharajites, Ali defeats their main force at **Nahrawan**. Despite his efforts to pursue and kill those Kharajites who survive, he fails to eradicate the movement as a whole; in Basra especially a Kharajite community survives.

660 Muawiyyah mounts Islam's first, unsuccessful, campaign against the Byzantine capital, **Constantinople**.

661 Ali is murdered in the central mosque at Kufa. His assassin, known as **Ibn Muljam**, is presumed to be a Kharajite, although his precise motivation is unclear—he might be avenging deaths within his own family resulting from Ali's purge of the Kharajites, or perhaps offering a "bride-price" for the daughter of another similarly affected family. In Kufa, **al-Hassan**—Ali's eldest son, and grandson of Muhammad—is proclaimed caliph, the first time the caliphate has passed in direct male descent from father to son. Al-Hassan's elevation is immediately repudiated by Muawiyyah ibn Abu Safyan, and rather than fight a war he knows he cannot win, al-Hassan agrees to **surrender his title** in Muawiyyah's favor.

As a result of Hasan's abdication, Muawiyyah becomes undisputed caliph, the Arab-Islamic empire is reunited and the **first *fitna*** draws to a close. But while Hassan's caliphate will go unrecognized in the mainstream Sunni Islamic tradition, in the alternative Shia tradition he will be regarded as the second *Imam*, his father Ali being the first.

CHAPTER THREE

The Umayyads

{632-750 (40-132 AH)}

ON THE FACE OF IT, the acceptance of **Muawiyyah ibn Abu Sufyan** as caliph in 661 did not constitute a dramatic break with the past, even though Muawiyyah's accession to power depended as much on force of arms as on consensus. Like the four Rashidun caliphs who had preceded him, Muawiyyah continued, for a while at least, to rule over Islam in consultation with the *shura* (council of elders). Yet just because Islam now comprised an empire as well as a faith, and also because Muawiyyah was anxious to promote the interests of his own family, a profound change was perhaps inevitable. This was realized in 680, when Muawiyyah was succeeded by his son **Yazid**, establishing a dynasty—the **Umayyads**—that took personal possession of the caliphate until 750, when it was displaced by another dynastic house, the **Abbasids**.

As it happens, the third caliph, **Uthman**, had also been a member of the Umayya clan, but the notion of a hereditary monarchy was alien to both Arab custom and the Muslim *umma* (community) established by Muhammad. Well before his death, however, Muawiyyah was able to persuade a majority of his peers that his son should succeed him. In part, no doubt, this was a consequence of Muawiyyah's own forceful personality: Yazid himself had nothing in particular to recommend him for the role of supreme leader. But as important—if not more so—was the way in which Muawiyyah had placed himself at the center of the administrative apparatus required to run the burgeoning Islamic empire.

An empire could be run without an emperor, but the **Arab-Islamic empire** had expanded with unprecedented speed during the 7th century. Moreover, the territories outside Arabia over which the Muslim Arabs first exerted their authority were habituated to the rule of emperors—either the **Persian** emperor, or the emperor of **Byzantium**. And until only very recently the Arabs themselves had no experience in administering large territories or many different peoples. Rather than adapt the *shura* to the cares and responsibilities of imperial rule and create a new kind of government, Muawiyyah continued where Uthman had left off and simply commandeered existing Persian and Byzantine administrative machineries.

Probably Muawiyyah was aided in this enterprise by a reluctance among Arabs to volunteer themselves for all but the most senior appointments, which, barely thirty years after Muhammad's death, would still have seemed demeaning to the traditional desert ethos. But it was not just non-Arab bureaucrats Muawiyyah collected around him. Even before he assumed the role of caliph, he had begun deploying soldiers recruited in Syria, and by the time of his death there was something like a **palace guard** whose loyalty was as much to its immediate employer as to the more generalized concept of a Muslim community.

Muawiyyah's strategy was justified in the sense that it enabled the newly acquired Arab-Muslim empire to hold together and go on expanding. But in the long term it created an unresolved tension within Islam itself. While Abu Bakr, Umar, Uthman and Ali had felt no contradiction in combining political and spiritual leadership—indeed, such a combination was part and parcel of Muhammad's Islamic revolution—for many Muslims after 661, and particularly after 680, the emergence of palpably **royal institutions**, including a royal court and a royal family, smacked of un-Islamic practice.

In modern times, similar reservations have generated "Islamist" protests against the temporal concerns of "secular" Muslim governments. And even during the Umayyad period there was hostility towards a caliphate that was perceived (in some quarters) as having abandoned Muhammad's mission to create a godly society on earth. The puritanical **Kharajites**, who had leveled similar criticisms against the Fourth Caliph Ali, not only survived, but demonstrated their resilience by mounting a series of rebellions, great and small, and by fostering new, anti-authoritarian sects including the **Najdaites**, the **Azraqites** and the **Qadarites**.

Just as significantly, there were those who opposed the Umayyads on more overtly political grounds, chief among them the followers of Ali himself. The **Alids** did not object on principle to a hereditary succession in the matter of Islam's leadership, but argued that instead of passing down through the Umayya line, it should be reserved to the direct descendants of Muhammad himself—the sons of the Prophet's daughter **Fatima** by Ali and their male descendants. The Alids became known as **Shiites** (or Shiis), from the Arabic *shi'at Ali*, meaning the "party of Ali," and today constitute the largest minority following within Islam. In time, Shiism developed distinctive religious doctrines, setting it apart from mainstream or **Sunni Islam**. But even though the gradual emergence of Shia Islam played an important role in forcing Sunni Islam to define itself, during the Umayyad period Shiism was primarily a focus of political dissent, drawing some support from those Arab clans and chieftains who felt they had been muscled out by Muawiyyah and his Umayya successors.

Soon enough, therefore, the Umayyads faced different kinds of opposition—opposition which could only be partially placated by a continuing drive for empire and the spoils that came with it. As early as 671, there was a **Kharajite** revolt in Kufa, and in 680 Ali's second son **Husayn** made a bid for power, only to be "martyred" on the **Plain of Kerbala**. This was immediately followed by what is known as the **second *fitna*** (civil war), when **Ibn al-Zubayr** attempted to oust the

Umayyads from Arabia itself; while in the Ummayad capital, Damascus, tension was rife between two rival Arab clans, the **Qays** and the **Kalb**.

Unrest continued throughout the Umayyad period, but in the end the dynasty succumbed to the inherent weaknesses of hereditary monarchy. The line simply failed to produce individual rulers of compelling stature, and in 750 a more energetic Arab chieftain, **Abbas al-Saffah**, exploiting unrest among Islam's disaffected Shiites for his own political ends, brought the dynasty down. Yet the rule of the Umayyads was by no means simply about ongoing power struggles within the Arab elite. In at least one profound respect, the nature of the Islamic empire, and with it Islam itself, began to change.

Although non-Arabs had from the earliest days been welcomed into the Islamic *umma*, such **converts** (*muwalis*) were relatively few in number, and were expected to affiliate themselves to an Arab tribe. Then, as the empire started growing, the Arabs naturally assumed the role of colonial masters, and relatively few efforts were made at further conversions. But under the later Umayyads this changed—especially as more and more Arabs became **urbanized**. In Damascus, Basra, Kufa, Qum, Fustat and other cities outside Arabia, despite some attempts at segregation, Arabs and non-Arabs increasingly rubbed shoulders with one another. As a result, many Syrians, Iraqis, Persians, Egyptians and others adopted the faith of their new masters, and Islam ceased being primarily a racial community, and became ethnically broad-based instead.

Apart from anything else, becoming Muslim meant no longer having to pay the *jizya* **tax** levied on non-Muslims—one initial reason why Arabs had been reluctant to make converts. Equally, continuing imperial expansion necessitated the recruitment of non-Arab soldiers, and it was essential that these embraced the Islamic faith. But perhaps another factor that encouraged conversion was the emergence of a compelling, even supremacist **Islamic architecture**, given early expression by the Dome of the Rock, completed in 691 on Jerusalem's

Temple Mount, a site sacred to both Jews and Christians. Thereafter mosques, often domed, not only dominated conquered cities and newly built garrison towns alike, but often their surrounding landscape.

Such developments were attended by other sorts of activity. As the empire bedded down, **commerce** prospered, spawning a transcontinental trading system that would eventually stretch from Spain in the west to China and other parts of the Far East, reviving the ancient Silk Roads and expanding the "southern sea" routes that led from the Persian Gulf to India and beyond. In the figure of **Hasan al-Basri**, too, Islam produced the first in a long line of scholars and thinkers who were to make **Islamic learning** a valued feature of the medieval world. Indeed, within less than a century of when Muhammad first preached his radical monotheistic doctrines at Mecca, Islam was already set to become an important and enduring civilization.

661 As **Muawiyyah ibn Abu Sufyan** becomes caliph, Ali's son **Hassan** retires with a generous stipend to Medina—where he will become known as "the Divorcer" on account of his many wives and even greater number of concubines. Muawiyyah stays in **Damascus**, which becomes the capital of the Arab-Islamic empire for the next century. Equally talented as a soldier and administrator, Muawiyyah restores the unity of Islam and its territories. His character, as recorded by Muslim historians, is that of a patriarch who combines great strength with charm. At the beginning of his reign he governs in consultation with the surviving "Companions of the Prophet" and their sons, in much the same way the Rashidun had done, and is careful to spread the appointments he makes among the factions that make up his *shura*, or advisory counsel. As a devout Muslim, he insists that his fellow Muslims should neither fight nor quarrel among themselves. Fairly rapidly, however, he adopts a more monarchical style of rule, sometimes making senior appointments from outside the Qurayshi elite, and increasing the size of his army (which includes Syrians as well as Arabs). He **resumes military campaigns** to expand the Arab-Islamic empire. During his reign new territories are acquired in the east and in North Africa, and campaigning also occurs in **Anatolia** (modern Turkey). He continues his predecessors' policies of not making land grants to his victorious warriors however; nor does he encourage the conversion of conquered peoples.

662 Muawiyyah acknowledges that **Ziyad ibn Abu Abihi** is a son of Abu Sufyan, after doubts about the latter's paternity, and appoints him **governor of Iraq**. Based in Basra, which now develops into an important city as well as military garrison, Ziyad will rule over the eastern parts of the Arab-Islamic empire on Muawiyyah's behalf for thirteen years.

663 As Arab forces launch raids against Sicily in the mid-Mediterranean for the first time, the Byzantine emperor **Constans II** moves his court from Constantinople to Rome in an attempt to reunify the Roman empire. Muawiyyah responds by increasing his attacks on Anatolia and against Byzantine shipping.

In the east, Arab forces begin regularly crossing the Oxus into the territory known as **Transoxiana**. Mainly inhabited by nomadic pastoralists of Turkic origin, under Islamic influence Transoxiana will develop into a region of towns and cities, partly due to revived trade with China along the ancient **Silk Roads**.

668 Following six years of Arab plundering in Anatolia, the Byzantine court returns to Constantinople under **Constantine IV**.

669 Muawiyyah dispatches an army to **besiege Constantinople**, but the siege fails, marking the beginning of a period during which the strength and fortunes of the Byzantine empire begin to revive.

670 Campaigning out of Fustat in Egypt, Arab forces under the command of **Uqba ibn Nafi** resume the conquest of North Africa. A new garrison is created at **Quairaywan** (Qayrawan in modern Tunisia) as a springboard for further conquest westwards. Quairaywan is sited away from the coast—perhaps to protect it against Byzantine naval assault, but also to enable the Arabs to control and pacify the desert **Berber tribes**.

Constantinople is again **besieged** by Arab forces. An Arab fleet passes through the Dardanelles into the **Sea of Marmora** and, perhaps for the first time, Muslims set foot on mainland Europe. The siege itself fails, however, and Muawiyyah orders his forces to withdraw.

In the east, as Arab control over **Khurasan** (northeast Iran) is consolidated, a new garrison is established at **Marv** (Merv), made up of several thousand soldiers and their families drawn from Basra, Kufa and other garrisons no longer on the frontline of Arab expansion.

Hasan—Ali's son and Muhammad's eldest grandson—dies of natural causes in Medina in the same year. The attention of the **Alids**, as the early Shiites are called, now focuses on his younger brother **Husayn** (Hussein), later styled the third of the Shiite Imams.

671 In **Kufa**, where the influence of the Kharajites is strong, a revolt breaks out against Umayyad rule, but is quickly crushed by Ziyad.

678 An Arab fleet involved in a blockade of Constantinople is heavily defeated by a Byzantine fleet at **Syllaeum**. Further Arab assaults on Byzantium are suspended as a consequence, and a peace between the two empires is brokered that lasts thirty years.

680 Muawiyyah dies, having secured the succession of his son **Yazid**, thus establishing the **Umayyad Dynasty**. Although Muawiyyah has gained the acquiescence of many Arab tribal and clan leaders, among others there is fierce opposition to the creation of a hereditary monarchy. There is also opposition among the Alids, who promote the claims of **Husayn** to the caliphate instead.

Hoping to take advantage of renewed unrest in **Kufa**, Husayn heads there with a small band of followers. Before he can reach the city, however, its governor persuades its inhabitants that Islamic unity is of greater importance than Husayn's claims, and Husayn's party (which includes women and children) is massacred on the **Plain of Kerbala** outside the city. According to Shiite tradition, Husayn is the last to

SHIA ISLAM

Shiism forms the most significant minority within Islam, today accounting for perhaps ten percent of all Muslims, or around 100 million individuals. In both Iran and Iraq, Shiites make up a majority of Muslims, while elsewhere there are Shia enclaves—for example the Ismailis in western Afghanistan. But while Shiites have evolved beliefs and practices that distinguish them from "mainstream" Sunni Muslims, and while tensions between the two groups have sometimes spilled over into bloodshed, both have often given each other a grudging respect as members of the same wider community.

The origins of Shiism date back to Muhammad's death, when some proposed that his cousin and son-in-law, Ali ibn Abu Talib, should become the first caliph. Throughout the following decades the idea persisted that Islam's leader should be drawn from the Prophet's close relatives, and once the Umayyad dynasty had assumed power, political opposition naturally tended to focus around the "family" that had been deprived of what many considered their birthright. But it was the "martyrdom" of Husayn, Ali's second son, at Kerbala in 680 that set Shiism firmly on an independent course.

From this event—which was perceived as an ultimate expression of persecution and betrayal—evolved the theory of a direct line, or succession, of infallible "Imams." In Shiism the word is used to denote a supreme, even semi-divine, leader, contrasting with Sunni practice, where an "imam" is simply the prayer-leader (and usually resident cleric) at a mosque. Complications arose however about the identity of some of the Shia Imams. Thus, when the Fourth Imam Ali Zayn died in 731, confusion arose as to whether his brother Muhammad al-Baqir or his young son Zayd ibn Ali should be regarded as the Fifth Imam. Most accepted Muhammad al-Baqir, but those who backed Zayd created a new minority, known variously as "Zaydis" and "Fiver Shiis." Then, following the Sixth Imam Jafar al-Sadiq's death in 765, a similar dispute arose—some backing one son, Musa al-Kazim, others another, Ismail, the latter becoming known as "Sevener Shiis," or Ismailis.

In the centuries that followed, Shiism intermittently played a crucial role in the development of Islam. In the 10th century, Ismaili Shiites, calling themselves "Fatimids" in honor of Muhammad's daughter, created a breakaway caliphate in Egypt; in the 16th century, the Safavid rulers of Persia made Shiism the state religion; and in 1979 the Iranian Revolution of Ayatollah Khomeini was essentially a Shiite rebellion against the secularism of the reigning Shah. Such episodes were informed by a growing divergence from Islamic "orthodoxy." Influenced by Christian and Persian (Zoroastrian) ideas, Shiism developed a messianic cult of saints centered on the Imams—particularly the twelfth and last, or "hidden," Imam. Such figures were perceived as being "friends of Allah" who could mediate between man and God and were therefore worthy of worship, even to the displacement of Muhammad. This, coupled with Shiism's inveterate disdain for secular government in any shape or form, has often exposed Shiites to persecution. Shiites are not obliged to attest their beliefs, however, but have often resorted to *taqiyah* (dissimulation), allowed by the Koran when self-preservation depends on it. Notwithstanding, whereas most Sunni Muslims grudgingly accept Ali as the fourth of the Rashidun caliphs, "Imamite" Shiis openly reject Abu Bakr, Umar and Uthman, as well as all the Umayyads and Abbasids, as usurpers.

die, clutching an infant son in his arms. The "**Battle of Kerbala**" and the "martyrdom" of Husayn will become the central episode in the emergence of **Shiism**, marking their separation from "mainstream" Islam. It is also one among several events that signal the beginning of the **second *fitna***, as Islam is again plunged into factional and sectarian conflict.

A serious revolt erupts at about the same time in the **Hijaz** region of Arabia, led by **Abdallah ibn al-Zubayr**, the son of Zubayr killed during the Battle of the Camel in 656. Ibn al-Zubayr, representing the old Muslim aristocracy, is strongly opposed to the Umayyads on political grounds, and quickly seizes control of **Mecca** and **Medina**.

Elsewhere there are fresh Kharajite rebellions. Even in Syria, the stronghold of Umayyad power, there is friction between two Arab tribes, the **Kalb** (originally from southern Arabia and sometimes referred to as Yemenis) and the **Qays** (originally from northern Arabia). As both tribes hold administrative posts within the empire, the Kalb-Qays face-off quickly spreads to Iraq and beyond.

681 The Umayyad caliph **Yazid I** makes some headway against the Kharajite rebellions, but delays confronting Ibn al-Zubayr.

In North Africa Uqba ibn Nafi leads a war-band across present-day **Algeria** and **Morocco**. Coming to the Atlantic he rides into the sea, declaring to his followers that, as Allah is his witness, he can proceed no further. As a result of Uqba's exploits the region known as the **Maghreb** (the western part of Africa's Mediterranean coastline) begins to fall under Arab sway, although some Berber tribes offer strong resistance to their latest conquerors. Indeed, shortly after reaching the Atlantic, Uqba is killed by a Berber chieftain called **Kusayla**. Taking advantage of the unrest in Arabia, Syria and Iraq, Kusayla and his successor—a priestess known only as **Kahina**—manage to reverse some of the Arab conquests in the Maghreb, but only temporarily.

683 An Umayyad army dispatched from Damascus, comprising mixed Arab and Syrian soldiery, **retakes Medina** from Ibn al-Zubayr in

THE TWELVE IMAMS
OF MAINSTREAM
("TWELVER") SHIISM

Ali ibn Abu Talib, d. 661
Hasan ibn Ali (first son of Ali), d. 669
Husayn ibn Ali (second son of Ali), d. 680
Ali Zayn al-Abidin (son of Husayn), d. 714
Muhammad al-Baqir (Ali Zayn's brother), d. 731
Jafar al-Sadiq (son of al-Baqir), d. 765
Musa al-Kazim (son of Jafar), d. 799
Ali al-Rida (son of Musa'l'Kazim), d. 818
Muhammad al-Jawad (son of Ali ar-Rida), d. 835
Ali al-Hadi (son of al-Jawad), d. 868
Hasan al-Askari (son of Ali al-Hadi), d. 874
Muhammad al-Muntazar * (son of al-Askari)

*also known as the "Hidden Imam," believed never to have
died and expected one day to reappear as the *Mahdi*.

August, following a battle fought at a place called **Harra** (literally "lava-field") outside the city. According to some records, the Umayyads pillage the city for three days before marching on Mecca. As the siege of Mecca commences, however, news comes that the caliph Yazid I has died, and the siege is lifted.

In **Damascus**, Yazid I's infant son **Muawiyyah II** is proclaimed caliph, confirming Umayyad dynasticism. When Muawiyyah II dies shortly afterwards, leadership of the Umayya clan passes to **Marwan**, a cousin of Muawiyyah I.

In **Mecca**, **Ibn al-Zubayr** proclaims himself caliph. Continuing to attract support from Qurayshi clans opposed to the Umayyads, he retains control of Islam's holiest city until his death nine years later. He is unable to significantly consolidate his influence outside Hijaz, however.

684 In June, Marwan's claim to the caliphate is confirmed at an Umayyad clan council held at **Jabiya** in Syria. According to some genealogists he founds a new sub-dynasty known as the **Marwanids**—as distinct from the first three Umayyad caliphs, known as the **Sufyanids**. Soon after his elevation, **Marwan I**, assisted by his son **Abd al-Malik**, inflicts defeat on a confederation of Ibn al-Zubayr's supporters at the **Battle of Marj Rabut**, north of Damascus.

A fresh campaign is launched against Mecca, during which a flaming arrow lands on the **Kabah**, which burns to the ground. It is immediately rebuilt by Ibn al-Zubayr on a grander scale than before.

In **Basra**, there is a **Kharajite uprising** led by **Nafi ibn al-Azraq**. The Kharajis try to topple the city's governor, who is sympathetic to Ibn al-Zubayr, but when they fail Nafi ibn al-Azraq is forced to flee.

685 Having wrested back control of Egypt from those sympathetic to Ibn al-Zubayr, **Marwan dies** in Damascus in April. His son, **Abd al-Malik**, is at once proclaimed caliph. Supported by the Qays, Abd al-Malik energetically continues his father's policy of suppressing unrest by force. To do so he relies heavily on Syrian troops, at the same time seeking to demilitarize some Arab garrisons, including Basra. As he also appoints some Syrians to senior positions within his administration, the initial opening-up of Islam to non-Arabs is sometimes dated to his twenty-year reign. Conversely, by ordering the translation of provincial tax registers from Greek and Persian into Arabic, he promotes the use of **Arabic**—the language of the Koran—within the empire. He is also remembered for instituting an efficient system of **couriers**—another centralizing expedient.

Abd al-Malik uses his Syrian troops to restore order in Iraq, and towards the end of the year Nafi ibn al-Azraq is captured and killed. His Kharajite followers, known as the **Azraqites**, continue to wage guerrilla war in the Iraqi hinterlands, however—proclaiming a *jihad* against sinners, they pursue a campaign that lasts another thirteen years.

In Iraq, there is a Shiite rebellion in **Kufa**, led by al-Mukhtar, in support of another of Ali's sons, **Muhammad ibn al-Hannfiyya**, promoted by al-Mukhtar as a *mahdi*—a prophet and "cleanser" predicted to appear shortly before the end of the world.

686 A new Kharajite group, led by al-Najda and therefore known as the **Najdaites**, takes control of the deserts and oases of central Arabia.

687 Abd al-Malik's Syrian regiments **restore order** in Kufa and Basra. Al-Mukhtar is captured and killed.

689 Following further campaigns, **Umayyad control is consolidated** over the whole of Iraq. Abd al-Malik is also able to reclaim most of Hijaz in Arabia, isolating Ibn al-Zubayr at Mecca.

691 In Jerusalem, the **Dome of the Rock (Qubbat al-Sakra)** is completed on the Temple Mount (Al-Haram al-Sharif) after six years' work, a monumental emblem of Islamic dominance in the Holy Land. Built to enclose the rock from which Muhammad is said to have ascended to Paradise on his *miraj* ("night flight"), it is inscribed inside with verses from the Koran. Also on the Temple Mount, work on Jerusalem's **al-Aqsa Mosque**, the largest in the city, nears completion.

692 **Al-Hajjaj ibn Yusuf** recaptures Mecca on behalf of the Umayyads, and Ibn al-Zubayr is cornered and killed. Following his death, opposition to the caliphate subsides. Al-Hajjaj **dismantles the Kabah** constructed by Ibn al-Zubayr, and rebuilds it on its original, smaller scale. For his victory, al-Hajjaj is rewarded by Abd al-Malik with the governorship of Iraq and the eastern provinces, a posting he fulfils with impartial severity until his death in 715.

Atlantic Ocean   • Poitiers

AL-ANDALUS

• Toledo

Seville •
• Córdoba
Gibraltar

Rome •

Constantinople •

BYZAN

ANATO

Cairouan •

Mediterranean
Sea   CRETE   CYPRUS

MAGHREB

Alexandria •
Fustat •

IFRIQIYA

EGYPT

N

Nile

THE ARAB CONQUESTS UP TO 800

The Kharajite **Najdaites** are finally suppressed. Although Azraqite
activities continue in parts of Iraq, the **second** *fitna* draws to a close.
Abd al-Malik's authority now runs throughout the empire, which
enters a period of renewed commercial and territorial expansion. As
Islam recovers its confidence, non-Muslim officials in the colonies are

increasingly replaced with Muslims, and there is also increased conversion to Islam among non-Arabs.

693 Abd al-Malik issues the **first Arab-Islamic currency**, replacing the Byzantine and Persian coins used in the empire until this date. The gold and silver coins (dinars and dirhams) minted in

BASRA

*F*ounded in 636 as a forward garrison during the conquest of Iraq, Basra provided an early indication of what might be achieved under Islamic rule. It rapidly developed from being one of several military depots into a thriving cosmopolitan city. Although the climate was often unbearably hot and humid, and flooding was commonplace, the surrounding countryside was lush and particularly suited to date cultivation. Basra's biggest advantage, however, was its location. Situated near the Shatt-el-Arab, the waterway where the Euphrates and Tigris converge on their way to the Persian Gulf, it offered access not only to Arabia and southern Persia (Iran), but ports in India, Southeast Asia and China. Basra was also well-positioned to benefit from the revival of overland trade with Afghanistan, Transoxiana and other areas of central or "inner" Asia.

Basra's commercial success was accompanied by its growing reputation as an urban melting pot. As the tribalism of its Arab founders dissipated and its military importance lessened, the city welcomed immigrants not just from within the empire but from as far afield as India, China and Southeast Asia. It also attracted a number of political dissidents, Kharajites and Shiites among them. Though Basra was often rocked by political turbulence, it developed into a center of learning—somewhere new "schools" of theology and jurisprudence could build up a following.

Yet eventually the city fell victim to its own success. The Abbasids, who succeeded the Umayyads, were partly persuaded by Basra's example that the Euphrates and the Gulf were worth investing in. But rather than relocate government to Basra, they decided to create an entirely new city at a village further upstream called Baghdad; and it was Baghdad, not Basra, that was to become the metropolitan center of the Arab-Islamic empire at its zenith.

Damascus show no ruler's face, but are instead inscribed with words from the Koran.

694 Al-Hajjaj begins consolidating Islamic power in **Khurasan**, **Transoxiana** and **Sind** (now in southern Pakistan), where lawlessness has spread during the second *fitna*.

697 There is unrest in **Egypt** (where a majority of the population still abides by the Christian Coptic faith), induced mainly by high levels of taxation.

698 As the last of the Khajarite **Azraqites** are crushed, **Hassan ibn al-Nusayr** begins reclaiming territories lost to the Berbers in the **Maghreb** region of North Africa.

The Dome of the Rock (Qubbat al-Sakra), Jerusalem

700 The territory of modern-day **Algeria** comes firmly under Arab sway. As a means of achieving pacification, Hassan ibn al-Nusayr encourages Berber tribes to convert to Islam.

701 A fresh anti-Umayyad revolt, led by **Ibn al-Asharth**, takes four years to quell. It is supported by a sect called the **Qadirites**—neo-

---

THE MOSQUE

*T*he Arabic word *masjid* literally means a "place of prostration." More generally, it is synonymous with a building designated for Islamic worship. Its essential requirements are simple, reflecting the simplicity of Muslim liturgy: a space, nearly always covered, for prayer; a perimeter marking out an area that is *haram*, equivalent to "sanctuary"; and the *qibla*, denoting the direction of Mecca. Originally the *qibla* was a stone, but in time became replaced by a *mihrab*—a recess modeled on the Roman niche and set within a wall (the *qibla* wall), forming the mosque's focal point. Although mosques have inevitably acquired an aura of sanctity, strictly speaking no object other than the Kabah can be said to be "holy"; the *mihrab* is not imbued with the same values as, say, a Christian altar. And a Muslim may offer prayers to Allah in any place, provided s/he faces Mecca and is prostrated on a prayer mat or other "clean" surface. Indeed, a popular saying is that "the whole world is a mosque."

Other features associated with mosques are the minaret, a tower-like structure from which the muezzin issues a call to prayer (*adhan*); a portal, separating the mosque from the outside world; a receptacle for water, often with a fountain, used for ritual cleansing before offering prayers; and a *minbar*, or pulpit, used by an imam to deliver a sermon (*khutha*) during Friday prayers. But mosques are also notable for what they do not contain. A prohibition on figurative art—derived from the idea that to represent a living creature in any medium is to challenge Allah as the supreme creator—

Kharajites who repudiate the supposedly divine sanction claimed for their rule by the Umayyad caliphs.

Muslim-Arab merchants operating out of Basra and other Persian Gulf ports, having already established trading links with India, venture as far as the **Moluccas** in the Far East. In time, traders will establish

means that mosques are devoid of paintings, sculptures and the like. As a result, for a Christian, Buddhist or Hindu, the interior of a mosque can seem austere (and indeed it has even been argued that the absence of icons and human images at the heart of institutionalized Islam has encouraged the growth of literal-minded fundamentalism).

Yet the mosque has also been one of the planet's great architectural adventures. Because Islam spread so rapidly and so widely, mosque-building adopted a variety of styles that combined Islamic requirements with indigenous traditions and materials, so that each one of the mosque's "standard" features—prayer-hall, *mihrab*, *minbar*, portal and minaret—has witnessed seemingly endless variation. Of equal importance was the evolution of a specifically Islamic ornamentation. Though mosques couldn't be filled with effigies, their interior and exterior surfaces could be decorated with abstract geometric designs, and inlaid with calligraphy quoting verses from the Koran. There was, too, a drift toward monumentalization, as Islam's rulers sought to glorify Allah (and perhaps themselves) in ever grander fashion. Among many outstanding examples are the Shah Mosque in Isfahan, raised by Shah Abbas, and the Blue Mosque of Sultan Ahmed in Istanbul, both built in the 17th century. Nor has the impulse slackened in modern times. Many capitals of newly independent Muslim nations are graced by a National Mosque; while in Iraq, following the Gulf War of 1992, Saddam Hussein commissioned the Mosque of the Mother of All Battles near Baghdad.

outposts across Southeast Asia, leading eventually to the creation of Muslim sultanates in the territories known today as **Malaysia** and **Indonesia**. Muslim merchants, preferring the southern sea-route to the still hazardous Silk Roads, will also establish trading communities in the **Chinese Empire**.

702 In the Maghreb, the death of the priestess **Kahina** and divisions among Berber chieftains assist the Arab reconquest of **Morocco**.

705 Abd al-Malik dies, and is succeeded as caliph by his son **al-Walid I**, who continues his father's policies of administrative centralization and territorial expansion. Al-Walid's elevation occurs without any major dissent, indicating that there is a growing acceptance of the dynastic principle within Islam, as well as of the authority of the caliphate itself.

Al-Walid appoints his cousin **Umar** as governor of Arabia—perhaps a sign that Arabia is no longer central to the Islamic empire. Umar oversees the rebuilding and enlargement of the central mosque at **Medina**, and provides new facilities for pilgrims wishing to visit Mecca.

In Damascus, as the construction of the great **Umayyad Mosque** begins, the **Cathedral of St John the Baptist**—until now shared by Christians and Muslims alike—is reserved for solely Islamic use.

Musa ibn Nusayr, already governor of Ifriqiya (modern Libya and Tunisia), takes charge over the **Maghreb** (Algeria and Morocco), where he persuades many more Berbers to join Islam.

710 Although the exact details are unclear, it is likely that in this year Arabs cross from the Maghreb to the **Iberian peninsula** (modern Spain and Portugal) for the first time, perhaps to reconnoiter a possible conquest.

711 As Arab-Islamic hegemony over **Transoxiana** and most of **Afghanistan** is established, one of al-Hajjaj's deputies, **Muhammad ibn Qasim**, leads an army to the banks of the Indus river.

Islamic conquest of the Iberian peninsula is initiated when Musa Ibn Nusayr sends a deputy, a Berber named **Tariq ibn Ziyad**, into the

Christian Visigoth kingdom of **Hispania** with a force of 7000 men, made up of Arab, Syrian and Berber cadres. The Visigoth king, **Roderick**, and a majority of his nobility are slain in battle somewhere near the **Guadalquivir River**. Some sources suggest that the Muslims have been invited into Hispania by Roderick's enemies; others that the campaign is one of simple conquest. Having disposed of Roderick, Tariq advances on the city of **Córdoba**, which falls into his hands perhaps before the year is out. As a result of his victories, the outcrop of rock at the mouth of the Mediterranean between Europe and Africa becomes known as **Jebel Tariq** (Gibraltar).

712 Campaigning against the Khazars beyond the Oxus, al-Hajjaj's deputy governor of Khurasan, **Qutayba ibn-Muslim**, captures the strategically important citadel and trading center of **Bukhara** (Bokhara).

Apprehensive about his subordinate Tariq ibn Zayid's ambitions, **Musa ibn Nusayr crosses into Hispania** with his own army of 18,000. Taking over command of the conquest from Tariq, Musa forces other Visigoth cities to surrender, among them **Seville** and **Toledo**.

713 Qutayba ibn-Muslim captures **Samarkand**, at the time the greatest trading center in Central Asia, and brings **Fergana** (the northern part of Transoxiana) under Arab control. However, the fierce independence of indigenous tribes in both Transoxiana and Afghanistan means that Arab-Islamic control will remain fragile at best, and the Arabs have insufficient manpower to subdue a region dominated by the Hindu Kush and other mountain ranges. The same difficulties inhibit the first attempts to conquer the **Indian subcontinent**, although in this year Muhammad ibn Qasim penetrates as far as **Multan** in the Punjab.

Musa ibn Nusayr and Tariq ibn Zayid advance into northern Hispania. When word of their success reaches al-Walid, he **recalls Musa to Damascus**. Musa obeys orders, taking with him a huge quantity of booty to present to the caliph, but leaves his son **Abd al-Azir** to continue the campaign. In Damascus, Musa is relieved of his command, but

Abd al-Azir is confirmed as his successor. His command is short-lived, however—over the next thirty years eighteen governors are appointed to **al-Andalus**, a new Islamic province incorporating the western Maghreb and Hispania. Unlike other Arab-Islamic colonies, in Hispania the victors are allowed to acquire landed estates.

714 Al-Hajjaj dies, and some of the impetus for making further inroads into Central Asia dissipates.

Following **Ali Zayn al-Abidin's death**, the eldest son of Husayn and regarded by Shiites as the Fourth Imam, the Shiites are divided

UMAR II (D. 720)

*U*mar II came to power during a difficult period. On the one hand, he faced "religious" renewal, particularly in the eastern territories of his empire, and on the other tensions between Arab colonists and muwalis (non-Arab subjects who had converted to Islam) were growing. To resolve this latter difficulty, Umar decreed that Arab and non-Arab Muslims should be accorded equal rights. While until then muwalis had largely been spared the *jizya* tax levied on dhimmis ("protected" peoples such as Jews, Christians and Zoroastrians), they were frequently liable for excessive land taxes. Arab Muslims, on the other hand—or at least Arabs from Arabia—either paid no land taxes, or paid them at reduced rates. Umar's solution was to insist that Arabs pay the same land-taxes as the muwalis, a leveling maneuver that helped replenish the caliphate's severely depleted coffers.

Umar II also made it known that while conversion to Islam was to be welcomed and indeed encouraged—he was the first caliph to explicitly adopt such a stance—converts would be expected to pay the *zakat* (alms tax).

between whom they should acknowledge as the **Fifth Imam**—Ali Zayn's son **Zayd**, or his older brother, **Muhammad al-Baqir**. While a majority favor the latter, some choose Zayd, giving rise to the birth of "**Fiver**" **Shiism**. Within Shia Islam, Zayd will be remembered as a mystic and an author of finely wrought prayers.

715 The liabilities of the Umayyads' monarchical system of government are exposed when al-Walid is succeeded by his brother, **Suleiman**. Suleiman begins his reign by making a series of unpopular appointments, and then, breaking the peace with the Byzantine empire,

Conversely, he abolished the system whereby muwalis were incorporated into Islam as clients of the Arab tribes and clans, and he granted muwali soldiers equal army pay. These latter measures resolved any lingering doubts as to whether Allah was everyone's god, or just the god of the Arabs—though some historians have speculated that Umar II's new laws merely regularized what may already have become widespread, or that they were introduced primarily to promote unity in the face of external threats, particularly on Islam's eastern borders.

Despite his well-attested piety, during his reign Umar II was accused by Ghaylan al-Dimashqi and other clerical scholars of not carrying his Islamic reforms far enough. Yet Umar II did listen to Ghaylan—in marked contrast to his successor, Yazid II, who executed him. Umar's credentials as a ruler who strengthened Islam are also reflected in his policies towards Jews and Christians, whom he required to wear distinctive clothing by which they could be readily identified, and whom he prohibited from serving in his armies.

launches an **attack against Constantinople** at great expense to his treasury. The assault fails, and many men and ships are lost.

In western Europe, the Muslim Arabs—or **Saracens** as they are called locally—make better progress. Having overrun most of Spain, they venture beyond the Pyrenees and begin launching raids against the Franks. **Narbonne**, a Visigoth province in southwest France, comes under nominal Arab-Islamic rule.

716 In the western part of Iberia, the port city of **Lisbon** falls to an Arab-Berber army.

717 Caliph Suleiman is succeeded by his cousin Umar, a nephew of Abd al-Malik and formerly the governor of Arabia (see opposite), who is known as **Umar II**. During his brief reign, he does much to enhance the authority of the caliphate, and will be regarded as a great reforming ruler who helps dissolve the divisions between Arab and non-Arab Muslims. But by mounting another costly, and ultimately disastrous, campaign against Constantinople he is also accused of undermining the power of the Umayyad dynasty.

719 Despite the first stirrings of **Christian resistance** to the Muslim conquest of Hispania, the Arabs increase their presence in southern France.

720 Umar II dies and is succeeded by his dissolute cousin **Yazid II**, another son of Abd al-Malik. Shortly after his succession, a major rebellion breaks out in **Basra**. Led by an army commander, **Yazid ibn-Muhallah**, who proclaims a *jihad* against the Umayyad dynasty, the revolt has Kharajite overtones—though the increasing dependence by the Umayyads on Syrian soldiers is high on the list of the rebels' grievances. Yazid ibn-Muhallah is defeated and killed, however, and his family exterminated.

In the western Mediterranean, Arab forces occupy **Sardinia** and begin the conquest of **Sicily**. Many Sicilians will convert to Islam, and an Islamic presence will also be established in southern Italy.

c.722 In the mountainous north of Hispania, a Muslim force is defeated by a Christian force at **Covadonga**. Although this is little more than a skirmish which does nothing to slow the Islamic occupation, among some Spanish historians Covadonga has been hailed as the beginning of the long process of the *Reconquista* which, 770 years later, will see the final expulsion of Muslims from Spain. In reality, it is unlikely that the Muslims have been either able or particularly willing to flush out the Christian enclaves that survive amid the relative impregnability of the Pyrenees, and the Asturian and Cantabrian mountains.

724 Yazid II is succeeded by his brother **Hisham**, the fourth and last of Abd al-Malik's sons to become caliph. Devout and autocratic by nature, Hisham goes some way to repairing the damage done to the caliphate by Yazid, although during his reign there is growing unrest among the Shiites, who regard the Umayyad dynasty as an ungodly usurpation. Among the Shiites an extreme faction emerges, known as the *ghulat* (literally "exaggerators") on account of their impassioned criticisms of the court and outspoken advocacy of their own doctrines.

725 In **Egypt** there is renewed unrest among the Coptic peasantry as the provincial government insists on maintaining high levels of tax. The revolt is uncoordinated, but lingers on for two years.

728 **Hasan al-Basri**, the leading theologian and thinker of the Umayyad period, sometimes associated with the Kharajite **Qadarite sect**, dies.

730 The nomadic **Khazar people** (ancestors of the modern Kazakhs of Kazakhstan) launch a series of raids against the northeastern parts of the Arab-Islamic empire. For a while they overrun Armenia, and there is evidence to suggest that they penetrate the empire as far as **Mosul**. Although the Khazars are eventually repulsed, their intrusions remind the Damascus-based caliphate that the security of the eastern empire cannot be taken for granted.

731 **Muhammad al-Baqir**, regarded by most Shiites as the Fifth Imam, dies. During his lifetime he has augmented Shia doctrine through his insistence that not only is true authority within Islam vested in Muhammad's male descendants, but that each Imam passes on to his successor "esoteric" knowledge similarly derived from Muhammad. His son **Jafar al-Sadiq** becomes the Sixth Imam.

732 In the west, the Arabs defeat an army led by **Eudo, Duke of Aquitaine** and sack **Bordeaux**. When a small Muslim force begins campaigning in northern France, however, it is defeated by Charles Martel at the **Battle of Tours**. Although the battle is a relatively minor engagement, it will be seen as a turning point in European history—the moment when the "Saracen" advance is decisively reversed. The Franks, however, are aided by two unrelated developments: a renewed revolt among the Berbers of North Africa, and a strengthening of Byzantine resolve under the emperor **Leo III**.

HASAN AL-BASRI (642–728)

*A*bu Said ibn Abi al-Hasan Yasar al-Basri, to give his full name, is regarded as Islam's first great scholar, even though nothing he wrote survives in more than fragmentary form.

Born in Medina, the son of a freed slave, like many others he migrated to Basra when he was 16. Between 670 and 673 he joined the armies fighting in Khurasan, but then returned to Basra to pursue a religious vocation, quickly acquiring a reputation as the city's finest preacher. While he emphasized the virtues of humility and simple living, he was not afraid to offer criticisms of the Umayyad regime, and between 705 and 714 he was forced into hiding by the no-nonsense governor of Iraq, al-Hajjaj. Only after his adversary's death was Hasan al-Basri able to return to Basra at the age of 72. He still had another fourteen years ahead of him, however, and it was during this last period of his life that he established his "school" of followers.

Exactly what Hasan al-Basri taught remains unclear, since many contradictory strands in Islamic thought are credited to his name. He has been described as, variously, the founder of Islamic jurisprudence, an early

About this time **Abu Hanifah** pioneers *fiqh*, the study of Shariah law. **Muhammad ibn Ishaq** assembles a biography of Muhammad that will be used by later hagiographers as a source for the *Hadith*.

736 In **Kufa**, Shiite protests against Umayyad rule lead to unrest, fuelled by the seizure and execution of some Shiis by Umayyad agents working undercover. The "revolt," led perhaps by the "alternative" Imam **Zayd bin Ali**, lasts four years, during which time further unrest in Iraq is caused by a succession of Kharajite uprisings.

Islamic mystic, a collector of the "traditions" of Muhammad and a crypto-Kharajite. He might well have been all these things at a time when disciplines had yet to be defined, and an innovative thinker might very well have explored different aspects of the developing Islamic compact.

From the passages of Hasan al-Basri that do survive, he was plainly an ascetic who promoted the claims of inner rather than outward devotion. Fasting and prayer, he said, meant nothing unless accompanied by conviction and true obedience to Allah; Muslim hypocrites were as bad, or worse, than infidels. In a famous passage he offers a haunting summary of death as something absolutely certain but absolutely uncertain in its consequences. In defiance of some Koranic verses, Hasan al-Basri is also supposed to have advanced the theory that man is entirely responsible for all his actions, and that life itself should be lived in a state of self-critical anxiety. But while he may or may not have arrived at a systematic philosophy, his importance for Islam is precisely as a legendary fountainhead of wisdom.

738 Khalid ibn Abdullah al-Qain, the governor of Iraq, is dismissed by Caliph Hisham for speculating in grain and perhaps other commodities—defined in the Koran as the "sin" of usury. Khalid attempts to stir revolt in Iraq, but this is suppressed by the caliph's Syrian troops.

740 When Zayd ibn Ali is killed by Umayyad forces, the Shiite revolt in Kufa collapses. Although some Zaydi ("Fiver") Shiis continue to hold that Zayd was the rightful Fifth Imam, many more accept the claim of Muhammad al-Baqir's son, **Jafar al-Sadiq**, as the Sixth Imam.

In **Anatolia**, a Muslim force is heavily defeated by an army of the Byzantine emperor **Leo II** at Acrazas. In **North Africa**, in addition to continuing Berber unrest, Kharajite dissent increases, encouraging some Arab colonists to resettle in the Iberian peninsula.

742 The Berber revolts in the **Maghreb** are crushed.

743 Hisham dies, and is succeeded by **al-Walid II**, the son of Yazid II. The new caliph is unable to reverse the tide of ill-feeling towards the Umayyads, and within the Arab elite opposition begins to cluster

A victorious line of march had been prolonged above a thousand miles from the rock of Gibraltar to the banks of the Loire; the repetition of an equal space would have carried the Saracens to the confines of Poland and the Highlands of Scotland; the Rhône is not more impassable than the Nile or Euphrates, and the Arabic fleet might have sailed without a naval combat into the mouth of the Thames. Perhaps the interpretation of the Koran would now be taught in the schools of Oxford, and her pupils might demonstrate to a circumcised people the sanctity and truth of the revelation of Mahomet.

—**Edward Gibbon on the Battle of Tours,**
in *The History of the Decline and Fall of the Roman Empire*
(1776–88), chapter 52

Abd al-Malik was an arrogant tyrant who did not care what he did. Sulaimaan's only ambition lay in his belly and his balls. Umar ibn Abd al-Aziz was like a one-eyed man among the blind. The only great man of the dynasty was Hisham. As long as their standards remained high and their conduct not base, the Ummayads held the government which had been given to them with a firm hand, protecting, preserving and guarding the gift granted them by God. But then their power passed to their effeminate sons, whose only ambition was the satisfaction of their own desires and who chased after pleasures forbidden by Almighty God. They knew not that God works slowly and believed themselves safe from His snares, although they had renounced their right to the Caliphate and had made light of God's truths, and the duties of good government. Then God stripped them of their power, covered them with shame and deprived them of their worldly goods.

> —The second Abbasid Caliph al-Mansur's
> portrayal of the Umayyad dynasty,
> in al-Masudi's 10th-century *The Meadows of Gold*,
> trans. Paul Lunde and Caroline Stone

around the **Abbasids**, a Qurayshi clan descended from the Prophet Muhammad's uncle Abbas. The Abbasid faction decides that, instead of confronting the Umayyads in Damascus head-on, it should first build up strength in the east. To this end, agents are sent into Iraq and Iran, among them **Abu Muslim**, a former Persian slave, tasked with enlisting Shiite support for the Abbasid cause.

744 Al-Walid II dies, and is succeeded by **Yazid III**, a son of al-Walid I. But Yazid III also dies, and is succeeded by his brother **Ibrahim**, another son of al-Walid I. When Ibrahim dies shortly afterwards, there is a crisis in the Umayyad court—resolved only when **Marwan II**, formerly the governor of Armenia, defeats his rivals and claims the caliphate for himself.

745 Aware of the Umayyad government's weak position—brought on by internal dissent and the overcommitment of its military resources—the Byzantine emperor **Constantine V** attempts the reconquest of **Syria**.

746 Although Constantine V fails to take Syria, he does recapture **Cyprus**, which is returned to Christian rule.

747 In June the Abbasid agitator Abu Muslim stirs revolt in Khurasan by unfurling the "**black banner**" in Marw—the emblem of Shiite rebellion. It is unlikely, however, that the Shiites who respond to Abu Muslim's call to arms are aware that his loyalties lie not with their Imam, but with the Abbasids. Abu Muslim succeeds in raising a force of several thousand by this deception, and by the year's end the Umayyad governor of Khurasan has been expelled.

748 As Abu Muslim makes headway in the east and begins threatening the Fertile Crescent, Marwan II captures the Abbasid clan leader, **Ibrahim al-Abbas**.

749 The death of Ibrahim al-Abbas in prison, probably as a result of plague, only encourages his faction to overthrow the Umayyads. Still playing the Shiite card, Abu Muslim and his army seize **Kufa** on the west bank of the Euphrates. As Abu Muslim does so, he cryptically proclaims that the Islamic empire will shortly be ruled by "him of the [Muhammadan] family who shall be approved." In accordance with this proclamation, on November 28 Ibrahim's brother **Abu al-Abbas al-Saffah** is declared caliph in Kufa's main mosque. The Shiites realize they have been duped, but some are persuaded that the Abbas line represents a closer blood relationship to Muhammad than the Ummayads.

750 In January **Marwan II** leads an army against Abu al-Abbas, but is defeated on the banks of the upper Zab, a tributary of the Tigris, east of Mosul. Marwan flees to Egypt, but in August he is seized and killed by Abbasid agents.

CHAPTER FOUR

The Abbasid period

{750-1258 (132-655 AH)}

THE **ABBASIDS** CAME TO POWER amid widespread disillusionment with the **Umayyads** and at a time of renewed religious enthusiasm in the Middle Eastern areas of Islam. Yet although the caliphal dynasty established by **Abu al-Abbas al-Saffah** lasted half a millennium, the period of the Abbasids witnessed a progressive decline in the authority and prestige of the caliphate itself. Long before 1258, when a **Mongol horde** led by Hulegu Khan sacked the Abbasid capital Baghdad, the caliph had been reduced to little more than a remote figurehead.

Opposition to the Abbasids took many forms—some of them familiar to their predecessors—and destroyed any illusion that Islam could still constitute the single seamless community (*umma*) that Muhammad had envisioned. As early as 756, a member of the Umayya clan, **Abd al-Rahman**, seized power in the Iberian peninsula. Incorporating much of the Maghreb, the western "province" of **al-Andalus** slowly severed its links with the Abbasids, and in 929 the "Spanish" Umayyads formally declared a separate caliphate. Closer to home, the **Fatimids**, an Ismaili Shiite dynasty, had by the same date staked out an autonomous territory in North Africa. Creating their own capital at **Cairo** in Egypt, the Fatimids declared a rival caliphate, too, and for a while controlled not only Palestine and Syria but much of Arabia itself, including Mecca and Medina.

If such developments offered a direct affront to Abbasid power, they also reflected endemic instability. The Abbasids sought to govern the provinces of their empire through loyal governors, or **amirs**. But the amirs themselves had dynastic ambitions, and sometimes made it a condition of their loyalty that their titles should pass down through their own families. Thus ensconced, a succession of amirates in **Iraq** and **Persia** (Iran) increasingly neglected to hand over revenues due to Baghdad, preferring instead to institute their own petty kingdoms—a tendency that was replicated in the east, where Muslim warlords carved out kingdoms in **Afghanistan**, **Transoxiana** and, more tentatively, northern **India**.

In an effort to re-establish control over the provinces, the Abbasids resorted to enlisting mercenary or "slave" armies made up of warriors drawn from the **Turkic peoples** of the Caucasus and other parts of Central, or Inner, Asia. Yet these proved a liability, too. First the **Buyids**, then the **Seljuks** simply took advantage of their military clout to create their own power bases in Baghdad itself. But although both Buyids and Seljuks eagerly embraced Islam, they neither commanded the automatic respect of other Muslims, nor proved themselves capable of running an imperial administration.

Thus political disunity became rife within Islam, often reinforced by local (and sometimes wider) religious and doctrinal differences. This in turn rendered Islam vulnerable to external assault—initially during the **First Crusade** of the late 11th and early 12th centuries, then the **Mongol invasions** of the 13th century, then when Jerusalem and large swathes of Palestine and Syria were "reclaimed" by Christian forces.

And yet the Abbasid period also witnessed the coming of age of Islam as a religion and social culture. Of critical importance under the early Abbasids was the emergence of Islamic law, known as the **Shariah**, which was extrapolated from the Koran and other sources, and encoded by a group of eminent religious jurisprudents. In addition to providing Muslims with a comprehensive set of regulations covering nearly every aspect of life, the Shariah underpinned a growing sense of **Sunni orthodoxy**, upheld by a burgeoning corps of *ulama*, or scholarly clerics. In accomplishing this, the Shariah helped instil a deeply conservative mindset within Islam, offsetting the more radical aspects of the Koran and Muhammad's mission.

Although Islam became entrenched under the Abbasids, it was also enriched—another essential addition to the Islamic compact during this period was the evolution of **Sufism**, often described as Islam's "mystic wing." Although it is claimed by some Muslims that Sufism merely articulated a "hidden teaching" contained within the Koran, historically it is almost impossible to separate it from Muslim encounters with pre-existing **Persian**, **Hindu** and **Buddhist** mysticisms as Islam expanded eastwards, just as the veneration of Islamic "**saints**" by many Shiites has something to do with Islam's absorption of the values of such **Christian communities** as survived in Iraq and Iran.

In the 9th, 10th and 11th centuries especially, Islam was receptive to all manner of non-Islamic influence, including the legacy of classical **Greek philosophers** such as Plato and Aristotle, giving rise to an eclectic and enterprising high culture. But well before the onslaught of the Mongols, the conservative custodians of Muhammad's message had determined what was permissible—and what was not.

The early Abbasids
750–929

Any expectations that the Abbasids would heal the rifts that had developed within Islam since the death of Muhammad were quickly dispelled. In a move unprecedented even in pre-Muslim Arab tribal history, the new caliph, **Abu al-Abbas al-Saffah** attempted to liquidate the whole of the Umayyad clan: large numbers were massacred at a single banquet and others were hunted down. But a handful of Umayyads escaped, among them Abd al-Rahman, who, in 756, re-established his dynasty in al-Andalus. Attempts were made to remove him, but to no avail; and although for 173 years the Umayyads in Spain paid lip service to the Abbasid caliphate as the supreme Islamic authority, theirs was in effect an independent state.

The Abbasid caliphs also endeavored to suppress **Shiism**—a grave political threat, since Shiites earnestly believed that only the descendants of Ali had the right to rule Islam. Moreover, some Shiites resorted to *taqqiyya* ("concealment") as a means of preserving their ideals during times of oppression, as recommended in the Koran. But the Shiites themselves were divided regarding the Alid succession—some preferring Imams from one branch of the family, some preferring others; and although the group known as "**Twelvers**" eventually emerged as majority Shiites, in the 8th and 9th centuries the issue was far from decided. The **Ismaili** (or "Sevener") Shiites built up a large following, and in 909, under the leaderships of the **Fatimids** (named after Muhammad's daughter Fatima), an autonomous Ismaili state was founded in **Ifriqiya** (modern Tunisia). In league with another rebellious Shiite sect, the **Qaramites**, the Fatimids aimed to impose their rule on the whole of Islam, and so restore its unity. At first, however, they struck out west to augment their power in the Maghreb—but although they managed to capture **Fez**, then the chief city of Morocco, their advance upon al-Andalus was halted by the Iberian Umayyads.

This conflict between the Fatimids and the Umayyads was part territorial, part doctrinal. The Fatimids had upped the ante by proclaiming a separate caliphate. The Umayyads, opposed to Shiism in any shape or form, saw themselves as defenders of the true faith, and because it appeared to them that the Abbasids were taking less than adequate measures against the Shiite heretics, in 929 they responded in kind by proclaiming a third caliphate in **Córdoba**, so dissolving the last formal tie between al-Andalus and Baghdad.

The fragmentation of Islam could scarcely have presented itself in starker terms. In many ways, the Abbasids were themselves to blame. The decision to site their capital at **Baghdad**—nearer Iran and territories further east where Islam was making steady inroads, but further from Arabia and the commercially important province of Egypt—confirmed the waning of Islam as an Arab enterprise. Although the Abbasids themselves were Arab, they increasingly detached themselves from the Arab world, perhaps for fear of finding themselves embroiled in tribal and clan jealousies. Far more than the Umayyads, they depended on Persian bureaucrats to administer their empire. They also depended for their safety on soldiers drawn at first from the great northeast Persian province of **Khurasan**, and then from **Transoxiana**, the land beyond the Oxus river.

In the long term, the choice of Baghdad decisively realigned the contours of Islam, making it the dominant faith of Central Asia as well as the Middle East and providing it with a springboard for meaningful incursions into the Indian subcontinent. For a while, too, Baghdad basked in the reflected glory of such strong-armed caliphs as **al-Mansur** (754–75) and **Harun al-Rashid** (786–809). Abbasid rule began to unravel, however, when **al-Mamun** (813–32) came to power. Embracing the distinctly heterodox ideas of a sect known as the **Mutazilites**, he created a climate of religious turmoil, and in 836 his successor, **al-Mutasim**, who also espoused Mutazilite values, was forced for his own safety to abandon Baghdad, creating a new capital at **Samarra** instead.

In 892 the Abbasids returned to Baghdad, but never again were they able to dominate Islam as they had during the first sixty years of their rule. In the very next year the first rumblings of the Fatimid revolt in Ifriqiya, where the **Aghlabids** had established a quasi-autonomous amirate, were heard. But the Aghlabids were only one among many "provincial" dynasties who wrested power from the center—other notable examples being the **Idrisids** in Morocco, the **Tahinids** in Khurasan and, later on, the **Saminids** in central Persia. Indeed, from this time the decentralization of power, even in Islam's heartlands, became the rule.

Some of the shortcomings that have been identified by historians in Islam's early imperial structure include the failure to rotate those in office and to install a military machine along, say, Roman lines. Yet, although the Abbasids had shown themselves every bit as vulnerable as the Umayyads, it was precisely in this early period of their "rule" that Islam acquired its most effective and enduring institution, the **Shariah**. Codification of Islamic law was undertaken not at the court's behest, but by several independent clerical scholars, among them the founders of the four main Shariah law schools: **Malik ibn Abbas**, **Abu Hanafi**, **al-Shafii** and **Ahmed Hanbal**.

Concurrently the **traditions** and **sayings** of Muhammad and some of his closest colleagues, upon which the Shariah was based in combination with the Koran and established custom, were given definitive expression. The *Hadith*, as they are known, had long been passed from one generation to the next by word of mouth, but now they were set down in writing by other clerical scholars. Although in 929 it may not have been entirely clear what direction Islam was taking, the foundations of Sunni orthodoxy had been laid.

750 Following his victory over the last of the Umayyad caliphs, Marwan II, in Iraq, **Abu al-Abbas al-Saffah** is proclaimed caliph. Acting to impose his authority on the empire and to secure his personal safety, he orders the elimination of every member of the Umayyad clan—an inter-tribal slaughter without precedent in Arab history. However, at least one Umayyad, **Abd al-Rahman** (a grandson of Caliph Hashim), evades his pursuers and makes his way first to Egypt, and then westwards towards the Maghreb. Although Abu al-

Abbas succeeds in founding a new dynasty, the Umayyads will survive in the **Iberian peninsula**, where eventually they will create a rival caliphate.

Abu al-Abbas establishes his court at **Kufa**, on the lower Euphrates, where he begins recruiting Persian soldiers drawn from Khurasan, preferring these to the Syrian troops used by the Umayyads. Throughout his short reign, Abu, the first of the **Abbasid caliphs**, expends his energies crushing pockets of political and sectarian resistance.

751 Following the capture of Chinese craftsmen during border fighting in Transoxiana, the first Islamic **paper mill** is established. Easier and cheaper to produce than papyrus, paper rapidly becomes the preferred medium of Arab and other Islamic scholars, and encourages a rapid growth of learning. Eventually paper technology will find its way into Europe through al-Andalus (Islamic Spain).

752 A serious uprising breaks out in **Oman** in the Arabian peninsula, fuelled in part by Shiite opposition to Abbasid rule.

754 Abu al-Abbas al Saffah dies and is succeeded as caliph by his younger brother **Abu Jafar al-Mansur**, who will rule for thirty years. He intensifies operations against militant Shiites.

755 To further strengthen their position, particularly in relation to the Shiites, the Abbasids claim that the office of "**Imam**" was conferred on their ancestor al-Abbas by Muhammad himself.

Al-Mansur orders the execution of **Abu Muslim**, the Abbasid agent largely responsible for creating support for the house of Abbas during the closing years of the Umayyad caliphate. Al-Mansur's stated reason is that Abu Muslim is suspected of creating his own power-base among Persians.

756 The Umayyad fugitive **Abd al-Rahman**, having gathered an army of followers, crosses over from the Maghreb to Spain and deposes the Abbasid governor of Córdoba, **Yusuf al-Fihri**. Quickly securing the loyalty of many Arab leaders in the Iberian peninsula, some of whom have been in open revolt against Yusuf, Abd al-Rahman in effect establishes **al-Andalus** as an independent Islamic state, with himself as its amir—although he and his immediate successors continue to pay notional homage to the Abbasid caliphate.

Al-Mansur orders the execution of **Ibn al-Muqaffa**, a Persian scholar condemned for *zandaqa* (irreligion) after challenging the authenticity of the Koran, criticizing Muhammad and allegedly attempting to introduce Zoroastrian or Manichean elements into the Islamic faith. He will be remembered as the author of *Kalila wa-Dimna* ("Kalila and Dimna"), a compendium of animal tales that, although it extols Persian cultural traditions, is written in Arabic.

757 Unrest among Turkic peoples in the east becomes manifest during a revolt in **Transoxiana** led by a warlord known as Ishaq al-Turki.

Berber tribes, encouraged by the teachings of Ibadite Kharajites take control of **Tripoli** (which, as Tarabulus, is the capital of modern Libya). As Kharajism spreads further westwards, the Abbasids lose control over Ifriqiya.

758 Caliph al-Mansur, concerned about his personal security in Kufa following an attack against his fortress at al-Hashimiyya, decides to build a new "imperial" city. The site he selects is a small village called **Baghdad** at a point on the Tigris that is still navigable, and is connected to the Euphrates by a canal.

In North Africa, Berber Kharajites occupy **Qairouan** (modern Tunis). They push further westwards, but are resisted by a Persian-born Ibadite called **Rustam** in western Algeria. Rustam establishes a quasi-autonomous dynastic amirate ruled by the Rustamids until 909.

759 An uprising in **Narbonne** challenges Muslim rule in southern France. As a strong Frankish kingdom emerges under **King Pepin** and his successors, the Christian enclave states in the mountains of northern Spain receive support from their northern neighbors—to the chagrin of the Umayyad rulers of al-Andalus.

762 Al-Mansur moves his court from Kufa to **Baghdad**, which quickly becomes the largest city on the Eurasian landmass outside China.

There is unrest in Medina after a self-styled prophet known as "**Muhammad the Pure Soul**" attempts to raise rebellion.

Malik ibn Anas, a leading scholar and one of the principal jurists of the Shariah, declares that the oath of allegiance to the Abbasid caliph is not binding on all Muslims. He is publicly flogged as a result, although he is later rehabilitated by Harun al-Rashid.

763 An Abbasid attempt to restore direct authority in **al-Andalus** by force is defeated by the Umayyad amir, Abd al-Rahman I.

Either in this year or at the end of the preceding year, **Jafar al-Sadiq**, regarded as the **Sixth Shia Imam**, dies in the prison where al-Mansur has placed him, despite Jafar's quietist protestations that the political authority of the Abbasids should not be opposed. It is assumed by many Shiites that Jafar, a scholarly man credited with introducing mysticism into Shiism, has been poisoned—augmenting the Shia tradition that all its Imams have met unnatural deaths. In the mainstream ("Twelver" or "Imamite") Shia succession, Jafar's son, **Musa al-Kazim**, becomes the Seventh Imam. A minority of Shiites, however, will insist that Jafar al-Sadiq's eldest son **Ismail** is the true Seventh Imam, even though Ismail has been dead since 760. As a result of this dissent is born a new Shia sect, known variously as "**Seveners**" or "**Ismailis**." In the first instance the Ismailis claim a new line of Shia succession through Ismail's own son Muhammad al-Mahdi. By some they are accused of harboring a tolerance for "**dualism**" (the notion that good and evil coexist independently of each other), a doctrine rejected in the Koran but integral to Persian Zoroastrianism and its Manichean derivatives.

767 Abu Hanifa, the leading jurist of the later Umayyad and early Abbasid period and eponymous founder of the **Hanafa School of Law**—one of the four principal branches of the Shariah—dies in Baghdad. A strict Sunni, or orthodox, Muslim and a silk merchant by trade, he is regarded as the first to systematically codify Islamic laws based on the Koran and the *hadith* ("traditions").

Ibn Ishaq, the first "biographer" of the Prophet Muhammad also dies in the same year. His work will survive only as passages quoted by later scholars (notably Ibn Hashim).

768 In the western Maghreb (present-day Morocco), a Berber strongman called **Chakya** raises a revolt, undermining the authority of the Umayyads of al-Andalus.

775 Caliph al-Mansur, after a reign during which he has done much to consolidate Abbasid authority in the Islamic heartlands, dies, and is

---

BAGHDAD

*T*he Abbasids first based their government at Kufa, most likely erecting several fortified administrative palaces outside the city, probably similar to the numerous garrisons constructed by the Umayyads throughout the Arab-Muslim empire. The second caliph, al-Mansur, decided in 758 to create a new capital further north, however, at a point near the ancient Sassanian capital Ctesiphon where important land routes intersected with the navigable Tigris—giving access to the Persian Gulf.

Officially named Medina al-Salam, the new city, which took between four and six years to build, was 1.7 miles in diameter and defended by two concentric perimeter walls made of the kind of mud-brick still manufactured in many parts of the Middle East. On the inside rim of this perimeter was a continuous line of offices, store-houses and living quarters for officials and the caliph's personal guard, broken only by four gates at the head of roads leading to Basra, Kufa, Damascus and Khurasan. In the middle of this ring was the caliphal palace, and standing immediately next to the palace a great mosque. The space between the palace and the round walls was left

succeeded by a son who adopts the title **al-Mahdi** ("the Guided One"). During the ten years of his reign, al-Mahdi encourages *fiqh*, or jurisprudence, increasingly the mainstay of Islamic society.

776 The Berber rebel Chakya is captured and executed by Umayyad forces from al-Andalus. His head is sent to Córdoba.

778 Emperor Charlemagne of the Franks attempts an invasion of Spain, but fails to dislodge the Umayyad amir, and his army suffers defeat during a rearguard action fought at La Roncesvalles. The Franks' defeat is commemorated in *La Chanson de Roland* ("The Song of Roland"), an early 12th-century chivalric epic in Old

empty, however, probably to deter any assault—though doubtless it was used as a military parade ground and for other ceremonial purposes. Designed in the form of a circle, Baghdad was unlike any previous Muslim construction, though it may well have been modeled on an earlier Sassanian city, Furizabad.

By all accounts, the palace was an imposing, multi-storied structure, with the throne-room on an upper floor, and its effect was to distance the caliph from those he governed. While a thriving metropolis quickly grew up around the "Round City," at its center was an increasingly ritualized imperial court that to Baghdad's Persian inhabitants must have seemed as redolent of their own imperial past as the new Islamic regime.

The modern conurbation bears virtually no resemblance to the Abbasid city, although how much of the latter was destroyed by the Mongols in 1258 and how much has simply been built over is unclear. After 1258, though, Baghdad soon regained its commercial stature, and today of course it is the capital of Iraq.

French in which Christians and Muslims (*Sarrazins*) abide by the same courtesies of war.

At the other end of the Mediterranean, during a period of Byzantine resurgence, **Emperor Leo IV** defeats an Islamic army at **Germanikeia**, as a result of which for the time being Islamic influence is expunged from Anatolia.

In **Khurasan**, a Persian follower of Abu Muslim known as **al-Muqanna** ("the masked one" on account of a veil he wears) stages a major revolt, seizing much of the province. A charismatic leader, al-Muqanna claims to be an incarnation of the divine.

780 Following a series of military defeats at the hands of the Abbasids, al-Muqanna incarcerates himself, his family and his few remaining followers in a fortress, then burns himself to death, bringing to an end his revolt.

781 In **al-Andalus**, Abd al-Rahman routs a second Abbasid army sent to overthrow him. He severs the heads of the fallen Abbasid commanders and dispatches them to Baghdad. On receiving them, Caliph al-Mahdi reputedly offers thanks to Allah for setting such a large sea between himself and his Umayyad rivals.

782 During continuing hostilities between Islam and the Byzantine empire, an Arab army marches on **Constantinople**, but is bought off by Emperor Constantine IV and his mother Irene.

785 Caliph al-Mahdi dies, and is succeeded by his eldest son **al-Hadi**.

786 Al-Hadi dies, and is succeeded by his younger brother **Harun al-Rashid**. Often considered the greatest of the Abbasid caliphs, Harun al-Rashid is sometimes said to have completed the transformation of the caliphate into an overtly imperial institution. At his court, supplicants are expected to kiss the ground before his feet, and he indulges in a Persian-style *harem*, preferring this to the maximum of four wives prescribed by the Koran. For the first time, emissaries are exchanged between Islam and the imperial Chinese court at **Xian**, and gifts are exchanged with the Frankish emperor

Charlemagne. During his 23-year reign Harun al-Rashid does much to promote learning (including medicine, astronomy and mathematics as well as *fiqh*) and the arts, and he is remembered not only as an able military commander, but also for leading Friday prayers at the central mosque in Baghdad—a city now firmly established as a center of commerce. Although, like his Abbasid predecessors, Harun al-Rashid depends for his power on a private army of mainly Persian troops, he also acquires **Turkic slave-soldiers**, called **mamluks**, renowned for their fighting abilities, to the eventual detriment of Abbasid authority.

A further symptom of Persian influence is Harun al-Rashid's appointment of **Yahya**, a Persian administrator, as his vizier. For most of his master's reign, Yahya undertakes the responsibilities of everyday government, expanding the scope and the size of the *diwan* (centralized Islamic bureaucracy).

The closing years of the 8th century witness the growth and spread of **devotionism** among urbanized Muslims, based on a strict observance of the *sunna* (customary practices of Muhammad). As greater efforts are made to suppress Shiism, Kharajism and new heterodox sects such as the Mutazilites, "orthodox" Muslims become known for the first time as *ahl al-hadith*—"People of Tradition"—and as "Sunni" Muslims, from the *sunna* (practices) of the Prophet Muhammad and his community.

791 **Al-Khalil ibn Ahmad**, a noted Arab-Muslim scholar, dies in Basra. His work as a philologist, mindful of the linguistic achievements of Persian and Syriac, does much to advance **written Arabic**.

793 The Ummayad amir of al-Andalus, **Hashim I** (son of Abd al-Rahman), briefly reasserts Muslim control over **Narbonne**.

795 The jurist **Malik ibn Anas** dies. In his wake, and based on his book *al-Muwatta* ("The Beaten Path")—a comprehensive compendium of *sunna*—the Maliki school of jurisprudence takes root as one of the four main interpretations of Islamic law constituting the Shariah. In the present day, it is followed in Medina, Egypt and North Africa especially.

THE SHARIAH [ISLAMIC LAW]

*F*rom its inception at the hands of Muhammad, Islam was as much a social faith as a personal creed. By submitting to Allah, the believer became part of a community of like-minded men and women. Like any other community, the Islamic *umma* needed directives as how best to order its affairs. In the early years these were provided either by the Koran, or by the remembered practices [*sunna*] of Muhammad himself, or by the examples set by his Companions—rules that might be enforced by a magistrate who, as often as not, had a military rather than a clerical background. Inevitably, what was perceived as correct Islamic behavior was also partly a matter of Arab custom—or at least those customs that Muhammad had elected not to jettison.

As time went by, however, circumstances changed. An empire grew, and many Muslim Arabs began living in far-off cities larger and wealthier than anything they had hitherto experienced. They also found themselves rubbing shoulders with non-Arabs—many of whom had converted to Islam, but who retained their own customs. Shia Islam, as well as other dissenting sects, also offered challenges to orthodoxy. And finally there was the spectacle of powerful rulers, first the Umayyads, then the Abbasids, whose Islamic credentials were cast in doubt by the extravagant manner in which they ran their courts.

The Koran did not provide unambiguous answers to every question that arose, or specific guidance for every circumstance. What was needed was a comprehensive law code that, although Koran-based, filled in as many of the gaps as possible. This was the Shariah, or Islamic law, compiled in the 8th and 9th centuries.

It covered social and familial relations [including the punishment of crimes and aberrations such as adultery] in addition to key religious tenets, and was based on, in descending order, the Koran, the *hadith* (traditions of the Prophet and his Companions), an analogical form of interpretation called *qiyas*, and popular tradition or consensus (*ijma*).

The Shariah was developed by a number of distinct schools (*madhhabs*) founded by, and named after, individual jurisprudents. Four have survived to the present day: the **Hanafi** (after Abu Hanifa, d. 767), the **Malaki** (Malik ibn Anas, d. 795), the **Shafii** (Muhammad ibn Idris ash-Shafi, d. 820) and the **Hanbali** (Ahmad ibn Hanbal, d. 855). Although each school differs in its detail, and sometimes in orientation—the Hanbali *madhhab*, for example, practiced in Saudi Arabia, is notoriously "hard-line," while the Shafii *madhhab* is considered the most liberal—by convention each is accorded a similar degree of respect by Sunni Muslims. The main branches of Shiism also have their own Shariah codes, as do some other minority sects including the Ibadite Kharajites.

The Shariah has indubitably provided Islam with a sheet anchor, giving ordinary Muslims comprehensive guidelines on how to order their lives. But it has also given Islamic purists a yardstick by which to measure the conduct and performance of Islam's rulers—explaining why it is that Muslim clerics have often been at the forefront of protests and rebellions against power-holders. As a result, sultans, shahs, kings, amirs and presidents have surrounded themselves with clerical advisers, to give themselves at least the appearance of abiding by the rules. In recent times especially, the call by Islamists for the full institution of Shariah law has been a thorn in the side of modernizing "secularist" governments; while the apparent inflexibility of sections of the Shariah, particularly those affecting women, has incited liberal exasperation.

A 25-year period of Kharajite unrest in **Khurasan**, orchestrated by a religious warrior known as **Hamsa ibn Adruk**, begins.

799 The Seventh Shia Imam Musa al-Kazim dies, presumed poisoned. His son **al-Rida** will be known as the **Eighth Shia Imam** in the mainstream Twelver tradition.

800 The Abbasid caliphate re-establishes nominal control over the north African province of **Ifriqiya** and appoints **Ibn al-Aghlab**, a Persian army commander, its governor. He succeeds in pacifying Tunisia, but creates a dynastic amirate—known as the Aghlabids—whose loyalty to Baghdad becomes increasingly tenuous.

Around this time, the physician **Jabir ibn Hayyan** designs a still for separating particle solids from liquids.

801 **Rabiah al-Adawiyya**, an early female Sufi mystic who promotes a concept of Allah as the God of Love, dies.

806 In al-Andalus, amid growing opposition to the Umayyad amirate, **al-Hakem I** orders the massacre of 1500 potentially rebellious and mainly Arab subjects—an event known in Islamic chronicles as "**The Day of the Ditch**."

In the western Maghreb, **Idris II**, a local amir and member of the Idrisid dynasty, founds the inland city of **Fez** on the banks of the

---

A Muslim philosopher maintains that the inventor of chess was a Mutazilite, an upholder of the doctrine of Justice—that is, Free Will—while the inventor of backgammon was a fatalist who wanted to show, by means of this game, that one can do nothing against fate and that true understanding is to mould one's behavior to the decisions of destiny.

—From al-Masudi's 10th-century *The Meadows of Gold*, trans. Paul Lunde and Caroline Stone

Sebou river. In time Fez will become a center of learning and a bastion of the Islamic faith in northwest Africa.

809 The caliph Harun al-Rashid is killed during a campaign against insurgents in Khurasan. His eldest son, the religiously conservative **al-Amin**, becomes caliph, but the succession is disputed by a younger son **al-Mamun**, the governor of Persia/Iran, whose mother is a Persian concubine. Al-Mamun, enjoying the support of Shiites and other dissident sects, and commanding a large army of Turkic slave soldiers, refuses to acknowledge his brother's title and **civil war** breaks out.

813 After four years of fighting, al-Amin is murdered after agreeing to surrender Baghdad to al-Mamun. Despite the opposition of orthodox Sunni clerics and other conservatives, **Al-Mamun becomes caliph**, also assuming the Shiite title "Imam." Influenced by the Mutazilites (see below), al-Mumun orders that *qadi* (judges) and *ulama* (clerical scholars) adopt the "heretical" position that the Koran is "created" (specifically tailored to the time and place of its revelation), as opposed to "uncreated" (a one-off, eternally valid and unalterable deliverance of Allah's message to mankind)—an argument that emphasizes the degree of theological discord in the early 8th century.

Al-Mamun, who enjoys the backing of many heterodox *muwali* (non-Arab converts to Islam), appoints **al-Fadh ibn Sahl**, a Persian Zoroastrian, as his vizier. Setting up a special "House of Learning," the new caliph does much to advance the progress of learning, including the further translation of Syriac, Persian, Indian and Greek texts into Arabic, among them works by Plato, Aristotle, Euclid, Hippocrates and Galen. Medical and botanical studies flourish, and there emerges a school of "rationalist theologians" (called *faylasuf*, "philosophers"), who are soon regarded as dangerous heretics by the Islamic establishment.

It is during al-Mamun's reign that the use of **Indian numerals**, known in the West as "Arabic numerals," becomes widespread in Islam.

814 Tensions between al-Mamun's court and traditionalists boil over into open rebellion in **Kufa** and **Basra**. There is also a revolt among Kharajites in **Khurasan**. Al-Mamun responds by instituting a *mitnah* (inquisition), as a result of which many prominent *ahl al-hadith* are imprisoned, among them the eminent Shariah jurist Ahmad ibn Hanbal.

815 Minority "Zaydi" Shiites stage an uprising in Kufa, but, partly to assuage conservatives in Baghdad, al-Mamoun uses force to suppress them.

THE MUTAZILITES

*A*s with its monotheistic rivals, Judaism and Christianity, Islam's assertion that there is one God and one God only spawned as many questions as it answered—not least the nature of its founding revelation, and whether or not humans can be said to exercise free will under an omniscient and omnipotent deity. While early conflicts inside Islam tended to revolve around issues of leadership, during the period of the Abbasids, Islamic theology became complex and sophisticated—a condition made fully manifest by the protracted, and at times bitter, dispute as to whether the Koran was "**created**" (specifically adapted to the time and place of its delivery to Muhammad) or "**uncreated**" (expressing or reflecting its absolute truths absolutely). While conservative *ulama* held that the Koran was uncreated, others followed a contrary view. One such group were the **Mutazilites**, who developed a school of thought that had its immediate origins in the work of a scholar called **Amr ibn Ubayd** (d.762), but which also had significant roots in Kharajism, Shiism and Greek rationalism. But the Mutazilites were not a single-issue party. Some maintained a belief in man's free will, arguing that an individual could reach paradise simply by leading a virtuous, sin-free life—a position that seemed to force Allah's hand and was therefore regarded as "heresy" by the orthodox.

816 In **Azerbaijan**, a twenty-year rebellion among the minority Khurramiyyah erupts, led first by Jawdam, and then by Babak. The Khurramiyyah are *muwalis* (converts) who have retained some of their Persian Manichean beliefs, and they are widely feared and reviled by Muslim Arabs.

817 The caliph further alienates himself from the citizens of Baghdad by nominating **Ali al-Rida**, the "Eighth Imam" of the Twelver Shiite

This kind of speculation involved vital considerations as to where Islam was heading—whether it should stick closely to its founding traditions and principles, or whether, by conceding that the Koran might in parts at least be amended, it should be allowed to evolve freely.

Yet the Mutazilites were not out-and-out progressives. Their very name derived from the Arabic word *atazala*, meaning "to withdraw" or "hold back." 9th-century Mutazilites like al-Nazzam (d.840) and Abu Hudhayl (d.849) took pride in portraying themselves as mediators of "a position between" extreme opinions. Certainly they had little time for the *faylasufs*, contemporaries who openly embraced Greek rationalism, and when the Mutazilites had the ear of Caliph at-Mamun after 813, they readily supported the institution of a *mihnah* (inquisition) to root out "heresies" other than their own.

Although the dominance of the Mutazilites was eclipsed after the accession of al-Mutawakkil in 847, they left a lasting legacy. Not only had they encouraged the very emergence of Islamic theology (*karam*) as a discipline distinct from Islamic jurisprudence (*fiqh*), but also several of their ideas—among them the notion that Muhammad himself might eventually be superseded by a final prophet or *mahdi*—contributed to the ideology of the Twelver Shiites.

succession, as his own successor in preference to his sons. Conservative Muslims respond by attempting to proclaim his uncle **Ibrahim** caliph in his place while al-Mamun is absent from the city, but the move is thwarted by al-Mamun's return.

818 The caliph's Persian vizier, **al-Fadh ibn Sahl**, is murdered at a public bathhouse in Baghdad, either by the caliph's political and religious opponents or the caliph's own agents. Six months later **Ali al-Rida** also dies, perhaps poisoned by al-Mamun—who is beginning to realize that he may have pushed his Shiite and Mutazilite leanings too far. According to the Twelver Shiite tradition, al-Rida's son al-Taqi al-Jawad becomes the Ninth Imam.

In al-Andalus, the Umayyad *amir* al-Hakem I quells urban unrest in **Córdoba** by levelling an entire suburb of the city. Around this time unrest in "Moorish" Spain encourages many resident Arabs to emigrate to **Fez** in Morocco, creating an "Andalusian" quarter there.

819 Reaching a political settlement with his opponents, al-Mamun gives up the possibility of a Shiite Imam succeeding to the caliphal throne. In return, it is agreed that no further attempts will be made to enthrone al-Mamun's uncle Ibrahim.

Ali Rida ibn Musa died at Tus from indigestion brought on by eating too many grapes. They say that the fruit was poisoned. This occurred in the month of Sfar 203 AH / 818 AD. [The caliph] Mamun recited the funeral prayers. Rida died at the age of fifty-three, or, according to another version, forty-nine years and six months. He was born at Medina in 153 AH/770 AD. Mamun had given to Rida in marriage his daughter Umm Habib, so that of the two sisters, one had married Muhammad ibn Rida and the other this young man's father, that is to say, Ali Rida.

—**From al-Masudi's 10th-century** *The Meadows of Gold*,
trans. **Paul Lunde and Caroline Stone**

AL-SHAFII (767–820)

*W*idely regarded as the greatest of the four main founding Shariah jurists, Muhammad ibn Idris al-Shafii was born at Askelon in Palestine, but grew up in Mecca. As a young man he studied law under the older Shariah jurist **Malik ibn Anas**, but appears to have fallen out with his teacher regarding what (after the Koran) should form the main basis of Islamic Law.

Whereas Malik laid great stress on the *sunna*, or practices of the original Islamic community, al-Shafii preferred *hadith*, with the proviso that the authenticity of each tradition should be properly established by painstaking scholarship. At the time the *hadith*, though sometimes written down, had been more usually preserved orally, and it was largely as a result of al-Shafii's own teachings that scholars began to assess which *hadith* were "true" and which "false." In this way, al-Shafii placed special and decisive emphasis on the values and the *sunna* of the original Islamic *umma*—his argument being that Muhammad had not been chosen at random by Allah to convey the divine message, but because of his innate piety. It was a Muslim's duty, therefore, to lead a life that resembled the Prophet's as closely as possible.

In addition to the Koran and *hadith*, al-Shafii permitted two other guides for determining the content of Shariah law: *qiyas*, or reasoning by analogy to extrapolate new laws from existing laws; and *ijma* (consensus), on the assumption that Allah would simply not allow a Muslim community to be wrong in every respect. But according to the *usul al-fiqh* ("Sources of the Law"), a hierarchical scheme devised by al-Shafii and broadly adopted by other Shariah schools, *qiyas* and *ijma* were given inferior status.

Curiously, perhaps the most influential of the four major Shariah jurists did not himself write very much, and it was only after his death that his followers enshrined a system that today is still applied by religious magistrates in **Egypt**, **Malaysia** and **Indonesia** especially.

820 In **Basra**, there is an uprising among the Zotts, an immigrant community of Indian "gypsies."

Muhammad ibn Idris ibn al-Shafii, one of the four principal Shariah jurists (see opposite), dies in Cairo.

821 Al-Mamun appoints one of his generals, **Tahir**, as governor of Khurasan. Like other amirs of the period, Tahir founds a local governing dynasty, known as the **Tahirids**, which will last half a century. Facing a **recruitment crisis** within his army, Tahir increases the number of Turkic mercenaries and slaves (*mamluks*).

822 In **al-Andalus**, al-Hakem's successor, **Abd al-Rahman II**, begins a restoration of Umayyad authority that will see his capital Córdoba become one of the great cities of western Eurasia and a foremost center of learning. In his efforts to emulate the Abbasid court at Baghdad, Abd al-Rahman II engages the services of **Ali ibn Zaryab** (or Ziryab), a renowned musician and singer of the period, and a noted authority on etiquette. Abd al-Rahman II also seeks to contain the rise of the Christian kingdoms in northern Spain by selectively intervening in their internecine squabbles, but faces domestic difficulties too.

In **Khurasan**, Tahir is "succeeded" as amir by his son Talha.

823 **Al-Waqidi**, author of a surviving account of the Prophet Muhammad's military campaigns, dies.

826 Muslim pirates operating out of al-Andalus and the Maghreb seize the Greek-Byzantine island of **Crete**.

827 Caliph al-Mamun, reverting to his Mutazilite sympathies, again declares the Koran to be "created," and re-establishes a *mihnah* (inquisition) to curb his theological opponents.

The Aghlabids of Ifiqiya initiate a fifty-year conquest of **Sicily**. Muslim raiders and settlers will also launch attacks against southern Italy, where small Islamic colonies are formed. Some will reach as far north as **Lombardy**.

829 Warfare between Islam and the Byzantine empire rekindles after **Emperor Theophilus** issues decrees against the propagation of Islam in his territories. An Arab-Muslim army sacks the city of **Amorium**, according to Christian sources putting 30,000 of its inhabitants to the sword.

830 Al-Mamun establishes the **Bayt al-Hikmah**, an academy dedicated to scientific research and the translation of non–Arabic works of science.

831 The Sicilian city of **Palermo** falls to an Aghlabid army composed of Arab and Berber warriors.

833 Shortly before his death, al-Mamun directs the attentions of the *mihnah* (inquisition) to those clerics who refuse to acknowledge Mutazilite doctrines. He is succeeded as caliph by his younger brother **al-Mutasim**, who continues al-Mamun's policies. Faced with a general uprising in **Baghdad**, and by the growing power of the caliphate's mainly Khurasani guard, al-Mutasim recruits a 70,000-strong slave army of mainly Turkic soldiers drawn from Transoxiana and other "fringe" provinces. In this he is helped by the Tahirid amir of Khurasan, **Talha**, who already possesses a standing force of mamluks.

The orthodox "hard-line" jurist **Ahmad ibn Hanbal**, who insists that the Koran and *sunna* are the sole permissible sources of Islamic law, publicly denounces Mutazilite doctrines and is imprisoned. Although ibn Hanbal writes little, his followers will develop his teachings into the **Hanbali** school of law, one of the four main schools of the Shariah, and widely embraced in Arabia.

In the same year **Ibn Hashim**, a compiler of *hadith*, dies.

835 The Ninth Imam of the Twelver Shiite succession, Muhammad al-Taqi al-Jawad, dies. His son, **Ali al-Hadi**, will be regarded as the Tenth Imam.

836 Faced by unrest in Baghdad, al-Mutasim transfers his capital to **Samarra**, sixty miles north on the Tigris, and inside the modern Iranian frontier. A new city rapidly burgeons, stretching twenty miles along the riverbank and at places five miles deep. Samarra will remain the Abbasid capital for 56 years; nowadays its ruins are notable for a large barracks built to house al-Mutasim's Turkish regiments as well as a striking mosque compound.

SUFISM

Sufism is often described as the "mystical wing" of Islam, even "Islam without the politics." While both definitions broadly hold good, they don't tell the whole story. The word *sufi*, meaning a practitioner of Sufism, is said to derive from *suf*, or "wool," denoting a rough woolen garment of the kind supposedly worn by Muhammad on his visits to the cave where he received the Koranic revelations. A main objective among early Sufis was to attain a closer, even intimate, understanding of the Koran and of Allah not by assiduously obeying the Shariah or the Five Pillars, but by recreating the circumstances of the Prophet's receptivity to Allah in their own lives—a form of asceticism that indeed involved wearing the woolen cloak.

In time, as Sufis came into contact with mystics and ascetics from other religions in Persia and India, they began to elaborate spiritual exercises that would lead the adept to a direct understanding of the divine—including music, dancing, chanting and night vigils, as well as techniques of contemplative introspection. By claiming to be the inheritors of an esoteric knowledge originating with Muhammad, however, adherents of this new worship became increasingly disapproved of by orthodox *ulama*, who regarded Sufism as being overly individualistic—and, in some of its doctrines, overtly blasphemous. In so far as Sufis also promoted the worship of saints, a practice probably borrowed from Christianity and widely embraced by Shiites, they were also seen as heretical. In response to such

837 The capture and execution of the Khurramiyya leader **Babak** ends the revolt in Azerbaijan.

839 The independence of the amirate in al-Andalus is underlined when Córdoba and Byzantine Constantinople **exchange emissaries**.

criticisms, Sufism split in two—between the original "drunken sufis," who indulged in public displays of "ecstatic" behavior, and "sober sufis," who attempted to reintegrate themselves within the Islamic *umma*, and who urged their audiences to respect and follow the Shariah.

By and large, though, because Sufis only rarely expressed political opinions, the *ulama* chose to leave them alone, and Sufism was allowed to become an important component of Islam. By the 11th and 12th centuries, it was not unusual for Muslims to adhere to both orthodox Sunni and Sufic forms of worship without feeling any disjunction. Sufis also played a crucial role in disseminating Islam in **India**, **Central Asia** and the **Far East**, particularly after the emergence of well-organized Sufi orders in the 12th century. Because they sought a heightened "religious" experience, Sufis were open to the spiritual impulses of other faiths, including Hinduism and Buddhism, in a way that imams and the *ulama* were not, and on the remoter boundaries of Islam strange amalgams of different faiths evolved—including Indonesian *abangan* Muslims, who combine an Islam originally brought to them by Sufis with pre-Hindu and pre-Buddhist animism. But the Sufi orders were not always so benign; often well-endowed with land and other forms of wealth, they could on occasion turn in more militant directions. In this respect the outstanding example are the **Safavids**, who began as a near-monastic Sufi community close to the Caspian Sea, but who revived the Persian empire during the course of the early 16th century.

842 Al-Mutasim is succeeded as caliph by his son **al-Wathiq**. Al-Wathiq remains at Samarra as Baghdad falls increasingly under clerical rule.

Later in the year, the Byzantine emperor is succeeded by his three-year old son **Michael III**. During his minority the empire is governed by Michael's mother Theodora, but the young emperor will resume his father's tough line against Islam when he comes of age.

846 The mathematician **al-Khwarizm**, traditionally regarded as the originator of **algebra** (derived from the Arabic word *al-jahr*), dies.

847 Al-Wathiq dies without having made adequate provision for his succession. In the event his younger brother, **al-Mutawakkil**, supported by the Abbasid Turkic slave-guard, gains the caliphal throne at the expense of al-Wathiq's son al-Mamun. Acting quickly to reverse the religious policies of his predecessors, al-Mutawakkil permanently suspends the *mihnah* (inquisition) and orders the arrest of the "Tenth Imam" **Ali al-Hadi**, who is brought from Medina to Samarra. Officials with Mutazilite leanings are replaced, and, in what amounts to a **Sunni restoration**, orthodoxy is promoted.

850 In **al-Andalus**, the first of fifty-odd Christians are executed in Córdoba for showing persistent (some have said wilful) disrespect towards Muhammad and Islam. Although such punishments are atypical of Islamic rule in Spain at the time, the **Córdoban Martyrs** will enter into the mythology of the Christian struggle to "liberate" the Iberian peninsula from Muslim rule. In the short term, many *muwalis* (converts), Jews as well as Christians, are removed from office in the Córdoban bureaucracy.

855 The jurist **Ibn Hanbal**, restored to favor by al-Mutawakkil even though he has declined to become a royal tutor, dies in Baghdad. In a further crackdown against Shiites, a shrine at the tomb of Muhammad's grandson Husayn at **Kerbala**, which over the years has become a popular place of pilgrimage, is destroyed (it is later rebuilt). New regulations limiting the freedom of Jews and Christians are promulgated.

Spiral minaret of the Great Mosque, Samarra

857 Al-Muhasibi, widely regarded as a leading early Sufi master, dies.

858 Viking raiders from Scandinavia, having already disrupted many parts of western Europe, reach al-Andalus and the Mediterranean, but are repelled by Arab and other Muslim defenders.

861 A decade of anarchy begins when al-Mutawakkil is murdered by his Turkic soldiers in December. His oldest surviving son, **al-Muntasir**, is

---

The thing whereof we speak can never be found by seeking; yet only the seeker may discover it.

> —Bayazid al-Bistami (d.874), a Persian Sufi master.

Someone complained to a Sufi sage that the stories which he gave out were interpreted in one way by some people, and in other ways by others.

"That is precisely their value," he said; "surely you would not think much of even a cup out of which you could drink milk but not water, or a plate from which you could eat meat but not fruit? A cup and a plate are limited containers. How much more capable should language be to provide nutrition? The question is not 'How many ways can I understand this, and why can I not see it in only one way?' The question is rather 'Can this individual profit from what he is finding in the tales?'"

> —Idries Shah, *Thinkers of the East* (1971)

Imam Muhammad Baqir is said to have related this illustrative fable: "Finding I could speak the language of ants, I approached one and inquired, 'What is God like? Does he resemble the ant?'
He answered, 'God! No, indeed—we have only one sting but God, he has two!'"

> —Idries Shah, *Thinkers of the East* (1971)

proclaimed caliph, but is almost immediately challenged by his brother **al-Mutazz**. In the eastern provinces, against the background of a Kharajite revolt, **Yaqub ibn Layth**, formerly a metalworker from Afghanistan and known as **al-Saffar** ("the coppersmith"), expels the Tahirids from Sistan and establishes his own amirate.

862 Al-Muntasir dies suddenly, almost certainly poisoned by al-Mutazz, but the caliphate passes to **al-Mustain**, a grandson of al-Mutasin. The new reign is immediately **plunged into unrest** as an uprising among Zaydi ("Fiver") Shiites in **Kufa** breaks out.

864 Facing persecution in Iraq, many Zaydis migrate to **Azerbaijan**, where a Zaydi Shiite state is created by Hasan ibn Zayd.

866 Al-Mutazz is proclaimed caliph in January after al-Mustain is driven out by his Turkish commanders. Repression against Shiites continues.

867 In **Constantinople**, following the murder of Michael III, the emperor Basil founds a new dynasty. By greatly strengthening the imperial army and navy, Basil ensures the continuing survival of the Byzantine empire against Muslim incursions.

868 Ali al-Hadi dies in mysterious circumstances. His son **Hasan al-Askari** will be recognized as the Eleventh Imam of the Twelver Shiite succession.

Ahmad ibn Tulun is appointed governor in **Egypt**, where he will create a dynastic amirate called the Tulunids.

869 Turkic commanders in Samarra depose al-Mutazz and in his place proclaim al-Muhtadi—a son of al-Wathiq—caliph.

In **Basra**, the **Zanj**—black African *muwalis* originally brought to the region to work on plantations—begin an uprising that lasts fourteen years.

Ahmad ibn Tulun annexes **Palestine** and adds it to his Egyptian amirate.

870 Caliph al-Muhtadi dies fighting Turkic rebels, and is succeeded by **al-Mutamid**, a son of al-Mutawakkil. Real power, however, devolves into the hands of his younger brother **al-Muwaffaq**, who is able partially to restore Abbasid authority.

The Mediterranean island of **Malta** is conquered by Arabs operating out of Ifriqiya.

Yaqub ibn Ishaq al-Kindi, a leading "rational theologian" and *faylasuf* who has tried (unsuccessfully) to incorporate Greek Platonism into Islam and rid Islam of anthropomorphism (the tendency to attribute human characteristics to the divine), dies. Few of his works, proscribed by Islamic clerics, will survive.

873 Operating out of Sistan, al-Saffar ejects the Tahirids from **Nishapur** and so brings to an end the rule of the Tahirids in Khurasan. In their place Yaqub creates his own dynasty, known as the **Saffarids**.

Hunayn ibn Ishaq, a Nestorian Christian physician and probably the most prolific translator of mainly scientific Greek texts into Arabic in the early medieval period, dies. Among his translations are works by Galen, Plato and Hippocrates.

874 The Eleventh Shiite Imam **Hasan al-Askari** dies on January 1, allegedly murdered and seemingly without an heir. According to Shiite tradition, however, he leaves behind an infant son by a Byzantine concubine (Narjis Khatun), **Muhammad al-Muntazar**, already sent into hiding for his own safety. Out of this arises the doctrine of the Twelfth or **Hidden Imam**—one who has never died, but will one day return to establish a divine order on earth as a *mahdi*. Forced to remain concealed—a circumstance known as the **Lesser Occultation**, which lasts until 940—al-Muntazar is represented within the Shiite community by a succession of *wakil* (intermediaries).

Two other important Islamic figures die in the same year: **Abu al-Husayn Muslim**, a leading compiler of *hadith* (see below); and **Abu Yazid al-Bistami**, a "drunken" Sufi influenced by Indian mysticism and renowned for "wooing" Allah in the manner of a lover. Al-Bistami's suggestion that the identities of Allah and the true ascetic may merge into one makes him a heretic for many Muslims.

876 Al-Saffar, the ruler of Khurasan, determined to enlarge his domains, launches an attack against **Baghdad** but is repulsed by al-Muwaffaq. Yaqub retains control over Khurasan and territories further east, however.

877 As construction begins on the great **Ibn Tulun** mosque in **Cairo**, Ibn Tulun adds **Syria** to his portfolio of "Egyptian" territories.

883 The **Zanj rebellion** in the Basra region is finally suppressed.

Ahmad ibn Tulud dies in Cairo, and is succeeded as amir by his son **Kulumarawayh**.

886 The Abbasid caliphate grants **official recognition** to the Tulunids as the rightful rulers of Egypt, Palestine and Syria.

890 An Ismaili ("Sevener") Shiite, **Hamdan Qarmat**, creates a popular reformist sect in southern Iraq, known as the **Qaramites** (also known as the Qarmatians and the Camarthians). By calling his center in the Wasit region the *Dar al-Hijra* ("House of the Exiled") he appeals to a deep-seated Muslim belief in the importance of dislocation as a necessary passage on the road to salvation. In the century to come, his sect will be a major and often disruptive Islamic movement.

891 Al-Muwaffaq dies, and is succeeded as titular amir of the eastern provinces by his son **al-Mutamid**.

892 Al-Mutamid dies and **al-Mutadid** becomes caliph in name as well as in deed. Abandoning Samarra for **Baghdad**, al-Mutadid energetically attempts to refurbish the caliphate as the embodiment of Islamic orthodoxy. Among his first acts is to ban all books written by Mutazilites and *faylasufs*.

The same year marks the death of two important historians: **Muhammad al-Tirmidi** and **al-Baladhuri**, the latter the author of an account of the original "Arab" conquests.

893 A new configuration of Ismaili (Sevener) Shiites, known as the **Fatimids**, begins soliciting support in Ifrqiya through its "agent" Abu Abdullah al-Shii.

897 Al-Yaqubi, an Armenian-born geographer and historian, dies. His work, while acknowledging the importance of Jewish and Christian scriptures and taking into account the achievements of the Chinese empire, is unequivocal in defining Islam as the superior and "final" civilization.

898 The Imam of Zaydi (Fiver) Shiism, **al-Hadi Yahya ibn al-Husayn al-Rassi**, establishes what rapidly becomes effectively an autonomous state in **Yemen** (southwest Arabia) which will lend its support to Fatimid expansion in northern Africa.

THE HADITH

*T*he *Hadith*—literally "sayings" or "reports"—are regarded by Muslims as sacred scriptures second only to the Koran. Made up of many thousands of the Prophet Muhammad's utterances and anecdotes about his life and practices (*sunna*), they also contain material relating to his Companions. After the Koran, they are also the most important source for Islamic Law, even though they were definitively compiled some time after the principal Shariah schools were first founded. Indeed, it was a perceived need to distinguish "true" *hadith* from the apocryphal for the Shariah law codes that led scholars to produce reliable collections—the more so as those opposed to some of the rules laid down by the Shariah jurists habitually quoted *hadith* to make their point.

Although *hadith* can be found in many early Muslim-Arab texts, six compilations are regarded as authoritative: those made by **Ibn Ismail al-Bukhari** (d.870), **Husayn Muslim al-Hajjaj** (d. 875), **Ibn Maja** (d.886), **Abu Dawad al-Sijistani** (d.888), **Muhammad al-Tirmidhi** (d. c.900) and **al-Nasai** (d. 915). While these scholars adopted a range of criteria for sorting out the wheat from the chaff—at one point it was estimated than no less than a million

900 An amirate dynasty, known as the **Samanids** after their leader Ismail Samani, displaces the Saffarids as the effective rulers of **Khurasan**. Claiming descent from the Persian Sassanians, they originate in Balkh and have been employed by the Abbasids to provide defence on the far borders of Transoxiana. While continuing to recognize the Abbasid caliphate, they establish a center of power at **Bukhara**, from where they also control much of Afghanistan and parts of present-day Pakistan. The Saffarids, now led by Yaqub al-Saffar's brother **Amr**, retain control over **Sistan** for another hundred years.

hadith were in circulation—the ultimate decider was *isnad* ("chain of transmission"). Since *hadith* had been transmitted orally, the authenticity of an individual *hadith* was assessed on the known character and reliability of those who passed it down.

Given a contemporaneous Arab penchant for fabricating spurious genealogies—everyone wanted to be related to the Prophet and his family—many Western and some Muslim scholars have questioned the validity of this method of authentication. The contribution of the *Hadith* to Islamic ideology, however, remains unassailable. "Know that paradise is under the shade of swords" is just one of many treasured sayings attributed to Muhammad; according to another *hadith* he predicted that "My community will divide into seventy-three sects, only one of which will be saved," while "If you see three men riding any kind of animal," he advises elsewhere, "stone them until one of them falls off." And it is from the *Hadith* that the haunting image of the crescent moon springs: asked if those destined for Paradise would finally see Allah, Muhammad answered yes, but only as one sees the sun reflected in the moon. On earth, the new moon is but a token of what may come hereafter.

In **northern Persia**, a succession of amirs known as the Ziyarid dynasty also achieve quasi-autonomy.

In Baghdad the court physician **Abu Bakr Muhammad ibn Zakariya al-Razi**, better known in the West as "Rhazez," establishes a diagnosis for smallpox, distinguishing it from measles.

THE FATIMIDS (910-1171)

*J*ust as in 750 the Abbasids came to power after a propaganda campaign waged by "agents" who deliberately misled Shiites into thinking their time had come, so the Fatimids prepared for power by first sending out their spokesmen into North Africa. The difference was that the Fatimids actually were Shiites, of the Ismaili sect, who believed that only an Imam descended from the Prophet should have the right to rule. Since the Fatimids also claimed to be descended from Muhammad's daughter Fatima—hence their name—it was clear from the beginning that they intended to lay claim to the whole of Islam. But they never fulfilled their greater ambitions. At the beginning of the 10th century, **Abu Abdullah al-Shii** proselytized on behalf of the Fatimids among the Berbers in Ifriqiya and in 910 the first of the Fatimid "caliphs," **Ubaid Allah**, established a court at Raqqada. The next objective was to conquer the Maghreb, but when the Umayyads of al-Andalus made this impossible, they turned eastwards and took Egypt instead. By 970 they had pushed into Arabia itself, where Mecca and Medina fell into Fatimid hands. Subsequently they intermittently controlled Palestine and Syria, but were unable to dislodge the Abbasids from Baghdad, and in 1171 were themselves overthrown by Saladin.

Despite their ultimate failure, the Fatimids were much more than a symptom of political and doctrinal disunity within Islam. The capital city

902 Al-Muktafi succeeds al-Mutadid as caliph. In **Arabia** the Shiite Qaramites openly revolt and set up an independent state in the Bahrain area of the Gulf which threatens to become the center of a much larger dominion—the more so as they are encouraged by the Egyptian Tulunids.

they founded, **Cairo**, or Misr al-Qahira ("City of the Victorious"), rapidly became, and has endured as, a great Muslim conurbation, with pride of place perhaps belonging to the al-Azhar, a theological college that expanded to become arguably the world's longest surviving university. Likewise Egypt itself ceased being an Islamic province, and became instead a distinctive Arab-Muslim state that in modern times rivals Saudi Arabia, Iraq and Iran.

In the 11th and 12th centuries, perhaps a majority of Egypt's inhabitants were still Coptic Christians, and for the most part these, along with a scattering of Jews, were left in peace. Nor did the Fatimids strive zealously to impose Ismailism on Egypt's mainly Sunni Muslims. Rather Ismaili Shiism remained the preserve of a ruling elite who generally succeeded, by the lights of the times, in furnishing Egypt with an equitable government. Yet, ensconced in a palace fortress in the center of Cairo that covered over a square kilometer, the Fatimids, like the Abbasids, soon yielded to the temptations of opulence, and, no longer able to rely upon the Berbers to maintain what never really ceased to be a colonial authority, they began employing slave mercenaries. Although Saladin established a new dynasty, the Abbuyids, the Abbuyids were short-lived, and in the 13th century Egypt fell into the hands of the Mamluks.

904 Muslim pirates operating out of Ifriqiya assault **Thessalonika**, plundering the Greek city's wealth and carrying off a reputed 20,000 of its citizens as slaves.

905 Responding vigorously to the Qaramite threat, the Baghdad caliphate sends large armies to **Syria**, **Palestine** and **Egypt**; the Tulunid dynasty is toppled and direct rule over its territories is re-established. Even so, the appointment of **Abu al-Hayja** of the Hamdan clan as governor of Syria and northern Iraq leads to the creation of yet another quasi-autonomous dynastic amirate, known as the **Hamdanids**.

908 Al-Muktafi dies and is succeeded as caliph by his 13-year old brother **al-Muqtadir**. Although al-Muqtadir will "rule" for 24 years, his reign witnesses further contractions of Abbasid power and the creation of two rival caliphates.

909 On behalf of the Fatimids, **Abu Abdullah al-Shii** seizes power from the pro-Abbasid Aghlabids in **Ifriqiya**. Soon afterwards, the Fatimids oust the Rustamids from **western Algeria**.

910 Abu Abdullah presents the Fatimid Imam, **Ubayd-allah**, to the people of Qariouan and Ifriqiya. Assuming the titles of *al-Mahdi* ("savior") and *amir al-muminim* ("Commander of the Faithful"), previously restricted to the caliphs themselves, he establishes a second, rival caliphate. Making it clear that the Fatimids intend to establish their Ismaili Shiite rule over all of Islam, armies are sent west towards **Morocco** and east into **Egypt**, but these are repelled. They are also supported in **Yemen** by Ismailis, and by Qaramites in other parts of Arabia and the Middle East.

In the same year, **al-Junayd**, reputedly the first of the "sober" Sufis, dies in his home city of Baghdad. During his life he has endeavored to restrain the excesses of the "drunken Sufis" by advocating mysticism as a means of returning to the original virtues of Islam.

912 The Fatimids found a new capital in Ifriqiya, which they call **al-Mahdiya**. As Fatimid power grows, trade routes across North

Africa and in the western Mediterranean are disrupted, to the economic cost of al-Andalus. In al-Andalus itself, as Muslim-Christian tensions escalate, the new Umayyad amir, **Abd al-Rahman III**, assumes the title *al-Nasir li-dini llah*—"he who fights victorious in the name of Allah." But while he successfully resists Christian expansionism in northern Spain, he also wars against the Fatimids in the **Maghreb**.

920 Abd al-Rahman III inflicts a heavy defeat on the combined forces of the Spanish Christian kingdoms of Asturias-León and Pamplona-Navarra at **Valdejunquera**. The heads of slain Christians are put on spikes in Córdoba, and Christian prisoners are either ransomed or sold into slavery.

921 The Fatimids capture **Fez** in Morocco, but their victory only encourages Abd al-Rahman III of al-Andalus to intervene more forcefully in the Maghreb.

922 At a time of increasing conflict between the *ulama* and Sufi teachers, the "drunken" Sufi **Husain al-Mansur**—better known as "al-Hajjaj," the "Wool-Carder"—is put on trial in Baghdad and then crucified. The grounds for his execution include a "heretical" claim made by al-Hajjaj that the *hajj* may be undertaken in the mind alone, rendering the physical journey to Mecca unnecessary.

923 Gathering strength in Bahrain, the Qaramites launch an attack against **Basra** and destroy much of the city. They also assault *hajj* pilgrims returning to Iraq from Mecca.

In the same year, the highly esteemed scholar **al-Tabari**, author of a voluminous commentary on the Koran, and of *Tarikh al-Rusul wa'l muluk* ("History of Peoples and Kings"), which pays special attention to pre-Islamic civilizations, dies.

925 The grand vizier **Ibn al-Furat**, unable to repress the Qaramite revolt, turns for help to **Munis**, one of the caliph's Turkish generals. Munis organizes a successful military campaign, but in June seizes, tortures and executes the vizier and his son. As a result Munis becomes the virtual ruler in Baghdad, to the chagrin of Caliph al-Muqtadir.

927 A Qaramite army threatens **Baghdad**, but is repulsed by Turkish troops led by Munis.

929 In al-Andalus, Abd al-Rahman III **proclaims himself caliph**, and so cuts the last formal ties between Córdoba and Baghdad. His declaration is probably intended more as a warning to the Fatimids than as a snub to the Abbasids, who have long since abandoned any pretensions to influence events in the Iberian peninsula. Within Islam there now exist three discrete caliphates.

The Middle Abbasids
930–1099

No sooner had the Umayyads declared a rival caliphate in Córdoba than the Abbasids suffered another humiliation. In 930 the Qaramites, who had first raised the standard of their Shiite revolt in Yemen, stormed Mecca and made off with the Black Stone from the Kabah. Two years later, the ruling caliph, **al-Muqtadir**, was toppled by his own Turkic army officers and replaced by a younger, more pliable member of the Abbasid family.

These two events set the scene for a further contraction of Abbasid influence. Egypt surrendered to the **Fatimids** in 969, and by this time the caliph had already been reduced to little more than a figurehead. Baghdad, Iraq and Iran had been taken over by the **Buyids**, a Muslim military clan of mixed Persian-Turkic lineage from the Daymalite mountain range south of the Caspian Sea.

The Buyids had used force to gain power, and liked to style themselves *shahanshah*—an ancient Persian title meaning "king of kings." To legitimize their usurpation, when they entered Baghdad in 945 they immediately struck a deal with the weak-minded al-Mustakfi. The caliph could continue on his throne as the titular religious head of Islam, on condition that he relinquished temporal power. This was a clever move: without the caliph by their side, the Buyids lacked sufficient followers to impose their rule. The Buyids were "Twelver" Shiite Muslims, and by supporting the Abbasid caliphate they were able to reassure the majority of their Sunni subjects that they intended their faith no harm.

Despite their initial political acumen, however, the Buyids lasted less than a century, and soon they controlled little territory outside Iraq. The decline of their power was due to several factors: the continuing quasi-independence of the provincial dynastic amirates; their inability to master the reins of government; and, most tellingly perhaps, the dynastic squabbling that broke out in their own ranks. For all their Persian pretensions, in the matter of succession the Buyids leaned toward Turkic custom—according to which the strongest of the clan, not necessarily a chosen son, took over when the ruler passed away.

The same applied to the **Seljuk Turks**, who displaced the Buyids during the first half of the 11th century. Like the Buyids, the Seljuks saw the wisdom of leaving the caliphate well alone, as a result of which the caliphs of this era often lived to a healthy old age. Unlike the Buyids, however, the Seljuks were Sunni Muslims; and although they too were forced to rely upon existing Persian administrators—among them the brilliant reformer **Nizam al-Mulk**—they were prepared to use strong means to enforce their views, taking the battle to the Egyptian Ismailis.

The advent of the Seljuks may well have secured Sunni Islam's abiding status as Islamic orthodoxy. Certainly the ardent Sunni faith of the Seljuks harmonized well with the *ulama*, who for centuries had been striving to achieve just that. The piety of the Seljuks also helps explain how it was that a purely Turkic clan, forcing their way in from the peripheries of Islam, gained acceptance among the existing elites. But the Seljuks' military reputation certainly had an impact. After Baghdad had been taken, a junior branch known as the **Lesser Seljuks**, resumed

Islam's war against the Byzantine empire, invading and subjugating much of northern Syria and Anatolia. Indeed, so successful were the Lesser Seljuks that the Greater Seljuks saw fit to rein them in, and in 1071 an army was dispatched from Baghdad to Anatolia. Instead of fighting their fellow Turks, however, the Greater Seljuks were met by a Byzantine army at **Manzikurt**, after Romanus Diogenes IV had misread their intentions. The Byzantines were heavily defeated, and news of the Muslim victory spread panic throughout Christendom. In the Iberian peninsula, too, a long-lasting stand-off between Muslims and Christians had been wrecked by the dictator **al-Mansur**, who had launched a *jihad* against the Spanish Christian kingdoms of the north. Yet the same kingdoms had fought back doggedly, and out of these events the crusades were born.

The **First Crusade**, launched by Pope Urban II at Clermont in 1095, resulted in the capture of Jerusalem four years later. But joy among Christians was barely matched by despair in Islam. Palestine was no longer at the center of the Islamic world, if indeed Islam could still be said to have a center. In the Middle East the Seljuks had more pressing problems to contend with—not least the **Nizaris**, an ultra-militant Ismaili sect better known in the West as the "Assassins." The Assassins created an impregnable stronghold at **Alamut**, in northern Iran, at a time when much of Iran, and all the territory beyond, had ceased to obey Baghdad. In Khurasan, Transoxiana and Afghanistan, new dynasties were on the make— chief amongst them, in the 11th century, the **Qarakanids** and the **Ghaznavids**. Atypically, the latter took their name from a city, Ghazna in Afghanistan, not a tribe or clan chief. But like other Muslims on the edge of Islam they pursued the faith with added zeal, and it was an Afghan strongman, **Mahmud of Ghazna**, who first waged serious warfare in India, conquering not only Gujarat and the Punjab, but also reaching the banks of the Ganges River.

930 As the Baghdad caliphate of al-Muqtadir becomes enfeebled, the Qaramites in Arabia storm Mecca and remove the **Black Stone** from the Kabah.

In the Mediterranean, the independence of al-Andalus encourages a growing volume of **trade** with Constantinople and other centers of Greco-Christian learning, which in turn facilitates a flow of ancient Greek texts from east to west. As Córdoba's reputation as a center of **learning** grows, Christian scholars begin to take more notice of non-Christian texts.

932 In a desperate attempt to reassert Abbasid authority, al-Muqtadir appears before his mainly Turkic army in Baghdad wearing the Prophet Muhammad's cloak. Unfazed by the caliph's gesture, the Turkic strongman Munis seizes and executes him. Al-Muqtadir's younger brother **al-Qahir** is made caliph.

933 Caliph al-Qahir creates his own faction, which succeeds in toppling Munis, who is executed. The infighting in Baghdad continues, however.

934 Al-Qahir is seized and blinded by a former vizier, **Ibn Muqla**. Because a blind man is disqualified from being caliph under Islamic law, al-Qahir is dethroned and succeeded by **al-Radi**, a son of the deceased caliph al-Muqtadir. Because of the turmoil in Baghdad, many provincial amirs are able to withhold taxes due to the caliphate, which consequently finds itself under increasing financial duress.

A group of Turko-Persian tribal warriors known as the **Buyids** (or Buwids) from Daylam, in the Alborz mountains to the southwest of the Caspian Sea, establish themselves as the rulers of **Shiraz**.

935 Ibn Tughj, the Turkic governor of Egypt, establishes a new dynastic amirate which, known as the **Ikhshids**, lasts until 969.

The same year marks the death of **Abu Hasan al-Ashari** (born c.874), founder of the widely respected **Asharite school** of Islamic theology. A Mutazilite and even "rational theologian" in his early days, he has done much to reconcile contending doctrines within

Islam, while finally putting his weight behind Sunni orthodoxy. His doctrine insists that while the "word" of Allah is indeed "uncreated," recording instruments such as pen, ink and paper are "created." Al-Ashari also sustains the notion of Allah's omnipotence and unaccountability: Allah may condemn the virtuous and spare the wicked as He wishes. According to al-Ashari, while Allah certainly has attributes, these are strictly non- or supra-human, and it should never be thought that Allah can be fully understood by men.

Ibn Mujahid, a noted grammarian, dies in this year. Since early written Arabic assumes rather than inscribes vowels, Ibn Mujahid has been able to extrapolate no less than seven different readings of the Koran.

936 The arrest and execution of the former vizier Ibn Muqla creates a power vacuum in Baghdad which, in November, is filled by **Ibn Raiq**, the governor of Basra, who uses his prestige to impose terms on the caliphate whereby Ibn Raiq becomes "chief amir" (*amir al-umara*). But although his coup makes Ibn Raiq co-ruler of the remaining Abbasid empire in all but name, he is resisted by a faction of Turkic commanders.

939 In al-Andalus, the Christian kingdoms avenge their defeat of 920 by gaining a victory over Abd al-Rahman III at **Simincas**. During the battle, the caliph loses his copy of the Koran and vows never to fight again.

940 Al-Radi is succeeded by his brother **al-Muttaqi** as caliph in Baghdad. During al-Muttaqi's four-year reign, Ibn Raiq is eclipsed by a member of the increasingly influential Buyid clan, **Ahmad ibn Buwayh**, who creates a personal power-base east of Basra.

According to the traditions of mainstream, "Twelver," Shiism, the period of the "Lesser Occultation" of the Hidden Imam ends, and the indeterminate period of His "**Greater Occultation**" begins. While it is possible that the Twelfth Imam—if he existed—may have died, the immediate reason for this watershed in Shiite history is the unwillingness of the Hidden Imam's fourth and last *wakkil* (agent), **Abul Hasan Ali ibn Muhammad Samarri**, to nominate his own successor. On his own deathbed, the final *wakkil* declares: "the matter now rests with Allah."

944 The Baghdad caliph al-Muttaqi is blinded by a Turkic general known as Tuzun, and therefore succeeded by **al-Mustakfi**, a son of al-Mutaffi.

945 Ahmad ibn Buwayh, having extended his authority across much of Iraq and Iran, marches on the caliphal city and enters it unopposed. He establishes himself as effective ruler, and in the process inaugurates the **Buyid Dynasty**. Under their rule the succession of Abbasid caliphs continues, but the activities of the caliphs themselves are largely confined to presiding over ritual and ceremony.

The Fatimids consolidate their hold over central and northern **Africa**, and also over the island of **Sicily**.

946 Ahmad ibn Buwayh unashamedly vaunts his authority in Baghdad by having the caliph al-Mustakfi blinded and therefore deposed. The caliph al-Muti is enthroned in his place. Ahmad augments his position by taking the title *Muizz al-dawla* ("Strengthener of the State"), and by promoting his two older brothers, **Ali** and **Hasan**, to the rank of amir.

950 The Turkmenistan-born speculative philosopher **Abu Nasr al-Farabi**, known in the West as "al-Farabius" or "Avenasser," dies in Aleppo, perhaps at the age of 80. A musician by training, al-Farabi is remembered for his attempts to blend a highly abstract concept of Islamic theology with elements of Platonic and Aristotelian thought. Although his prescripts include the notion that the ascendancy of Islam makes the practice of reason possible, his claim that reason should take precedence over revealed religion—fiercely opposed by conservative *ulama*—will consign him to the peripheries of Islamic thought.

951 The Qaramites, having refused to accept ransoms for the **Black Stone**, arrange for its return to the Kabah in Mecca by leaving it in a mosque at Kufa. According to some Muslim historians, a note is attached, stating: "By command we took it, and by command we have restored it."

About this time, a secretive Basra-based association calling themselves the **Ikhwan al-safa** ("Brotherhood of Purity"), possibly of Ismaili Shiite origin, begin disseminating a series of hand-copied paper tracts in which a wide-ranging knowledge of different civilizations is deployed to suggest that all religions are equal under the eyes of God. The Brotherhood itself quickly disappears, and is only declared heretical some two hundred years later.

THE BUYIDS

Known also as the Buwids and the Buwayhids, the Buyids were a ruling clan of mixed Persian-Turkic extraction who appeared from the Daylam mountain area near the Caspian Sea. Like other Central Asian potentates, they were skilled at raising warrior bands for the purposes of protecting their homeland and either exacting tribute from their more settled neighbors, or simply plundering them.

From around the beginning of the 10th century, the Buyids began expanding their domains, with the result that they were sometimes asked by Baghdad to supply mercenaries for the caliphal army. But if the enfeebled Abbasids aimed to contain the Buyids, their hopes were dashed. The Buyid leadership, divided between three brothers, continued to harry northern Iran and Iraq until they had sufficient strength to advance on Baghdad itself, in 945.

But the Buyids were no mere barbarian invaders. They had already converted to Shia Islam, and it seems that their leader, Ahmad ibn Buwayh,

952 Having attempted to win public support by their release of the Black Stone, the Qaramites, backed by an army from Oman, launch an attack against **Baghdad**, but are repulsed by Ahmad ibn Buwayh.

953 The Fatimid Imam al-Muizz becomes "caliph" in Ifriqiya. During his 22-year reign, largely because of the exploits of his commander Jawhar, the **Fatimid "empire"** comes into being.

956 **Al-Masudi**, an Arab scholar known for the breadth of his learning, dies. Of his works that survive, *Muruj al-Zaman* ("Meadows of Time") and *Muruj al-Dhahab* ("Meadows of Gold") are most celebrated—structured miscellanies of historical, geographical, biographical and

had a sharp political sense. Instead of expelling the Abbasid caliph, he struck a deal with him: the caliph would be permitted to remain in Baghdad as a religious figurehead, if Ahmad was given the amirate of Iraq and the title *amir al-umura*—"prince of princes." And the Buyids did not attempt to assert their Shiite values, perhaps because they feared a general uprising if they did. As a result they established themselves as the rulers of central Islam for over a hundred years, until the middle of the 11th century.

Khurasan, Afghanistan, Transoxiana and the Fatimid Egyptian empire remained beyond their grasp, however. While they eventually succumbed to internal wrangling as to who should be their leader, in the interim they raised the profile of Turkic soldiery as an instrument of imperial policy—even though tensions between Shiite Daylamites and Turkic Sunni slave troops in the Buyid army contributed to their downfall. Indeed, the significance of the Buyid period is precisely that the Turkic peoples, hitherto existing uneasily on the Islamic fringe, began exerting their influence.

antiquarian anecdotes in which the author's curiosity is matched by his capacity for detached amusement at the antics of his fellow men.

961 In al-Andalus, Abd al-Rahman III is succeeded by his son **al-Hakem II**, during whose reign the **palace library** at Córdoba reputedly becomes the largest in the world, housing some 400,000 titles gathered from as far afield as Persia.

A Byzantine force commanded by **Nicephorus Phocas** recaptures Crete from Muslim pirate rule. Its island population is reconverted to Christianity.

962 Muizz al-dawlah (Ahmad ibn Buwayh) reveals his Shiite sympathies by ordering an official commemoration of the death of Muhammad's grandson Husayn at the **Battle of Kerbala** (680). The anniversary, which falls on the tenth day of the Islamic month of Muharram, and which is still mourned by Iraqi and Iranian Shiites, endures as the most important date in the Shia calender.

In Afghanistan, **Alptegin**, a war-leader of Turkic origin, establishes a court and power-base at **Ghazna**.

963 Muizz al-dawla orders the "**Great Khumm**," the anniversary of Muhammad's supposed designation of his son-in-law Ali as his successor—the second most important date in the Shia calendar—to be officially celebrated.

967 Muizz al-dawla dies after naming his son **Izz al-dawla Bakhtiyar** as his heir, thus initiating the Buyid succession. The new Buyid "chief amir" lacks military ability, however, preferring a life of pleasure, and is challenged both by his cousin **Imran ibn Shahin** from a base in the marshlands of lower Iraq, and by the Hamdanids in upper Iraq. Imran ibn Shahin assumes the title **Adud al-dawla** and extends his control as far as Oman in Arabia.

969 After a prolonged campaign, the Fatimid commander Jawhar conquers **Egypt**, now poorly defended by Abbasid interests. The Fatimids decide to move their court from Ifriqiya to Egypt and a new capital, **Cairo** (*al-Qahira*), begins construction close to the existing administrative capital at Fustat—where it is ordered that the Abassid caliph's name no longer be mentioned during Friday Prayers.

970 Having established political supremacy in Baghdad, Adud al-dawla commissions a great **hospital**, intended as a medical research institute as well as providing state-of-the-art health care. As trade with India and China flourishes, the hospital's pharmacy becomes stocked with medicines drawn from the main centers of civilization in Eurasia.

The famous arches in the mosque of Cordoba, Spain

972 As the new city of Cairo begins to take shape, work begins on **al-Azhar**, initially a mosque/seminary for the propagation of Fatimid Ismaili ideology, but destined to become the foremost university in Islam.

973 The Fatimid caliph takes up residence in Cairo.

The holiest cities of Islam, **Mecca** and **Medina**, fall under Fatimid control and a Fatimid army advances into **Syria**.

CÓRDOBA

By the middle of the tenth century, when the Umayyads still held power in al-Andalus, Córdoba, with its 700,000-odd inhabitants, had emerged as the greatest city in Europe after Constantinople. Rome was still floundering in the wake of the 5th-century "barbarian" invasions, and cities of the future such as Paris, Vienna and London were little more than ambitious villages. By this time Islamic authority over the Iberian peninsula had been established for over two centuries, and although a scatter of Christian kingdoms in the mountainous north of Spain were slowly gathering strength, the threat they posed was, for the moment, limited.

One reason for this was that, following the bloodshed of their initial conquests, Spain's Muslim rulers treated their **Christian** subjects (who made up a majority of the population) if not well, then at least wisely. They were obliged to pay the *jizya* and land taxes, were prohibited from building new churches, were not allowed on pain of death to marry Muslim women (although Muslim men were free to take Christian girls as brides), and were sometimes obliged to wear distinctive clothing. But Christians who converted to Islam—and some who didn't—could rise to prominent positions in the

974 A faction of Turkic generals attempts to seize control of **Baghdad** while the Buyid amir is absent, by deposing the Abbasid caliph al-Muti and replacing him with the puppet **al-Tai**. Baghdad becomes violently divided by hostilities between orthodox Sunnis, who broadly support the caliphate, and Shiites, who support the Buyids.

975 The Buyids reassert their authority over Baghdad at the beginning of the year by deploying their own Turkic slave soldiers. In the

Umayyad bureaucracy. In general, despite odd episodes of "communal" violence, Christian communities were left to administer themselves—following their own laws upheld by their own magistrates.

Since the same conditions applied to a smaller **Jewish population**, it is scarcely surprising that "Islamic Spain" in its heyday has been cited by Muslims as an example of their tolerance towards others, or that Córdoba should have become distinctly cosmopolitan. While Christians and Jews lived in their own quarters within the city, by day Córdoba's thoroughfares and markets thronged with artisans and traders of different creeds and nationalities—merchants arrived from as far away as **Italy**, **England** and even **Scandinavia**, as well as from Muslim **North Africa** and the **Levant**. Córdoba also became a center for international learning, particularly once scholars living under the Abbasid and Fatimid caliphates began reading and translating ancient Greek (as well Hebrew and Indian) texts. While it would be wholly wrong to suggest that Greek learning in its entirety was transmitted to western Europe through the Umayyad capital, Córdoba undoubtedly played a key part in the process.

interests of compromise, however, they agree that al-Tai should remain caliph.

977 As feuding breaks out within the Buyid clan, Adud al-dawla defeats his cousin Bakhtiyar at **Ahwaz**, making himself the political and military master of Baghdad and Iraq. To bolster his position, he marries a daughter of the Abbasid caliph al-Tai, but conservatives resent the idea that Arab blood associated with Muhammad himself should be mixed with non-Arab blood.

In **Afghanistan**, Alptigin (the master of Ghazna) is overthrown by **Sebuktigin**, another warlord of mixed Turkic and Afghani blood.

AL-MANSUR (938-1002)

*A*lthough hostilities between Umayyad al-Andalus and the Christian states of northern Spain were commonplace, they were to some extent ritualized. Summer campaigns resulted in the gain or loss of relatively small amounts of territory, booty was plundered, prisoners were exchanged and notables ransomed. On both sides, limited warfare was good for business, and seldom interrupted other kinds of exchange. The picture changed, however, with the coming to power of the Muslim dictator al-Mansur (Muhammad ibn Abu Amir al-Mafari), known in Europe as Almanzor, in 981.

Beginning his career as a court letter-writer, al-Mansur became the favorite—and probably lover—of the boy-caliph Hisham II's mother. But it was his connections with a veteran army commander, Ghalib, whose daughter he married, that catapulted Muhammad ibn Abu Amir al-Mafari into the role of co-regent; and once he had secured that position there was no looking back. Like the greatest of the Spanish caliphs, Abd al-Rahman III, he undertook

Although Sebuktigin remains nominally loyal to the Samanid rulers of Khurasan and pays lip service to the Abbasid caliphate in Baghdad, he begins campaigning in the **Punjab** in order to acquire a personal empire. By doing so he establishes the **Ghaznavid dynasty** of "Afghan" sultans (kings).

978 As the Buyids overcome and expunge the Hamdanid amirate in northern Iraq, which for some time has been confined to the city of Mosul, the Fatimids capture **Damascus** and with it much of upper Syria.

981 In **al-Andalus**, following the accession of a boy, **Hisham II**, as Umayyad caliph, his regent **al-Mansur** (Almanzor) assumes dictatorial

regular campaigns against the Christians, 53 all told. But his style of warfare was altogether more ruthless: prisoners were as likely to be butchered as traded, and his assaults on Spanish towns and cities were notorious for their brutality towards citizens. At the same time, al-Mansur was determined to sideline the Umayyad caliphate, and to this end he made a point of projecting himself as a devout, even zealous, Muslim. Consulting regularly and conspicuously with Córdoba's *faqihs* (religious judges), he dispensed with the palace guard, made up of mainly Slavic slave-soldiers, and instead recruited Berbers from the Maghreb, known for their religious fervour. But although his military campaigns met with immediate success, in the long term al-Mansur's legacy was ruinous. He destroyed the trust and understanding that had built up between Muslims and Christians in al-Andalus, and by undermining the Umayyads he plunged the western caliphate into tumult. More seriously, by waging *jihad* (holy war) against the Christian states, he inspired a backlash that eventually generated the Crusades.

powers in Córdoba. Although al-Mansur restores Umayyad influence in the Maghreb and successfully combats the growing power of Spain's Christian states, he fatally undermines the authority of the Iberian caliphate.

983 In Baghdad, Adud al-dawla dies. Power is contested between his two sons, **Samsan al-dawla** (lit. "Scimitar of the state"), his nominated successor, and **Sharaf al-dawla**, after Sharaf seizes control of Shiraz.

985 Pursuing war against the Christians of Spain, al-Mansur sacks **Barcelona** and massacres many of its inhabitants.

987 Sharaf al-dawla triumphs over his brother Samsan al-dawla and becomes grand amir of **Iraq**.

989 Sharaf al-dawlah dies of dropsy, and is succeeded as grand amir by another of his brothers, **Baha al-dawla**. Although Baha al-dawla will "rule" over Iraq until his death in 1012, further feuding among the Buyid steadily erodes his authority. By the same token, the Fatimids are able to consolidate their hold over **Syria**, filling a vacuum left by the Hamdanids. In the east, the Ghaznavids greatly increase their influence in **Afghanistan**.

990 The Fatimids, advancing into Iraq, seize **Mosul**, but are quickly expelled by a Buyid force.

In Córdoba, the physician **Abul Kasim** completes a **medical encyclopedia** which provides advice on a number of topics—among them the delivery of babies and the surgical removal of stones from the urinary bladder. Translated into Latin, it will become widely consulted in Europe.

991 **Al-Qadir** succeeds al-Tai as the Abbasid caliph.

995 The Byzantine emperor, declaring his intention to reclaim Syria for Christendom, captures **Aleppo**.

997 Al-Mansur penetrates the Christian northwest of Spain and ravages **Santiago de Compostela**, home to the shrine of St James (the patron saint of Spain) and a place of Christian pilgrimage.

998 In **Afghanistan**, Sebuktigin is succeeded by his son **Mahmud** as the amir of Ghazna. A devout, even pious, Sunni Muslim but also a warrior with an eye for plunder, Mahmud sets about the conquest of India in earnest. Declaring a *jihad*, he instructs imams in mosques under his control to invoke al-Qadir's name during Friday prayers, so underlining his orthodoxy and attracting "holy warriors" (*ghazis*) from across non-Shiite Islam (excluding al-Andalus). Presenting himself as a patron of the arts, he assuages Persian opinion by encouraging Firdawsi and other Persian poets. During the course of his reign, Mahmud launches a total of eighteen campaigns against India, which is at the time weakened by infighting between its many Hindu kings and princes.

999 The Persian Samanid rulers of Transoxiana are overthrown by a Sunni Muslim tribe of eastern Turks called the **Qarakanids**. The Qarakanid victory heralds a steep decline in Persian influence east of the Oxus.

1001 Having imposed his control over the Afghan city of **Kabul**, set in a fertile river valley, Mahmud of Ghazna extends his territory west into parts of **Khurasan** and north into **Transoxiana**.

1002 Al-Mansur dies in al-Andalus, but his son, **Abd al-Malik**, assuming the same dictatorial powers, continues his father's aggression against the Spanish Christian states, mounting punitive campaigns against **Catalonia**, **Castile**, **León** and **Aragon**.

1004 The Byzantines having been driven out of Aleppo, a former slave-soldier known as **Lulu** establishes control over northern Syria at the expense of the Fatimids.

1005 In Cairo, the Fatimids begin building the *dar al-Hikma* ("House of Learning"), a palatial complex that includes a library intended to rival Córdoba's.

1008 Mahmud defeats an Indian army assembled by a consortium of Hindu rulers at **Peshwar**, a victory that gives him access to the Punjab. As his campaigns begin to prosper, Muslims begin settling in northwest India for the first time.

In **al-Andalus**, the death of Abd al-Malik causes an abrupt cessation of the wars against the Christian states. The Córdoban caliphate descends into anarchy that will last twenty years, as local Muslim commanders, many of them Berbers, begin feuding amongst themselves.

1009 The Fatimid caliphal ruler **al-Hakim**, responding to an uprising in Palestine, gravely damages the Christian **Church of the Holy Sepulchre** in Jerusalem.

1012 Baha al-Dawla is succeeded in Baghdad by **Sultan al-Dawla** (literally "ruler of the state") as grand amir.

1015 The Fatimids seize **Aleppo** in northern Syria and oust Lulu, but are unable to maintain control over the city.

1020 The Persian poet **Firdawsi**, author of the *Shanameh* ("Book of Kings"), the most celebrated Persian epic, dies in Tus. According to legend, as his body is taken out from one city gate, camels bearing gifts for Firdawsi from the Ghaznavid "sultan" Mahmud enter by another—slightly too late.

1021 Perhaps mindful of Mahmud's exploits in India, the new Buyid grand amir in Baghdad, **Mushariff al-dawla**, gives himself the ancient Persian title *shahanshah* ("king of kings").

1025 Musharriff al-Dawla is deposed by his fellow Buyid, **Jalal al-Dawla**.

In the east, Mahmud of Ghazna annexes the Indian state of **Gujarat**. During his campaign he plunders the vastly rich Hindu temple at **Somnath**, putting an alleged 700 of its monks to the sword—a massacre that is remembered to the present day.

1030 Mahmud of Ghazna, having occupied the Punjab and the lower Indus, dies in Afghanistan. He is succeeded as sultan of the east by his oldest son **Masud**. Although Masud seeks to extend his father's Indian conquests, he is hampered by the rise of a new force in Islam, the **Seljuk Turks**. Led at this time by **Chagri-beg** and his brother **Tughril-beg**, the Seljuks are the ruling clan of the Oguz (or

Guzz)—a Central Asian nomadic people of Turkic stock who have already converted to Islam and whose homelands are in present-day southeast Russia.

Perhaps in this year, **Abu Ali ibn Sina** (known in the West as **Avicenna**) completes his influential medical encyclopedia, known as the *Canon of Medicine.*

1031 In Baghdad, **al-Qaim** succeeds al-Qadir as caliph.

In al-Andalus, **Hashim III**, the last of the Umayyad caliphs, is expelled from Córdoba. While the Arab aristocracy generally maintains its grip in the cities of the caliphate, Berber and slave warlords vie for supremacy in rural areas. Over the following half-century, "Moorish Spain" fragments into rival states ruled by *taifas* ("party kings" or faction leaders).

1035 Led by Chagri-beg and Tughril-beg, the Seljuk Turks begin moving west from Transoxiana into **Khurasan**.

1037 The Seljuk Turks capture **Nishapur** from the Ghaznavids.

1039 In the Maghreb, a Berber revivalist preacher recently returned from Mecca, **Ibn Yasin**, founds a *ribat* (militant religious community) on the Atlantic seaboard, drawing support from members of his own Sanhaja tribespeople. His sect, called *al-Murabitun* ("people of the *ribat*"), but known to Western historians as the **Almoravids**, offers strict religious observance based on the Malikite Shariah school of law, simplicity of lifestyle and military discipline.

1040 The Seljuk Turks win a decisive victory over the Ghaznavid ruler Masud at **Dandanqan** in northern Iran, as a result of which Ghaznavid rule in Khurasan is expunged. The battle marks the beginning of Seljuk influence in central Islam. Masud abandons Ghazna as his capital and re-establishes his court further east at **Lahore**, in present-day Pakistan.

1041 Caliph al-Qaim formally acknowledges the Seljuk leader Tughril-beg as the sultan of the "eastern provinces."

1042 In the **Maghreb**, Ibn Yasin and the Almoravids begin expanding their influence and power outside their *ribat*.

1043 Tughril-beg's Seljuks, known as the **Greater Seljuks**, campaign in Iraq, seizing the northern city of **Mosul**.

1044 In Baghdad, **Imad-ad-din Abu Kalijar** becomes the latest in the line of ruling Buyid amirs.

SCIENCE AND LEARNING
DURING THE ABASSID PERIOD

*A*s Islam spread, it encountered and, particularly during the Abbasid period, attempted to accommodate the systems of learning that had dominated the ancient world—Greek, Persian and Indian. In the process, it produced a succession of outstanding scholars who made important original contributions to the sciences and philosophy. A seminal figure was **Abu Rayhan al-Biruni** (973–1048), a Persian from Transoxiana who became known as *al-ustad*, "the teacher." A great polymath, al-Biruni journeyed to India on the coattails of Mahmud of Ghazna and spent ten years studying Hindu technology, astronomy and mathematics, as well as Indian religious and social customs. But al-Biruni's acquisition of Indian learning was only part of a much greater project. Consulting Greek and Persian texts, he explored pharmacology and botany as well as history. Using his own instruments, he calculated the radius of the earth (which he knew to be round) to within ten miles of its actual measurement.

At the practical level, such thirst for knowledge presented Islam with few problems. In the field of medicine, especially, Abbasid scholars preserved and augmented existing knowledge, and their own treatises became standard texts in Europe. After all, like any others Islamic rulers wanted the best treatments available. But difficulties did arise when it came to Greek

In **Anatolia**, a separate group of Seljuk Turks, known as the **Lesser Seljuks**, orchestrate a revolt against Byzantine rule—an episode seen by some as laying the foundations for the modern state of Turkey.

1048 Al-Malik al-Rahim becomes the last of the Buyid rulers. As communal violence between Sunnis and Shiites breaks out in Baghdad

rationalism. From the early 9th century Greek thinking had a profound impact on Islam, giving rise to a movement loosely called *falsafah* (meaning, simply, "Philosophy," derived from the Greek) which attempted to reconcile Greek rationalism with the tenets of the Muslim religion. Two early scholars drawn towards Plato particularly, and also the neo-Platonist school which had flourished in Egypt, were al-Kindi (d. 870), an Iraqi Arab, and al-Farabi (870–950), a figure of Turkic origins who migrated to Baghdad. Both had an influence on the Mutazilites that won caliphal backing during the 830s and 840s.

But the sharper intellect, perhaps, belonged to Ibn Sina (Avicenna), a scholar with a mixed Persian-Turkic and Ismaili Shiite background. He also compiled medical lexicons, drawing on the work of Hippocrates and Galen, which gained wide circulation. More boldly, though, he endeavored to equate Allah with Plato's "Prime Mover," the force that had set the world in motion, but which then left it to look after itself. For orthodox Muslims such notions were anathema, since Allah was constantly present and, according to the Koran, the arbiter of every event. Greek rationalism therefore, at least in its speculative aspect, became associated with the taint of heresy in Islam, and within a century of Avicenna's death Abbasid *glasnost* was drawing to a close.

and other southern Iraqi cities, Tughril-beg's Seljuks increase their control over the territory as a whole.

1050 The Greater Seljuks, pursuing war against the Ghaznavids, seize **Isfahan** in Persia and carry their assault into Afghanistan, where Ghazna itself is sacked. Much of eastern Afghanistan remains under Ghaznavid control, however.

1052 The prosperous Italian city-state of Pisa annexes **Sardinia**, expelling its Muslim Arab rulers.

THE SELJUK TURKS

*T*oo little is known about the ethnography of early medieval Central Asia to offer any definitive statement about the original identity of the Seljuks—other than that they were Turkic. But even the term "Turkic" is misleading if considered simply or primarily in ethnic terms: it denoted a widespread population of steppe nomads who spoke approximately the same language, in distinction from "Mongolian," the other main body of nomads further to the east. Down the centuries, a combination of inter-tribal marriages, seizure of women during warfare and raids, and the dictates of individual strongmen led to genetic blurring and overlap.

Given that tribes were the essential building blocks of steppe society and politics, tribal affiliation mattered most. At some point during the 10th century a tribal grouping known as the Seljuks (almost certainly after a strongman of the same name), but associated with a wider grouping called the Oguz or Ghuzz Turks, established itself on the lower Jaxartes river. Around 985 they moved into the vicinity of Bukhara and entered into a relationship with Mahmud of Ghazna. They converted to Islam, and began supplying mercenary troops to Mahmud and local amirs—in fact the word "Seljuk" came to denote a tribal confederacy whose fighters were prized for their hardiness and courage.

1054 Lesser Seljuk Turks take control of **Azerbaijan**.

The Byzantine "**Greek Orthodox**" Church dissolves its remaining ties with the Roman papacy, opening a fissure in Christianity that survives to the present day.

1055 Having gained control of nearly all Iraq, Tughril-beg **enters Baghdad** at the "invitation" of Caliph al-Malik al-Rahim and of the caliph's vizier Ibn al-Muslima, both of whom are aware that the Seljuks intend to defend orthodox Sunni Islam. As Tughril-beg is

Eventually the Seljuks were encouraged to overstep their "client" relationship with Islam and embark on a conquest of the Muslim heartlands in Iran and Iraq at a time when the authority of the caliphate was in disarray. At the same time a junior body of Seljuks, known as the **Lesser Seljuks**, chanced their hand in Anatolia, bringing pressure to bear on Christian Byzantium.

In retrospect, the impact of the Seljuks was momentous. Although the "Greater" Seljuks quickly adopted the Persian (not the Arabic) language—with scant experience of administering either cities or an empire, they were dependent on the existing Persian bureaucracy—their dominance stemmed the advance of Persian culture eastwards into Central Asia. Second, the Seljuks permanently established the Turkic peoples as key players in the development of Islam. Although the Greater Seljuks fell prey to internal dynastic divisions as well as the onslaught of their steppe cousins, the **Mongols**, in Anatolia the Lesser Seljuks prepared the ground for the Turkic **Ottoman Empire**—out of which the modern state of Turkey was born. Third, the fact that the Seljuks were ardent Sunni Muslims reinforced the emergence of orthodox Sunni Islam.

granted the title of **sultan**, what remains of Buyid authority is destroyed, and persecution of Shiites begins. Tughril-beg maintains the Abbasid caliphate to add legitimacy to his usurpation, but retains his personal capital at **Rayy** (near modern-day Tehran) in Persia.

1058 Tughril-beg's half brother **Ibrahim Inal** is executed after launching a rebellion against the Seljuk sultan.

1059 The Seljuks, in command of western Afghanistan, conclude a fifty-year **peace treaty** with the Ghaznavids.

In Baghdad, the vizier Ibn al-Muslima is murdered by **al-Basahiri**, an army commander who has connections with the Egyptian Fatimids and who now launches a rebellion against Tughril-beg.

In the Maghreb, Ibn Yasin dies, having asserted the authority of the Almoravids over much of present-day **Morocco** and parts of **western Algeria**. He is succeeded by Abu Bakr, who appoints his cousin **Yusuf ibn Tashufin** as commander of the northwest sector of the Almoravid territory. Yusuf quickly sets about creating a new military-religious base (*ribat*) at **Marrakesh**, little more than a village on the banks of the Tensift River above the Atlas Mountains.

1060 Al-Basahiri is defeated and killed by Tughril-beg near **Kufa**. Chagri-beg, who has shared Seljuk power in the east, dies, and his brother becomes sole Seljuk ruler.

In the Mediterranean, the **Normans** launch their first attack against **Sicily**. During the next thirty years they will drive Islam out of the island and establish an independent kingdom there. The loss of Sicily also spells the end of Islamic influence in southern Italy.

1063 Tughril-beg dies in September and is succeeded as sultan by his deceased brother Chagri-beg's son, **Alp Arslan**, who appoints a Persian, **Nizam al-Mulk**, as vizier. A gifted administrator, Nizam takes on the responsibilities of government, and in so doing makes early Seljuk rule a period of stability and prosperity. Through a program of public works, which include new roads and irrigation facilities, he revives agricultural activity in the Fertile Crescent.

Determined to combat the insurrectionary tendencies of Ismaili Shiites, supported by Egypt's Fatimid dynasty, Nizam promotes the authority of orthodox Sunni *ulama* and of religious courts, while ordering many new mosques to be built. He also sponsors the opening of new **madrasas**, or religious schools, and it is during his ascendancy that Baghdad reasserts itself over Syria and much of Arabia.

1064 Alp Arslan begins a four-year campaign to secure control of **Azerbaijan**, during which Turkomen soldiers under his command advance deep into **Georgia**. The Lesser Seljuk Turks of Anatolia wrest control of **Armenia** from Byzantine rule.

The jurist and theologian **Ibn Hazm** dies in al-Andalus. Though a fervent supporter of Umayyad rule in Spain and a stern critic of those who have hastened political disintegration, Ibn Hazm is remembered in the West as the author of *Tawq al-hamamah* ("The Ring of the Dove"), a light-hearted but subtle rumination on the capacity of lovers to delude themselves. According to tradition, it was conceived when Ibn Hazm was a young man much pre-occupied with his master Hisham II's harem; translated into Latin and other languages, it becomes popular in Medieval Europe.

1065 Either in this year or the next, Nizam al-Mulk founds the **Nizamiyyah**, a madrasa in Baghdad that, adhering to the Hanbali school of Shariah law, soon takes on the size and status of a university to rival the al-Azhar in Fatimid Cairo. At the Nizamiyyah, students are supported at the sultan's expense.

In **Egypt**, a seven-year **famine** begins, bringing with it social and political disorder.

1066 In al-Andalus, there is a **massacre of Jews** in the southern city of **Granada**. While the exact circumstances of this atrocity remain obscure, it is likely that the rise to prominence of many Jews in the Granadan government has caused resentment among Muslims, and that tensions have been exacerbated by preachers claiming it is "un-Islamic" for Muslims to serve under non-Muslims.

1070 Alp Arslan begins campaigning against the Fatimids in **Syria**. **Aleppo** is captured, and the Seljuk sultan extends his rule to the Mediterranean. He is unable to press home his victories, however, when a fragile peace with the Byzantines collapses.

1071 To rein in "renegade" Lesser Seljuks fighting against the Byzantines in **Anatolia**, Alp Arslan assembles an army and marches against his fellow Turks. Misreading Alp Arslan's intentions, the Byzantine emperor **Romanus Diogenes IV** fields his own army, numbering perhaps 60,000 men, but is heavily defeated

---

MADRASAS

*U*nder the Seljuks, the madrasa—literally a "place of study," but more generally a religious school or college—developed into one of Islam's key institutions. Its origins go back to the earliest years of Islam when a mosque was not just a place of worship, but also a meeting-point for members of the Islamic *umma*—following the example of Muhammad's mosque in Medina. Mosques, like early Christian monasteries, were used to impart Islamic knowledge to aspiring clerics, and over time this arrangement became formalized, some larger mosques acquiring dormitories for students and special teaching rooms. From there it was a natural progression to build complexes specifically dedicated to training novices. An important early example was the al-Azhar in Cairo, created to promote Fatimid Ismaili Shiism. So effective was the al-Azhar that the Seljuk vizier Nizam al-Mulk was prompted to establish a great Sunni madrasa in Baghdad, named after him as the **Nizamiyyah**. But the Nizamiyyah was only one of many madrasas founded by the Seljuks, and soon there were madrasas in every important Islamic city.

at **Manzikurt** (Malaz Kard) on August 21. As a result of Alp Arslan's victory, Byzantine power in **Asia Minor** (east of the Bosporus) is decisively broken, and Anatolia becomes part of a new Islamic territory known as "**Rum**" (derived from the name "Rome") that, ruled by a second Seljuk house, will soon expand into the Balkans. But while the Battle of Manzikurt revives Islamic interest in capturing Constantinople itself, the overwhelming defeat of the Christians will inspire the first of the **Crusades** a generation later.

In the centuries that followed, with madrasas flourishing in Persia, Afghanistan, Transoxiana and India, there was no shortage of clerics willing to propagate Islam eastwards. Since secular education was virtually nonexistent, individual madrasas might also provide a broader curriculum, offering courses in medicine, science and Islamic jurisprudence—hence their much-vaunted claim to have provided the prototype of the modern university. More recently, though, the madrasa has tended to assume a somewhat different character. Most Islamic states support education systems that are similar to their Western counterparts, superficially at least; and, since madrasas are obvious breeding grounds for extremist forms of political Islam, some countries—notably Egypt, Saudi Arabia and Turkey—have set up regulatory ministries of religion. Elsewhere though, especially in poorer nations, madrasas remain unregulated. Famously, during the war against the Soviet Union in Afghanistan in the 1980s, thousands of *jihadis* were indoctrinated in hundreds of madrasas dotted along the Pakistani border. It was in these "schools," which offered Afghan peasant children a "free" education (often doubling as weapons depots), that the Taliban developed.

1072 Alp Arslan is murdered by a prisoner brought before him during a minor campaign in his eastern territories. He is succeeded as sultan by his young son **Malik Shah**. During Malik Shah's minority, Nizam al-Mulk, now sometimes called *ata-beg* ("father-chief") continues to govern central Islam on behalf of the Seljuks, and pursues anti-Shiite policies.

A Lesser Seljuk prince known as **Suleiman** establishes hegemony over **Armenia**.

The Fatimid caliph **al-Mustansir** urgently summons **Badr al-Jamali**, an Armenian-born general serving as the Fatimids' governor at Acre in Syria, back to Cairo to restore order in an Egypt devastated by famine and political unrest. Al-Jamali succeeds in his task, gaining the soubriquet *amir al-juyush* ("amir of the armies") on account of his ruthlessness. He also succeeds in establishing a position equivalent to that of vizier, creating a precedent whereby the Fatimids will increasingly fall foul of military cliques in Egypt and other territories under their control.

1073 The Greater Seljuk general **Atzis** captures Jerusalem from the Fatimids.

The **Ghurids**, a warrior band from the mountains of central Afghanistan, overthrow and replace Ghaznavid rule in **India**.

1075 The Greater Seljuks extend their control over Syria by occupying the southern province of **Palestine**, increasingly regarded as a separate territory. The long-lived al-Qaim is succeeded as caliph by **al-Muqtadi**.

1076 The Greater Seljuks gain control of **Damascus**.

Arab-Muslim adventurers attack and destroy the centuries-old kingdom of **Ghana** in West Africa, looting its capital **Kumbi**. Ghana now becomes a center for the spread of Islam in the western part of the continent.

1077 In Baghdad there are **riots** as Hanbalite students from the Nizamiyyah wage doctrinal war against Mutazilites, Asharites, Shafiites and other theological "minorities." Similar disturbances will occur in 1083 and 1101. As Sunni orthodoxy increases its remit in the capital, the city's Shiites migrate to other centers—usually, but not exclusively, in **Iran**.

1079 As Almoravid power in the Maghreb spreads, Yusuf ibn Tashufin campaigns eastwards and captures **Tangier**.

1080 In Anatolia, **Suleiman ibn Qatalmish**, leader of the Lesser Seljuks, enters into a **defensive alliance** with the Byzantines against Malik Shah and the Greater Seljuks. Suleiman proclaims himself a rival sultan.

In Baghdad, **al-Nasir** accedes as caliph. Surviving until 1125, al-Nasir restores the Abbasids' temporal authority over much of Iraq as the power and influence of the Greater Seljuks temporarily wanes.

In Italy, a Benedictine monk known as **Constantine the African**, who has studied in Iraq, begins translating Avicenna and other Arabic authors into Latin at a monastery in **Monte Cassino**.

1084 Antioch surrenders to Suleiman ibn Qatalmish of the Lesser Seljuks.

1085 Alfonso VI, king of León-Castile, captures the key city of **Toledo** from the Muslims in Spain. As a result of his victory, the *taifa* rulers of al-Andalus begin seeking military support from the Almoravids in the Maghreb. Many Muslim and Jewish scholars, protected by Alfonso, choose to remain in Toledo, which now displaces Córdoba as a center of international learning.

1086 "Sultan" Suleiman is defeated and killed by a Greater Seljuk army led by **Tutush**, putting an end to Lesser Seljuk expansion into Syria and northern Iraq.

Yusuf ibn Tashufin brings an Almoravid army across the Straits of Gibraltar and defeats Alfonso VI of León-Castile at **Sagrajos**, near Badajoz. He is unable to recapture Toledo, however.

The Ghurids, having established themselves in northern India, overcome the Ghaznavids in **Afghanistan**, bringing the dynasty to an end.

1087 Muslim control over the western Mediterranean is dented when a combined Pisan and Genoese force captures the North African pirate port of **Mahdiyya**.

1089 A Castilian mercenary, **Rodrigo Diaz** (known as "El Cid"), having previously offered his services to Muslim *taifas*, begins creating a personal kingdom in **Valencia**, eastern Spain, between the Christian and Muslim spheres of influence.

THE ASSASSINS (NIZARIS)

xpert at murder and harboring strange, esoteric beliefs, the Assassins were in one sense the early medieval equivalents of the Chinese Triads or the Ku Klux Klan—mere utterance of their name sufficed to evoke fear and panic. It remains debatable whether they were a symptom of the disunity that plagued the Islamic world in the 11th and 12th centuries, or a main contributing cause.

They burst onto the scene in 1190, when their founder, Hasan al-Sabbah, an Ismaili Shiite, decided to back a claimant to the Fatimid throne called Nizar during a succession crisis in Cairo. When Nizar was sidelined by his brother, Hasan angrily left Egypt and, accompanied by other dissident Ismailis, established a fortress base at Alamut (known as the "eagle's nest") in the mountains of northern Iran. From there he established fortresses in Syria and Iraq as well as elsewhere in Iran, and decided that the time had come to challenge the Sunni Seljuks. Instead of resorting to open warfare, however, he trained his followers in the art of political killing, focusing on highly placed individuals. The Assassins' weapon of choice was the dagger, and they were prepared to die during their assignments. From the beginning Hasan al-Sabbah instilled in his operatives a sense of *jihad*, of righteousness in their undertakings.

1090 **Hasan al-Sabbah**, an Ismaili Shiite dismayed by the Fatimids' failure to create a truly upright and God-fearing regime in Egypt and supported by other Ismailis from across the Seljuk empire, seizes a fortress at Alamut in northern Iran. Using Alamut as his base, Hasan al-Sabbah creates a militant religious movement that during the course of the next two years turns into a full-scale rebellion. In time, his followers will be known in the West as **Assassins** and by Muslims as the **Nizari Ismailis** (Nizaris).

Although the various rituals that are supposed to have attended their cult are veiled in legend—there is talk, for instance, of a mysterious head-dress which, if worn, resounded with the "music of evil"—it is fairly clear that along the way the Assassins soaked up both Manichean and messianic tendencies.

In the decades that followed, Nizari targets included the grand vizier Nizam al-Mulk, the sultan Malik Shah, at least two caliphs and a Christian king of Jerusalem, Conrad of Montferrat, in addition to many hundreds, even thousands, more. An attempt was also made on the life of Saladin, perpetrated by the Syrian Assassin leader, known as the *shaykh al-jabal*, or "old man of the mountains."

The word "assassin" has since passed into the English language, although the Arabic original, *hashshashin* ("takers of hashish"), was probably used more as a slur than an accurate description of Hasan's men. Their historical legacy is perhaps more certain: the Assassins disturbed the peace of Islam at a time when peace was fragile enough. It is worth recording that the present-day Aga Khan, the titular head of the remnant Nizaris since 1818, spends much of his time extirpating the sins of his forefathers by promoting social welfare.

In al-Andalus, Yusuf ibn Tashin overthrows the Muslim ruler of **Granada**.

1091 The Byzantine emperor, **Alexius Comnenus**, dispatches the first of several emissaries to Rome to ask the pope to raise support among Christians against the threat posed by the marauding Seljuk Turks.

The Normans complete their conquest of Sicily.

1092 As the influence and activities of the Ismaili Assassins grow, the vizier **Nizam al-Mulk** dies, reputedly murdered by one of Hasan al-Sabbah's followers, and with the possible connivance of Sultan Malik-Shah. Local governors are ordered to seize and deal harshly with suspected Assassins—an initiative that merely encourages further acts of Nizarite terrorism. At Alamut itself, the Assassins create an

In order to bring about the death of the lord or other man which he desired, [the Sheikh of the Mountain] would take some of these Assassins of his and send them wherever he might wish, telling them that he was minded to dispatch them to Paradise: they were to go accordingly and kill such and such a man; if they died on their mission, they would go there all the sooner. Those who received such a command obeyed it with a right good will, more readily than anything else they might have been called on to do. Away they went and did all that they were commanded. Thus it happened that no-one ever escaped when the Sheikh of the Mountain desired his death, and I can assure you that many kings and many lords paid tribute to him and cultivated his friendship for fear that he might bring about their death. This happened because at the time the nations were not united in their allegiance, but torn by conflicting loyalties and purposes.

—**Marco Polo**, *The Travels*,
trans. **Ronald Latham**

independent principality that survives until the 13th-century onslaught of the Mongols.

Later in the same year, Malik–Shah himself dies. The succession is disputed by two of his sons, **Mahmud** and **Barkiyaruq**, and their uncle **Tutush**.

1094 Mahmud triumphs and is proclaimed sultan in Baghdad by **al-Mustazhir**, who succeeds al-Muqtadi as caliph in the same year.

Having remained in al-Andalus, the **Almoravids** establish their hegemony over the *taifa* states and create a reunified Islamic state.

In **Egypt** the Armenian "vizier" **al-Jawali** dies. His offices and responsibilities are assumed by his son, **al-Malik al-Afdal**. Under al-Afdal's 21-year stewardship, the political stability created by his father continues and Egypt enjoys a period of social and commercial prosperity.

1095 The Seljuk sultan Mahmud is defeated and killed by his uncle **Tutush**, who becomes sultan in his place. Civil war among the Baghdad Seljuks continues, however, when Mahmud's sons, anxious to avenge their father, seize **Damascus** and **Aleppo**. During the confusion, other claimants to the sultanate emerge, including two half-brothers of Barkiyaruq, **Muhammad** and **Sanjar**.

Pope Urban II, finally responding to Emperor Comnenus's appeals for help, preaches a "**crusade**" against Muslims in the "**Holy Land**" (Palestine) during a Church synod held at Clermont. Those who fight are promised redemption of their sins. To encourage support for a Christian military expedition against the Seljuk Turks, Urban also emphasizes that success in Palestine will offer opportunities to acquire personal estates at a time when western Europe is undergoing a marked growth in population, giving rise to the phenomenon of the "poor knight"—younger sons who, because of the rules of primogeniture, have no lands of their own.

Al-Ghazali, a prominent teacher of Islamic jurisprudence at the Nizamiyyah in Baghdad, experiences some kind of profound emotional collapse. Relinquishing his post, he leaves the capital at the beginning of a personal journey in search of the roots of his Muslim faith.

1096 During the summer months, Christian crusaders converge on **Constantinople**. A majority are either French or French-speaking Normans. Three principal contingents are present: the first, commanded by **Godfey of Bouillon** with the assistance of his brother **Baldwin**; the second, led by **Count Raimond of Toulouse** seconded by the papal legate **Adhemar of Puy**; and the third, by **Bohemund of Otranto**. The Byzantine emperor provides food, accommodation and other necessities for the crusaders, whose leaders, with the exception of Count Raimond, all take an oath of allegiance to him.

1097 The Seljuk prince **Sanjar** becomes governor of Khurasan, a position he holds for 60 years, including the period after 1118 when he becomes "Grand" Sultan.

A Lesser Seljuk army is defeated at **Nicaea** in Anatolia by a combined force of crusaders and Greek Byzantine soldiers. As news of the victory filters back to western Europe, more knights are persuaded to set out for Constantinople, journeying there by land and sea.

Forced out of Nicaea, the "northern" Seljuks establish a new capital at **Konya**.

It is indeed the will of God. And let this memorable word, the inspiration surely of the Holy Spirit, be forever adopted as your cry of battle, to animate the devotion and courage of the champion of Christ. His cross is the symbol of your salvation, wear it, a red, a bloody cross, as an external mark, on your breasts or shoulders, as a pledge of your sacred and irrevocable engagement.

—**Urban II,**
proclaiming the First Crusade at Clermont in 1095

1098 During a second campaign, the crusaders capture the city of **Antioch**, and the first of a series of Christian kingdoms south of the Taurus mountains is set up.

Qilich Arslan, the son of the Lesser Seljuk prince Suleiman killed in 1086, gains control of **Rum** (Anatolia) and establishes a second Seljuk dynasty that will survive 200 years.

1099 During a third campaign, the crusaders, perhaps numbering in excess of 200,000, drive south to attack **Jerusalem**, which falls on July 15 after a siege that lasts a month. The crusaders pour into the city and **massacre** an estimated 40,000 of its inhabitants, among them Jews as well as Muslims. Others are seized—either as slaves or for ransom. Some Muslims and Jews purchase their freedom from individual crusaders with offers of gold, silver, coins and other valuables, only to be murdered or enslaved by other crusaders. Mosques and synagogues are vandalized. A new **Kingdom of Jerusalem** is proclaimed, to be ruled by Geoffrey of Bouillon, who assumes the title "Defender of the Holy Sepulchre"—the site where Jesus Christ was supposedly laid to rest after his Crucifixion. Within weeks of the Christians' triumph, however, disease and famine spread among their ranks, persuading many to return home; by the year's end the crusaders' numbers have fallen to no more than 60,000. Notwithstanding, the fall of Jerusalem leads to the creation of four main Christian states: the Kingdom of Jerusalem, at one point stretching as far south as the Red Sea, and to the north of this the **County of Tripoli**, the **Principality of Antioch** and the **County of Edessa**.

News of the fall of Jerusalem travels through Islam quickly, causing widespread dismay, but concerted resistance to the crusaders is stymied by internal disunity—particularly among the Greater Seljuks. In August an Egyptian army, unsupported by the Seljuks, is defeated by the crusaders at **Askalon**. The Egyptian Fatimids are at loggerheads with the Baghdad Seljuks, who in turn are subject to constant harassment by the Ismaili Assassins, now at the height of their disruptive power.

The later Abbasids
1100–1258

To Christian Europe at least, it seemed that the first Crusaders had carried all before them. Not only was Jerusalem captured, but so too was
all of Palestine and much of Syria, including the coastal lands today
known as Lebanon, and the pressure on Byzantium was relieved. What
was more extraordinary, however, was that no great Islamic army,
marching from the east, had been assembled against them. The Lesser
Seljuks in Anatolia continued to fight, and the Egyptian Fatimids
defended their interests in southern Palestine and Arabia. But the
riposte from Baghdad was relatively slight. If they were greatly concerned, the Greater Seljuks didn't show it.

The Christians had unwittingly stumbled into a no-man's land
between the Seljuks and Fatimids. Neither of the two central Islamic
powers was prepared to expend its all against the Crusaders for fear that
their Muslim rivals would then take advantage. Instead they bided their
time; it was only after the Cairo Fatimids, who had entered into an
unholy alliance with the Christian king of Jerusalem, had been overthrown by **Salah ad-Din**, that the telling counter-crusade got properly under way. Ironically, perhaps, Saladin—as he is known to the
West—was neither an Arab nor a Persian nor a Turk, but a member of
the minority Kurds from northern Iraq. But, armed with a burning
faith and military genius, he recaptured Jerusalem and in a few short
years reversed most of the Crusaders' gains—demonstrating the folly of
mounting long-range campaigns in terrain unsuited either to the people or the fighting habits of western Europe.

Yet Saladin's magnificent victories, though they cemented his power
in Egypt and ensured the birth of the Abbuyid dynasty there, impressed
his foes more than his co-religionists. Islam as a whole did not capitalize on what had happened in the Levant, but remained disunited at the
political and military levels. When in Spain, in 1212, a coalition of

Christian forces led by Alfonso VIII of Castile, scored a resounding battlefield success over the forces of al-Andalus at Las Navas de Tolosa, neither Cairo nor Baghdad blinked. Al-Andalus, which had fallen victim to two successive "fundamentalist" movements incubated in the Maghreb, the Almoravids and the Almohads, was largely written off, although in the southern Spanish principality of Granada, the Nasrids clung on to their Muslim amirate for another 280 years.

By 1212, the power of the Greater Seljuks was wearing thin as, like their Buyid predecessors, they fell foul of internal dynastic disputes. Indeed, because of Seljuk weakness, the caliph al-Nasir (r. 1180–1225) was able to restore Abbasid authority in Iraq. But eastern Iran and the lands beyond, where a new Muslim empire—the **Khwarazm-shahs**—was beginning to gather strength, were already beyond the reach of Baghdad.

Such, generally speaking, was the political condition of Islam on the eve of the **Mongol onslaught**, which arrived in two great waves, the first under the aegis of **Genghis Khan**, beginning with the swift dispatch of the Khwarazm-shah in 1216; the second commanded by his grandson **Hulegu** in the 1250s, culminating in the bloody sack of Baghdad itself in 1258.

Yet away from politics, the health of Islam was more robust than the easy victories of the Mongols might suggest. The Assassins had set aside their daggers and returned to the Sunni fold, while in the Middle East a majority of Shiites—though ideologically committed to the reappearance of the "Hidden Imam," when Allah's word would be made good on earth as a prelude to the end of time—had explicitly adopted an attitude of quiescent non-resistance. Equally, the growth of **Sufism** perhaps encouraged more widespread piety.

That some at least of Islam's revolutionary fire had been extinguished was reflected in the writings of **al-Ghazali** (d. 1111), a theologian who constructed an essentially conservative synthesis of Islamic doctrines that, from the 13th century onwards, became widely accepted as a definition of Muslim orthodoxy. As well as rebutting Ismaili Shiism, al-Ghazali removed a Greek rationalist strain in Islamic thought that, at various points over the preceding four centuries, had gained real purchase in intellectual circles. But the way he did this was sometimes to deploy Greek logic—like the much later Christian Jesuits, al-Ghazali danced with his doctrinal enemies, using their own arguments to deflate them. The result was a defence of Islam that, by medieval standards at least, was clothed in reason. On behalf of the *faylasufs*, as the "rationalists" were called, **Ibn Rushd** (Averroes) attempted a rearguard action, but his work only became widely known in Europe. In Islam, al-Ghazali and the tradition he personified prevailed, to the extent that the edifice the Mongols assaulted was far more solid underneath than its flimsy defences suggested. Yet the triumph of al-Ghazali also brought about a closure. The final demise of the Baghdad Abbasid caliphate coincided with the waning of open-minded enquiry among Islamic scholars.

1100 Having campaigned against the Seljuks in Syria, Geoffrey of Bouillon dies in July, and is succeeded as effective head of the crusaders' mission by his elder brother Baldwin, Count of Flanders, as **Baldwin I**. Abetted by the legendary chivalric crusader **Tancred**, Baldwin rules the Kingdom of Jerusalem for eighteen years.

In the Iberian peninsula, the Almoravids, having already established themselves in southern al-Andalus, occupy **Valencia**.

1101 **Qilich Arslan**, ruler of the Lesser Seljuks, successfully repels Crusaders in **Anatolia**.

1104 Baldwin I of Jerusalem takes the Syrian port of **Acre**. **Byblus** falls to Raimond of Toulouse, who afterwards lays siege to **Tripolis**, another Syrian port. Away from the Christian-Muslim front, however, a spat develops between Bohemund of Otranto and the Byzantine emperor **Alexius Comnenus**, who has ordered his troops to occupy towns in **Cilicia** already captured by the crusaders. In the emperor's view, cities and territories recovered by the crusaders should be restored to Byzantine suzerainty. In the (mainly Norman) crusaders' view, such acquisitions are to be regarded as their own.

1105 Among the Greater Seljuks, Barkiyaruq's half-brother **Muhammad** gains control of Baghdad and is proclaimed sultan. His own brother **Sanjar**, however, controls most of Khurasan.

The scholar-jurist **al-Ghazali** returns to Baghdad after a ten-year absence and begins composing his great work *Ihyah ulum al-Din* ("The Restoration of Religious Knowledge").

1106 Yusuf ibn Tashufin, the leader of the Almoravids, dies. The Almoravids continue to consolidate their position in al-Andalus, however, and to wage successful war against Spain's Christian states.

1107 The crusader Tancred recovers **Cilicia** from the Byzantines on behalf of the Normans. Around this time, the Normans begin building

The Crusader fortress of Crac Des Chevaliers, Syria

a series of imposing defensive castles in the Holy Lands, notably the **Crac de Chevaliers** in the County of Tripoli. Incorporating some elements of Islamic architecture, these inspire a wave of massive **castle-building** in western Europe itself.

1108 The Almoravids defeat Alfonso VI of León-Castile at **Uccles**, but again fail to recapture Toledo.

THE CRUSADES

*W*ithin fifteen years of Pope Urban II's promulgation of the First Crusade at Clermont, those who "took the vow" had captured Jerusalem and carved out four distinct Christian (sometimes called "Latin," sometimes "Frankish") states in the Levant. But from that point on, the Crusades went steadily downhill. Rather than go to the Holy Land themselves, those who signed up increasingly sent surrogates or paid hefty fines to the Vatican. Edessa was lost again in 1144, and most of the rest, including Jerusalem, had gone by 1192. More disastrously still, the Fourth Crusade never even got as far as the Holy Land, but instead sacked Constantinople—the defence of which against the belligerent Anatolian Seljuks had been one of the inspirations behind the Crusades in the first place. As a result, the Roman Catholic and Greek Churches entered into a relationship of permanent separation.

Arguably the Crusades delayed the final assault on Constantinople, which had been on the Islamic agenda since the days of Muhammad, by three hundred years. Historians have also suggested that the Crusades had a profound effect on Europe, focusing Christian identity during the 12th century and furthering the emergence of European states such as France and England, but since it is impossible to know what would have happened had

1110 The Almoravids complete their conquest of al-Andalus with the capture of **Zaragoza** and the overthrow of the last of the *taifa* kings. The Almoravid amir returns to **Marrakesh** in Morocco, having appointed governors to rule in Spain in his place.

1111 Death of **al-Ghazali**.

the Crusades never occurred, such theories are at best speculative. Rather, what can be said is that the Crusades brought West and East in closer contact, sometimes to positive effect, sometimes not—"Arabic" (originally Indian) numerals, oriental textiles, and nutmeg on the one hand; gunpowder and leprosy on the other.

From the Muslim viewpoint, the Crusades seem not to have been quite so significant—at least at the time. Since Jerusalem was the Christians' main objective, Islam itself, preoccupied with its own internal divisions and mounting insurgency on its eastern borders, was never in any great danger. Perhaps, though, it is the word itself, derived from the Spanish *cruzada*, that has been the most significant legacy. When George W. Bush declared "a crusade against terrorism" after the attacks on the US in September 2001, he was immediately obliged to retract his statement. According to some, he had offended Muslim sensibilities by invoking memories of the grisly slaughter of Muslims in Jerusalem in 1099. The irony was that Bush's antagonist, Osama bin Laden, had some years before already declared a *jihad* against "crusaders," meaning the infidels of the West. But Bush's greater error was to overlook the most obvious point—namely that the Crusades failed, at least in the Levant.

1116 Masad I, sultan of the Lesser Seljuks in Anatolia, establishes his capital at **Konya**, where he rules for forty years.

1118 Following his brother Muhammad's death, Sanjar becomes "supreme sultan" among the Greater Seljuks, and restores unity between Iraq and Iran. But although Sanjar, who moves his personal capital to **Marv**, will rule for thirty-nine years, during his reign the Seljuks' hold over Iran is steadily eroded.

AL-GHAZALI (1058–1111)

*K*nown in medieval Europe as **Algazel**, Abu Hamid Muhammad al-Ghazali is regarded by Muslims not only as Islam's most eloquent theologian, but also the figure who "saved" Islam from disintegration amid the welter of rival sects and opinions that sprouted everywhere in the half-millennium since Muhammad's death. His principal work, *Ihya Ulum ad-Din* ("The Restoration of Religious Science"), compiled towards the end of his life, synthesized several existing main currents in Islamic thought while firmly rejecting others. Al-Ghazali found space for Sufism at the expense of the *faylasufs*, and in so doing breathed fresh life into the sense of Sunni orthodoxy promoted by the Shariah jurists. He advanced an understanding of Islam that, while insisting on the validity of established forms of worship and behavior, endeavored to suffuse it with Sufic thinking. In a key passage aimed against rationalists, and derived from the work of the earlier theologian al-Ashari, al-Ghazali argues that the reason fire burns is because Allah wills it, not because of some fixed law of the physical world. Everything, therefore, is a perpetual miracle, however much appearances can be rationalized. Logic in the Greek sense has its

In Spain, **Alfonso I of Aragon** gains papal approval to launch a crusade for the recovery of **Zaragoza** and other towns from Muslim rule; Zaragoza falls to the Christians in December.

In the Maghreb, **Muhammad ibn Tumart**, the son of a Berber chieftain, begins plotting the overthrow of the Almoravids in Morocco. Failing to incite a general rebellion, he retires to the Atlas mountains where he founds a militant sect known as the **Almohads**.

uses, but only insofar as it elucidates the greater reality of Allah; any other use should be abandoned.

Arriving at his *summa theologica* was, however, an arduous journey for al-Ghazali—a personal *hijra* of the sort cherished by devout Muslims. Although he was born and died in the small Persian township of Tus, for much of his life he was a wanderer. Early brilliance attracted the attention of the great vizier Nizam al-Mulk, who installed al-Ghazali as a professor of jurisprudence at the newly opened Nizamiyyah college or madrasa. But al-Ghazali stayed in Baghdad for only four years. Experiencing some sort of personal crisis, during which his speech became impaired, he begged to be excused his teaching duties and instead embarked on a spiritual pilgrimage that took him to Damascus, Jerusalem and Hebron (the site of the tomb of Abraham) as well as Mecca and Medina. During these travels, which lasted well over a decade, and which introduced him to several Sufi masters, he divided his time between intense study and contemplation. Only when he felt he had resolved all the outstanding issues of his faith did he return to Baghdad.

1120 In Jerusalem, Hugh of Pajens founds the **Knights Templar** to protect pilgrims visiting the city. The Order rapidly becomes a major expression of militant Christianity that will acquire great tracts of land not only in Palestine and Lebanon, but also in western Europe.

1121 Crossing the Bosporus, Byzantine forces reclaim territory in southwest Anatolia, but **Emperor John II Comnenus** is prevented from pressing home any advantage he has over the Lesser Seljuks by the eruption of unrest in the Christian Balkans.

The death of **al-Malik al-Afdal**, effectively Egypt's ruler since 1094, marks the beginning of a period of renewed unrest in the Nile valley that the Fatimid caliphs are increasingly unable to control.

In **al-Andalus**, as conflict between the Almoravids and Alfonso I of Aragon intensifies, **Amir Ali ibn Yusuf** deports many Christians from his territories to the Maghreb. Those who remain in al-Andalus experience harassment.

In the Maghreb, the Almohad leader **Ibn Tumart** is hailed as a *mahdi* ("guided one") and establishes an independent state in southern Morocco.

1125 Ibn Tumart extends Almohad control over most of **Morocco**.

In north and west China, the **Khitai people** are expelled following the political and military success of the Jürchen people. A large number of the Khitai move west and found a new state in the central Asian steppes, where they become known as the **Qarakhitai** ("black Cathays"), and where they begin threatening the eastern territories of the Greater Seljuks.

1130 Ibn Tumart dies and is succeeded as Almohad leader by **Abd al-Mumin**.

1131 The Persian poet, astronomer, mathematician and hedonist **Umar al-Khayyam** dies. A master of the *rubbaiyat*, or verse quatrain, his fame in the West will be established in 1859 with the publication of Edward FitzGerald's intensely lyrical translation, *The Rubaiyat of Omar Khayyam*.

Ah, with the Grape my fading Life provide,
And wash the body when the Life has died
And in Windingsheet of Vine-leaf wrapt,
So bury me by some sweet Garden-side.

That ev'n my buried Ashes such a snare
Of Perfume shall fling up into the Air,
As not a True Believer passing by
But shall be overtaken unaware.

Indeed the Idols I have loved so long
Have done my Credit in Men's Eye much wrong:
Have drowned my Honor in a shallow Cup,
And sold my Reputation for a Song.

Indeed, indeed, Repentance oft before
I swore—but was I sober when I swore?
And then and then came Spring, and Rose-in-hand
My thread-bare Penitence apieces tore.

And much as Wine has play'd the Infidel,
And robb'd me of my Robe of Honor—well,
I often wonder what the Vintners buy
One half so precious as the Goods they sell.

—*The Rubaiyat of Omar Khayyam*,
trans Edward FitzGerald,
stanzas 67–81

1139 In the Iberian peninsula, Alfonso Henriques establishes the Christian kingdom of **Portugal** and inflicts a crushing defeat on an Almoravid army at **Ourique**.

1141 The Greater Seljuk sultan Sanjar is defeated outside **Samarkand** in Transoxiana by an army of the Qarakhitai. But although the Qarakhitai expand their power in Central Asia, they are tolerant in religious matters and Muslim communities remain relatively unaffected.

1142 The first known translation of the **Koran** into a western language, Latin, is made by **Robert of Ketton**, an English scholar resident in Spain.

1143 The death of **Ali ibn Yusuf**, the second Almoravid amir, creates a power vacuum in al-Andalus. Local governors re-emerge as "*taifa* kings" ("party" or "petty" kings).

1144 As Almoravid rule disintegrates in al-Andalus, there is open revolt in **Córdoba**. In the Algarve, **Ibn Qasi**, the founder of a revivalist sect known as the *al-Muridan*, invites the Almohads to cross from Morocco to restore order.

Imad ad-Din Zangi, the amir of Aleppo and Mosul, defeats the crusaders in **Armenia** and conquers **Edessa**.

1145 With the backing of Pope Eugenius III, a **Second Crusade** against "Muslim infidels" is promulgated by **Bernard of Clairvaux**, the founder of the Cistercian order of monks.

1146 In the Maghreb, the Almohads gain control of **Fez**, which until now has held out. Crossing to Spain, a body of Almohads help Ibn Qasi capture **Seville**. Alfonso VII of León-Castile occupies the former Umayyad capital **Córdoba**, however.

1147 As the Second Crusade gathers momentum, up to half a million Christian soldiers assemble under the leadership of **Conrad III of Germany** and **Louis VII of France**. Although this army succeeds in engaging some Seljuk forces, it is quickly ravaged by disease and hunger, and the crusade ends in a shambles. But the Norman king of Sicily, **Roger II**, decides to annex Greek islands belonging to Constantinople rather than return home empty-handed. This triggers an eleven-year war between Sicily and Byzantium.

1148 The Almohads, now campaigning in the Iberian peninsula on their own behalf, **recapture Córdoba** from Alfonso VII of León-Castile.

1151 In Afghanistan, **Ghazna** is sacked by the Persian amir of Ghur.

In the Iberian peninsula, the Portuguese extend their territory by capturing the **Algarve** from Muslim rule. Ibn Qasi is murdered at **Silves**, probably at the instigation of the Almohads.

1152 At the beginning of a revival in Abbasid power and authority, the purposeful caliph **al-Muqtafi**, creating his own guard of slave soldiers, expels Seljuk officials from Baghdad.

1153 The Seljuk sultan **Sanjar** is captured by renegade Turkic tribesmen during an anti-insurgency campaign in northern Khurasan.

1154 In al-Andalus, the Almohads seize **Granada**.

1155 In the Lesser Seljuk Anatolian state of Rum, Sultan Masud I is succeeded by **Qilich Arslan II**. During his 37-year reign, Rum is destabilized by almost constant family feuding.

1157 The Seljuk sultan Sanjar dies shortly after his release by his rebel captors. Although Sanjar's successors continue to rule over Iraq, Iran and other territories to the east are lost to them as now the **Khwarazm-shahs** emerge as a potent threat in the steppes.

In al-Andalus, the Almohads take Almería.

1159 The Almohads create a fortified township on the island of **Gibraltar**, which now becomes the springboard for the completion of their conquest of al-Andalus.

1164 In Alamut, the Assassin ruler **Hasan** declares himself to be the Ismaili Imam and proclaims the arrival of a new spiritual age sometimes called "**the restoration**."

1165 In **Toledo**, Gerard of Cremona forms a group of scholars dedicated to the **translation** of Arabic, Syriac and Hebrew texts into Latin.

1166 **Abd al-Qadir** al-Jilani, a Persian Sufi and founder of the *Qadiriyyah*, the first *tariqah* or order of Sufis as such, dies in Baghdad.

1169 In **Cairo**, a 31-year-old Kurdish commander called **Salah ad-Din Yusuf ibn Ayyub**, better known as **Saladin**, deposes the Fatimid caliph's vizier Shawar and assumes the viziership for himself. Intimidated by Saladin's obvious ability, the caliph allows him to

THE ALMORAVIDS AND THE ALMOHADS

A persistent feature of Islamic history is the periodic eruption of geographically peripheral warrior sects who, determined to assert what they consider the Muslim faith in its purest form, cause havoc in more settled Muslim communities.

Al-Andalus in the 11th and 12th centuries experienced two such "fundamentalist" or Islamist movements. The Almoravids (*al-Murabitun*), whose very name derives from the Arabic word *ribat*, a religious military camp, first gathered strength among the nomadic Sanhaja peoples living in the Moroccan desert, then moved across the Straits of Gibraltar to take maximum advantage of the collapsed Umayyad regime. Their welcome had much to do with the threat posed by the Christian kingdoms; as al-Mutamid, the *taifa* ruler of Seville put it, "I would rather drive camels in Fez than tend pigs in Castile." Once established in Spain, however, the Almoravids behaved more like brigands than true upholders of the faith; within a generation their idealism gave way to greed and profligacy. Nor, on the theoretical front, were they immune from criticism. The Almoravid insistence on a strictly literal reading of the Koran had led them to adopt the title *al malik* (the king), although Saladin is more usually styled "sultan." Saladin is also given command over the Fatimids' forces in Syria since he has already made clear his intention to wage a *jihad* against the Christian crusader states.

1171 Saladin masterminds a **coup** against the Fatimids, bringing their rule over Egypt to a close. The Ismaili caliphate is abolished and in its place Saladin institutes a return to the Sunni faith. He sends emissaries to Baghdad, where in return for Saladin's expres-

attribute human qualities to Allah, a "heresy" that helped open the door to their successors, the Almohads.

Like the Almoravids, the Almohads originated in the mountainous deserts of the Maghreb, building a *ribat* and promising to cleanse Islam of its pollution. Their founder, Ibn Tumart had spent long years in the Middle East, where he came across the revivalist thought of al-Ghazali, in particular al-Ghazali's emphasis on the "unity of Allah," and it was from this the Almohads took their own name: *al-Muwahhiddun*, "Upholders of Divine Unity." But, like al-Ghazali, Ibn Tumart had also experienced Sufi mysticism, and he preached an inner spirituality alien to his Almoravid predecessors. It was this that made the Almohads a potent force. Ibn Tumart proclaimed himself a *mahdi*, and ordered a *jihad* not only against infidels but against errant Muslims. Yet once the Almohads had invaded Spain, their rule proved no more enduring. Shunned by more urbane Muslims who had too much to lose by embracing Almohad principles, the Almohad leadership fell foul of dynastic division. Far from saving Spanish al-Andalus, the Almohads softened it up for a renewed Christian onslaught.

sions of loyalty towards the Abbasids, the reigning caliph **al-Qaim** acknowledges him as the just and rightful ruler of the Egyptian empire.

Ferdinand II of León creates the **Order of Santiago**, a religious-military organization that plays an important part in the *Reconquista* ("Reconquest") against Muslim rule in Spain.

ABD AL-QADIR AL-JILANI (1077–1166)

*A*s his full name suggests, Abd al-Qadir was born in the Persian town of Jilan, although much of his life was spent in Baghdad, where he became the most highly regarded Sufi of his day. A famous story tells of how, as a youth, he determined to journey to the capital to gain a greater knowledge of Islam. His mother told him always to tell the truth, and then stitched the money he would need into the inside of his cloak. Accompanied by other poor students, Abd al-Qadir was accosted by thieves along the road. Disappointed that they had not stopped a richer party, the thieves were on the point of turning away when one of them asked if any of the students had any money. Abd al-Qadir immediately told them yes he had, and opened his cloak. The leader of the robbers was so struck by the boy's honesty, and the reasons behind it, that he let him continue his journey unmolested.

Apocryphal or otherwise, this and other legends surrounding Abd al-Qadir sit comfortably with his status as a Muslim holy man. But his greater significance has to do with his incarnation as the founder of the first *tariqah* (literally "path," meaning Sufi order or mystic brotherhood), although it is not entirely clear whether Abd al-Qadir ever intended such a

1173 The Almohads, under the leadership of **Yusuf I**, complete their conquest of Muslim **Spain** and begin purposefully attacking the Christian states.

1174 Saladin begins a twelve-year program that mixes force and diplomacy to unify and expand the Egyptian empire of which he is sole ruler. Over the following years he brings under his authority parts of

thing, or whether it was implemented by his followers and disciples in Baghdad. Whichever is the case, from the time of his death there existed a school of Sufis who called themselves the Qadiriyyah, and soon other Sufi orders sprang up in his wake—some merely associations of poor peripatetics, others richly endowed communities that focused on missionary work among "infidels." All such brotherhoods, though, adopted their name and distinguishing rituals, or exercises, from a revered master.

The largest, or at any rate best known, were the "silent" Naqshbandi, "founded" by Muhammad ibn Muhammad Baha ad-Din Naqshband (1317–89), who taught that Allah was better invoked with the heart and mind than with the tongue. Similarly, the *tariqahs* did much to promote the idea of Islamic sainthood—strictly speaking not permitted by the Koran, but tolerated because, at the popular level, veneration of Muslim worthies was preferable to godlessness. In this respect, again it was Abd al-Qadir who led the way when he proclaimed that whoever called out his name in distress, even after he was dead, would receive succour. To this day, his shrine-tomb in Baghdad, like those of other Sufis and also the Shiite Imams, attracts a flow of supplicants.

Syria and **Palestine** not under Christian rule, and also **upper Iraq**, in order to encircle the crusader states. At the same time he forges a disciplined army capable of taking on and overcoming Frankish, Norman and Byzantine opposition.

1175 Muhammad of Ghor invades the northern plains of **India**.

1180 In Baghdad, **al-Nasir** becomes caliph. The only one of the later Abbasids to successfully assert the authority of the caliphate, al-Nasir promotes himself as a religious leader by acquiring a proficiency in each one of the four main schools of the Shariah.

Around this time, the physician **Abu Mervan ibn Zuh**, known in the West as "Avenzoar," assembles a compendium of medical therapies supported by anatomical explanations.

1183 Saladin begins the active phase of his *jihad* to recover Syria and Palestine from Christian rule by capturing **Aleppo**.

1186 In the east the **Ghaznavid** dynastic empire collapses.

1187 Saladin escalates his *jihad* against the crusader states by **declaring war** against the Kingdom of Jerusalem. On July 4 he routs a Christian army at **Hattim** near the old port of Tiberias in Palestine after six Christian leaders defect to his side the night before. During the battle, many of his adversary's finest soldiers are killed, and in its aftermath Saladin easily captures a string of Christian cities and fortresses, including **Beirut**, **Sidon**, **Nazareth**, **Nablus**, **Jaffa** and **Askalon**. On October 2 **Jerusalem** itself capitulates, after nearly ninety years of crusader rule. As they take control of the city Saladin's troops act with restraint, and the massacre feared by many Christians does not occur.

Following his victory, Saladin quickly overruns the remaining Christian states and establishes himself at **Damascus**. Only a handful of fortresses and fortified cities remain in the crusaders' hands, including the port city of **Tyre**, which Saladin fails to reduce.

In Europe, the response to Saladin's success is swift: a **Third Crusade** is proclaimed.

In the Indian subcontinent, Muhammad of Ghor (leader of the Ghurids) secures control over the **Punjab**.

1188 As enthusiasm for the Third Crusade gathers momentum in western Europe, **Philip I of France** imposes the "**Saladin tithe**," a tax to raise money for a crusading army.

1189 **Philip of France**, **Richard I of England** (known as *Coeur de Lion*, "Lionheart") and **Frederick I Barbarossa** of the Holy Roman Empire emerge as the principal leaders of the forthcoming crusade, which is further helped by a **truce** between Byzantium and Norman Sicily, at war since 1185.

1190 Frederick I Barbarossa drowns in **Cilicia** ("Little Armenia") after capturing the Lesser Seljuk capital, **Konya**. He is succeeded as Holy Roman Emperor by his son **Henry VI**.

1191 Richard I disembarks at Tyre and joins his fellow crusaders in a successful siege of **Acre**, which falls in June. Shortly afterwards Philip returns to France, and Richard quarrels with Emperor Henry VI's representative in the Holy Lands, **Leopold of Austria**. Richard defeats Saladin at **Arsuf**, but, without the support of his fellow leaders, is unable to press home his advantage with an attack on Jerusalem.

Yahya Suhrawardi, the founder of a school of mysticism that endeavors to fuse Sufism with traditional Persian mystical beliefs, is executed as a heretic in Aleppo, most probably because some of his writings invoke atheist elements of Greek rationalism.

After the Almohads recapture **Alcacer do Sal** from the Portuguese, **Pope Celestine III** pronounces the whole of the Iberian peninsula a crusading zone.

1192 The Third Crusade collapses after Richard I and his army become stranded in the desert east of **Antioch**; of an original force of 100,000 men, only some 5000 remain. Many have died in battle, succumbed to disease or returned home; while others have deserted, some converting to Islam. Saladin generously **makes peace** with

The Infidels, not weighed down with heavy armor like our knights, but always able to outstrip them in pace, were a constant trouble. When charged they are wont to fly, and their horses are more nimble than any others in the world; one may liken them to swallows for swiftness. When they see that you have ceased to pursue them, they no longer fly but return upon you; they are like tiresome flies which you can flap away for a moment, but which come back the instant you have stopped hitting at them: as long as you beat about they keep off: the moment you cease they are on you again. So the Turk, when you wheel about after driving him off, follows you home without a second's delay, but will fly again if you turn on him. When the King rode at them they always retreated, but they hung about our rear, and sometimes did us mischief, not infrequently disabling some of our men.

—from the *Itinararium Regis Ricardi*
("Itinerary of King Richard"),
a near-contemporary account of the Third Crusade

Richard, and guarantees Christian pilgrims access to the Holy Sepulchre in Jerusalem. Richard sets out for England, but in December is **taken prisoner** by Leopold of Austria and handed over to the emperor Henry VI.

In Rum the death of the sultan **Qilich Arslan II** marks the beginning of a period of prolonged decline of the Lesser Seljuks, as their throne becomes prey to virulent family conflicts.

1193 Saladin dies on March 4. According to tradition, he leaves insufficient wealth even to afford a plot of land for his grave.

1194 The rule of the Greater Seljuks over the central states of Islam is brought to a close as the last sultan, **Tughril III**, is killed fighting the Khwarazm-shah.

1195 In the Iberian peninsula, the Almohads inflict a crushing defeat on Alfonso VIII of Castile at **Alarcos**.

1196 The Almohads begin raids deep into Christian territory, ravaging the land around the Castilian city of **Madrid**. The Almohad ruler, **Abu Yusuf**, also launches a persecution of unorthodox Muslim scholars in al-Andalus, among them **Ibn Rushd**, suspected of being a free-thinking *faylasuf*.

1198 The **Order of the Knights of St Mary of the Teutons**, a mainly German militant body, is founded in Acre (which remains in Christian hands) to promote a **Fourth Crusade**. Like the Knights Templar, the Teutonic Knights acquire considerable wealth and political influence in the lands of their birth.

c.1200 A Turkic leader called **Tekish**, descended from a family of amirs appointed by Malik Shah to rule over Khwarazm, a territory between the Caspian and Aral seas, dies having forged a powerful tribal confederacy. He is succeeded by Ala al-Din Muhammad, who takes the title Muhammad Kwarazm-shah. Later he will also style himself caliph. For the time being however he is content to submit to Qarakhitai overlordship.

In spite of his power and his victories he was a quiet, modest man. Many years later a legend reached the ears of the Frankish writer, Vincent of Beauvais, that when he lay dying he summoned his standard-bearer and bade him go round Damascus with a rag from his shroud set upon a lance calling out that the Monarch of all the East could take nothing with him to the tomb save this cloth.

—**Steven Runciman** on Saladin, in *A History of the Crusades* (1951–54), vol. III

1202 The **Fourth Crusade** is affirmed by Pope Innocent III.

1203 Muhammad of Ghor completes his conquest of India's northern plains.

In the western Mediterranean, the Almohads conquer the **Balearic islands** (Majorca, Minorca and Ibiza), the last surviving stronghold of the Almoravids.

SALADIN (1138–93)

$\mathcal{S}$aladin—whose full name in Arabic, **Salah ad-Din Yusuf Ibn Ayyub,** translates as "Righteousness of Faith Joseph Son of Job"—is conventionally held as the epitome of Islamic heroism. Thus, when in 1991 Saddam Hussein promised to fight the "mother of all battles" against America and its allies after his seizure of Kuwait, he was hailed by some enthusiastic clerics as "the new Saladin."

Emulating Muhammad, Saladin sought to combine politics, warfare and faith. Against the Crusaders he proved a brilliant adversary, but he was also a great patron of religious scholars and an avid builder of mosques; indeed, in his youth, Saladin was more noted for his religious aptitude than any martial prowess. His rise to power, however, was meteoric. Born into a prominent Kurdish family in the employ of the Fatimids in Syria, he grew up in Aleppo and Damascus, entering the service of the amir Imad ad-Din Zangi. On Imad ad-Din's death, he attached himself to his own uncle Asad ad-Din Shirkuh, although the new amir, Nureddin, perhaps had a greater influence on Saladin's emerging values.

1204 Crusaders gather in **Venice**, hitherto a port frequented by Arab merchants, under the command of the city's ruler, the doge **Enrico Dandolo**. Partly to protect his trading interests, instead of directing the crusaders to the Holy Land Dandolo asks **Count Baldwin IX of Flanders** to attack the Byzantine emperor, **Alexius Comnenus**. After **Constantinople** is ransacked, Innocent III excommunicates Dandolo and his fellow crusaders, but Baldwin stays on and has

The Fatimid vizier Shawar, anxious to prevent the spread of Sunni power, was known to have made an alliance with the Christian king of Jerusalem, Amalic I; and it was this unholy compact that drove Saladin to seize power in Cairo in 1169. Thereafter Saladin showed himself a master of strategy. Before attacking the Christian kingdoms, he patiently gathered strength, appealing above all to his fellow Muslims' sense of destiny by proclaiming a *jihad* while instilling keen discipline into his relatively small army. When he struck, the results were immediate: Jerusalem fell within three months of opening his campaign. Inevitably a fresh Crusade was announced in Europe, but this Saladin withstood, to the extent that no other Muslim attracted greater plaudits outside Islam. In his legendary contest with Richard of England, there is little doubt who emerges the better man. Saladin habitually extended mercy towards those whom he vanquished, and even Edward Gibbon, who rarely found anything good to say about anyone, commented in his *History of the Decline and Fall of the Roman Empire* that Saladin's "perusal of the Koran on horseback, between the approaching armies, may be quoted as proof, however ostentatious, of piety and courage."

A heroic representation of Saladin

himself proclaimed emperor. Alexius Comnenus escapes to **Trebizond** on the southern shores of the Black Sea and there creates an independent Christian state that survives until 1461. The Fourth Crusade itself collapses after an outbreak of plague rules out further campaigning.

1206 Muhammad of Ghor is murdered, and an independent sultanate in northern India is created by **Qutruddin Aibak**, a former Turkic slave promoted by Muhammad to be his vice-regent in the Punjab. Because of his background, the dynasty Aibak founds will be known as the first of the Muslim "**slave dynasties**" to rule in India. In the subcontinent, the first sultans make little attempt to disseminate Islam among the conquered Hindus, preferring instead to enjoy the proceeds of plunder and taxation.

In Mongolia, **Genghis Khan** (also known as Jinghiz or Temujin) forges a powerful and aggressive confederacy of steppe tribes that, as the **Mongols**, will become the single most destructive force in medieval Eurasia.

1210 In Alamut, the Assassin leader **Jalal ad–Din** renounces the title of Shia Imam and declares the "veil" opened by his predecessor Hasan in 1164 to be "closed." He embraces Sunni Islam, and imposes the Shariah on his people. Although the independence of Alamut continues, the **Assassins** cease to be a distinctive movement.

Muhammad Khwarazm-shah, declaring his independence from the Qarakhitai, occupies **Transoxiana**.

In India, **Sultan Aibak** dies after an accident during a game of polo.

1211 Aibak's successor in India, **Sultan Iltmash**, operating out of his capital **Delhi**, extends Muslim rule into Sind in the west and Bengal in the east. In Delhi itself he commissions the **Qutb Minar** tower. During his and subsequent reigns the number of Muslims settling in India is greatly augmented by those fleeing the onslaught of the Mongols in western Central Asia.

1212 As a coalition of Christian princes is forged in the Iberian peninsula, **Alfonso VIII of Castile** leads a massive Christian army against the Almohads and achieves a decisive victory at **Las Navas de Tolosa**—a battle that ends Muslim dominance in Spain.

1213 The Almohad regime is further weakened by a tribal revolt among the **Banu Merlin** in the Maghreb.

1215 Muhammad Khwarazm-shah launches an invasion of **Afghanistan**, capturing territory from the Ghurids.

As Genghis Khan begins to look west after campaigns against China, Muslims in **Kashgar** become the first followers of Islam to experience the Mongols' rapacity.

IBN RUSHD (AVERROES) (C.1126-98)

*A*mong the constellation of thinkers who intermittently thrived during the period of the Abbasids, none shines brighter than **Ibn Rushd**, known as "Averroes" in the West. Born into a family of jurists in the al-Andalusi capital Córdoba, he served as a *qadi* (chief religious judge) in Córdoba and Seville. Averroes had also trained in medicine, and it was in that capacity that he became intimate with the amir Ibn Yaqub. Yet his true passion was for philosophy. Recognizing in Averroes a man of exemplary learning, the amir asked him one day to explain Greek philosophy. Fearing that he might transgress beyond the bounds of Islamic orthodoxy, Averroes demurred, but Ibn Yaqub insisted, and from their exchange flowed a series of works that, soon translated into Latin, established Averroes as an authority on Aristotle and Plato, and in so doing transformed early medieval European learning.

As Averroes was acutely aware, to pursue philosophy at the level of abstraction practised by the Greeks was theologically dangerous, since "truth" was supposedly revealed for all time in the Koran. His response to this

1216 The slaughter of a delegation of up to a hundred Mongols, either emissaries or members of a trading caravan, on the banks of the **Otrar River** on the orders of Muhammad Khwarazm-shah provides Genghis Khan with a pretext to launch a full-scale assault against Islam.

1217 Islam in the Iberian peninsula experiences another setback when a Muslim army is defeated by the Portuguese at **Alcacer do Sal**.

1218 Genghis Khan destroys the empire of the Qarakhitai.

Pope Innocent III preaches a Fifth Crusade.

conundrum, offered sincerely, was to seek to demonstrate that Aristotle's philosophy in particular was at one with Islam, for all that the Athenian had pursued truth by other means. In similar fashion, Averroes's greatest Christian champion, the Italian **Thomas Aquinas**, elaborated the theory that philosophy deals only with "secondary causes," and that any understanding of "first" causes must necessarily remain the preserve of theology.

In due course Aquinas was acknowledged not only as the "father" of the dominant "scholastic" school of European medieval philosophy, but also as the principal apologist of Roman Catholic dogma. The man who inspired him, however, was less fortunate. As the war between al-Andalus and the Christian states of Spain intensified, hard-line *ulama* looked increasingly askance upon the seemingly free-thinking Averroes, and in 1195 he was banished from Córdoba. But although Averroes was rehabilitated shortly before his death, in Islam his achievements have been marginalized—along with those of several other of his intellectually adventurous contemporaries and near-contemporaries.

1219 In Anatolian Rum, the accession of **Ala ad-Din Kay-Qubadh**, known as "Kaikobad," restores some vigour to the Lesser Seljuk sultanate, which lasts until his death in 1237.

Having destroyed the Qarakhitai, Genghis Khan initiates a war against the nascent Khwarazm-shah Muslim empire, which is weakened by

THE MONGOLS

Various theories have been advanced to explain the phenomenal eruption of the Mongols, who, following the election of Genghis as supreme khan of a loose confederation of tribes inhabiting the eastern steppes in 1206, devastated much of China, Central Asia, Europe and of course Islam, for a century afterwards. Some believe there must have been profound changes in climatic conditions and population densities in the steppes, creating an overwhelming need for a people who were essentially nomadic pastoralists to unite and find new lands; some that the nomadic way of life itself had come under pressure from the spread of cities and sedentary agriculture; and others that the Mongol success should be ascribed to the military genius of the man himself, **Genghis Khan**, and of his immediate successors—notably his four sons, **Jochi, Chagatai, Ogedai** and **Tolui**, and at least two of his grandsons, **Kublai Khan** and **Hulegu**, the first of the Ilkhans.

Each of these explanations played a part, but in the context of Islamic history there are interesting comparisons to be made with the Arab conquests of the 7th century. In both cases plunder provided a powerful incentive, and in both cases the marauders profited from the relative disunity of those they attacked. Again, both the Arabs and Mongols prospered by their ability to wage long-range warfare on horseback. Like Muhammad, Genghis was adept at persuading potential followers to lay aside their specific tribal allegiances. But there the similarities end. Contrary to widespread

religious dissent and a feud between Muhammad Khwarazm-shah and his mother **Terken Khatun**. A Mongol horde, led by Genghis's son Tolui, simultaneously attacks Muhammad Khwarazm-shah's forces from three directions, and Muhammad and his son **Jalal ad-Din** are driven out of their territories into Azerbaijan. As the Mongols

opinion, the Mongols were not a single, ethnically seamless people. Their hordes almost certainly contained as many warriors of Turkic as of Mongolian origin, and, as they swept along the steppe corridor running from China to Hungary, their numbers swelled with fresh recruits. But more significantly still, the so-called Mongols were not propelled by any strong ideological or religious imperative.

If Genghis and his successors had a weakness other than an impatience with the cares of civil government, it was their lack of any strong, binding faith. Traditionally the "people of the felt-walled tents," as the steppe nomads were called, abided by **shamanistic** beliefs, which in practice meant abiding by the qualities of individual shamans. This gave the Mongols a natural respect for almost any kind of priest, and in the long run left them exposed and vulnerable to more systematic, institutionalized belief systems—in the east the Mongol leadership converted to Buddhism, usually of the Tibetan variety; westwards, albeit more reluctantly, they surrendered to Allah.

Today, the landscapes of Afghanistan and Iran are still scarred by the Mongols' initial ferocity, littered by ruined medieval cities and savaged irrigation works. Yet in time the Mongols helped underwrite the spread of Islam in Central Asia, especially among what became the southern former Soviet Republics—**Kazakhstan, Turkmenistan, Uzbekistan** and **Tajikistan**; and a group of their descendants, the **Mughals**, established a Muslim dynasty in **India**.

advance, they leave a trail of great destruction, killing those who do not immediately surrender and burning their towns and cities.

1220 Shah Muhammad of Khwarazm dies, and **Jalal ad–Din** becomes leader of a dwindling band of Khwarazm Turks. For a while he mounts effective resistance against the Mongols.

1221 Genghis Khan himself sacks **Samarkand**, the greatest of the Central Asian trading cities, but instead of advancing into the Islamic heartlands, he launches an assault against eastern Europe, where his armed horsemen reach the Danube. His son Tolui invades Afghanistan, however, where he destroys **Herat**.

1223 A Mongol horde crushes a Muscovite (Russian) army on the **Kalka River**.

1224 When the Almohad ruler **Yusuf II** is trampled to death by a cow in Marrakesh, a succession crisis leads to the separation of Almohad power in al-Andalus and the Maghreb.

1225 The reforming Abbasid caliph **al-Nasir** dies in Baghdad, and the caliphate, falling prey to a series of disputed successions, again becomes a weak institution respected by few.

1227 The death of Genghis Khan abruptly halts the tide of Mongol invasions as the Mongol hordes return to their homelands to determine a new leader. In the event Genghis's vast empire is partitioned amongst his four surviving sons. **Jochi**, the eldest, receives the western portion north of the Caspian and Black Seas, including much of present day Russia, a territory that becomes known as the **Golden Horde**; **Chagatai** receives a Central Asian territory later known as the **Chagatai Khanate**; his third son **Ogedai** is proclaimed "Great Khan," with authority over his brothers; while the youngest, **Tolui**, is bequeathed the Mongol heartlands, in present-day Mongolia.

1228 A **Sixth Crusade**, led by Holy Roman Emperor Frederick II, lands by sea in Palestine.

1229 Having agreed a treaty with the ruler of Egypt, Saladin's nephew **Malik al-Kamil**, early in the year Frederick II regains **Jerusalem**, **Bethlehem** and **Nazareth**. He crowns himself king of Jerusalem in March and establishes a safe corridor for pilgrims between the holy city and the Christian port of **Acre**.

James I of Aragon captures the Balearic islands from Almohad rule.

1230 Kaikobad of the Lesser Seljuks defeats the Khwarazm-shah Jalal ad-Din at **Erzincan** and extends his authority into northern Iraq.

1231 Mongol incursions against Islam resume, although with less intensity than under Genghis Khan.

1236 In al-Andalus, **Córdoba** falls permanently into Christian hands on June 29 after an assault launched by Ferdinand III of León-Castile. That same evening, the **Great Mosque** is reconsecrated as a Christian cathedral.

1237 As Almohad rule in al-Andalus disintegrates, **Muhammad ibn Yusuf ibn Nasr** establishes an independent dynastic amirate at **Granada** that, governed by the Nasrids, will survive as a "Moorish" enclave in Christian Spain until 1492.

1238 James I of Aragon captures **Valencia** and its surrounding territories from the Almohads. He allows the defeated Muslims to retain their residences and faith.

1241 Campaigning once more in Europe, the Mongols achieve a massive victory at **Liegnitz**, but immediately afterwards news of the Great Khan Ogedai's death deprives the Mongol horde of its momentum.

1243 The Mongols launch an attack against the Lesser Seljuks in **Anatolia**. Defeated at **Kosa Dagh**, the Lesser Seljuks become the Mongols' vassals, and Rum ceases to exist as an autonomous state. The Seljuks, however, will continue as governors in Anatolia until the early 14th century.

1244 Jerusalem is retaken for Islam by an Egyptian army led by the pasha (governor) **Khwarazmi**. Although this Christian defeat inspires the **Seventh Crusade**, Jerusalem will remain in Egyptian hands until 1517, when it passes to the Ottoman Turks.

1245 The **Seventh Crusade** is launched under the leadership of Louis IX of France.

1248 Rather than fight in the Holy Land, Louis IX decides to attack **Egypt** directly. He takes the Nile delta port **Damietta** and then marches on Cairo. His army is defeated at **Mansura**, however.

In al-Andalus, after a three-year siege, **Seville** falls to Ferdinand III of León-Castile. Although Muslim resistance to Christian forces continues for a further ten years, the capture of Seville spells the end not just of the Almohads, but also of Islamic rule in Spain outside Granada.

1249 The death of the Abbuyid sultan Malik al-Salih Najm al-Din in Egypt leaves the throne vacant, although for a year al-Salih's wife **Shagarat al-Durr** rules in his stead.

1250 The **Seventh Crusade** ends in humiliation when Turanshash, a claimant to the Abbuyid throne, inflicts a second defeat on Louis IX's forces at **Fariskur** on April 6. As his troops, already weakened by scrurvy, are massacred, Louis himself is taken prisoner. A ransom of 800,000 gold pieces is set on his head, and Damietta is returned to the Egyptian authorities.

Turanshash is unable to establish his tenuous claim to the Egyptian throne, and a mamluk commander named **Aybak** assumes the sultanate. Although Aybak is soon toppled by another Turkic commander, his coup initiates the rule of the **Mamluk Sultans** in Egypt, lasting 267 years.

1251 Following the death of the Great Khan **Mongke**, Genghis's grandson by Tolui, the Mongol patrimony (excluding the Golden Horde and the Chagatai Khanate) is divided between Mongke's brothers. **Kublai** is made khan of the east, including parts of China; **Aughboke** is given Mongolia; and the youngest, **Hulegu**, is given whatever he can conquer west of the Oxus—an Islamic territory that will become known as the **Ilkhanate**. Hulegu immediately begins preparing a campaign that will take him to the shores of the Mediterranean.

1256 Hulegu Khan storms the Assassin fortress at **Alamut**. Its last ruler, the "Grand Master" Rukn ad-Din, is put to death.

1257 With his mind clearly set on Baghdad, Hulegu continues his campaigns in **Persia/Iran**, but is temporarily delayed from achieving his goal when tensions erupt with his distant cousin Berke, the Khan of the Golden Horde.

1258 Hulegu enters Iraq and camps outside Baghdad. When the caliph refuses to surrender, Hulegu takes the city by force. In the ensuing **Sack of Baghdad**, many buildings are destroyed, and several hundred thousand of its inhabitants, including the caliph himself, are killed. Although the Abbasid caliphate will be revived in Cairo as a means of legitimizing the rule of the Mamluks, no future Abbasid will be anything other than a token figurehead.

CHAPTER FIVE

From the Sack of Baghdad to the Fall of Constantinople

{1258–1453 (655–856 AH)}

THE **SACK OF BAGHDAD** IN 1258, itself a calamity, presaged a regime of uncommon brutality in **Iraq** and **Iran**. The Ilkhanate established by Hulegu was one of three "western" Mongol khanates, the others being Chagatai and the Golden Horde. The sole interest of the first **Ilkhans** was to wring those whom they had subjugated dry: punitive taxes were imposed on Muslims and non-Muslims alike, crippling commerce and agriculture. Yet the Mongol strikes against Islam, dreadful though they were, were territorially contained. Neither **Hulegu** nor his successors were able to cross through southern Afghanistan into the Indian subcontinent, where Muslim rule over the Punjab, the lower Indus valley and the great plains of the Ganges was being steadily consolidated. And the Mongols' ambition to add Cairo to their portfolio of conquered cities was decisively halted by a Mamluk army at **Ain Jalat** in 1260. As a result, Egypt, Arabia, Ifriqiya, the Maghreb and other Muslim territories in Africa were spared.

Even without the resounding Mamluk victory, though, it is questionable how far the Mongols would have progressed. Their military strength depended on the horse—up to five fresh mounts per warrior during each campaign—but in the sun-baked wildernesses of the Middle and Near East, maintaining such a menagerie presented overwhelming logistical problems. Come winter, there was little option but to withdraw to more northerly pastures, allowing the enemy time to regroup. The Mongols had other shortcomings, too. They had neither the experience nor the aptitude for large-scale government, especially where towns and cities were concerned.

In all three western khanates, the Mongol leadership converted to Islam, with the result that, once the ravages were past, the religion was enlarged. Nor had Muslim clerics suffered unduly in the interim. Rather they were the one segment of the Islamic community to escape virtually unscathed, for the simple reason that it was Mongol custom to respect "holy men," whatever their creed.

The same could not be said of **Timur**, the second great scourge of Muslim communities during the high Middle Ages. Falsely claiming descent from Genghis Khan, Timur—who was more Turk than Mongol—first carved out a kingdom in Transoxiana, then lashed out in every direction open to him, leading his armies into the **Middle East**, the **Caucasus**, **India** and finally towards **China**. Yet Timur himself was a Muslim—of the most zealous kind, in fact. In India hundreds of Hindu monks numbered among tens of thousands slain by the ruler in 1398 as he waged *jihad* against "idolaters." Following his death in 1405, Timur's great empire collapsed like the Mongol empire before it. Yet failures such as these only created opportunities for others. In Iraq and western Iran, factions of mainly Turkic descent vied for supremacy, while further east the mountains of Afghanistan bred a line of warrior clans that, one by one, rode into India to claim the Delhi sultanate during the 15th century.

It was in **Anatolia**, however, that the future structure of Islam's central nations first began to take shape. Having smashed the power of the Lesser Seljuks, the Mongols had created another vacuum, soon filled by vying Turkish warlord dynasties. Among these, one house became preeminent: the Osmanlis or **Ottomans**. Like any successful dynasty, the Ottomans were eager to expand their domains and acquire an empire. In pursuit of their ambitions, though, they turned at first not towards Damascus, Baghdad or Cairo, but Europe—eyeing the Balkans and the Greek peninsula, and, more keenly still, the Byzantine capital. Since the time of Muhammad, the capture of **Constantinople** had been a cherished, even sacred, objective. Throughout much of the 14th century, the Ottomans chipped away at the Byzantine empire, only to be halted in their tracks by Timur at the end of it. But once the Timurids were in retreat, the Ottomans resumed their charge, and in 1453, amidst great bloodshed, the city fell to **Mehmed II**.

No greater victory could have marked the recovery of Islam after the disasters that had befallen it. Yet although the assault on Constantinople had been projected as a *jihad*, the years after 1453 did not witness any great resurgence of the revolutionary radicalism that had characterized the birth of Islam in the 7th century. Rather, Islam in 1453 was essentially conservative—though influenced by the continuing spread of **Sufism**. Particularly in **India**, where conditions were more favorable to heterodoxy, a number of distinct Sufi schools flourished, although perhaps the best-known Sufi master of them all—**Jalal ad-Din al-Rumi** (1207–73), founder of the **Whirling Dervishes** — had been a Persian who settled in Anatolia. But amid the turmoil of the preceding centuries, the *ulama* had quietly succeeded in installing the **Shariah** as the basis of Muslim life. Furthermore, the Shariah itself was widely perceived as having attained its final expression; in determining the laws appropriate to the followers of Muhammad, the doors of *ijtihad* ("independent reasoning") were deemed to have closed, and any new rules were to be decided on the grounds of precedent alone. The standoff between majority Sunnis and minority Shiites continued, but less acrimoniously than before. Perhaps appropriately, the one figure of outstanding doctrinal controversy during these times was **Ibn Taymiyyah**—a "fundamentalist" for whom even the conservatives were a touch too radical.

1258 Following the **Sack of Baghdad**, the Mongols under Genghis Khan's grandson **Hulegu** overrun **Iraq**, adding it to the lands they have already conquered in Transoxiana, western Afghanistan and Iran. Cities which surrender without putting up a fight are treated with some leniency, but those that resist are destroyed. Hulegu establishes a personal empire in these territories, called the **Ilkhanate** and sharing borders with two other Mongol khanates: the **Golden Horde** to the north; and to the east **Chagatai**, centered on the Hindu Kush. Hulegu's principal interest in his conquests is extracting revenues, and to this end he retains the mainly Persian governmental apparatus already in place. Grand viziers are appointed to supervise the

Ilkhanate, although in the early years particularly they are often executed when they fail to raise sufficient revenues. Unaffected by Islam, Hulegu and his entourage move from place to place.

1259 As Hulegu campaigns to capture **Syria** and **Palestine**, news reaches him that his eldest brother Mongke, the Great Khan, has died. The second oldest brother, **Kublai Khan**—already in control of

THE MAMLUK SULTANS OF EGYPT (1250–1517)

*T*he Arabic word *mamluk* literally means "owned," and was used to describe almost any slave soldiers bought or recruited by a ruler in the Islamic world. Usually they were well trained, well treated and—since the ruler's power depended on their continuing loyalty—increasingly well rewarded. Their officers were often drawn from among their own ranks, up to and including the position of commander. Not surprisingly, then, *mamluks* soon came to wield political as well as military power. Indeed, the ascendancy of Turkic rulers in the Near and Middle Easts from the 11th century onwards was entirely due to the fact that the preferred catchment areas for *mamluks* were in the Caucasus and other parts of Central Asia, where those speaking Turkic dialects were concentrated.

In Egypt especially the *mamluks* made good, to the extent that between 1250 and 1517 its rulers were known as the **Mamluk sultans**. The man responsible was the last of the Ayyubids, Saladin's nephew al-Salih, who introduced unusually large numbers of Kipchuk Turks into the Nile Delta. In 1250 the Kipchuks seized power and proclaimed one of their commanders sultan. Because they had originally been barracked on an island, they were called the "Bahri" or "river" Mamluks. Their power was consolidated particularly by **Baibars** (r. 1260–77), more famous in his day than Saladin for his exploits against Islam's enemies, and also by **Qalawun** (r. 1279–90).

much of China—assumes the title, but will make little attempt to assert his authority over the Mongol empire at large, which remains divided into four main components. Hulegu continues his Syrian war, but encounters resistance from the forces of the **Egyptian Mamluks**. As winter approaches, Hulegu withdraws his army to **Azerbaijan** in order to pasture his horses.

Although Qalawun was succeeded by his son **Nasir Muhammad**, dynastic succession was the exception, not the rule. Usually when a Mamluk sultan died, intense factional infighting followed until a new strongman emerged. In 1382 the Kipchuk Bahris themselves were displaced by another group of Turks, the **Burjis**, who (with Ottoman help) placed their own man, Barquq, on the throne. Under the Burjis, the Mamluk sultanate continued until 1517, when the Ottomans annexed Egypt to their empire.

In essence, the Egyptian Mamluks were a militocracy with religious overtones, and among historians they have received a mixed press. Without question, they built upon the success of their Fatimid and Ayubbid predecessors: Cairo continued to grow, both as a commercial center and as a city of learning, and during the troubled times of the Mongols and Timur, Egypt was a safe haven for Muslim refugees. Both the Bahris and Burjis were, however, ardent Sunni Muslims, and the Coptic Christians, who in 1250 still made up a majority of the population, suffered severely at their hands. Following a series of persecutions, notably in 1321 and 1354, their numbers dwindled. Many were massacred, while others opted for conversion to Islam in order to survive. By 1517, no more than ten percent of Egyptians still followed the Coptic faith, which was now mainly confined to the relatively poorer region of the Upper Nile.

1260 Assembling a larger army, Hulegu resumes his Syrian campaign and swiftly captures **Aleppo** and **Damascus**. He sends envoys to **Cairo** demanding Egypt's surrender, but the Mamluk sultan **Qutuz** orders their deaths. In August, Hulegu dispatches his army southwards from Damascus, but on September 3, unused to fighting in desert terrain, it is heavily defeated in open battle at **Ain Jalat** in Galilee by a Mamluk force led by Qutuz. Qutuz, heralded as the savior of Islam against the Mongols, returns in triumph to Cairo, but at the end of October he is assassinated and the Mamluk commander **Baibars** is proclaimed sultan.

1261 Hulegu sets up his headquarters at **Maragha** in Azerbaijan and begins warring against Berke, khan of the Golden Horde, over grazing rights in Azerbaijan and the Caucasus. By this time Berke has converted to Islam, which now spreads across **southern Russia**.

In Cairo, the Mamluk sultan Baibars receives an Abbasid fugitive and proclaims him caliph. But although the succession of **Abbasid caliphs** continues in Egypt until the Ottoman conquest of 1517, the later Abbasids are no more than Mamluk puppets.

1265 Hulegu Khan dies and is succeeded by his son **Abaqa**. Abaqa maintains his capital at Maragha for a while, then moves to **Tabriz**, but resists attempts to convert him to Islam. During his reign he will sometimes war against the Egyptian Mamluks in Syria, although continuing tensions with the khanate of the Golden Horde and fresh difficulties with the Chagatai khanate occupy most of his attention.

1266 In **Delhi**, a new Afghan dynasty is founded by **Balban**, who seizes power when Sultan Mahmud dies after a reign lasting twenty years. During his own reign, which lasts 21 years, Balban maintains law and order, strengthens the Muslim army and extends Muslim rule into the **Deccan**, overcoming several Hindu principalities in the process.

1270 An **Eighth Crusade** is proclaimed in Europe—the last in the series of "major" crusades. Intended to take Cairo from the west, and led by **Louis IX** of France, it lands in Ifriqiya, but collapses in August when Louis dies of the plague.

1273 Jalal ad-Din al-Rumi, a Persian poet and founder of the Sufi order of the **Whirling Dervishes**, dies in Anatolia.

1281 The Mamluks inflict a heavy defeat on the Ilkhanate Mongols at **Hims**.

A 16th–century painting of Whirling Dervishes

1282 The second Ilkhan Abaqa dies, probably of alcohol abuse, and is succeeded by his brother **Teguder**. Teguder sues for peace with the Mamluks and, taking the name "Ahmed," almost certainly converts to Islam. This stirs up resentment among his Mongol commanders, who adopt Teguder's nephew **Arghun** as their leader. Unwisely, Teguder spares Arghun's life after defeating him in battle.

1284 Arghun wars against his uncle Teguder, defeats then executes him, and becomes the fourth Ilkhan. A devout Buddhist, he resumes hostilities against the Mamluks in Syria and appoints a fellow Mongol, **Buqa**, head of his bureaucracy rather than a Muslim.

1288 In **Anatolia**, where the Mongols have encountered Turkic resistance—particularly in the Taurus mountains—a powerful clan emerges under the leadership of a *ghazi* (holy warrior) called **Osman** (Uthman). The dynasty Osman founds will be known as the **Ottomans**.

1289 The Ilkhan Arghun orders the execution of his Mongol vizier, Buqa, and appoints **Sad al-Dawla**, a Jew, in his place. Sad al-Dawla increases the khan's revenues, but, notorious for his use of torture, is detested by Muslims and Christians alike.

The Ottoman Turks, advancing out of Anatolia, capture Syrian **Tripoli**.

1290 In **Delhi**, a new dynasty known as the **Khalji** is founded by Firuz Shah Jalal-ud-adin Khalji.

1291 The sole remaining Crusader enclaves in the Near East, **Acre** and **Tortosa**, are recaptured for Islam by the Egyptian Mamluks—a victory that secures Egyptian rule over **Mecca** and **Medina** as well as Palestine.

As the Ilkhan Arghun falls gravely ill, his unpopular Jewish vizier, Sad al-Dawla, is seized by enemies and murdered. Other Jews are massacred in **Tabriz** and **Baghdad**. Arghun dies after swallowing an elixir prepared by an Indian yogi, and his dissolute brother **Geikhatu** becomes the fifth Ilkhan. Geikhatu's four-year reign is marked by an economic crisis exacerbated by the introduction of **paper money**,

JALAL AD-DIN AL-RUMI (1207–73)

*N*o other figure in medieval Islam has such widespread appeal as the poet, scholar and Sufi mystic Jalal ad-Din al-Rumi. As his name suggests, he grew up in Rum (the name given to Anatolia by the Seljuks), although he was born in Balkh in Khurasan, the son of a Persian, **Baha ad-Din Walad**, himself a celebrated man of learning. The family migrated to Konya when al-Rumi was a boy, and it was there, under the protection of the Lesser Seljuks, that he founded the **Mawlawi**, a Sufi order better known in the West as the "Whirling Dervishes."

"Whirling," or dancing in graceful circular motions to the music of drums and flutes and accompanied by chanting, forms part of a spiritual regimen devised—perhaps in response to Mongol oppression—by al-Rumi some time after he came into contact around 1246 with an older and somewhat elusive Sufi mystic called **Shams ad-Din al-Tabrisi**. Al-Rumi believed that, by dancing, the individual could transcend his mortal nature and meld with the divine. The dances themselves consist of highly stylized sequential episodes, each one of which embodies a stage in an ultimately profound spiritual journey.

Among Persians, Turks, Syrians and Indians, al-Rumi is equally prized for his writings. In the *Mathnawi*, he presented a comprehensive digest of Sufic lore and teaching crystallized into anecdotes and poems. But both his methods and substance have attracted the opprobrium of Muslim hardliners. Not only is the use of song and dance deemed "un-Islamic," but al-Rumi's inference that man has evolved from lower states of being runs contrary to the creationist doctrines of the Koran. Ironically, though, in Turkey at least the Mawlawi was not proscribed by any Islamic authority until it was banned by Mustafa Kemal Ataturk's secularist government in 1925—a curious state of affairs, perhaps, since al-Rumi himself once wrote "I am neither a Christian nor a Jew, neither a Pagan nor a Muslim."

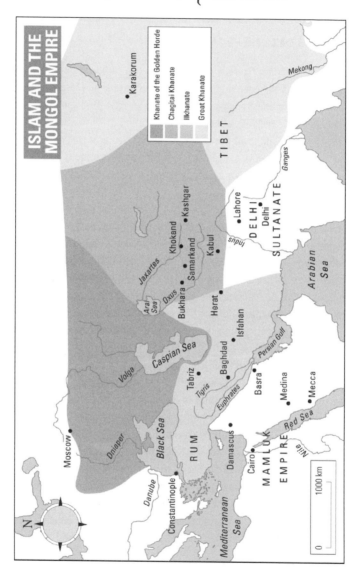

ISLAM AND THE MONGOL EMPIRE

Khanate of the Golden Horde
Chagitai Khanate
Ilkhanate
Great Khanate

Karakorum

T I B E T

Mekong

Ganges

Lahore
Delhi

D E L H I
S U L T A N A T E

Indus

Kashgar
Khokand
Samarkand
Kabul

Jaxartes

Arabian
Sea

Oxus
Bukhara
Herat

Aral
Sea
Isfahan

Volga
Caspian Sea

Baghdad

Persian Gulf

Tabriz

Basra

Tigris
Euphrates

Medina
Mecca

Moscow

Dnieper

Black Sea

R U M

Damascus

M A M L U K

Cairo

Red Sea

Constantinople

Danube

Mediterranean
Sea

Nile

E M P I R E

N

1000 km

0

an innovation borrowed from the Chinese. As trade and commerce grind to a halt under a regimen of excessive taxation, Geikhatu's nephew **Ghazan**, Arghun's eldest son, raises rebellion in **Khurasan**.

1292 The Italian traveler **Marco Polo** records the existence of an Islamic community in **Sumatra**, in the Indonesian archipelago.

1295 Geikhatu is overthrown by his cousin **Baidu**, but Baidu himself is soon killed by **Ghazan**, who becomes the seventh Ilkhan. Ghazan, already converted to Islam, liquidates other potential rivals from the House of Hulegu and resists envoys sent by Pope Boniface VIII to convert him to Christianity. More moderate than his predecessors and more fully assimilated to Muslim Persian culture, Ghazan appoints the capable and energetic **Rashid al-Din** as his vizier. Rashid soon persuades Ghazan to accept wide- ranging tax and administrative reforms that enable the economy to revive, and the *jizya* tax on non-Muslims is reimposed. Led by Ghazan's example, other senior Mongols embrace Islam. **Buddhists** are expelled from the Ilkhanate, and Buddhist temples and monasteries, many of them built since 1258, are destroyed. Historians will query the sincerity of Ghazan's own conversion, however, speculating whether his primary motive is simply to identify himself with the majority of those he rules over. Towards the Egyptian Mamluks he maintains an attitude of uncompromising hostility, even attempting to enter into an **alliance** with Christian states to bring about their defeat.

1296 In **Morocco**, Almohad power disintegrates when the **Merinids** seize Marrakesh and Fez and create a new dynastic amirate.

In India, Firuz Jalal-ud-adin is murdered and succeeded by his nephew **Alauddin**, who rules for 20 years.

1300 Ghazan campaigns in **Syria** and temporarily drives the Mamluks back into Egypt.

1301 Having enlarged his *ghazi* principality in western Anatolia, Osman I defeats a Byzantine force at **Baphaion**, and so extends his domains yet further.

1304 Ghazan dies childless and the Ilkhanate passes to his brother **Oljeitu**, who retains the reforming Rashid al-Din as his vizier. Like Ghazan, Oljeitu is a Muslim—although he sometimes shows signs of reverting to Mongol shamanism, or embracing either Christianity or Buddhism during his twelve-year reign. His commitment to Islam, however, is reflected in the domed mausoleum he builds himself at his new Ilkhanate capital, **Sultaniyyah**. That he also styles himself "sultan" as well as "khan" is taken as a sign of further integration of the ruling Mongol dynasty into Islamic-Persian culture.

1316 The Ilkhan Oljeitu dies and is succeeded by his 11-year-old son **Abu Said**. Because Abu Said is a minor, government is left in the hands of Rashid al-Din and a newly appointed fellow vizier, **Taj al-Din Ali Shah**. Neither, however, is able to prevent the rise of two powerful court factions—one led by the amir Chopan

> The bowels trailed, drooping his legs between;
> The pluck appeared, the sorry pouch and vent
> That turns to dung all it has swallowed in.
> While gazing on him I stood all intent,
> He eyed me, and with his hands opened his breast,
> Saying: "Now see how I myself have rent.
> How is Mahomet maimed, thou canst attest
> Before me Ali, weeping tear on tear,
> Goes with face cloven apart from chin to crest
> And all the others whom thou seëst here
> Were, alive, sowers of schism and of discord,
> And therefore in this wise they are cloven sheer ...
>
> —**Dante Aligheri**,
> *La Divina Commedia: Inferno*
> **(trans. Laurence Binyon)**

(known as the **Chopanids**), the other by Hasan Jalayir (known as the **Jalayirids**).

1318 Taj al-Din Ali Shah, in alliance with Chopan, plots the overthrow and execution of Rashid al-Din.

1320 In **India**, the ruling Khalji are overthrown by the **Tughlaqs**, a new Turkic-Afghan dynasty founded in west India by Ghiyas-ud-din Tughlaq, who now moves the Muslim capital to a new city, **Tughlaqabad**, four miles east of Delhi. Soon the Tughlaqs extend their power eastwards by annexing large parts of **Bengal**.

1321 In Egypt, **Coptic Christians** are persecuted during a popular uprising against them that the Mamluk sultanate does little to restrain. Tens of thousands are massacred and Copts are largely driven out of the Nile Delta into the provinces of the Upper Nile.

The Christian Italian poet **Dante Alighieri** dies in Ravenna shortly after completing his verse masterpiece *La Divina Commedia* ("The Divine Comedy"), in which the Prophet Muhammad is condemned to the eighth circle of Hell for promoting violence in the name of religion.

1322 As the Ilkhan court falls prey to further factional infighting, a **peace treaty** is concluded with the Mamluks of Egypt, whose rule over **Palestine** and **southern Syria** is acknowledged by the Mongols.

1325 In **India**, Sultan Ghiyas-ud-din Tughlaq is murdered and succeeded by his son **Muhammad Tughlaq**, who reigns until 1351.

1326 Osman I captures the ancient city of **Bursa** in northwest Anatolia. Later in the year, however, Osman dies aged 67, and is succeeded by his son **Orhan**. Orhan will further expand the "Osmanli" (Ottoman) territories and in so doing establish his authority over other Turkic princes in Anatolia, assuming the title "Sultan of the Ghazis." He also begins minting his own **silver coinage**.

1327 Reaching the age of 22 and wishing to impose his authority, Abu Said overthrows Chopan, who has assumed the powers of regent, and appoints Rashid al-Din's son **Ghiyath** as his vizier. For a few years, stability returns to the Ilkhanate.

1328 **Ahmad ibn Taymiyyah**, sometimes called "the father of Islamic fundamentalism," dies in prison in Damascus.

1331 Pursuing his wars against Byzantium, Orhan captures **Iznik** (Nicaea) and adds it to the expanding Ottoman sultanate.

AHMAD IBN TAYMIYYAH (1263–1328)

*I*deologue, polemicist and activist, Ibn Taymiyyah was an Iraqi *alim* (clerical scholar) who followed the Hanbali school of Shariah law and who settled in Damascus in 1268, mainly to evade the oppressive government of the Mongols. Living under the Mamluk regime, however, did little to enhance his personal liberty. Singularly outspoken in his attacks on almost anything he considered a departure from Islam as originally constituted by Muhammad—his targets included the Mongols, rival Shariah law schools, the Shiites, Sufis, caliphs Uthman and Ali, nearly every sect that had arisen within Islam, *ijma* (community consensus), the Mamluks themselves and even al-Ghazali—Ibn Taymiyyah was regularly interned and eventually died in prison, apparently distraught that he had been deprived of books and writing implements.

Between 1306 and 1313 he was removed to Egypt, in the first instance to face trial, then so that the authorities could keep a closer eye on him. Cleverly, his opponents managed to hoist Ibn Taymiyyah with his own petard. His trenchant reformism, based on a literal understanding of the Koran, had, they said, involved him in the "anthropomorphic" heresy, the attribution of human qualities to God—a difficult charge to dodge, since in

1333 In alliance with the Nasirid ruler of Granada Yusuf, the Merinid sultan, Abu al-Hassab, seizes **Gibraltar** and begins planning a Muslim reconquest of Spain.

Perhaps in the same year Yusuf begins work on the **Alhambra**, a new palace at Granada that will become one of the glories of medieval Islamic architecture.

such phrases as "the Hand of Allah" the Koran does indeed appear to sustain the anthropomorphic view. Famously, Ibn Taymiyyah had told his congregation at Friday prayers in Damascus that "Allah descends to earth just as I descend the steps of the pulpit," and it was his idiosyncratic handling of Islamic truths that so often landed him in trouble.

Among Ibn Taymiyyah's many writings is the *Minhaj al-sunna* ("The Way of Tradition"), an important source for the much later radical reformism of al-Wahhab. In the contemporary period, too, Ibn Taymiyyah has been held in high regard by the Muslim Brotherhood and other Islamists, including Osama bin Laden. Like the Kharajites of the 7th century, Ibn Taymiyyah strove to keep what he perceived as the egalitarian flame of Muhammad's revolution alight, and to his personal credit he refused to buckle under pressure. Back in Damascus he continued to make waves, and it is said that his funeral was attended by 20,000 mourners, many of them women—mindful that Ibn Tamiyyah's first term of imprisonment had been incurred for advocating women's Koranic divorce rights. Yet his body was laid to rest in a Sufi graveyard, where his tomb became a Muslim shrine. The man who had railed against Islam's adoption of saints himself became one.

1334 Shaykh Safi al-Din Ardabili, a Sufi master who has spent much of his life instructing senior Mongols in the intricacies of Islam, dies. The order of Sufis he has founded, the **Safavids**, will become progressively more militant and eventually provide Persia with a new ruling dynasty.

1335 The khan-sultan Abu Said dies without a direct male heir and the Ilkhanate is thrown into disorder. Vizier Ghiyath ad-Din attempts to install **Arpa Keun**, a descendant of Genghis Khan, on the throne, but other equally distant claimants quickly remove him and the period of the Ilkhanate ends in a series of civil wars during which several autonomous amirates are established—notably by the **Jalayirids** in Iraq and Azerbaijan, by the **Muzaffarids** (followers of Mubariz al-Din) in central Persia/Iran, and by **Togha Temur** in western Khurasan.

1340 The attempted Merinid reconquest of Spain is decisively repulsed by Alonso XI of León-Castile at the **Battle of the River Salado**. Although Granada survives as a Moorish enclave inside Spain, no further serious attempt to bring the Iberian peninsula back inside the Islamic fold will be made. Instead, Europe's Christian powers will often seek to gain territorial possessions in North Africa at Islam's expense.

1341 A six-year **civil war** begins in the Byzantine empire. As different factions contest the throne in Constantinople, the Serbian leader **Stephen Dushan** attempts to create an autonomous empire comprising Greeks, Bulgars and Albanians as well as Serbs. The Ottomans take advantage of Byzantium's disarray to mount **sea raids** against the Albanian and Greek coastlines.

1345 John Cantacuzenus, a pretender to the Byzantine throne who has established a power base in **Thrace**, invites the Ottomans to help him war against the legitimate emperor, **John V Palaeologus**. As a result, an Ottoman force led by Sultan Orhan crosses the Bosporus and Muslim soldiers conduct land campaigns on East European soil for the first time.

1347 Helped by the Ottomans, and having given Sultan Orhan his daughter Theodora in marriage, Cantacuzenus establishes himself in Constantinople as the emperor **John VI Cantacuzenus**, bringing the civil war in Byzantium to a conclusion.

In **Kashmir**, sometimes called the "head of India," **Shah Mirza** institutes an independent Muslim dynasty that survives until 1589.

Around this time, the great **Eurasian plague epidemic**, known in Europe as the "Black Death," begins ravaging the Middle East and North Africa. Although not as well documented in Islam as in Christendom, surviving evidence suggests suffering of equally harrowing proportions in Egypt, Ifriqiya and other areas.

1351 In Egypt, renewed persecution of the **Coptic Christians**, including those who have resettled in Upper Egypt, encourages many Copts to convert to Islam for their own safety. Many of those who refuse conversion are murdered, and Christian churches are destroyed.

1352 Sultan Orhan, introduced to his clients by the Byzantines, enters into trading agreements with the powerful Italian city state of **Genoa**. As **civil war** resumes in Byzantium, Orhan's son **Suleiman** is given command of a campaign that will lead to the Ottoman conquest of **Thrace**.

1354 In March, Ottoman forces capture **Ankara** (Angora) and, following an earthquake, the **Gallipoli peninsula**, where direct Turkish rule is imposed. As factional infighting in Byzantium resumes, in Constantinople John VI Cantacuzenus is ousted by forces loyal to John V Palaeologus and retires to a monastery. But the Ottomans, having established a foothold in Europe, disregard the removal from power of their principal Christian ally, and continue their military campaigns.

In **Spain**, the Nasirid **Muhammad V** becomes amir of Granada and oversees the completion of the **Alhambra**. Although the amirate itself still survives, its territories are being gradually eroded through a series of small wars fought with **Castile**.

1357 Following the death of his son Suleiman, Sultan Orhan calls a temporary halt to his Byzantine campaigns.

1359 Ottoman hostilities against the Byzantines resume under the command of Orhan's son **Murad**, who captures the Thracian towns of **Tsouroullos** and **Didymoteichos**.

MUSLIM CONQUESTS
IN THE INDIAN SUBCONTINENT

*T*he modern frontiers between India, Pakistan and Afghanistan are just that—modern. They traverse what was originally a huge area of relatively advanced and ethnically diverse civilizations bounded by the Hindu Kush and Himalayas, known for convenience as the **Indian subcontinent**. Central to the history of the area are the vastly fertile northern river basins of the **Indus** and **Ganges** which, over the millennia, attracted successive waves of invaders, giving rise to powerful but transient empires. But although political unity was the exception, not the rule, in India, by the time of Islam's arrival, **Hinduism** was fully developed, its combination of a richly articulated polytheistic religion and comprehensive custom-based laws giving a majority of India's diverse people a common cultural identity.

As early as the 7th century, Arab Muslim raiders, drawn to the subcontinent by legends of fabulous wealth, briefly occupied the western state of **Sind**, and following this, Arab-Muslim merchants succeeded in establishing a number of permanent trading posts on India's western coast. It was only after Islam had fully established itself east of Baghdad, however, that more concerted efforts at conquest were made. The breakthrough was made by **Mahmud of Ghazna** in the 11th century, who succeeded in overrunning the **Punjab**. Thereafter, successive dynasties of mixed Afghan and Turkic blood

1361 After a prolonged siege, Murad captures **Adrianopole**, the provincial capital of Thrace and after Constantinople the most important Byzantine city. Renamed **Edirne**, it becomes the Ottoman capital.

In the western part of the Chagatai Mongol khanate, **Timur** (known variously as "Tamburlaine" and "Tamurlane," from "Timur the Lame")

gradually extended Muslim rule into and across the Gangetic plains. Because these often chose Delhi as their capital, they are known as the Delhi Sultanates, and included the Khaljis, Tughlaqs, Sayyids and Lodis. The Mongol eruption in Central Asia in the 13th century provided further encouragement for Muslim migration into India, and there soon existed several smaller "independent" Muslim sultanates in Kashmir, Gujarat, Bengal and the Deccan. Finally, three centuries later, the Mughals created a unified empire that eventually reached nearly to the southern tip of India, and east as far as Burma.

Although the Muslim conquests were completed by force, conversion rates remained relatively low, due mainly to the attachment of Hindus to their own religion and to the highly stratified 'caste' system already in place. In general, converts were made among the poorer classes, and it is unlikely that the proportion of Muslims to non-Muslims surpassed 25 percent. Rather, Muslim rulers like Muhammad ibn Tughlaq (r. 1325–51) learned that the way to administer India was to practice Indian tolerance, and even co-opt unconverted Hindu leaders into government. In such circumstances, Hinduism itself impacted on Islam. As the subcontinent became a breeding ground for Sufi orders such as the Sahrawardis, Chistis and Shattaris, Sufis were influenced by Indian yogis and other "local" mystics.

becomes the leader of a Turkish-speaking Muslim clan of steppe nomads called the Barlas. Timur wars against other tribes whilst offering to protect the cities of Transoxiana from their assaults.

1362 The Ottoman sultan Orhan dies and is succeeded by his son, **Murad I**.

1363 Having crushed a rebellion in Anatolia, Murad I resumes campaigning in Europe, leading a Muslim army into **Bulgaria**.

1366 After Pope Urban V announces a **crusade** against the Ottomans, Amadeo VI of Savoy briefly captures **Gallipoli**, but is unable to hold on to his conquest.

1369 At the age of 33 Timur makes himself master of **Samarkand** and **Bukhara**, the two great trading cities of Transoxiana.

1371 In September Murad I extends Ottoman influence in the **Balkans** when he defeats two Serbian princes, Ugljesa and Vukasin, at **Chermanon**.

1375 The **Mamluks**, having consolidated their repossession of Syria, overrun **Armenia**, where they slaughter those Christians who refuse to convert to Islam.

1376 Interceding in a Byzantine succession crisis, the Ottomans help enthrone **Adronicus IV** in Constantinople with the assistance of the Genoese. The new emperor restores **Gallipoli** to Ottoman rule in return.

1377 The jurist and great Arab traveler **Abdullah Muhammad Ibn Battuta** dies. Born in Tunisia in 1305, Ibn Battuta has spent 29 years of his life journeying around Islamic communities in Africa, Spain, the Middle East, Central Asia, India and Southeast Asia, and has also visited China. Towards the end of his life he dictates his observations and adventures, a work usually known simply as *al-Rihala*, "The Travels."

1380 An army of the khanate of the Golden Horde, already under pressure from Timur, is defeated at **Kulikovo** by the prince of Moscow, Dmitri Donskoi. As the **Russian kingdom** expands further, the northern khanate rapidly disintegrates. Local Muslim resistance to the imposition of Muscovite rule, however, will continue to the present day.

1381 Having consolidated his hold over **Transoxiana**, Timur begins a series of raids westwards. His cavalry horde sweeps through **Afghanistan** and **Khurasan**, and reaches as far as **Azerbaijan**. Mainly intent on seizing plunder, though, he returns to Samarkand. Similar attacks are launched on an almost yearly basis for the next decade, during which period Timur forces local rulers to pay him an annual tribute.

1382 In Egypt, the last of the Bahri Mamluk sultans, **Hajji II**, is overthrown by the first of the Burji Mamluk sultans, **Barquq**.

1385 Following their capture of **Serres**, **Monastir** and **Okhrida**, the Ottomans establish themselves on the coast of modern-day **Albania**. In the same year a second Ottoman force advances north against the Bulgars and captures **Sofia** (the capital of present-day Bulgaria).

But let Tamerlane [Timur] arrive in India to subjugate it, and then you will see only arbitrary laws. One will oppress a province to enrich one of Tamerlane's tax-collectors; another will make it a crime of lèse-majesté to have spoken ill of the mistress of the first valet of the rajah; a third will lay hands on half the farmer's crop, and dispute his right to the rest; and finally there will be laws by which a Tartar beadle will come to seize your children in the cradle, make the most robust one into a soldier, and the weakest a eunuch, and will leave the father and mother without resource and consolation.

Now which would be better, to be Tamerlane's dog or his subject? It is obvious that his dog is much better off ...

—**Voltaire**, *Philosophical Dictionary* (1764): "**On Laws**," trans. **Theodore Besterman**

1387 The Ottomans, now determined to occupy the Greek peninsula, besiege and capture the city of **Salonika**.

1388 In the Balkans, Serbs, Bulgars and Bosnians mount an uprising against Ottoman rule. Their combined forces defeat the sultan's army at **Ploshnik** in August. The Ottomans succeed in occupying northern Bulgaria, however, and in the same year conclude a mercantile treaty with **Venice**, now challenging the Genoese for valuable east Mediterranean trade.

TIMUR "THE GREAT" (1336–1405)

*N*icknamed the "Scourge of Allah," Timur was the last steppe warrior to wreak havoc from the Middle East to the edge of China. His calling-card was a pile of skulls, left pointedly outside the gates of whichever town or city he had most recently sacked. Such was his awesome reputation that, almost two centuries after his death, in faraway England the dramatist Christopher Marlowe wrote two plays about his conquests. Yet unlike his Mongol counterparts, Timur was a Muslim. His achievement—if it can be called that—was to blend the fervour of the *ghazi*, Islamic holy fighter, with the predatoriness of the mounted nomad.

Born in Shahr-i Sabz of Turkic ancestry (despite an inscription on his tomb claiming descent from Genghis Khan), Timur grew up in the central Mongol Chagatai khanate at a time when Chagatai had descended into lawlessness. Early on, he made his way as the charismatic leader of a warband, mixing violence with offers of protection in order to increase his standing. On both these counts he seems to have been peculiarly effective, simultaneously acquiring a reputation for extreme violence and dependability. At the same time, he strengthened his bonds with other warlords through a series of marriages that made him the youthful master of eastern

1389 Determined to crush resistance to Ottoman rule in the Balkans, **Sultan Murad I** leads an enlarged Turkish army against the coalition of Serbs, Bulgars and Bosnians, led by Prince Lazar, joined now by Albanian and Wallachian contingents, led by Prince Hrelbeljanovic. On June 15, the two sides meet on Kosovo Field. Although Murad is killed at the beginning of the battle, the Ottomans rout their enemies, while Prince Lazar is captured and swiftly executed. The **Battle of Kosovo**, as it usually known, ensures Ottoman supremacy over

Transoxiana. By 1359 he was master of the two richest cities of the region, Samarkand and Bukhara, and with these under his belt he embarked on more ambitious campaigns, partly to keep his restless followers supplied with booty, but partly to gratify his insatiable lust for power and dominion, which he sought to justify by projecting an image of himself as a destroyer of idols and a cleanser of Islam.

Timur was more than a simple robber-baron with messianic delusions, though. Large-scale warfare came to him naturally: he combined cavalry and infantry more adroitly than any other commander of his day, and his army was always accompanied by a cohort of siege specialists. Away from the battlefield, he was a patron of literature and commissioned many new mosques, although his greatest monument, the Bibi Khanum mosque in Samarkand, was destroyed by an earthquake soon after his death. He played chess, too—reflected in the name he gave the son who eventually inherited his domains, Shah Rukh ("King Rook"). Yet the endgame eluded him. Although he rotated those whom he appointed to high office, his did so to protect himself rather than build a stable government. At his death it was discovered that he had made no provision for his succession.

the Balkans and also puts paid to an emerging Serbian empire. In Serbian folk memory, the defeat becomes the wellspring of a nationalist antipathy toward Turks and Muslims alike.

Following the battle, Murad's successor **Bayazid I** returns to Anatolia, where he campaigns to subjugate several surviving *ghazi* principalities.

1391 Taking advantage of the final breakdown of the Golden Horde, Timur campaigns north of the Caspian Sea. His army, numbering well over 100,000 men, defeats and kills **Tokhtamish Khan**.

1393 Timur's cavalry races through Iran and overruns much of Iraq. **Baghdad** is captured and looted.

Sedentary people are much concerned with all kinds of pleasures. They are accustomed to luxury and success in worldly occupations and to indulgence in worldly desires. Therefore, their souls are coloured with all kinds of blameworthy and evil qualities. The more of them they possess, the more remote do the ways and means of goodness become to them. Eventually they lose all sense of restraint. Many of them are found to use improper language in their gatherings as well as in the presence of their superiors and womenfolk. They are not deterred by any sense of restraint, because the bad custom of behaving openly in an improper manner in both words and deeds has taken hold of them. Bedouins may be as concerned with worldly affairs. However, such concerns would touch only the necessities of life and not luxuries or anything causing, or calling for desires and pleasures. The customs they follow in their mutual dealings are, therefore, appropriate. As compared with those of sedentary people, their evil ways and blameworthy qualities are much less numerous.

—**Ibn Khaldun**, *The Muqaddimah*, II.iv,
trans. **Franz Rosenthal** (1958)

Following a series of further campaigns, **Sultan Bayazid I** consolidates Ottoman rule over the whole of **Bulgaria**, including the lower Danube river.

1394 Bayazid I begins an eight-year blockade of **Constantinople** in an attempt to reduce the Byzantine capital without launching an all-out assault. In the same year, the Ottomans complete their conquest of **Thessaly**.

1395 Campaigning further up the Danube, Bayazid I defeats a Hungarian army at **Argesh** in May. The principality of **Wallachia** is added to the nascent Ottoman empire.

1396 A fresh **crusade** led by King Sigismund of Hungary, supported by Venice and aimed at lifting the blockade of Constantinople (though not usually numbered among the "great crusades"), is overwhelmed by the Ottomans near **Nicopolis** on the lower Danube in September.

1397 Bayazid I mounts a frontal assault on **Constantinople**, but the city is saved by a defense organized by Jean Bouciquaut, the Marshal of France, and also by Timur's first incursions against the Ottoman Turks to the east.

1398 Already the master of Afghanistan, Iran and Iraq, Timur turns on **India**. He crosses the Indus in September and in December sacks **Delhi**. Grabbing a vast amount of plunder, he puts a reputed 100,000 of its Hindu inhabitants to the sword whilst proclaiming a *jihad* against "idol-worshippers."

1399 Having abandoned Delhi, where the Tughlaq dynasty is able to re-establish its rule, Timur takes **Meerut** in January, then turns homeward with his booty.

Campaigning for the first time in northern Iraq, Ottoman forces capture two townships on the upper Euphrates, **Elbistan** and **Malatya**, from the Egyptian Mamluks, who have taken advantage of the disorder in Baghdad to expand their territory.

1402 Timur campaigns successfully against the Mamluks in Syria. While besieging **Damascus**, he is interviewed by the historian **Ibn Khaldun**, who will write an account of Timur's exploits.

1402 Warring against the Ottomans, Timur defeats and captures Bayazid I at **Ankara** in July, but, already contemplating a campaign against **China**, prefers not to attempt any wholesale takeover of the emergent Ottoman empire. He does, however, restore power to a number of non-Ottoman amirs in **Anatolia**, thus hobbling Ottoman expansionism for a generation.

1403 Bayazid I, in captivity at Aksehir, commits suicide in March. Timur attempts to divide what remains of Bayazid's patrimony among the Ottoman sultan's three surviving sons: Suleiman receives

AL-RAHMAN IBN KHALDUN (1334–1406)

*T*he greatest Arab historian of any age was also (it has been argued) the progenitor of sociology, although Ibn Khaldun himself preferred the term "science of culture." Unlike other medieval historians—Muslim or European—he sought the underlying pattern of events as well as their immediate causes. While his *magnum opus* is his *Kitab al-Ihar* ("Book of Examples"), it is his lengthy introduction to this work, called *The Muqaddimah* ("Introduction to History," but known in Europe as the *Prologomena*) that has attracted most plaudits. In it, he advances a cyclical view of history, based on the interaction of two opposing modes of consciousness, the "nomadic" and the "sedentary." Since cities exist and it is in the nature of nomads to conquer, nomads will eventually become city-dwellers, whereupon they will suffer moral degeneration. At that point society can only be rejuvenated by a fresh incursion of the nomad spirit. And so it goes on. But the cycle can be broken by creating a stable, God-fearing community (namely, Islam).

The Arabic antecedents of such a theory are clear enough, harking back to the desert culture of Arabia itself. It is, however, in the details of his argument

Edirne, Isa receives **Bursa** and Mehmed receives **Amasya**. But the Ottoman princes decline to accept this partition and begin fighting among themselves to re-establish the sultanate—a civil war that lasts ten years. By entering into an alliance with Constantinople, though, Suleiman gains the upper hand, although he is compelled to restore **Salonika** to Byzantine rule.

1405 Timur sets out from Samarkand to conquer China, but is taken ill and dies aged 68 at **Utrar** on the Jaxartes in February. The great empire he has accumulated begins to fall apart, although his sole surviving son,

and the breadth of his enquiry that Ibn Khaldun achieves greatness. While his method owes at least some of its vigor to the Greek-based tradition of the *faylasufs*, his innovation was to combine social observation with philosophical and psychological insight. More than many historians, he saw that people and circumstance shape each other in roughly equal measure.

But then, Ibn Khaldun himself led a varied and eventful life. Born in Tunis, he spent most of his adulthood serving in various capacities at various courts in Fez, Granada and Cairo. Dragged into intrigue after intrigue, he was in and out of office, often fearing for his life. He also witnessed the grotesque consequences of the great plague as it swept through North Africa. But the real climax of his career came in 1400, when he found himself stranded in Damascus as the city lay under siege by Timur. At Timur's request, the elderly scholar was dramatically lowered down the walls by rope, and the two men shared conversations over the following weeks—providing most of what we now know about Timur. True to form, in his portrait of the tyrant, Ibn Khaldun neither praises not condemns Timur, but presents him as an avatar of his own grand theorem.

Shah Rukh, continues to uphold a powerful and intermittently expansionist court at **Samarkand**. But while Shah Rukh maintains control over eastern Persia after fighting a series of wars against other contenders for his throne, further west power passes to two rival dynastic clans, the **Jalayirids** (an established family of Mongolian descent) who rule over Iraq, and the **Qara Qoyunlu** (Turkomen known as the "Black Sheep"), who rule over Azerbaijan and the north.

In the same year the Ming Chinese emperor Yongli appoints a Muslim eunuch, **Zheng Ho**, to command an expeditionary fleet that, in a series of voyages designed to extract homage from "all the countries of the world," will visit the **Red Sea**, **Arabia** and the east coast of **Africa**.

Around this time, a Muslim sultanate is founded at **Malacca** (Melaka) on the Malayan peninsula by a ruler named Iskander. Equipped with a madrasa, the town becomes an important center for the dissemination of Islam in **Southeast Asia**.

1410 Qara Yusuf, the powerful leader of the Qara-Qoyunlu, seeking to widen his domains, wars against Ahmad Jalayir, whom he kills in battle. Qara Yusuf takes control over much of Iraq as the Jalayirid dynasty is brought to an end, but is unable to extend his rule into Iran.

1413 The youngest of the Ottoman princes, Mehmed, triumphs over his brothers in **Anatolia** and becomes ruler of all the Ottomans. As the sultan **Mehmed I** (sometimes called Muhammad I), he begins to rebuild the Ottoman empire. But in both Anatolia and the Balkans, power has generally reverted to local princes and warlords, and throughout his nine-year reign Mehmed faces rebellion and insurgency.

In **northern India**, the Tughlaq dynasty is overthrown and replaced by the **Sayyid dynasty**.

1415 The **Portuguese** capture **Ceuta**, a stronghold of the Moroccan Merinids. As a result, the Straits of Gibraltar come under Christian control.

ISLAM IN THE FAR EAST

*D*uring the late 13th century, if not before, Islam began to penetrate Southeast Asia, then the islands of the western Pacific. But unlike the eruption of Islam from Arabia into the Middle East, Africa, Spain, Central Asia and India—which occurred as a result of conquest—in the Far East Islamization resulted from trading contacts. Arab and Persian spice merchants, who had long plied the southern sea routes to the Straits of Malacca, which separate Sumatra from the Malayan mainland, began to build their own communities in Malacca (Melaka) and other ports at a time when the modern countries of Malaysia and Indonesia were ruled by a patchwork of warring princes. Merchants ingratiated themselves with their hosts, sometimes marrying into their families, and often putting their considerable wealth at their patrons' disposal. In time, some local kings themselves converted to Islam, followed rapidly by their courts and the upper strata of society. By the early fifteenth century, Malacca itself was an Islamic principality.

But the spread of Islam in the east was by no means only top-down. Particularly after the emergence of the Mughal empire in India in the 16th century, adventurous Sufi missionaries began proselytizing among the poor, building mosques in towns and villages, and creating unprecedented opportunities to acquire literacy and education. Yet, in Indonesia especially, Islam was grafted onto existing animist, Hindu and Buddhist belief systems, giving rise to often esoteric forms of worship. Not until the era of European colonization did demotic Islam in the Far East begin to align with Islamic orthodoxy. As colonization took hold, a "reformed" Islam emerged as an expression of anti-imperialism as well as a vehicle of greater piety. More recently, in turn, this has in itself encouraged political unrest in many areas of postcolonial Asia—notably Malaysia, Indonesia and some areas of the Philippines.

1416 The **Venetians**, increasingly alarmed at Ottoman interference with their eastern Mediterranean trade, dispatch a fleet, which defeats a Turkish fleet in the Dardanelles. Mehmed I agrees to allow **Venice** its established trading rights.

The Timurid ruler Shah Rukh moves his capital from Samarkand in Transoxiana to **Herat** in eastern Persia (today in western Afghanistan). A devout Muslim, Shah Rukh endeavors to repair some of the damage done to Persia by his father Timur by distributing his wealth to build new mosques.

From Herat, Shah Rukh begins a series of finally unsuccessful campaigns to recover western Iran and Iraq from the Qara-Qoyunlu and a new Turkic faction, the **Aq-Qoyunlu** ("White Sheep"). Shah Rukh's son, **Ulugh-beg**, appointed governor of Transoxiana, creates a virtually independent sultanate based on Samarkand.

A keen astronomer, Ulugh-beg builds an **observatory** in Samarkand which collects more accurate data on the movements of Mars and Venus than have yet been recorded.

1421 The Ottoman sultan Mehmed I dies and is succeeded by his 18-year-old son **Murad II**, whose thirty-year reign will witness a significant restoration and expansion of Ottoman power. To assert his credentials as an Islamic leader, Murad II begins his reign by immediately preparing a war against **Byzantium**.

1422 Murad II besieges **Constantinople** between June and September, but fails to breach Byzantine defenses. He is also distracted by a rebellion raised by his brother **Mustapha**.

In **Egypt** the accession of the Burji Mamluk sultan **Barsbay** (Baibars II) signals a period of economic decline, as the sultanate begins creating restrictive monopolies in sugar and other essential commodities.

1423 Murad II defeats and kills his brother Mustapha. Instead of resuming his campaign against Constantinople, however, he wars against **Venice**, which has been rewarded for its promise of military assistance to Byzantium with **Salonika** and surrounding territory in **Thessaly**.

1424 Murad II concludes peace terms with the Byzantines in order to concentrate his forces in Anatolia and the Balkans, where a resurgent **Hungary**, led by King Sigismund, has succeeded in ousting Ottoman rule along the lower Danube and capturing the Serbian city of **Belgrade**.

1428 Taking advantage of the vacuum created by the demise of the Golden Horde, **Abul Khayr** creates a confederacy among the **Uzbeks**, Turkic steppe warriors inhabiting an area to the north and west of the Caspian Sea. Moving southwards, Abul Khayr leads his horde in attacks against the Timurids.

1430 Murad II invades **Thessaly** and expels the Venetians from **Salonika**. He also captures **Ioannina** in western Greece.

1432 Murad II lays siege to **Constantinople** for a second time, but is thwarted by the defensive tenacity of the Byzantine emperor, **John VII Palaeologus**.

1434 Full-scale hostilities erupt between the Ottomans and the Hungarians for control of **Wallachia**, **Bosnia** and **Serbia**.

1437 The Portuguese launch a "crusade" against Islamic rule in North Africa, but are heavily rebuffed outside **Tangier**. Attempting a second assault, the Portuguese king's brother **Fernando** is captured by the Moroccan Merinids and held prisoner at Fez. The Merinids demand that Portugal evacuate the port city of **Ceuta** before his release, but King Duarte refuses to negotiate and five years later Fernando dies in captivity after allegedly enduring near-constant torture.

1439 Murad II reimposes Ottoman rule over much of **Serbia**, driving the Serbian puppet ruler **Georg Brankovich** into exile in Hungary.

1440 Murad II fails to recapture **Belgrade** from the Hungarians despite a lengthy siege.

Jahan Shah of the Qara-Qoyunlu accedes to power in **Iraq**, **Azerbaijan** and parts of **eastern Anatolia**. He extends his rule over northern and central Persia/Iran, and from 1447 establishes his capital at **Tabriz**, where he proclaims himself "ruler of the world." His aim is to create an empire equal in size to that of the Ilkhans, but his ambitions are resisted by the rival Aq-Qoyunlu.

1441 An Ottoman army campaigning in **Transylvania** is repulsed by the Hungarian **János Hunyadi**.

1443 Supported by Georg Brankovich and King Ladislaw VI of Poland, Hunyadi leads a Christian counter-offensive against Ottoman encroachment in the Balkans, but is defeated by Murad II at **Zlatica** on Christmas Day.

1444 Faced by domestic unrest, Murad II concludes a truce with the Hungarians at **Edirne** in July. The Hungarians relinquish control of **Belgrade** to direct Serbian rule and agree that the Ottoman border should lie along the southern banks of the lower Danube. Shortly afterwards, Murad II abdicates in favor of his teenage son **Mehmed II** (also called Muhammad II, "the Conqueror").

The Hungarian-Ottoman truce is broken within three months when Pope Eugenius IV pressures the Hungarians to resume hostilities. They march through Bulgaria, but on November 10 are crushed by Mehmed II at **Varna**. King Ladislaw of Poland is killed, and many Europeans taken prisoner.

1446 Murad II **returns to the throne**, displacing his son after the latter is criticized by Anatolian chieftains for over-zealousness in his desire to capture Constantinople.

1447 Shah Rukh, the Timurid ruler of western Afghanistan and eastern Persia, dies in Herat (although he will be buried in Samarkand). Nominally his throne passes to his son **Ulugh-beg**, who is already the ruler of Transoxiana, but almost immediately Ulugh-beg is confronted with a rebellion in Khurasan by his own estranged son, **Abd al-Latif**. In the same year, Abul Khayr, taking advantage of Shah Rukh's death, launches a fresh Uzbek invasion of **Transoxiana**.

1448 Resuming his campaigns in **Europe**, Murad II wins signal victories over Albanian and Hungarian armies.

1449 Ulugh-beg is captured and killed by Abd al-Latif, who also murders his brother Abd al-Aziz. But having established his authority over Iran and Transoxiana, Abd al-Latif is himself challenged by **Abu Said**, a great-grandson of Timur who enjoys Uzbek support.

1451 Aided by the Uzbeks, Abu Said overthrows Abd al-Latif and lays claim to the Timurid inheritance. He fails to reconstitute his grandfather's empire in its entirety, however. Attempting to regain **western Persia**, he is regularly thwarted by the Qara-Qoyunlu.

The seige of Constantinople

> In the jihad against Constantinople, one third of Muslims will allow themselves to be defeated, which Allah cannot forgive; one third will be killed in battle, making them wondrous martyrs; and one third will be victorious.
>
> —**The Prophet Muhammad,**
> **a saying from the *Hadith***

The Ottoman sultan Murad II dies at Edirne in February and **Mehmed II** returns to the throne at the age of 21. Almost immediately, having brought fractious officials into line and murdered his infant son by a concubine, he begins preparing for what will be Islam's final assault on **Constantinople** with the construction of offensive fortifications on both sides of the Bosporus (including the **Rumeli Hisari** fortress), and by pursuing other measures aimed at cutting off supplies to the Byzantine capital. With his cannon in place by the end of the year, Mehmed is able to control all shipping in and out of the Byzantine capital. When the emperor **Constantine XI Palaeologus** sends envoys to Mehmed's court to protest, the sultan has them decapitated.

In **India**, the **Lodis** displace the Sayyids as rulers of Delhi, the last of the "Delhi Sultanates."

1452 In June, Constantine XI sends sorties out against the Ottomans from **Constantinople**, and in August Mehmed orders the Dardanelles closed to all shipping. A Venetian vessel, attempting to break the blockade, is sunk and its crew beheaded. Constantine desperately appeals to his fellow Christian rulers to send support, but to little avail. A handful of Genoese, Venetian and Spanish arrive by land to supplement the emperor's 7000 men, but these forces are insufficient to man a 14-mile-long line of defense.

1453 As the **siege of Constantinople** intensifies, the Byzantines throw a chain across the "Golden Horn" aimed at preventing the Turkish fleet from entering the Sea of Marmara for an attack on Constantinople's northern fortifications, but Mehmed II overcomes this obstacle by ordering seventy of his ships to be hauled overland. By the first week in April, having assembled an army of 100,000 at **Edirne**, among them 12,000 janissaries, the sultan has Constantinople completely surrounded by land and sea. He begins an artillery bombardment against its walls, making use of a 25-foot-long "super-cannon" built by a Hungarian renegade named Urban, and capable of firing quarter-ton stone balls over a mile. These have a devastating impact on the city's complex but antique defenses. Although the Byzantines hold out for well over a month, repelling almost continuous Turkish assaults, Constantinople's **Romanos Gate** is captured in the early hours of May 29 and the city (having withstood Muslim attacks for eight centuries) soon follows. Constantine IX, preferring death to captivity, discards his imperial armor and is killed in battle. For three days, Mehmed's army rampages through its streets in an orgy of plunder, rape and murder, and desecrating its Christian churches. Those who survive are rounded up to be sold as slaves.

In September **Pope Nicholas V** proclaims a crusade for the recapture of Constantinople, but finds no takers among Europe's rulers. Instead Venice and Genoa dispatch envoys to Mehmed II to protect what remains of their commercial interests in the "Queen of Cities."

CHAPTER SIX

From the Fall of Constantinople to the Siege of Vienna

{1453–1683 (856–1094 AH)}

LIKE THE FALL OF SAIGON TO VIETNAM'S COMMUNISTS IN 1975, the fall of **Constantinople** in 1453 sent out shockwaves that traveled across continents. The spectre of ideological conflict loomed large—in this case between the rival Muslim and Christian faiths. Yet, like Saigon, Constantinople threatened more than it finally delivered. The Byzantine empire was long past its sell-by date, and the real centers of Christian Europe—**Florence**, **Paris** and **Antwerp**, to name but a few emergent cities—were not about to be overrun by hordes of zealous Turks, however much Christians feared the contrary. Rather, the demise of Byzantium initiated a prolonged contest between two spheres of interest that was as often fought on commercial and cultural fronts as through bruising military encounters. Constantinople itself, where non-Muslims formed a majority of the population until well into the 17th century, rapidly recovered its status as a principal East-West trading city, with Venice its closest rival.

Yet 1453 did herald the arrival of a new and formidable Islamic empire. For years afterwards, the Ottomans, backed by their **janissary troops** and equipped with the latest in deadly artillery, strenuously attempted to broaden their domains. Their endeavors included further assaults on Christendom, but only in underdeveloped Hungary, Wallachia and the Balkans. Greece also fell to the Ottomans, but then at this time Greece constituted part of the Byzantine empire. Paradoxically, the Ottomans scored greater successes within Islam itself. In 1517 **Selim I** entered Cairo, putting an end to Mamluk independence and laying claim to Arabia and its holy places as well as Syria and Palestine.

This accorded well with the Ottomans' Sunni faith. Just as the siege of Constantinople had been undertaken by Mehmed II as a conscious revenge for the ignominy of the early crusades, and in fulfillment of an ambition originally laid down by Muhammad, so the project of reuniting Islam weighed heavily on the early Ottoman sultans. But, as chance would have it, the capture of Cairo, Mecca and Medina coincided with the rise of a second Islamic empire in Persia—a Shiite one.

The **Safavids** originated as a Sufi order close to the shores of the Caspian Sea. At what point their leader **Ismail** embraced Shiism (or why) remains unclear, but his decision could scarcely have had more impact. Just as Europe was torn apart by "religious" wars between Catholics and Protestants for much of the 16th and 17th centuries, central Islam was riven by Sunni-Shiite rivalry as the Ottomans and Safavids slogged it out for the control of Iraq. Neither side could claim ultimate victory: each sapped the others' energies as both increasingly sank under the deadweight of their own burgeoning despotism. Although the Safavids were finally forced to abandon their ambitions to rule Iraq, they created a Shiite state that survives to this day as **Iran**. And although the Ottomans failed to suppress Shiism, they nonetheless retained their pre-eminence within the Islamic world.

While all this was going on, a third great Muslim empire gathered in the Indian subcontinent. For over a century following the accession of Akbar to the Delhi throne in 1556, the **Mughal** emperors of India brilliantly combined Muslim authority with a sympathetic understanding of indigenous Hindu culture. Yet by the end of the 17th century the Mughal compact was falling apart, too, thanks mainly to the zealotry of the emperor **Aurangzeb**.

In all three empires, the whims and personalities of individual rulers played a critical role in seeping decay. But the three empires had another characteristic in common. Each was essentially agrarian: a resplendent court was supported by a great peasant mass who toiled year in, year out for scant personal reward. And this, too, was to prove a liability.

Threats to Islam were also gathering outside. A fourth, equally autocratic, but non-Muslim, agrarian empire—**Russia**—was gathering strength and size in Central Asia, where during the course of the 17th century it began to challenge Islam. But a greater challenge still came from a new kind of seaborne mercantile empire, hatched by smaller European states such as **Portugal**, the **Netherlands** and **England**. Following the example of Spain in the 16th century, these combined maritime enterprise with commercial ambition—and increasingly newfangled technologies, including the manufacture of more advanced weapons than had yet existed.

Perhaps in retrospect the greatest collective failure of Islam was not to capitalize on the proven sea power of the Ottomans, whose navies often dominated the Mediterranean until at least the 17th century, but which did virtually nothing to arrest Europe's takeover of the **Indian Ocean** and the eastern **spice trade**—for several centuries a mainstay of Islamic commerce. And since both the Safavid and Mughal empires paid even less attention to nautical developments, it became only a matter of time before Islam surrendered its economic wellbeing.

In this context, whereas the first Ottoman siege of **Vienna** in 1529 might have profoundly altered European history—had it only been successful—the second and equally unsuccessful siege of 1683 was almost an irrelevance, even though the repulse of the Ottomans by John Sobieski III of Poland was greeted at the time with as much relief as the fall of Constantinople 230 years earlier had been met by alarm. From a geopolitical perspective, sea power was already taking over from land power.

Curiously, during the siege the first **coffee house** in Vienna opened after an Austrian spy slipped back through Turkish lines with a sack of coffee beans. And legend has it that the first **croissant** (*kipfe*, or "crescent") was also baked in Vienna, either in anticipation of a Turkish victory or in derision of the Muslim faith. If this is true, then the West's standard "continental breakfast" is an Ottoman inspiration.

1453 After the pillage of Constantinople, unofficially renamed **Istanbul** (but informally until the 1930s), the Ottoman sultan **Mehmed II** forbids the persecution of Christians and declares himself protector of the Greek Church. **Genadios**, the first post-conquest patriarch, receives the pastoral staff from the sultan himself. Conversely, the *jizya* tax is levied on Christians and Jews. Mehmed establishes his court in the city, which henceforward becomes the capital of the Ottoman empire. Construction soon begins on the **Yeni Saray** ("New Palace," completed in 1465) on the site of the ancient Greek acropolis. Noted for its fine gardens, the Yeni Saray is also conspicuous for its high walls, presaging the future isolation of the Ottoman sultans. The walls are patrolled by the sultan's **janissaries**, his elite "convert" troops; while the gardens are tended by those who double as the sultan's executioners.

His great victory secured, Mehmed II immediately begins campaigning in **Albania** and **Greece**.

1455 Ottoman forces campaigning in the Balkans annex **Moldavia**.

With the backing of the papacy, **Henry IV of Castile** begins a crusade to conquer **Granada** and so expel the last vestige of Muslim rule from Spain. He fails to take the city itself, but demoralizes its inhabitants by ravaging its surrounding lands.

1456 The Ottomans capture **Athens**, and with it control of the whole of upper Greece. Mehmed II also asserts control over much of the **Balkans**, but fails to subjugate Hungary after an Ottoman fleet is destroyed by János Hunyadi in July. Laying siege to **Belgrade**, the sultan is defeated by the Hungarians.

1456 Mehmed II resumes the siege of **Belgrade** with an army of 60,000 and breaches the city's walls with his artillery. In fierce street fighting Mehmed's janissaries are repelled, however, and Belgrade is saved—a Christian victory of considerable importance, as Mehmed's forces are deterred from occupying the Hungarian plains.

1458 While Ottoman forces consolidate their grip over the Balkans, Mehmed II begins campaigning in the **Morea** (southern Greece).

1461 The Greek Christian enclave state of **Trebizond** on the Black Sea falls to the Ottomans.

1462 Taking personal charge of the Hungaro-Balkan campaign, Mehmed II occupies **Wallachia**.

1463 Protesting that the Turks have interfered with its Levantine trade, **Venice** declares war against the Ottomans and lends military assistance to the Greeks of the Morea.

1464 The Ottomans expel the Venetians from the Morea, which now becomes an Ottoman province.

1467 In the Middle East, Jalan Shah of the **Qara-Qoyunlu** is killed fighting Uzun Hasan, the leader of the rival **Aq-Qoyunlu** faction, which now gains ascendancy over Iraq and western Persia. The Qara-Qoyunlu are pushed back into their original heartlands in Azerbaijan.

1469 The Timurid ruler of Transoxiana and Khurasan, **Abu Said**, exploiting Qara-Qoyunlu weakness, strikes at their strongholds in Azerbaijan, only to be captured in battle. Following his execution, the Timurid throne passes to **Husayn Bayqara**, a great-grandson of Timur. Husayn, the last of the Timurids, rules in Herat for 36 years. Although he gains a reputation as a generous patron of writ-

THE OTTOMAN COURT

*W*riting about just and unjust wars from the safety of England in the early 17th century, Francis Bacon commented acidly: "The Turk hath at hand, for cause of war, the propagation of his law or sect; a quarrel that he may always command." By the "Turk" he meant the Ottomans, who had mounted regular, and seemingly gratuitous, assaults on eastern Europe since 1453. These trod a fine line between *jihad* and imperial aggrandizement: whereas there is no doubt that Mehmed II, the conqueror of Constantinople, was religiously inspired, his successors were more calculating. The Ottoman sultans surrounded themselves with clerics and instituted the rule of Shariah law, yet as the Ottoman court blossomed, it became hard to distinguish the sultans from any other kind of despotic potentate. In their hands, Islamic institutions became a means of political and social control.

The Ottoman court evolved its own language and rigorous dress code: the size and colour of turbans and tunics—even the length of sleeves—were precisely legislated according to rank and occupation. It was also near-Chinese in its ritual. Four mornings a week, officials and others gathered in the Hall of Diwan, then moved through to an "inner" space to pay obeisance to the sultan himself, regardless of whether he was present. Often he remained concealed behind a grille, known as the "Dangerous Window" for the good reason that if his eye fell critically upon you, death might follow. The executioner was always on hand and public beheadings were a feature of city life—not just in Constantinople, but in provincial capitals as well.

Indeed, by the gates of the palace were special marble columns for the display of severed heads.

Beyond these "outer courts" was the Abode of Bliss, a more private audience chamber where the sultan and his advisers received intelligence not fit for wider airing. Deeper still was the *haram* ("forbidden"), a huge complex which housed the sultan's living quarters, his bureaucracy and the thousands of slaves, converts and eunuchs who ran it. Inside this lay the *harem*, an area for concubines overseen by black slaves recruited from Africa or bought on the open market. Like their Seljuk precursors, the Ottomans did not trust their own.

Yet if slavery lay at the heart of Ottoman rule, it was scarcely regarded as an indignity by those enslaved. It offered security, real chances of promotion, power and personal wealth; and it is known that many "free-born" Muslims bribed their way into palace service. Nor were prospects for women within the court entirely hopeless, at least in terms relative to the age. True, their quarters were cramped and their movements severely restricted. But a favorite concubine wielded influence, while the dowager empress (the valide sultana), could, if her son the sultan was weak, govern the empire itself—as happened in the 17th century.

Inevitably, Ottoman ostentation gradually succumbed to the paranoia underlying it. Display gave way to rigidity, creating an environment scarcely conducive to producing rulers capable of meeting new challenges—whether inside or outside Islam.

ers and artists—including perhaps the greatest of the Persian minia-
turists, **Bihzad**—he is unable to exert political control in either
western Persia or Transoxiana, which increasingly falls under the
sway of the **Uzbeks**.

1471 The Portuguese, determined to create colonies in North Africa,
capture **Tangier** from the ruling Hafsid dynasty.

1473 Uzun Hasan of the Aq-Qoyunlu, seeking to create an empire
based on his domains in Iraq and western Persia, is defeated by an
Ottoman army at **Bashkent**.

THE JANISSARIES

*F*or much of the later 15th and 16th centuries, the janissaries (*yen
ceri*, "new troops") were the most feared infantry in western
Eurasia, made instantly recognizable by their pointed helmets
wound round with turbans. The main prop of early Ottoman power, they
were sons of mainly Christian subjects, drawn from Greece and the
Balkans, requisitioned by the sultan, then converted to Islam and raised
according to an exacting military discipline. But, like other slave-merce-
nary armies that had preceded them, the janissaries became a liability for
their masters. Like Rome's Praetorian Guard, they were the tail that
learned to wag the dog.

The janissaries doubled as the Ottomans' crack battle troops and their
personal protection. After 1453 they were barracked in Constantinople at **Et
Meydan**, or "Meat Square." Each regiment, or *orta*, had an outsized cooking
pot or soup kettle that became its talisman. An upturned cooking pot meant
the regiment was dissatisfied; many upturned cooking pots spelled grave

Still warring against the Ottomans, the Venetians seize control of **Cyprus**.

1475 The Ottomans expel the Genoese from their trading colonies on the **Crimean peninsula** in the Black Sea.

Kiva Han, the first known **coffee house**, opens in Constantinople. As diplomatic and trade contacts between the Ottoman and European courts develop, a taste for coffee spreads to the West.

1477 An Ottoman army invades northeastern Italy and briefly threatens **Venice** itself.

---

trouble. From around the end of the 16th century, the janissaries got progressively out of hand. To keep them in line, the sultan had to pamper them—with more and more free food and clothing, and greater rates of pay. Yet the more he pampered them, the more they expected.

One part of the problem was that the janissaries saw themselves as *ghazi*, holy warriors. Another was that their activities became increasingly unholy. While most janissaries abandoned their vows of non-marriage, others developed "commercial" interests in Constantinople and other cities where they were stationed for policing. Many had trained as artisans—metalworkers, carpenters, masons, cobblers and so forth—and this gave them purchase on local trading networks. Before long they established themselves as the *mafiosi* of the Ottoman empire. As seriously, they resisted technological change, refusing to countenance the bayonet or use Western drill techniques. By the mid-18th century, disposing of the janissaries was high on the sultans' agenda.

1478 Following the death of Uzun Hasan, the **Aq-Qoyunlu** state in Iraq and western Persia begins to disintegrate amid dynastic squabbling.

By sanctioning a tribunal of the papal "Holy Office" to operate in her territories, Queen Isabella of Castile effectively launches the **Spanish Inquisition**. Although designed to root out heresy among Christians, the Inquisition is used to oppress Muslim (and Jewish) converts.

1479 The **Treaty of Constantinople**, signed in January, brings to an end the war between the Ottomans and Venice begun in 1463. The Ottomans gain several Venetian possessions, including **Lemnos** and **Negroponte**, and Venice agrees to pay the sultan an annual tribute for trading rights in the Levant and Black Sea.

Isabella of Castile's husband **Ferdinand** accedes to the Crown of Aragon and the modern nation of **Spain** effectively comes into being. Although Ferdinand is less zealous than Isabella, both embark on policies aimed at making Spain a bastion of the Christian faith. Intimidation of Muslims and Jews grows.

1481 The Ottoman sultan Mehmed II dies in May. Backed by the **janissaries**, his son **Bayazid II** assumes the throne, but another son, Djem, also proclaims himself sultan and proposes a division of the empire. Bayazid responds by ordering Djem's strangulation.

In Iraq and northwest Persia, **Yaqub** partially restores the power of the Aq-Qoyunlu. His nine-year reign is remembered chiefly for the work of his chief minister **Qadi Isa**—a devout Sunni Muslim whose "reformist" policies are designed to eradicate surviving nomadic customs among his Turkomen masters.

1482 As civil war breaks out in **Granada** between Amir Mulay Hassan and his son Bobadil, Ferdinand and Isabella of Spain prepare a fresh campaign to reduce the Muslim principality.

1483 Although a Spanish army is beaten off by Mulay Hassan, **Bobadil** is captured. He agrees to aid the Spanish monarchs.

A Janissary officer

1484 Sultan Bayazid II begins a seven-year war with the Egyptian Mamluks.

1485 Ferdinand of Spain attacks Granada's outlying towns and cities.

1487 Ferdinand captures **Malaga** from Granada and sells its Muslim population into slavery.

The Portuguese mariner **Bartholomew Diaz** rounds the Cape of Good Hope and enters the Indian Ocean—a voyage often seen as the start of Europe's successful maritime assault on Eurasia's eastern markets.

1490 The Aq-Qoyunlu ruler **Yaqub** dies and his territories are thrown into confusion during a succession crisis that intermittently continues until the final collapse of the Aq-Qoyunlu in 1514.

The Granadan city of **Almería** falls to Ferdinand; Amir Mulay Hassan's territories have shrunk by 75 percent in the space of five years. Although **Granada** itself is seemingly impregnable, perched on a high mountain, Ferdinand lays siege to it, creating a military camp called **Santa Fe**.

A Portuguese expedition navigates the lower reaches of the **Congo** in western-central **Africa** and begins converting local rulers to Christianity. In the centuries ahead, European intervention in western and southern Africa will prevent the spread of Islam throughout the continent, although it remains strong in the north and on the eastern seaboard.

1492 Following an eight-month siege by Spanish forces, on January 2 **Granada** formally surrenders to Ferdinand and Isabella, who enter the city four days later dressed in Moorish costume and extend Granada's citizens the traditional rights of Muslims living under Christian rule in Spain. Three months later, the monarchs expel all Jews from their territories, creating an exodus of some 100,000 refugees. Known as the **Sephardic ("Spanish") Jews**, many travel to the eastern Mediterranean to settle in lands ruled by the Ottoman Turks, where their religious and social rights are protected.

Christopher Columbus, a Genoese seaman sponsored by Spain, sets out on his first voyage across the Atlantic and "discovers" the **Americas**. The subsequent Christianization of two continents will give Islam's Western competitors decisive strategic, material and man-power advantages.

1494 As Ottoman naval power in the Mediterranean grows, Pope Alexander VI proclaims a **crusade** against Muslims in North Africa, though to little effect.

1497 The Ottomans begin a three-year war against Poland after Albert of Poland invades **Moldavia**.

Following the death of Shah Rustam, the ruler of Transoxiana, **Zahiruddin Muhammad Babur**, a Mongol-Timurid warlord, captures Samarkand.

1498 The Portuguese adventurer **Vasco da Gama** lands in **India** at Calicut and begins trading in spices, despite the hostility of Muslim Arab merchants.

1499 Hostilities between the Ottomans and **Venice** resume, and last four years.

At **Gilan** on the southwestern shores of the Caspian Sea, the titular head of the Safi order of Sufis, a 12-year-old boy named **Ismail**, proclaims his intention to seek revenge on the Aq-Qoyunlu, who have persecuted his family. Falsely claiming descent from Muhammad's son Ali, Ismail rides out of Gilan accompanied by militant followers to begin a series of campaigns that will lead to the creation of the **Safavid Persian empire**. He is hailed by some as a "god-king" in the making.

In **Spain**, the Inquisition is introduced into Granada and Muslims are forced to observe Christian sacraments. They respond by raising a rebellion in **Alpujarras** and other enclaves, but the revolt is brutally repressed.

1501 Aged 15, Ismail leads his holy warriors against an Aq-Qoyunlu army, defeats it and shortly afterwards captures **Tabriz**, which becomes the first Safavid capital.

Isabella of Castile orders the **expulsion of all Muslims** who refuse to convert to Christianity from her kingdom and imposes a heavy departure fine on emigrants, who are also forbidden to take their children with them. Many Moors opt to convert and

SHAH ISMAIL I (1487–1524) AND THE SAFAVIDS

*T*he Shiite Safavid empire, the basis of modern Iran, had its origins in a Sufi sect that adhered to Sunni Islam. In 1301 Shaykh Safi-al-Din, of mixed Persian and Kurdish descent, assumed control of a Sufi order established by Shaykh Zahid al-Gilani in Azerbaijan and moved it from Talish to Ardabil. Despite some setbacks, the new Safa order steadily expanded its prestige and wealth, but it was not until after 1447 that the Safavids emerged as a political force. In that year, the fourth Safavid "master," Ibrahim, died. His son Junayd expected to inherit his father's title, but was forced out of Ardabil by an uncle, Jafar. Junayd responded by forming a breakaway militant Safavid group, composed largely of Qilibash Turkic tribesmen from the Caucasus whom Junayd instilled with the *ghazi* spirit, and whom he led in raids against Christian settlements in Georgia.

Eventually Junayd regained control of Ardabil. But while it is suggested he also infused his followers with a reverence for Muhammad's son-in-law Ali, there is no clear evidence that either he or his grandson, Shah Ali, leader of the Safavids from 1488, was a Shiite as such. Rather the turning point came in 1494, when Shah Ali was killed in battle fighting the Aq-Qoyunlu. For his own safety his young son Ismail was secreted at Gilan, a

remain in Spain, although this exposes them to the watchful eye of the Inquisition.

A second, larger expedition to the Indian Ocean by Vasco da Gama wrests control of the spice trade by blocking access to the **Red Sea**. As a result, the price of eastern spices in European markets falls by 75 percent and the Egyptian trading center **Alexandria** enters a period of sharp decline.

1502 Ferdinand and Isabella formally outlaw the Islamic faith in Spain.

"Twelver" Shiite community close to the Caspian Sea—an experience that doubtless awakened Ismail to the options open to him once he had begun forging his own power-base after 1499.

In a sense, what Ismail achieved was a rerun of the Abbasid usurpation of 750. By advertising his Shiite sympathies, he drew together dissidents in the lands he aimed to conquer. In particular he allowed the suggestion that he might be the "Hidden Imam" to gain currency—later he would be called "The Shadow of Allah on Earth." But unlike the Abbasids, once Ismail had achieved his goal, he did not renege. Instead he implemented a full Shiite state: Sunni *ulama* were either exiled or beheaded unless they converted, and Sufi *tariqas* that followed Sunni practice were disbanded. Officials serving under Ismail were required to publicly repudiate Abu Bakr, Umar and Uthman, the first three of the four *rashidun* caliphs. Yet non-Iranian historians have questioned the sincerity of Shah Ismail's "conversion." The man described by Giovanni Angiolello, a Venetian traveler, as "brave as a gamecock and stronger than any of his lords" may have calculated that by laying claim to the Alid inheritance he stood a better chance of creating a counterweight to the Ottomans.

1503 Hostilities between the Ottomans and the Venetians end in August. The Ottomans are confirmed as the masters of the whole of **Greece**.

Shah Ismail of Tabriz wins a second victory over Aq-Qoyunlu forces at **Hamadan**, as a result of which **western Persia** falls into his hands.

1504 The Uzbeks, led by **Muhammad Shaybani**, take control of Samarkand from Babur following decades of Uzbek expansion in Central Asia.

1505 Muhammad Shaybani begins a series of annual campaigns designed to annex **Khurasan** and **Afghanistan**.

Finally responding to Pope Alexander VI's 1494 call for a "crusade" in Africa, Ferdinand of Spain dispatches an armada to the **Maghreb**, but it succeeds only in capturing the port city of Mers al-Kabir.

The merchant admiral **Francisco de Almeida** establishes fortified Portuguese trading posts at **Mombasa** on the east coast of Africa, and at **Calicat** and **Cochin** on India's southwestern coast.

1506 Husayn Bayqara, the last of the Timurids, dies in Herat.

1507 The Safavid Shah Ismail extends his authority into **eastern Anatolia** after defeating a remnant army of the Aq-Qoyunlu. His startling successes on the battlefield arouse Ottoman apprehensions.

In the third year of his Afghan-Khurasan campaigns, Muhammad Shaybuni of the Uzbeks captures **Herat**.

The Portuguese capture **Hormuz**, the strategically vital island guarding the Straits of Hormuz at the entrance to the Persian Gulf.

1508 Shah Ismail defeats the last of the Aq-Quyunlu, captures Baghdad and establishes his rule over **Iraq**. In the same year he extends his authority over **Khuzistan** in southwest Persia, all with the help of largely Qizilbash Turkic warriors. As Ismail's empire grows, he entrusts its running to existing Persian administrators, who happily defect from their former masters. But he also insists on the compulsory conversion of his new subjects to **Twelver Shiism**. Many who refuse are executed; conversely, clerics who do convert are quickly elevated to positions of authority within the **Safavid empire**, reinforcing its theocratic character.

1509 In February, an Ottoman fleet dispatched to combat Portugal's growing ascendancy in the spice trade is defeated by Francisco de Almeida off the Indian port of **Diu**. Later in the year, the Portuguese seafarer Ruy de Sequeira reaches **Malacca** (Melaka), regarded as the gateway to the South China Sea and the Pacific Ocean beyond

Following the relative failure of a second North African "crusade," Ferdinand limits Spain's objectives to the acquisition of a handful of trading ports in the **Maghreb**. His policy encourages the activities of the "**Barbary Corsairs**," Muslim pirates who cause havoc among Christian merchant shipping.

1510 Shah Ismail drives the Uzbeks out of **Khurasan** after defeating Muhammad Shaybani near **Marv**. The Uzbek leader is killed, and his skull—artfully converted into a gold-rimmed drinking vessel—is sent by Ismail to his arch-enemy **Sultan Bayazid II** in Constantinople. The Safavid ruler establishes the eastern frontier of his Shiite Persian empire along the banks of the Oxus.

Portuguese forces seize **Goa**, an island off India's Malabar coastline, which becomes the springboard for further conquests.

1511 Supported by Shah Ismail, Babur marches into Transoxiana and recaptures **Samarkand**. He is quickly driven out of the Uzbek capital, however, by an angry populace wrongly suspicious that Babur is a Shiite.

Portuguese control over the strategic **Straits of Malacca** is assured when the soldier-sailor **Alfonso d'Albuquerque** wrests control of Malacca from its Muslim sultan.

1512 Sultan Bayazid II, under pressure following an uprising in Anatolia of Qizilbash Turks sympathetic to Shah Ismail, is overthrown

by his son **Selim I** in April. Bayazid dies a month later. To strength-
en his hand, the new sultan, known as "Selim the Grim," murders his
brothers and other Ottoman dynasty males. He also brutally repress-
es the Qizilbash and other Shiite minorities in **Anatolia**, ordering
the deaths of up to 40,000 Muslim "heretics." As well as planning an
all-out offensive against the Safavids, Selim begins plotting the overthrow of the Mamluks in **Egypt**.

The Uzbeks, regrouping under their new leader **Ubayd Allah**,
invade **Khurasan**. Shah Ismail is defeated at Ghujduwan.

1513 Shah Ismail recovers Khurasan.

1514 The last of the Aq-Qoyunlu leaders, Murad, is killed by Shah Ismail,
who now controls **Iraq** and **western Persia** in addition to Azerbaijan.
Almost immediately, however, Ismail is confronted by the Ottoman sultan Selim who, determined to stamp out Shiism, personally leads an army
against his rival. The two sides meet in the climatic **Battle of Chaldiran**
on August 23. Ismail, whose cavalry is heavily outnumbered and whose
forces are met by advanced Ottoman artillery, is defeated, but manages to
escape. Selim occupies **Tabriz**, but withdraws to Anatolia as winter sets
in, whereupon Ismail reoccupies his capital, although he soon abandons
it for the more easterly city of **Qazwin**. Fighting between the Ottomans
and Safavids continues unbroken for three decades. Although territory
will be won and lost by both sides, Chaldiran establishes a lasting boundary between Sunni Turkey and Shiite Iran.

1516 Determined to subjugate the **Mamluk Egyptian empire**,
Selim I uses heavy artillery to defeat a Mamluk army at Marjdabik,
north of **Aleppo**, in August. Selim takes Aleppo and enters
Damascus on September 26. From there he advances towards
Egypt, marching across the Sinai desert.

1517 Selim I sacks **Cairo** on January 25. The janissaries and other
Ottoman troops pillage the city for three days, during which as many
as 10,000 Mamluks and their supporters are hunted down and killed.
The Mamluk ruler Tuman Bey is hanged from the city gates, and the

THE OTTOMAN CALIPHATE

*T*he Ottoman Caliphate is a grey area of Islamic history. There is no evidence that Selim I formally adopted the title of "caliph" in 1517, although the fact that he captured and deposed the last puppet Abbasid caliph, al-Mutawakkil, led many to believe he had—a rumor subsequent Ottoman sultans did little to disavow. Matters came to a head more than 250 years later when the Russian tsars, embarked on the conquest of Muslim territories in Central Asia, enshrined their status as protectors of Orthodox Christians living under Ottoman rule in the Treaty of Kucuk Kaynarja (1774). By the same agreement, the sultan was acknowledged as the legitimate protector of Muslims living under Russian rule, implying that he had pan-Islamic religious authority.

Supported by their possession of the Prophet's Cloak and the Sword of Umar, acquired by Selim I, the sultans began using the title "caliph" following the 1774 Treaty, and this was widely accepted both within their own dominions and in India. In 1916 an irate British secretary of state for India, Austen Chamberlain, had cause to complain that "The Muslim community of India is, I think, the only community under the British flag which habitually prays for a foreign sovereign, and does not offer prayers for the King." To the grief of Sunni Muslims everywhere, in 1924 Mustafa Kemal Atatürk, founder of post-Ottoman secularist Turkey, announced the formal abolition of the caliphate, thus giving it a retrospective legitimacy technically it may never have enjoyed.

last of the Abbasid puppet caliphs, Mutawakkil, is seized and sent to Constantinople, making possible the **Ottoman caliphate** (see opposite), which survives until 1924.

By gaining control over Egypt and Syria, Selim I also gains control of **Arabia**. He receives the formal submission of Bedouin tribal chiefs, and on July 17 is acknowledged as the "Servant and Protector of the Holy Places" by the sharif of Mecca, who presents him with important Islamic relics, including the cloak and banner of Muhammad, and the sword of Caliph Umar. Selim takes these with him when he returns to Constantinople.

1520 Selim I dies in September and is succeeded by his 24-year-old son **Suleiman I**, known as "the Magnificent" by Europeans but as *al-Qanuni*—"the Lawgiver"—among Muslims.

1521 Resuming his father's wars, Suleiman captures **Belgrade** from the Hungarians, a triumph that rekindles the apprehensions of Christian Europe.

1522 Suleiman I captures the island of **Rhodes** from the Christian Knights of St John.

1524 Shah Ismail of the Safavids is succeeded by his 10-year-old son **Tahmasp I**. During his 52-year reign, Tahmasp consolidates his father's Shiite regime in Persia, and the Safavid court becomes a center of literary and artistic excellence. At first, however, the throne is threatened by ongoing hostilities with the Ottomans, by restlessness among its Turkic followers and by Uzbek aggression in the northeast, after **Ubayd Allah Shaybani** mounts the first of five incursions into **Khurasan**.

1526 Pursuing Ottoman expansion into Europe, Suleiman attacks **Hungary** itself, advancing on its capital Buda. King Louis II and many Hungarian nobles are killed during the **Battle of Mohacs** on August 29 and Hungarian prisoners-of-war are massacred. Suleiman enters **Buda** on September 10. But while much of Hungary falls under Muslim-Ottoman rule, the battle also propels the **Habsburg** rulers of Austria into the frontline of the defense of Christendom. The Habsburgs assume responsibility for Hungary, Bohemia and the Balkans, laying the foundations of the **Austro-Hungarian empire**.

In the east, Zahruddin Muhammad Babur, having been driven out of Transoxiana and Afghanistan by the Uzbeks, leads an army into **India**. On April 19 Babur scores a decisive victory over Ibrahim Shah, the last of the Lodi sultans, at **Panipat**, following which he enters Delhi and establishes a new dynasty—the **Mughals**—which will endure until 1857.

1527 The Habsburg **Archduke Ferdinand of Austria** recaptures Buda.

In East Africa, Ahmed Gran, the Muslim ruler of **Somalia**, launches a ferocious attack against Coptic Christian **Abyssinia**. The Ethiopian negus appeals to Portugal for help.

1528 Deploying artillery manufactured by the Portuguese, a Safavid army defeats an Uzbek army of invasion at **Jami**.

1529 Suleiman I, counter-attacking Archduke Ferdinand, takes Buda for a second time and marches into Austria, where he lays siege to **Vienna** from September 26, even though wet weather has forced him to leave much of his heavy artillery behind. The sultan's janissaries breach the Corinthian Gate, but many die under Austrian fire. Further assaults proving equally fruitless, Suleiman abruptly withdraws on October 16, killing prisoners. Instead of returning to Constantinople, the sultan winters at **Buda**, which is reinforced pending a second assault on Vienna.

1530 In **India**, the first Mughal emperor, Babur, is succeeded by his son **Humayun**.

The **Koran** is printed for the first time, by **Paginus Brixiensis** in Rome.

1532 Suleiman I's army marches out of **Buda**, but is repulsed by a joint force of Croatians and Carinthians.

Recovering from their defeat at Jami in 1528, the Uzbeks attempt a full-scale invasion of **Khurasan**. They fail to take Herat from the Safavids, however.

1533 Aged nineteen, the Safavid shah Tahmasp I asserts his personal authority by executing the most powerful of his amirs, **Husayn Khan Shamlu**.

Khair ad-Din, known as Barbarossa, the leader of the Barbary Corsairs, is appointed grand admiral of the Ottoman fleet by Suleiman I.

1534 As Shah Tahmasp campaigns in Khurasan to expel the Uzbeks, Suleiman attacks the Persian empire from the west, capturing **Tabriz** and **Baghdad**.

A combined Ottoman and Barbary Corsair naval force commanded by Khair ad-Din recaptures **Tunis** from the Portuguese.

SULEIMAN I (1494–1566)

*T*he Ottoman empire reached its apogee under **Suleiman I**, known as *il magnifico* among his Italian contemporaries, hence "the Magnificent" in English. The only son of Selim "the Grim," he acceded to the throne in 1520, having previously served as military governor of the **Crimea** amongst other provinces. Throughout his reign he personally led Ottoman armies, and died aged 72 whilst campaigning in Hungary—a military enthusiasm which matched illustrious predecessors such as Mehmed II, but which was seldom replicated by Suleiman's descendants.

But Suleiman was not merely one of the great fighting Turks. Between campaigns he moulded the Ottoman empire as an Islamic empire. For the first time anywhere Shariah courts, following the Hanafi school, were established on a systematic basis; and his Islamic soubriquet, *al-Qanuni*, "the lawgiver," reflects a widespread understanding that, under Suleiman, justice was dispensed impartially, consistently and fairly. Furthermore, to enhance his court's Islamic prestige and reconcile his Muslim Arab subjects to "alien" Ottoman authority, he put senior clerics and religious judges

In Europe, divided by the **Protestant Reformation** launched fifteen years earlier by Martin Luther, Ignatius Loyola founds the **Society of Jesus**, known as the Jesuits. Not only will the Jesuits play a seminal role in the Roman Catholic Counter-Reformation, but in the Far East particularly they will militate against Islamic interests.

1535 Unable to lure Tahmasp I onto the battlefield, Suleiman returns to **Constantinople**. Baghdad and large parts of Iraq remain under

(*qadi*) on the state payroll. And it was under Suleiman's rule that the *mufti*, or religious adviser to the sultan, emerged as a prominent figure in Islamic hierarchies.

Suleiman is also remembered as a builder of **mosques**—not just the great Suleimaniyyah complex in Constantinople, but of new constructions in Damascus, Baghdad, Mecca and Medina. At the same time he maintained Ottoman tolerance towards Christians and Jews living in his domains, and he fostered diplomatic and commercial relations with several European states, which he was perhaps the first Muslim ruler to fully recognize had a life and vitality of their own. In a series of treaties with France, Venice and England, known as the **"Capitulations"** (from the Latin *capita*, meaning "heads within the agreement"), he granted diplomatic immunity from Shariah law to traders from those countries—a model of "extra-territoriality" that was later imposed by the "Great Powers" on China. Significantly, the fame of Suleiman's court contributed to the emergence of European absolutism. Listening to travelers' tales about the fabled sultan only encouraged Christian kings and queens to enhance their own profiles.

Ottoman control, however, encouraging the Safavid Persian empire to center itself further to the east.

Determined to stamp out Muslim "piracy" in the Mediterranean, **Charles V**, Holy Roman Emperor and the king of Spain, dispatches a fleet commanded by the Genoese admiral **Andrea Doria** to North Africa. Khair ad-Din is defeated and **Tunis** recaptured.

1536 At war with Emperor Charles V, the French king **François I** concludes a formal alliance with Suleiman I. As French forces take **Turin**, Ottoman forces harry the Italian coast.

Faced with sedition, the Uzbek leader Ubayd Allah abandons his attempts to conquer **Khurasan**, which now becomes fully integrated in the Safavid Persian empire.

1537 With French support and aided by Khair ad-Din, the Ottomans make war against the Venetians, laying siege to **Corfu**.

Building on his success against the Uzbeks, Shah Tahmasp campaigns in Afghanistan and briefly wrests control of **Kandahar** from the Mughals.

1538 Khair ad-Din defeats a combined Spanish-Venetian fleet off **Preveza** (Greece), a victory that secures Ottoman naval dominance in the Mediterranean.

Seizing **Yemen**, the Ottomans extend their control over Arabia, but Ottoman ambitions suffer a setback when Charles V and François enter into a **Holy League** against Suleiman I with Venice and Pope Paul III.

1539 Guru Nanak, the founder of the **Sikh religion**, dies in India. Although Sikhism attempts to fuse Islam and Hinduism, its militant adherents will oppose Muslim Mughal rule.

1540 Suleiman I concludes a peace treaty with Venice. The Austrians besiege **Buda**.

Shah Tahmasp, having seen off the Uzbeks, begins waging a twenty-year *jihad* against Christian communities in **Georgia** and the **Caucasus**.

SELYMVS
SVLTAN
IMPERII
EVERSOR

Suleiman the Magnificent

I am God's slave and sultan of this world. By the grace of God I am head of Muhammad's community. God's might and Muhammad's miracles are my companions. I am Suleyman, in whose name the hutbe [Friday prayer] is read in Mecca and Medina. In Baghdad I am the shah, in Byzantine realms the Caesar, and in Egypt the sultan; who sends his fleets to the seas of Europe, the Maghrib and India. I am the sultan who took the crown and throne of Hungary and granted them to a humble slave. The voivoda Petru raised his head in revolt, but my horse's hoofs ground him into the dust, and I conquered the land of Moldavia.

—Inscription from 1538
extolling Suleiman the Magnificent
in Bender, present-day Turkey,
cited in Halil Inalcik, *The Ottoman Empire* (1973)

While many are killed, many more are enslaved, some rising to senior positions at the Persian court once they have converted to Islam.

In **India**, the second Mughal emperor Humayun is overthrown by **Sher Shah**, an Afghan warlord.

1541 Suleiman I counterattacks Ferdinand of Austria and consolidates Ottoman authority in **Hungary**.

Vasco da Gama's son, **Cristofo**, leads a Portuguese expeditionary force to **Ethiopia** to support the Christian Copts. The Somali Muslim ruler **Ahmed Gran** is expelled and the Christian negus restored.

1541 An Ottoman army takes the former Safavid capital **Tabriz** in Iran.

1545 Suleiman I and Ferdinand of Austria agree a **truce**.

Sher Shah, the Afghan ruler of India, is succeeded by his son **Islam Shah**. With the help of Tahmasp I of Persia, the ousted Mughal emperor Humayun begins a campaign to reclaim India from a base in Afghanistan.

1546 Khair ad-Din dies in Constantinople and is succeeded as leader of the Corsairs and grand admiral of the Ottoman fleet by **Dragut**.

1547 A multilateral **peace treaty** is agreed between the Ottomans, the Habsburgs, the pope, Venice and France. **Hungary** is confirmed as a Turkish possession.

1548 In league with Shah Tahmasp's rebellious brother **Alqar Mirza**, Suleiman I invades Persia in the hope of crushing the Safavid Shiite regime. As before, however, Tahmasp avoids pitched battle, and, his supply lines severed, Suleiman retreats.

1550 Around this time, as Islam spreads throughout the Malay-Indonesian archipelago, the strong Muslim sultanate of **Aceh** in **Sumatra** is founded.

1551 The Ottomans fail to take **Malta**, but Suleiman I occupies **Tripoli** (the capital of modern Libya) as a forward base in their projected conquest of the western Mediterranean. Ottoman rule over **Ifriqiya** is secured.

1552 Tsar **Ivan IV** of Russia launches a four-year campaign to subjugate the post-Mongol Muslim khanates of **Kazan** and **Astrakan**. The Volga becomes a Russian river and for the first time Muslims come under Russian rule.

1554 Suleiman orders a **new campaign** to destroy the Safavid empire, but his army once again fails to engage the enemy.

The Corsair leader Dragut drives the Spanish out of their main North African stronghold at **Mehedia** (in modern Tunisia).

In India, Islam Shah is succeeded by his son **Muhammad Adil Shah**.

1555 After almost four decades of war, the Ottomans and Safavids conclude a peace treaty at **Amasya** on May 29. While Ottoman possession of Baghdad is confirmed, it is agreed that Shiite shrines under Ottoman control in Iraq will not be harmed.

In India, Humayun enters **Delhi** and regains the throne for the **Mughals** from the regime established by Sher Shah.

1556 Humayun's son and successor, **Akbar**, fully re-establishes Mughal rule over northern India. He will extend Muslim rule beyond the

THE MUGHALS

*A*lthough Mughal rule in India was first established by Babur, a warlord from Transoxiana who claimed descent from both the Mongols and the Timurids, it was his grandson, Akbar, who did most to secure the new regime. Reigning for almost half a century, Akbar drew his strength from three sources: his well-disciplined army; his refinement of a Persian style of kingship that projected the monarch as a semi-divine figure; and his deeply felt policy of inclusiveness towards his non-Muslim subjects. Although it would be wrong to suggest that the great mass of laboring Hindus did not suffer hardship and deprivation, Akbar extended understanding and tolerance towards the Hindu elite, appointing them to senior positions in both his army and his civil administration. Indeed, so "Indianized" was he that, to the consternation of orthodox *qadis* and *ulama*, towards the end of his reign he began promoting *Din-Ilahi*—a "syncretic" doctrine that combined Islam with a Hindu belief in a greater god who presided over Hinduism's lesser gods.

Akbar's great idea did not catch on, but his immediate successors—Jahangir (r. 1605–27) and Shah Jahan (r. 1628–58)—continued his conciliatory style of government. Across all three reigns an extraordinarily brilliant high culture arose, enshrined by the ethereal Taj Mahal and

Deccan into southern India, winning the trust of many Hindus through his policies of tolerance and cooperation.

In **Constantinople** work finishes on the **Suleimaniyyah mosque**, begun in 1550. Designed by the architect Sinan, it is a vast complex that covers four acres, including a madrasa with accommodation for 1000 students, an extensive library, a soup kitchen for the needy and a hospice.

a number of other buildings, including important complexes at Agra, Ajmer, Lahore, Allahabad and Fathepur Sikri. While the combination of Indian and Persian forms can be detected in monuments erected by the Afghan ruler Sher Shah (r. 1540–45), without doubt it was the Mughals who took these possibilities to the heights of architectural expression. The Taj Mahal in particular is noted for its use of rare materials brought from as far afield as East Africa and Europe. Similarly, under the "Great Mughals," painting, music, literature and other arts—including cuisine—flourished.

Yet the military continued to be an important facet of Mughal rule, which, by the end of the 17th century, had expanded to include, as well as the northern plains of India, much of Afghanistan and the Deccan, the southern peninsula and all of Bengal. But by then the accommodation between rulers and ruled had become severely strained. Akbar's great-grandson, Aurangzeb (r. 1658–1707), who snatched the throne from his brothers in 1658, pursued altogether different policies to his predecessors. Bent on creating a fully Islamic state, he succeeded only in kindling Hindu resentment at Muslim rule. In the north the Rajputs and in the south the Marathas began organizing rebellion, as did Sikhs in the Punjab. Although Aurangzeb's successors clung on to power in the 18th century, they were known as the "Lesser Mughals."

1557 The Mughal emperor Akbar transfers his capital from Delhi to **Agra**, where he begins building the **Red Fort** complex.

1565 A determined effort to capture **Malta** is mounted by the Ottomans, who besiege the island from May 20 until September 11. Defended by the Knights of St John, the port city of **Valletta** withstands the onslaught until the arrival of a Spanish relief force.

1566 Suleiman I dies on September 5 aged 70. The Ottoman throne passes to his lacklustre son **Selim II**.

1569 Ottoman and Russian forces clash in the **Caucasus**, the first in a long series of hostilities that will continue until World War I three centuries later.

Mughal painting depicting Friday prayers

1570 Encouraged by **Don Joseph Nasi**, a Sephardic Jew who wants the island to become a safe haven for Jews fleeing persecution in Europe, the Ottomans capture **Cyprus** from Venetian rule.

1571 As another Holy League forms against the Ottomans, they capture **Famagusta**. On October 7, however, they lose 300 warships to a Christian armada commanded by **Don Juan of Austria** during a major naval engagement off **Lepanto** in the Gulf of Corinth. But although Lepanto is hailed as a great Christian victory, the Ottomans rebuild their fleet within two years. Venice, a member of the Christian coalition, quickly agrees a **bilateral ceasefire** to protect its trading interests.

1572 Don John of Austria captures **Tunis** in October, but will hold it for barely a year.

1574 Selim II dies and is succeeded by his son **Murad III**, a dissolute sultan under whose rule Ottoman officials become progressively corrupt.

1576 Following the death of Tahmasp I, the Safavid succession is disputed by two of his sons. Ismail murders his older brother Haydar and assumes the throne, as **Shah Ismail II**, but rapidly alienates his court by his volatile behaviour and by his attempts to replace Shiism with Sunnism in Persia.

1578 Having exterminated most male members of his family, Shah Ismail II dies, probably murdered. He is survived by one younger brother, the virtually blind **Muhammad Khudabanda**, who is enthroned as a figurehead ruler. His inability to rule encourages factionalism, and the empire enters a decade of internal upheaval during which a succession of revolts and assassinations occur.

Venice formally concedes its interest in **Cyprus** to the Ottomans. Of a once considerable island empire in the eastern Mediterranean, only Crete, Paros and the Ionians remain in Venetian hands.

During a "**War of the Three Kings**" fought in Morocco, although the amir of Fès and a rival to his throne are killed in the **Battle of al-Kasr al-Kebil** (Alcazar), so too is Sebastian I of Portugal. The

Portuguese refuse to believe their young crusading monarch is dead, and a cult begins in his name.

1580 **Ceuta**, directly opposite Gibraltar in northern Africa, is captured by the Spanish and remains in their possession until 1688.

In India, the emperor Akbar permits **Jesuit missionaries** to visit his court.

SHAH ABBAS I (1571-1629)

*I*f Suleiman "the Magnificent" was the glory of the Ottomans, Shah Abbas "the Great" was the Safavid equivalent. Unlike Suleiman, though, Shah Abbas had virtually to begin anew. When he ascended the Persian throne in 1588 as an adolescent, the empire was in tatters—pressed by the Uzbeks and the Mughals to the east, by the Ottomans to the west, and internally by unruly Qizilbash ("Red Head") Turkomen. Not until ten years later was he able to make discernible headway with a memorable victory over the Uzbeks.

To achieve his aims, Shah Abbas initiated both military and political reforms. Whereas his predecessors had relied on tribal levies, Shah Abbas created a standing army of Georgian and Circassian *ghulams* ("slave-troops," similar to mamluks), thus ridding the Safavids of their dependence on the Qizilbash. At the same time he abandoned the traditional system of appointing tax-farming amirs, and instead brought Persia's provinces under central control. He also made a point of promoting Persians within his refurbished bureaucracy.

After 1598, such measures paid dividends. For the first time in a thousand years, Persia was strong and independent. At its center was **Isfahan**, on the Zayanda-rud river, which Shah Abbas made his capital after defeating

1588 Ten years of factional infighting in Persia end when Shah Muhammad Khudabanda is deposed and his 16-year-old son Abbas is enthroned. The outstanding ruler of the Safavid dynasty, **Shah Abbas I** restores the power of the empire, relocating its capital from Qazwam to **Isfahan**.

1589 In Constantinople, the **janissaries** stage the first of many mutinies that severely impair Ottoman rule over the next 250 years.

the Ottomans in 1602. Rebuilt from scratch, with its many new mosques, madrasas, royal palaces, boulevards, gardens and other open spaces, it rapidly acquired a reputation as the most captivating city in Islam. In the middle of the **Mayden**, Isfahan's great central square, was laid out a polo ground equipped with marble goal-posts. Isfahan, it was said, "was half the world." And indeed there was from the beginning of its Safavid incarnation a cosmopolitan atmosphere as Shah Abbas encouraged international diplomatic and trading links in emulation of the Ottomans. It was from this time, too, that the Persian rug, sold in Isfahan, became sought after by European diplomats, merchants and travelers. The other arts of Persia also flourished—this was a high period for poetry, miniature painting, illuminated manuscripts, book production in general and ceramics.

Shah Abbas also consolidated Shia Islam. His agents sought out Shiite *ulama* in other territories; persuaded to come to Persia, they were awarded copious gifts of land that in the future would make the Iranian mullahs an independent political force. Conversely, Shah Abbas abandoned Safavid pretensions to religious leadership. Rather than project himself as a Sufi leader, he promoted *shah-savani*, "love of the shah."

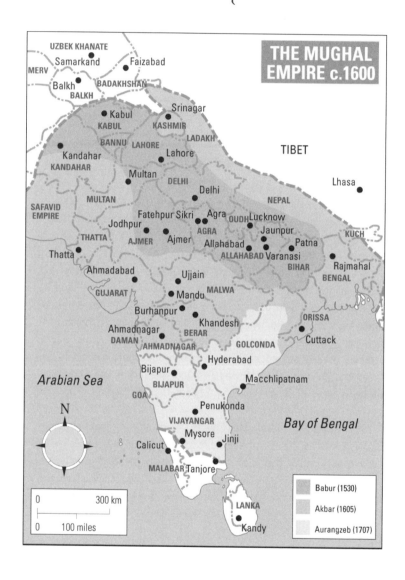

THE MUGHAL EMPIRE c.1600

UZBEK KHANATE
Samarkand
Faizabad
MERV
Balkh
BADAKHSHAN
BALKH
Kabul
KABUL
Srinagar
KASHMIR
LADAKH
BANNU
LAHORE
Kandahar
KANDAHAR
Lahore
TIBET
Multan
DELHI
MULTAN
Delhi
NEPAL
Lhasa
SAFAVID
EMPIRE
Fatehpur Sikri
Agra
OUDH Lucknow
Jodhpur
AGRA
Jaunpur
KUCH
THATTA
AJMER
Ajmer
Allahabad
Patna
Thatta
ALLAHABAD Varanasi
BIHAR
Rajmahal
Ahmadabad
Ujjain
BENGAL
GUJARAT
Mandu
MALWA
Burhanpur
Khandesh
ORISSA
Ahmadnagar
BERAR
DAMAN
AHMADNAGAR
GOLCONDA
Cuttack
Bijapur
Hyderabad
BIJAPUR
Macchlipatnam
GOA
Penukonda
N
VIJAYANGAR
Arabian Sea
Mysore
Jinji
Bay of Bengal
Calicut
MALABAR Tanjore
0   300 km
0   100 miles
LANKA
Kandy

	Babur (1530)
	Akbar (1605)
	Aurangzeb (1707)

1590 Shah Abbas of Persia wars against the Uzbeks, who have taken advantage of Persian disarray to impose control over **Khurasan** and **Sistan**. Although it will take Shah Abbas a dozen years to reclaim Persian territories in the east—and although he is forced to make concessions to the Ottomans with regard to **Azerbaijan**—he reforges the authority of the Safavid throne by repeatedly demonstrating courage as a military leader.

1592 The Mughal emperor Akbar conquers **Sind**.

1593 Hostilities resume between the Ottomans and the Austrians, who support an anti-Turkish uprising in **Wallachia**.

1595 Murad III is succeeded by the marginally less dissolute **Mehmed III**, who immediately puts all his brothers and half-brothers to death. He also transfers the administration of the grand mosques in **Mecca** and **Medina** from his chief white eunuch to his chief black eunuch.

1596 Mehmed III defeats an anti-Ottoman alliance in Hungary, at **Keresztes** near Erlau in the north. His victory is soured by unrest in **Anatolia**, however.

1598 Shah Abbas's campaigns against the Uzbeks begin to prosper after **Herat** is captured and the Uzbek khan **Abd Allah** dies.

Dutch merchants, competing with the Portuguese, establish their first trading colonies in the **East Indies**.

1600 In London, the **East India Company** is founded by royal charter specifically to foster English maritime trading enterprise.

1602 Finally victorious over the Uzbeks, Shah Abbas imposes his rule over the whole of **Khurasan** and begins planning fresh campaigns against the weakening Ottomans.

1603 Sultan Mehmed III dies in December and is succeeded by his 14-year-old son, **Ahmed I**.

1605 Shah Abbas wins a notable victory against the Ottomans at **Sifiyan** (near Tabriz), as a result of which his forces reoccupy **Azerbaijan**.

In India, the Mughal emperor Akbar dies after ruling for 49 years. He is succeeded by his pleasure-loving son **Jahangir**.

1606 Austro-Ottoman hostilities are ended by the **Treaty of Zsitva-Torok**.

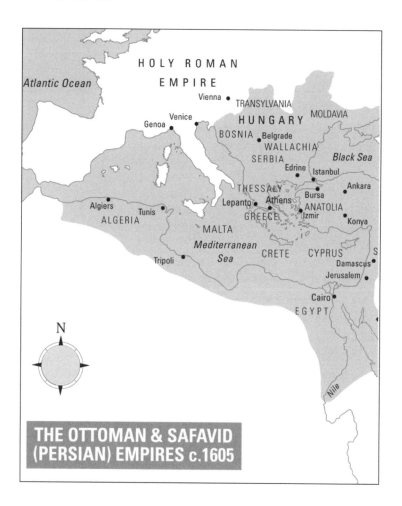

THE OTTOMAN & SAFAVID (PERSIAN) EMPIRES c.1605

Shah Abbas enters into a **trading agreement** with the English East India Company, whose merchants import English cloths through the Gulf of Persia in exchange for Persian silks, jewels and other luxury commodities.

1607 Faced with further attacks by Shah Abbas, the Ottomans agree to the restitution of the territorial boundaries specified by the 1555 Treaty of Amasya.

1608 The Mughal emperor Jahangir grants **trading rights** to the English.

1609 The Habsburg monarch of Spain, **Philip III**, orders the expulsion of all 275,000 *moriscos* (descendants of those Muslims who converted to Christianity) from the kingdom.

SHAYKH AHMAD (AL-)SIRHINDI (1564–1624)

*A*midst India's cultural and religious free-for-all, opposition to the early Mughals' apparent willingness to temper their Muslim faith with elements of Hinduism was not unknown, particularly among the conservative *ulama* of Delhi. The most strident criticisms, however, issued from the mouth and pen of a Sufi, **Shaykh Ahmad Sirhindi**.

Named after the village of his birth in Patiala, Sirhindi joined the most "orthodox" of the Sufi orders, the **Naqshbandis**, around 1593, and soon began preaching against what he saw as the heretical corruption of both Emperor Akbar and his successor Jahangir. In 1619 he was briefly imprisoned at Gwalior for his outspokenness, but did not recant his views. For Sirhindi the more important date was 1622, the thousandth anniversary of the *hijra* that traditionally marks the beginning of the Islamic era. He saw himself, and was seen by his followers, as the *Mujaddid Alf-e ath-Thani*, the "renovator" of Islam's second millennium. His polemics were not simply directed against the Mughal court; like other "fundamentalists" who had gone before him, notably **Ibn Taymiyyah**, Sirhindi inveighed against Shiism, the worship of saints, bogus Muslim festivals, the exaggerated mysticism of other Sufi sects and a host of other "abuses." This critique was

1612 English trading rights in **India** are extended after armed merchantmen of the East India Company defeat a Portuguese fleet in the Arabian Sea.

1616 The English establish mercantile links between **Surat**, their trading colony in India, and the Persian empire.

1617 The Ottoman sultan Ahmed I is succeeded by his mentally retarded cousin **Mustafa I**.

forcefully expressed in his *Maktubat*, a collection of letters addressed to associates outside India and very much written for publication, and which became a source of inspiration for **al-Wahhab**.

It was in India itself that his influence was most keenly felt. One leading follower was **Shah Walliallah** (1702–63), who emphasized the conceptual vitality of the Islamic caliphate—a progressively important aspect of Indian Muslim attitudes that would one day set the somewhat spurious Ottoman caliphate above the ruling British Raj. But ironically his greatest devotee was the Mughal emperor **Aurangzeb** (r. 1658–1707), who implemented many of Sirhindi's recommendations. During Aurangzeb's reign the *jizya* tax was reimposed, non-Muslims were removed from office and attempts were made to impose full Shariah law. As a result, the compact between Hindus and their Muslim overlords was lastingly impaired and India was destabilized politically, making it much easier for British imperialists to pursue a strategy of divide-and-conquer in the centuries that followed. Islamic reformism also engendered the spirit of Muslim entrenchment and **Muslim communalism** in India—a "movement" that, as well as prompting the eventual creation of Pakistan in 1947, stoked the fires of an intermittently violent civil discord that continues to the present.

1618 Mustafa I is replaced by his 14-year-old brother **Osman II**. As hostilities resume between the Ottomans and Safavids, Shah Abbas extends his authority from Azerbaijan into **Georgia**.

1622 Osman II is killed during a janissary revolt in **Istanbul**. Mustafa I is restored to the throne.

Shah Abbas reclaims Kandahar from Mughal rule. In the same year, with the complicity of the English East India Company, the Safavid ruler recaptures the strategic Persian Gulf island of **Hormuz** from the Portuguese.

1623 Mustafa I is persuaded to abdicate in favor of his young nephew, **Murad IV**, but actual power is assumed by the new sultan's mother, **Sultana Kassem**. As the Ottoman court falls prey to infighting, Shah Abbas invades Iraq and captures **Baghdad**, returning it to Persian rule after a century of Ottoman administration.

1625 Ahmad Sirhindi, a hardline Sufi Islamist who has opposed the willingness of India's Mughal emperors to accommodate Hinduism, dies.

1627 In India, the emperor Jahangir is succeeded by his son **Shah Jahan**, whose achievements will include the building of the **Taj Mahal** and the construction of the **Peacock Throne**.

1629 Shah Abbas dies and is succeeded by his grandson **Safi I**, a ruler raised in the *harem*, not on the battlefield, and remembered for his paranoid cruelty. He orders the immediate murder of every other Safavid prince, and has ministers executed on the grounds of personal dislike.

1634 The deficiencies of Shah Safi I are compensated for by the appointment of **Mirza Muhammad Taqi** (Saru Taqi) as his chief vizier—an efficient, honest official who shines at economic management.

1638 Sultan Murad IV recaptures **Baghdad** from the Safavids.

1639 The Ottomans and Safavids conclude the **Treaty of Zuhab**, which brings a lasting peace between the two empires and establishes the modern borders between Iraq and Persia/Iran.

1640 Sultan Murad IV is succeeded by his sole surviving brother **Ibrahim**, called "the Debauched." Their mother, the "valide sultana" Kassem, continues to wield power, murdering concubines the sultan grows too fond of.

1641 Dutch dominance of the Far Eastern maritime spice trade is sealed with their capture of **Malacca** from the Portuguese.

1642 In Persia, Shah Safi dies and is succeeded by his more able son **Shah Abbas II**, who adds the **Khaju Bridge** and **Chihil Sutun Palace** to Isfahan's architectural splendors. To the alarm of the Shiite *ulama*, though, he is addicted to the pleasures of the *harem* and the wine-cup and overly tolerant towards the Christian minorities in his empire.

1645 The Ottomans begin a nineteen-year struggle to wrest **Crete** from Venice.

In **Isfahan**, vizier Saru Taqi is murdered by political opponents and Shah Abbas II assumes personal control of government.

1647 The first translation of the **Koran** into French is made by **A. du Ryer**, whose book is later used as the basis for the "first" English translation by **Alexander Ross**. The first English translation from the original Arabic text will be made by **G. Sales** in 1734, a work still admired by many scholars.

1648 Shah Abbas II leads a campaign in Afghanistan and recaptures **Kandahar** from the Mughals, who have seized it during his father's reign.

In **Constantinople**, the valide sultana Kassem orchestrates the overthrow of her son Ibrahim by persuading the chief religious judge to issue a *fatwa* (ruling) saying that a madman has no right to rule. Ibrahim is replaced by Kassem's 8-year-old grandson, **Mehmed IV**.

The **Taj Mahal**, Shah Jahan's memorial to his deceased wife Mumtez Mahal ("Jewel in the Crown"), who died in 1631, is completed.

1656 The **Kadizadelier**, a puritanical sect who seek to prohibit dancing, music, wine and other "luxuries" prevalent at the Ottoman court, are banished to **Cyprus** by the grand vizier Koprulu Mehmet.

1658 After a bitter succession feud, **Aurangzeb** succeeds his father Shah Jahan as the Mughal emperor of India. A fervent Sunni Muslim influenced by the teachings of Sirhindi, Aurangzeb begins destroying the delicate balance between Muslims and Hindus and Sikhs, all respected and protected by his predecessors. The *jizya* tax is reimposed on non-Muslims, including Sikhs, while the Hindu elite is stripped of its privileges and squeezed out of office. At the same time Aurangzeb endeavors to repress Shiism in the subcontinent. While he fails to apply his policies uniformly in all parts of his dominions, he creates a climate of fear and intolerance.

1659 Aurangzeb prohibits gambling, alcohol, prostitution and other "vices" in India.

1664 Aurangzeb **prohibits** *suttee* (from the Hindi "faithful wife"), the Hindu Indian custom of self-immolation of widows on the funeral pyres of their husbands.

1666 Shah Abbas II dies, according to rumor from the effects of syphilis, and is succeeded by his equally indulgent son **Safi II** (Shah Suleiman). During his reign the prestige of the Safavids will suffer as a result of famine, inflation, outbreaks of plague and Cossack attacks in the Caucasus.

1668 Aurangzeb orders the **destruction of Hindu temples** and a ban on the playing of music. Many ancient edifices are smashed. In their place the emperor commissions new **madrasas** for the dissemination of "orthodox" Sunni Islam.

1669 The capture of **Crete** finishes the latest Ottoman-Venetian war, and with it brings the end of the Venetian empire.

1672 The Ottomans, at war with Poland, attempt an invasion of the **Ukraine**.

1674 The East India Company establishes a trading station at **Bombay** on the west coast of India.

1681 Following Russian battlefield successes, the Ottomans cede **Kiev** to Moscow.

1682 The Ottoman and Austrian empires slide into war.

1683 The grand vizier **Kara Mustafa** leads an Ottoman force of 100,000 men to the gates of **Vienna**. During a 58-day siege, in which starvation forces the Viennese to eat their pets, thousands die of hunger. Relief comes on September 12 when **John Sobieski III** of Poland, seconded by **Charles of Lorraine**, arrives at the head of an army of huzzars. Kara Mustafa withdraws, and is afterwards made to pay for his failure with strangulation by the "silken cord," the traditional Ottoman way of disposing of inept officials. On the same day, Sobieski dispatches a message to the pope, reading: "I came, I saw, God conquered."

CHAPTER SEVEN

From the Siege of Vienna to the Battle of the Nile

{1683-1798 (1094-1212 AH)}

THE 18TH CENTURY WAS A PERIOD OF ACCELERATING DECAY for Islam's three principal states. Although the **Ottomans** continued to campaign in the Balkans and elsewhere in eastern Europe despite their failure to capture Vienna in 1683, the Austro-Hungarians and Russians—intent on building empires of their own—put paid to further Turkish aggrandizement. In **Persia**, a line of ineffectual Safavid shahs paved the way for **Nadir Shah**, a tyrant who, though he briefly managed to extend the Persian empire into India, left it in even greater disarray at his death in 1747 than when he had usurped power eleven years earlier. In **India** itself, a similar pattern of dynastic decline affected the Mughals. Whereas Aurangzeb, the last of the "Great Mughals," had balanced his ideological assault on the subcontinent's majority Hindu population with territorial gains in the southern peninsula, his weak-minded successors were unable to prevent either the rise of the **Nawabs** (local Muslim potentates who ruled independently of Delhi) or a Hindu resurgence, led by **Rajput** and **Marathi** princes.

In each case, the liabilities inherent in any hereditary monarchy contributed to imperial lassitude. Raised in the stifling luxury of their courts, sometimes in the yet more stifling embrace of the *harem*, the late successors to Suleiman, Shah Abbas and Akbar were isolated from the world at large and lacked incentive—except perhaps fear for their own safety—to the further detriment of their capacity to provide leadership. Dynastic corrosion, though, did not in itself ensure calamity for Islam. In the past, such houses as the Umayyads, the Abbasids, the Buyids and the Seljuks had all unravelled, yet Islam had continued to grow, both as a faith and as a territorial entity. Indeed, in times gone by, the presence of internal political disorder had sometimes created opportunities for recently converted peoples on Islam's peripheries— Persians, Berbers, Afghans and Turks, for example—to infuse Islam with a renewed sense of purpose. But during the 18th century pressure from outside forced Islam to contract. Not only did the **Austro-Hungarian**, **Russian** and **Qing Chinese empires** make their presences felt on Islam's northern and Central Asian borders, but European nations that had no land frontiers with Islam increasingly pursued their desire for overseas colonies at Islam's expense—with much greater long-term consequences.

As early as the 16th century, the **Portuguese** had established themselves as a maritime power in the Indian Ocean, only to be displaced by the **Dutch** in the 17th century. But neither nation had sought to do much more than create and maintain fortified trading stations east of the Cape. At first the **British**, who challenged the Dutch, followed a similar course; but in time the London-based East India Company changed tack. Following Robert Clive's much-trumpeted victory over the Nawab of Bengal at **Plassey** in 1757, the Company set about subjugating the whole of India, a project well on its way to completion by 1800.

Clive's success prompted the Dutch, the French and other Europeans to consider acquiring lands of their own in the East. In a sense, these ventures followed on naturally from the achievements of **Spain**, which, in the wake of Columbus's epic crossing of the Atlantic in 1492, had demonstrated the viability of a sea-borne empire in the Americas—a project quickly emulated by the Portuguese, the English and the French in the same quarter of the globe. Yet between 1493 and 1757, the European world in particular had changed. Whereas the Spanish and Portuguese conquests had combined commercial interests with Catholic fervour, the exploits of the Dutch and English were more singularly **mercantile**. To be sure, British conquests unleashed a cohort of mainly Protestant missionaries who worked indefatigably, and often to little avail, to achieve converts in conquered territories, but by the 18th century Christianity was seldom uppermost in the minds of Europe's seafarers. Commerce alone had become the guiding principle.

This shift of emphasis was one aspect of an ongoing alteration in European culture, the consequences of which reverberate to this day. After a prolonged and violent conflict between rival Catholic and Protestant versions of Christianity during the 16th and 17th centuries, by the 18th century a new order began to emerge, in which religious belief became progressively less central to the way people in Europe's many competing states thought and acted. Intellectually, this "secular" transformation attained classic expression in what is called the **European Enlightenment**, a broadly agnostic, even atheistic movement made up of such figures as the Frenchmen Jean-Jacques Rousseau and Voltaire and the Scotsman David Hume, which explicitly sought to replace the certainties of revealed religion with the imperatives of reason and science.

For Islam, where such notions were anathema, this might have mattered little, had it not coincided with European expansionism—in turn the harbinger of what is often termed "**Western suprematism**." Although the connections between the Enlightenment and European colonial-mercantile opportunism were tenuous at best in the 18th century, in the long term the fact that Europe's most secularizing nations were also those that impacted territorially upon Islam created an enduring ideological confrontation quite different from the Muslim-Christian face-off during the crusades.

As it happened, the European nation that had done most to spawn the Enlightenment, France, lagged well behind England and Holland when it came to colonizing the "East." Things began to change after 1789, though, when the French Revolution got rid of Crown, Church and aristocracy in one fell swoop. In July 1798 **Napoleon**

Bonaparte staged an invasion of **Egypt**, an Ottoman province that succumbed to his greatly superior army in just three weeks. One of Napoleon's strategic aims was to hobble Britain—with which France was then at war—by wresting control first of the Red Sea, then the Persian Gulf, and through these gain commanding access to the Indian Ocean. Although the British Horatio Nelson made a mockery of his campaign by destroying his fleet in **Aboukir Bay** a bare fortnight later, from a Muslim perspective, Napoleon's Egyptian attempt was the writing on the wall. A European power had all but strolled into an Islamic heartland.

For **Muhammad Ali**, the ruler of Egypt once the French and British had left, the solution was transparent. Islam must strive to acquire European technology, even European institutions, whatever the cost to Islamic values. For other Muslims, however, the solution lay in a different direction. While Islam in the 18th century was scarcely awash with religious confidence, two important markers were set up for the future. In Persia the **Usulis** revitalized Shiism, laying the foundations for the Iranian Revolution of 1979; and in Arabia itself, **Abd al-Wahhab** concocted a brand of Sunni fundamentalism that is, today, perhaps the most assured expression of Islamic resilience.

1684 Following the Ottomans' attempt to capture **Vienna**, Austria, Poland and Venice form a **Holy League**, backed by Pope Innocent XI but opposed by Louis XIV of France, for whom opposition to the Habsburgs is a priority.

1686 The Hungarian city **Buda** falls to the Austrians after it has been gutted by the Ottomans.

In India, the English **East India Company** for the first time uses force against the Mughals to secure their trading interests. The Company establishes its main station at **Calcutta** in the mouth of the Ganges in Bengal.

1687 As the Holy League continues its offensive, an Ottoman army is routed at the second battle to be fought at **Mohacs**. With large parts of Hungary now "liberated," the Austrian Habsburgs gain hereditary possession of the Hungarian throne, making the **Austro–Hungarian empire** a legal reality.

In November, Sultan Mehmed IV is deposed following his denunciation as an "un-Islamic" ruler by the reformist grand vizier **Kupril Fazil Mustafa**. **Suleiman II** succeeds him.

In **Greece**, the **Temple of Athena** on the Acropolis at Athens is badly damaged when a Venetian shell hits a Turkish arsenal stored in its vaults.

1688 An Austro-Hungarian army captures **Belgrade**.

1690 Launching a **counter-offensive**, the Ottomans drive the Austrians out of Bulgaria, Serbia and Transylvania and threaten Hungary.

1691 The reoccupation of **Hungary** by the Ottomans is prevented by their defeat at the hands of Louis of Baden at **Szcelankemen** on August 19. Grand vizier Mustafa Kupril dies in battle, bringing to an end his attempted reforms.

Sultan Suleiman II is succeeded by his brother, **Ahmed II**.

1694 In **Persia**, Shah Safi II is succeeded, after the intervention of court eunuchs, by the weakest of his sons, **Sultan Husayn**. During his reign Persia's Shiite clerics, led by Muhammad **Baqir al-Majlisi**, gain political ascendancy in Isfahan. Christians and Jews, who have hitherto enjoyed the protection of the Safavids, face persecution, as do non-Shiite Muslims. A principal proponent of **Akhbari** Twelver Shiism, al-Majlisi conducts a vendetta against Sufism, which is driven out of Isfahan and other Persian cities. He promotes the public mourning of the Second Shia Imam Husayn while deprecating the worship of other Shiite "saints." From this grows the *taziyah,* a form of mass-participatory passion play based on the death of Husayn, which, continuing to the present day, still sometimes focuses popular resentment against unpopular regimes.

Lacking strong military leadership, the Persian empire experiences revolts in several provinces. In **Oman**, the anti-Safavid ruling Shiite Imam creates a power base that undermines Persian trade in the Gulf.

1695 Sultan Ahmed II is succeeded by **Mustafa II**.

1696 The expansionist tsar of Russia, **Peter the Great**, seizes control of the **Sea of Azov** in Central Asia and conquers **Kamchatka**.

1698 Portugal loses its trading colonies on the east coast of **Africa** following Muslim-Arab militancy.

1699 After further military setbacks, the Ottomans concede Hungary to the Habsburgs in the **Treaty of Carlowicz**.

ISLAM IN CHINA

Looked at one way, the Muslim population of China is very slight—well under five percent of the total, even though mosques can be found in all China's main cities. Looked at another, it is significantly large—numbering today perhaps 30 million individuals divided into two broad groups: the **Hui**, a more-or-less integrated community whose distant forbears converted to Islam; and "non-Chinese" peoples such as the Turkic **Uighurs**, who fell under Chinese rule during the century that followed the Qing emperor Kangxi's expedition against the Zungars in 1699 and the reimposition of Chinese authority over China's traditional "western" domains, now called **Xinjiang** ("New Territory").

Until recently, Muslims formed a substantial majority in Xinjiang—eroded only by the Chinese government's endeavors to transplant its own "Han" people into its largest, least populous province. Among the Uighurs especially this has caused acute resentment, and since the founding of the communist People's Republic of China in 1949 there has been a persistent,

Following a period during which **Chinese** control over the Tarim Basin and "Chinese Turkestan" has been allowed to lapse, the Qing emperor Kangxi leads an army across the Gobi desert and defeats Galdan, the khan of Muslim **Zungaria**. Over the next century Chinese authority will be reasserted as far west as the Pamir Mountains, bringing the **Uighurs** and other Muslim peoples under direct Chinese rule.

1703 Mustafa II is deposed and replaced with his brother **Ahmed III** by discontented janissaries. The 27-year reign of Ahmed III will be known as the "**Tulip Period**" on account of the Ottoman sultan's fondness for the flower and his generally peaceful disposition.

though under-reported, Uighur **separatist movement**, manifest in bombings and terrorist attacks; just as, before 1949, China was intermittently prone to Muslim uprisings both in Xinjiang and other outlying provinces.

To date the Uighur independence movement has been ethnic and nationalist in character, not so much religious—although this has not discouraged the Communist Party, ideologically opposed to all religions, from keeping a watchful eye over all its Muslim "minorities." Conversely, the government has seldom hesitated to sell arms to Muslim nations, notably Pakistan, when such sales have advanced China's strategic interests in Central Asia and elsewhere. Yet in the wake of the attack on New York the PRC moved swiftly to express solidarity with US president George W. Bush's "war against terrorism." Simultaneously many "ethnic" Muslims were forcibly evicted from Beijing, Shanghai, Guangzhou and other Han Chinese metropolises. Confident in its right to control faiths and people alike, the government was taking no chances.

Diplomatic contacts with European nations are enlarged, the first **printing presses** (hitherto resisted as being "un-Islamic") are set up in the empire, and the **Blue Mosque** is built in Constantinople.

1707 In India, the emperor **Aurangzeb**, the last of the "Great Mughals," dies. Already the Mughal empire is being undermined by rebellious **Rajput** and **Marathi** Hindu princes.

1711 The Ottomans defeat Peter the Great on the **River Pruth**, the last significant Turkish victory over the Russians.

In **Afghanistan** a revolt against Safavid rule, in part fuelled by Persian attempts to impose Shiism, is led by **Mir Wais**, chieftain of the Gilzai Pashtuns. Mir Wais succeeds in establishing an autonomous kingdom based on **Kandahar**.

1713 The Ottomans capture the crusading Swedish king Charles XII at **Bender** in Moldavia.

1715 Inspired by their victory over Russia in 1711, the Ottomans attempt a re-invasion of **Hungary**, but their 100,000-strong army is mauled by a better-armed Austrian force at **Peterwaradin** on the Danube.

1716 The English East India Company, expanding its activities in India, obtains **tax exemptions** from the Mughal court.

1717 The Austro-Hungarians, led by Prince Eugene, begin dismantling Ottoman control over the **Balkans**.

1718 Sultan Ahmad III attempts to upgrade his **armed forces** along European lines, but is resisted by the janissaries.

1719 Mir Wais's son and successor as ruler of the Ghilzai Afghans, **Mir Mahmud**, launches an invasion of **Persia**, reaching as far as west Kirman.

1722 The Ghilzai Afghans defeat a Safavid army at **Gulnabad** and begin a seven-month siege of **Isfahan**. In October Shah Sultan Husayn capitulates and Mir Mahmud is proclaimed shah in his stead. But although Sultan Husayn is imprisoned and most of the Safavid royal family murdered, Mir Mahmud is unable to assert control over all the Safavid empire.

NADIR SHAH (NADIR KHAN)
(1688–1747)

Known as the "Napoleon of Persia," Nadir Shah was the foremost Islamic commander of the 18th century. Born Nadir Qoli Beg into the Afshar clan of the Turkic Qizilbash, he carved out an early reputation as a fearless warlord before offering his services to the beleaguered Safavid shah, Tahmasp II. Having restored the integrity of the Safavid empire, he then proceeded to get rid of the Safavids themselves, contriving to have himself proclaimed shah in 1736. During his eleven-year reign he invaded India, inflicting a crushing blow on the Mughals at Karnal in 1739 from which they never recovered, and thereafter warred against the Uzbeks, Russians and Ottomans.

It remains unclear, though, whether Nadir Shah aimed to create a much larger empire than the one he had seized, or whether his principal interest was in booty. Despite the huge treasures plundered from Delhi, which included the Koh-i-Noor diamond, his wars were a drain on the Persian treasury, and his tyrannical rule placed a heavy burden on his subjects. Towards the end of his life he became manically deranged, and was eventually cut down by one of his own Qizilbash lieutenants.

From the Islamic viewpoint, he is remembered for his failed attempt to eradicate Shiism in Persia/Iran. Although Nadir himself was raised as a Shiite, like many Turks he became an orthodox Sunni Muslim—either out of conviction or because he saw this as a means of expanding his authority within Islam. Such was the backlash against Nadir, however, that not only was Shiism reasserted in Persia, but it acquired its enduring Usuli doctrines.

1725 Mir Mahmud is assassinated by his nephew **Ashraf**, who assumes the Persian throne. He is unable to retain **Kandahar**, however, which is seized by one of Mahmud's surviving sons.

1726 Shah Ashraf puts the former shah Sultan Husayn to death. **Nadir Khan**, a Turkic warlord who has served under the Safavids, begins promoting an alternative Safavid claimant to the throne, **Tahmasp II**.

1729 Shah Ashraf is overthrown by Nadir Khan, who proclaims Tahmasp II in Isfahan. But Tahmasp II is no more than a puppet, and **Nadir Khan** becomes the real ruler of Persia. Later in the year, he expels the Ghilzai Afghans from **Persia**.

The Ottoman court hires a French officer, **Comte Alexander de Bonneval**, to modernize its army. But although Bonneval stays in Constantinople until 1742, he is unable to change Ottoman tactical thinking or introduce European drill techniques, and his reforms are derided by the janissaries.

1730 Nadir Khan campaigns in northern and eastern **Persia** to consolidate his authority over dissident political and tribal factions.

In Constantinople, an Albanian janissary leader, **Parona Halil**, openly criticizes the court for its "un-Islamic" conduct. Faced by a full-scale revolt, Sultan Ahmed III has his grand vizier **Daman Ibrahim Pasha** murdered, then offers the janissaries his body. But the janissaries riot, and the sultan is overthrown and replaced by the more conservative **Mahmud I**.

1731 Mahmud I invites **Parona Halil** and other leaders of the janissary revolt to his palace, where they are strangled and decapitated, their heads being paraded through the streets of Constantinople.

1732 Nadir Khan transfers his allegiance from Tahmasp II to the shah's infant son **Shah Abbas III**.

1735 Supported by Russia, Nadir Khan inflicts defeat on an Ottoman force at **Bhagavand** and takes **Tiflis**.

THAMAS KOULIKAN
Sophi de Perse.

Nadir Shan, King of Persia, also known as Thamas Kuli-Khan

1736 Nadir Khan convenes an assembly of senior clerics and other Persian dignitaries at **Mughan** in Azerbaijan and is proclaimed shah, thus formally ending the Safavid dynasty. In its place **Nadir Shah** (as he is now called) founds the **Afshar dynasty**. Although he revives the fortunes and prestige of Persia, his attempts to restore **Sunni Islam** at the expense of Shiism are less successful. During the same year his forces begin a campaign that leads to the occupation of **Oman** in southeast Arabia.

1738 Campaigning against the Ghilzai Afghans, Nadir Shah captures **Kandahar**, **Ghazna** and **Kabul**. He then turns his attention against the Mughals and takes **Peshawar** (in present–day Pakistan).

1739 Continuing his Indian campaign, Nadir Shah captures Lahore, then marches on **Delhi**. The main Mughal force is defeated at **Karnal**, and Delhi is sacked. Nadir has no intention of staying in India, but plunders the capital and carries off, among other treasures, the **Peacock Throne**, which becomes an emblem of the Persian empire. Following his departure, the Mughals reclaim power, but Hindus and Sikhs, taking advantage of Mughal weakness, enlarge the territories they control as the subcontinent slides into chaos.

As war with the Austro-Hungarians continues unabated, the Ottomans achieve a rare success when they occupy **Belgrade**.

1740 Nadir Shah campaigns successfully against the **Uzbeks** in Transoxiana, capturing **Bukhara**. He transfers his capital from Isfahan to **Mashhad** in Khurasan, reflecting his "eastern" ambitions.

1742 The French writer **Voltaire**'s drama *Le fanatisme, ou Mahomet le prophèe* ("Fanaticism, or the Prophet Muhammad") is first performed in Paris.

1743 War resumes between the Ottomans and Persians.

1744 Muhammad ibn Abd al–Wahhab, the leader of an extremist Muslim sect, is expelled from Mecca after his followers desecrate holy shrines and indulge in other acts of iconoclasm.

1745 Abd al-Wahhab and his followers migrate to **Diriyyah**, a settlement in the Najd where they are offered protection by the local ruler, **Muhammad ibn Saud**, who is soon convinced by al-Wahhab's fundamentalist doctrines. The relationship between the **Wahhabis** and the House of Saud is cemented by the marriage of al-Wahhab to one of Muhammad's daughters.

1747 The **assassination of Nadir Shah** by a fellow Qizilbash Turk plunges Persia into anarchy. Although Nadir's near-blind son **Rukh Shah** manages to hold on to Mashhad and parts of Khurasan, further west **Karim Khan Zand**, a fervent Shiite, emerges as the strongman who will rule central Iran for 25 years. Establishing his capital at **Shiraz**, he renames its districts after the twelve Shiite Imams. To the east, **Agha Muhammad Khan** establishes a personal fiefdom in those parts of Khurasan not controlled by Rukh Shah.

In **Afghanistan**, as the rule of the Ghilzais crumbles, Ahmad Shah Abdali is proclaimed king by a council of elders, or *Loya Jirga*, convened in Kandahar. Ahmad Shah adopts the name "Durrani," thus founding the **Durrani dynasty**, which will rule Afghanistan as a discrete nation-state until 1973.

During the upheavals that beset Persia, two rival Shiite theological schools, the **Usulis** and the **Akhbaris**, vie for dominance. The more radical Usulis eventually triumph.

1757 The commander of the East India Company's armed forces in India, **Robert Clive**, wins a decisive victory over the Muslim Nawab of Bengal and his French backers at **Plassey**, opening the way for the British occupation of the subcontinent.

1761 Ahmad Shah Durrani attempts an invasion of India from Afghanistan, defeating a combined Mughal-Marathi army at the **Second Battle of Panipat** and briefly occupying Delhi, but is forced to withdraw after his troops mutiny.

1764 Clive's victory at Plassey is consolidated by Major Hector Munro, who defeats a coalition of Muslim forces in the **Battle of Baksar**.

In France, **Voltaire** publishes his *Dictionnaire philosophique portatif* ("Philosophical Dictionary"), a pocket-book of speculative essays relentless in their criticism of Christian, Judaic and Islamic monotheism as revealed religions.

THE USULIS AND THE AKHBARIS

Under Safavid rule in Persia, the prevailing Shiite dogma was that of the Akhbaris—traditionalists who, not unlike mainstream Sunni Muslims, maintained that true religion must be based on *hadith*, or *akbar* ("tidings") as they called them, hence their name. While the Akhbaris were tolerant of Sufism, they were doctrinally opposed to both *ijma* (consensus) and *ijtihad* ("independent reasoning"). Alongside the Akhbaris were the distinctly radical **Usulis**, who took their name from the word *usul*, meaning "principles," but associated with the concept of speculation—or indeed *ijtihad*.

The *Usulis* might have remained a minority had it not been for the attempts of **Nadir Shah** to impose Sunni Islam. During the disorder that followed his assassination, Persians looked to the *ulama* to provide them with leadership, and this gave the Usulis their opportunity. Their own leader was **Vahid Bihbahani** (1706–92), who not only honed Usuli doctrines, but was prepared to use force, forging a group called the *mirghadabs* ("executioners of wrath") that in due course provided a model for the Revolutionary Guard (*Pasdaran*) of Ruhollah Khomeini's 1979 revolution. With the help of the *mirghdabs*, Bihbahani drove the Akhbaris out of the main Shia centers not only in Persia but also in eastern Iraq, where many Shiite clerics had taken refuge, and so established Usuliism as the dominant mode of Twelver Shiism.

Although Bihbahani is known as *Sufi Kush*, or "exterminator of Sufis," the radicalism he espoused was inherently sympathetic to new ideas, within the framework of a more elaborate clerical hierarchy than had hitherto

1766 As hostilities between Russia and the Ottomans resume, an earthquake destroys much of **Constantinople**, including a mosque complex built by Mehmed II.

existed among Muslims. Indeed, the empowerment of such a hierarchy was a main feature of Usuli doctrine. The all-important figure was now the *mujtahid*, derived from the expression *marja al-taqlid*, "exemplars fit for emulation," a senior cleric with the status of a "representative of the Hidden Imam" whose interpretative authority in religious matters was absolute during the course of his lifetime; and it became the duty of ordinary Shiites to declare their allegiance to a particular *mujtahid*. Whether the *mujtahid* in question was "right" in what he taught was largely irrelevant. So long as his *muqallid* ("emulators") were steadfast in their loyalty, any theological error could not be held against them.

Since *muqallids* were also required to pay *zakat* (alms) and other taxes directly to the *mujtahid*, and since they were forbidden from following a dead *mujtahid*, Usuli Shiism generated a forcefully original theocratic current in Iran. There was, though, no limit on the number of *mujtahids*. By the end of the 19th century there were hundreds, prompting a nomenclatural refinement between ordinary *mujtahids* and a senior *Hajjataislam* ("Proof of Islam"). There also emerged the figure of the *ayatollah* (from *ayat-Allah*, "sign of God"), and then a supreme ayatollah, recognized by his fellows as *Ayatollah al-Uzma* ("Greatest Sign of God"). All of which, as Sunni theologians quickly pointed out, smacked of ancient, pre-Islamic priestly practices in Persia—abetted by the emergence of a caste of *mujtahid* families, or religious elite.

If your nurse told you that Ceres presides over corn, or that Vishnu and Xaca have several times taken human form, or that Sammonocodum came to cut down a forest, or that Odin is waiting for you in his hall somewhere in Jutland, or that Mohammed or somebody else made a journey into heaven; if then your tutor drove into your brain what your nurse engraved there, you will keep hold of it for life. Should your judgment seek to rise above these prejudices, your neighbors, above all the women, scream impiety and frighten you. Your dervish, fearing to see his income diminish, accuses you to the cadi [qadi], and his cadi has you impaled if he can, because he wants to command fools, and believes that fools obey better than others. And that will last until your neighbors and the dervish and the cadi begin to understand that folly is worthless and that persecution is abominable.

—"Prejudices" in Voltaire,
Dictionnaire philosophique portatif (1764)

1770 A Russian fleet brought from the Baltic inflicts a heavy defeat on the Ottoman fleet off **Chesme** on the Anatolian coast.

1772 In Afghanistan, Ahmad Shah Durrani's son and successor Taimur Shah moves his capital from Kandahar to **Kabul**.

1774 After further crushing victories over the Ottomans, Russia gains control of the **Crimean peninsula** in the Black Sea. According to reciprocal provisions contained in the **Treaty of Kuchuk Kaynarja**, the tsarina Catherine "the Great" is granted the status of protector of Orthodox Christians living under Ottoman rule, and the sultan is granted the status of protector of Muslims living under Russian rule.

1776 The ruler of central Persia, Karim Khan Zand, annexes the Iraqi city of **Basra**.

1779 Karim Khan's death provokes a further period of confusion in Persia, but the Ottomans are too enfeebled to take advantage.

1781 In **China**, a separatist uprising among Muslims in Gansu province is quickly suppressed by the government of the Qing emperor, Qianlong.

1783 Catherine of Russia orders the **expulsion of Muslims** from Crimea.

1784 The Ottomans, unable to protect Muslims under Russian rule, formally concede Crimea to Russia by the **Treaty of Constantinople**.

Britain's parliament passes the **India Act**, making the East India Company—now in control of much of the former Mughal empire—directly answerable to the British government.

The creed of Mohammed is free from suspicion of ambiguity; and the Koran is a glorious testimony to the unity of God. The prophet of Mecca rejected the worship of idols and men, of stars and planets, on the rational principle that whatever rises must set, that whatever is born must die, that whatever is corruptible must decay and perish. In the Author of the universe his rational enthusiasm confessed and adored an infinite and eternal being, without form or place, without issue or similitude, present to our most secret thoughts, existing by the necessity of his own nature, and deriving from himself all moral and intellectual perfection. These sublime truths, thus announced in the language of the prophet, are firmly held by his disciples, and defined with metaphysical precision by the interpreters of the Koran. A philosophic theist might subscribe [to] the popular creed of the Mohammedans: a creed too sublime perhaps for our present faculties.

—Edward Gibbon, *The History of the Decline and Fall of the Roman Empire* (1776–88), chapter 50

1786 The East India Company establishes a colony at **Penang**, an island off the west coast of the Malay peninsula.

1787 Hostilities between the Ottomans and Russians resume, this time lasting five years.

1788 Austro-Hungary enters into an **alliance** with Russia against the Ottomans.

Edward Gibbon publishes the final volumes of *The History of the Decline and Fall of the Roman Empire*. His apparent preference for Islam over Christianity provokes censure among Anglican churchmen.

ABD AL-WAHHAB (1703-92)

*B*y the mid-18th century, Arabia had reached the nadir of its post-Muhammad fortunes. Little more than a backward province of the Ottoman empire, its Bedouin nomads were reverting to the sort of tribalism the Prophet so abhorred. Even the holy cities, Mecca and Medina, were tatty, run-down places full of un-Islamic practices and all too ready to fleece the unwary pilgrim.

Into this milieu stepped an Islamic firebrand of the sort readily familiar to those acquainted with the Kharajites, Ibn Taymiyyah or Sirhindi—but the fundamentalism Abd al-Wahhab preached went further than anything his revivalist predecessors had advocated. Not only did he inveigh against all the usual things—Shiism, mysticism, the worship of saints, medieval jurisprudence and so forth—but he explicitly condemned anyone who did not agree with his doctrines as an apostate against whom force and coercion, even *jihad*, were justified. Intolerance and literalism were his benchmarks. Of the four main Sunni Shariah law schools only the severest—the

1789 **Selim III** accedes to the Ottoman throne. A more able ruler than any of his immediate predecessors and determined to restore the deteriorating military balance with regard to Austro-Hungary and Russia, he summons a *majlis* (state council) to discuss reform. Despite their recent humiliations, however, the **janissaries** refuse to contemplate any modernization, including adoption of the socket bayonet. Exasperated, the sultan decides to create a new army, known as the "**trained soldiers of Allah**." Drilled by Russian and German officers and composed of Turks, the existence of this force is kept a secret.

Hanbali, which allowed no room for *ijma*, or consensus—was to be countenanced, while anyone who did not pray to Allah five times a day was to be flogged or executed.

For holding such views, and for interfering with the annual *hajj*, Abd al-Wahhab and his followers were expelled from Mecca in 1745, which might well have been the last anybody heard of them—had al-Wahhab not found a sympathetic protector in **Muhammad ibn Saud at Diriyyah**. From their relationship was forged a compact that led to the creation of Saudi Arabia in the 20th century. Yet Wahhabism has proved a liability for the House of Saud. Its very emphasis on formalism, the unwavering outward observance of the Koran and *sunna*, demands a degree of faith few rulers can live up to for long. Yet such is its appeal to some Muslims—the promise of regaining Muhammad's *umma* in its pristine purity—that Wahabbism can threaten the most well-established regime. Since Saudi Arabia is founded on Wahabbi principles, it possesses the greatest number of Wahabbis ready to turn against the government.

1792 Muhammad ibn Abd al-Wahhab, the founder of the Wahhabi sect, dies.

1793 By fixing land taxes in **Bengal** and other parts of India they control, the British deal a body-blow to the prestige and wealth of Muslim landlords.

1794 To the dismay of the janissaries, Selim III unveils his new army in Constantinople. Now 1600 strong, and designated "**Riflemen of the Corps of Gardeners,**" it is armed with bayonets and trained by French drill-masters. Selim also orders the construction of a modern arsenal and weapons factory capable of producing its own gunpowder.

In **Persia**, Agha Muhammad Khan captures, tortures and murders the last of the Zandid rulers, **Lutf Ali Khan**.

1795 As the "Napoleonic" Wars between France and its enemies gather pace in Europe, **Malacca** and other Dutch colonies in the Far East are handed over to Britain.

1796 Agha Muhammad Khan kills **Rukh Shah**, the Afshar ruler of **Khurasan**.

1797 Assassinated by his own henchmen, Agha Muhammad Khan is succeeded by his nephew **Fath Ali Shah** as the ruler of Persia. Considered the founder of the **Qajar** dynasty, Fath Ali Shah rules until 1818, allowing Britain and Russia—increasingly at odds in their ambition to control Central Asia—to establish their influence at the Persian court.

1798 Intending to extend French power to the Red Sea, from where British shipping to India and the Far East can be intercepted (and perhaps to establish a colonial empire in the Middle East), **Napoleon Bonaparte** sails for Egypt from Toulon with an army of 38,000 men aboard 400 ships. On July 1 Napoleon captures **Alexandria**, and on July 21, marching on Cairo, he easily overcomes the main Egyptian army at the **Battle of the Pyramids**. On August 1, however,

Napoleon's fleet is destroyed by a British fleet, sent to protect Ottoman interests, under the command of Horatio Nelson, in Aboukir Bay, an engagement known as the **Battle of the Nile**. Although Napoleon remains in Egypt with his army, France's geopolitical strategy lies in ruins.

CHAPTER EIGHT

Islam and the "Great Powers"

{1799-1918 (1212-1336 AH)}

NAPOLEON'S ASSAULT ON **EGYPT**, quickly reversed by British intervention, was a harbinger of things to come. Throughout the 19th century, Islam suffered at the hands of European colonial powers at a time when its own political and religious institutions were experiencing a period of decay. **Britain**, **France** and **Holland** each sought to expand their portfolios of overseas possessions, primarily for economic reasons, but also to contain each other's power and influence. In Central Asia, too, the **Russian empire** was on the move, propelling it into head-on confrontation not only with Muslim communities in the Caucasus, but also with the Ottoman empire further west.

In the **Indian subcontinent**, Britain tightened its grip, finally toppling the last vestiges of Muslim Mughal rule in 1858, when the East India Company was dissolved and the **British Raj** established in its stead. Britain was less successful in imposing direct control over **Afghanistan**, whose rulers quickly learned how to play British and Russian interests off against each other—part of what became known as the "Great Game" contested between the two "Great Powers"—but in the East it created a new colony on the **Malayan peninsula**, hitherto governed by a medley of Muslim sultans. Further east still, the Dutch gradually asserted their authority over the sprawling **Indonesian archipelago**, likewise largely a patchwork of Muslim sultanates, while nearer home, on the African seaboard of the Mediterranean, France gained possession of **Algeria**, **Tunisia** and **Morocco**.

All these were "losses" to Islam, even though in each conquered territory the Muslim faith continued to be practiced, whether by a minority, as in India, or by a majority, as in the other countries affected. Yet outright conquest was by no means the only way in which Islam was dominated by Europe. Sometimes "**economic imperialism**" was enough to undermine the autonomy of existing states. Muslim rulers may have rued the misfortunes of Islam during the 19th century, but some of them also perceived a need to modernize along European lines. More often than not, however, modernization was achieved only with crippling loans from European (and later American) financiers, leading to a state of indebtedness that undermined political independence.

The two prime examples of this kind of economic surrender were **Egypt** and the failing **Ottoman empire**. In Egypt, the shock of Napoleon's easy victories prompted **Muhammad Ali** to embark on a program of rapid economic, technological and military reforms designed to give his country the strengths of a European nation. But although "Ali Pasha" set about modernization with remarkable skill and determination, his successors were less adroit, particularly as regards controlling development of the **Suez Canal**, and by 1875 Egypt teetered on the brink of bankruptcy, from which the only way back was to become a British protectorate.

The Ottoman empire, which from 1453 to 1683 had provided such a threat to Europe, was a more complex case. It too went bust, and around the same time—1875, when there was something of a meltdown in global money markets. Yet although the Russian and Austro-Hungarian empires continued to chip away at the Ottomans' European possessions, there was a reluctance amongst the "Great Powers" to attempt an outright invasion of **Anatolia**. Perhaps such a thing was in Tsar Nicholas's mind in 1853, but an Anglo-French alliance soon put paid to that in the ensuing Crimean War. What the powers preferred was a weak Ottoman empire, incapable of adequately defending its own colonies and amenable to economic exploitation. Periodically the Ottomans attempted to put their house in order—notably through the **Tanzimat reforms** introduced from 1837 onwards—but it was constantly a question of doing too little too late. In the end the Ottomans were sunk during World War I, after a group known as the **Young Turks**, who had seized power in Constantinople a few years previously, allied themselves with Germany.

Out of the ruins of the Ottoman empire there eventually emerged a new and far more compact state, the **Republic of Turkey** (formally proclaimed in 1924). To the chagrin of many Muslims, though, the new state was decidedly "secularist": it had a parliamentary democracy, and an education system that stressed the need to acquire technical skills at the expense of inculcating religious faith. In this new society there was no room for old-style madrasas, women were discouraged from wearing the veil and men expected to dress in western clothes.

What happened in Turkey reflected a deeply pessimistic mood that engulfed Islam during the 19th century, and which it is no exaggeration to say was largely induced by the "triumphs" of European imperialism. In such circumstances it was only natural that the pursuit of **secularism**, which meant abandoning Islamic tradition in favor of "westernization," became the preferred option among some Muslim leaders. Thus the history of **Persia** at this time is largely a history of tensions and conflict between "progressives" who favored opening up another decayed empire to British and Russian influence and a powerful lobby of conservatives guided by Shiite mullahs—with the figure of the shah, mainly interested in preserving his own power, caught somewhere in between. Similarly in India, particularly after the fiasco of the **Great Revolt** of 1857–58, Muslims (unfairly blamed by the

British for the uprising) were divided about what path to pursue. On the one hand was a figure like **Sayyid Ahmed Khan**, who explicitly urged Muslims to collaborate with their colonial masters and learn from them. On the other was **Qasim Nanavtavi**, who in 1867 established a new madrasa at **Deoband** expressly to revive and promote Islamic values in the subcontinent. Yet it was not until the early 20th century, with the founding of the **Muslim League**, that Indian Muslims began to find a viable political direction—leading finally to the creation of **Pakistan** in 1947 as a separate Islamic state.

Islam did not altogether lose its revolutionary and ideological vigour during the 19th century, however. In **Dagestan** in 1834, Imam Shamil launched a 30-year *jihad* against Russian occupation that had many of the hallmarks of 20th century guerrilla warfare; and in the Sudan in 1881 Muhammad Ahmad ibn Sayyid Abd Allah, better known as the **Mahdi**, began an Islamist rebellion that for seventeen years exasperated British and Egyptian authorities alike. In retrospect, though, a more important figure than either of these was Iranian-born **Jamal ad-Din al-Afghani**, a restless, articulate and sometimes inconsistent ideologue whose writings and lectures did much to inspire the Islamic revival of the 20th century. Yet at the time of his death in 1897, al-Afghani had singularly failed to spark the pan-Islamic movement he had worked for all his life, journeying from one court to another.

Fittingly, perhaps, the only place where a version of Islam close to its original Muhammadan formulation did survive was in **Saudi Arabia**, where the **Wahhabis** continued their symbiotic relationship with the House of Saud. But although Ibn Saud, the eventual creator of the Kingdom of Saudi Arabia, had already begun expanding his territory by 1914 by taking advantage of Ottoman weakness, it was only the far-reaching upheavals brought about by World War I that enabled him to complete his campaigns—and enabled the Arabs to recover some of their lost pride.

1799 His fleet destroyed by Nelson, **Napoleon Bonaparte** leads a contingent of his army overland into **Palestine** and **Syria** as he continues his war against the Ottoman empire, but suffers a second defeat at **Acre** at the hands of a janissary regiment. Napoleon returns to **Cairo**, then at the end of July secretly leaves Egypt.

1801 The French evacuate Egypt after the British land an army at **Aboukir**. Cairo's *mamluk* elite refuse to accept the new Ottoman governor sent from Constantinople, however, and violence erupts as different factions vie for control.

The **Wahhabis**, led by Muhammad ibn Saud's grandson **Abd al-Aziz**, launch a raid against **Kerbala** in Iraq. The tomb of the Shiite Imam Husayn is vandalized, and Kerbala's citizens are massacred.

Fath Ali, the second Qajar shah of **Persia**, signs a pact with Britain, agreeing to become an ally in return for arms and technical advice.

1803 The Wahhabis, now pursuing a *jihad* against the Ottomans, begin campaigning for the control of **Hijaz**.

Sultan **Selim III** dispatches an army of mainly Albanian troops to **Egypt** in a bid to reassert Ottoman control. When its commanding officer is assassinated, his immediate subordinate, **Muhammad Ali** (Mehmed Ali) imposes his authority on Cairo with the backing of the city's *ulama*.

1805 Muhammad Ali is granted the title of **"pasha"** (governor) by Selim III. Finally establishing his authority over all of Egypt, he rules as a monarch beholden to none and introduces wide-ranging **"modernizing" reforms** unprecedented in Islam. Appointing his sons to military commands outside Egypt, Muhammad Ali becomes the dominant Muslim leader of the period.

After the Wahhabis capture **Medina**, Abd al-Aziz's father **Abdullah ibn Saud** bars Muslims who do not acknowledge Wahhabi doctrines from making the annual pilgrimage to the Holy Cities.

The reigning Mughal emperor, **Shah Alam II**, a blind octogenarian, is stripped of his powers—though not his title—and is pensioned off by the East India Company following further British victories in **India**.

1806 Selim III's new Western-style **army** has grown to 22,000, but indiscipline sets in as its members begin aping the corruption and lifestyle of the janissaries.

1807 In February, Abdullah ibn Saud enters **Mecca** itself, where his followers cause havoc during a spree of terror. Tombs and shrines are desecrated, looting is widespread, and the Ottoman sultan's name is replaced by Abdullah's during Friday prayers. As news of the outrage reaches Constantinople, Selim III's credibility is shattered. Overturning their kettles, the **janissaries** provoke a general uprising during which they murder as many "New Trained" soldiers as they can while setting fire to their arsenal and barracks. Selim attempts to quell the mutiny by announcing the disbandment of the new regiments, but to no avail. A group of leading *ulama* issue a *fatwa* against the sultan, and a body of *yamaks* (auxiliaries) led by **Kabakji Mustafa** storm the palace, demanding the enthronement of Selim's cousin Mustafa. Reluctantly **Mustafa IV** agrees, and Selim is confined to his *harem*.

1808 In July, the reforming Ottoman army commander **Bayrakdar Mustafa Pasha** breaks off a campaign against the Bulgars and returns to Constantinople. His troops seize and execute all those involved in Selim III's deposition. Sultan Mustafa IV, refusing to yield to the pasha's demands for his uncle's restoration, has him beheaded instead, but fails to apprehend the only other surviving royal male, the 23-year-old Mahmud. **Mahmud II** is proclaimed sultan, and Mustafa IV is deposed. Mustafa Bayrakdar is appointed grand vizier, and Selim III's military reform program is reinstated. The "New Trained" army is reconstituted as the *Seghans* ("Masters of the Hounds"). In November, the janissaries stage a second revolt. After Mustafa Bayrakdar is assassinated, Mahmud II orders the execution of the deposed Mustafa IV, making himself the only surviving Ottoman male. The janissaries attack his palace, but are beaten back, whereupon the sultan orders his fleet to bombard the janissary barracks. After two days' confusion, during which large parts of **Constantinople** burn to the ground, the *ulama* mediate a truce. Mahmud II agrees to disband the *Seghans* and pardon the janissaries on condition that they end their mutiny. The janissaries consent, but then immediately butcher the *Seghans*. Powerless to intervene, Mahmud vows that one day the janissaries must be destroyed.

1809 Turning on those who have helped him to power, Muhammad Ali decrees that Egypt's *ulama* should no longer be exempt from **taxation**.

1811 Determined to create a modern army, Muhammad Ali purges the old *mamluk* regiments by massacring 480 of their leaders at a banquet in **Cairo**. A thousand others are murdered in the days and weeks that follow.

1813 Under the command of his son **Ibrahim**, Muhammad Ali's new reformed army recaptures **Mecca** and **Medina** from Abdullah ibn Saud, slaughtering many Wahhabi *ghazis* in the process. The keys of Mecca are sent as a gift to Constantinople, and the sultan's name is once again honored during Friday prayers in the Holy Cities.

1814 Following fresh hostilities, the Ottomans cede territories in the **Caucasus** to Russia by the Treaty of Gulistan.

1815 In the Balkans, the **Serbs** rebel against Ottoman rule.

1817 A charismatic leader known as **Jahangir**, claiming descent from the Prophet Muhammad and aiming to recover **Kashgar** in the

Tarim Basin from Chinese rule, raises revolt by declaring a *jihad* against the Qing dynasty.

1818 Ibrahim Pasha, continuing his campaign against the Wahhabis in Najd, lays siege to their stronghold **Diriyyah** and captures Abdullah ibn Saud, who is sent under escort to Constantinople. After being declared a heretic by the Sultan's religious advisers, Abdullah is executed and his head placed on the marble columns outside the palace. Despite this, both the Wahhabis and the house of Saud—now ruled by Abd al-Aziz—survive, and they soon reclaim **Najd**.

MUHAMMAD ALI (1769–1849)

*H*aving seized power in Cairo in 1803 with the backing of the *ulama*, **Muhammad Ali** wasted little time before sidelining them. As regards the *mamluk* elite, he simply invited them to dinner en masse, then murdered them. But it was all to a purpose: Muhammad Ali wanted to drag Egypt, a stagnant province in a stagnant empire, into the 19th century. He wanted it to be a modern nation like France or Britain.

Born in Turkish **Macedonia**, probably of Albanian parents, he arrived at Aboukir to help restore Ottoman rule in the wake of the collapse of the short-lived French colonial government. But it was his own power that interested him more. In the prevailing confusion he asserted his formidable personality, then set about clearing the decks for the great enterprise of **modernization**— all the more remarkable for a man who remained illiterate until his forties.

Between 1805 and 1840, he transformed Egypt. He established a new army with the latest weapons. He created a cotton industry that earned sufficient foreign currency to purchase new machines for new factories that refined sugar and manufactured glass. He dragooned the population into public works. He built new schools and colleges, based on European

1819 Singapore, a Malay island consisting of little more than a handful of Muslim villages, is annexed by **Britain** as a Crown colony.

1820 An expeditionary army sets out from Cairo under the command of Muhammad Ali's third son Ismail to annex **Nubia** and the **Sudan**, both important sources for a burgeoning trade in largely female **black slaves**.

1821 The Christian population of **Greece** revolts against Ottoman rule. In the Morea, 15,000 Muslim villagers are massacred, persuading Muslims elsewhere to flee.

institutions. He made **Cairo** and **Alexandria** cities people wanted to visit. Yet the methods used by "**Ali Pasha**" were idiosyncratic to say the least. To effect his revolution he requisitioned all of Egypt's land in his own name, expropriating the property of both mamluks and religious endowments; by owning everything he could do as he pleased, and for a time it seemed as if he might take over the Ottoman empire itself. But, curiously, when his son Ibrahim lay within a forced march of Constantinople in 1834, Ali ordered his retreat—perhaps fearing his child might become over-mighty, recognizing the empire was too unwieldy to take on, or reverting to his original Ottoman loyalty. In 1840, again the prize seemed his for the taking, only this time it was the "Great Powers" who stayed his hand. Ali Pasha went downhill from there on, eventually ending his days as a convalescent in Naples.

Ali bequeathed a lasting conundrum for Egypt and Islam alike. As a secularist dictator he provided a model for many later rulers, Atatürk and Nasser among them. But Muhammad Ali's kind of success meant sacrificing Islamic values. On the other hand, without his brand of aggressive nationalism, what hope did an Islamic nation have?

1824 Britain and Holland conclude a **bilateral treaty** whereby **Malaya** becomes a British "sphere of interest" and **Indonesia** becomes the Dutch equivalent.

1825 Muhammad Ali Pasha dispatches Egyptian troops commanded by Ibrahim Pasha to help the **Ottomans** against the Greek rebels. As both sides butcher each other, the captured Greek patriarch is hanged from the gates of his palace on Easter Sunday.

1826 The key fortress **Missolonghi** falls to Egyptian troops after a prolonged siege. Ibrahim Pasha's successes help Sultan Mahmud II to press home his arguments for army reforms in Constantinople.

Muhammad Ali, lounging at his royal abode

With the backing of the *ulama* the **janissaries** are disbanded, on the understanding that many of their fitter men will be immediately re-enlisted as "new soldiers" (***eskenjis***). On June 14, "remnant" janissaries attempt an uprising, but are cut down in their barracks at **Et Meydan** by the *eskenjis* and other loyalist troops. Those taken prisoner are either beheaded or strangled. The *eskenjis* are called the "Triumphant Soldiers of Allah," and their victory dubbed "**The Auspicious Event**."

In the wake of his coup against the janissaries, Mahmud II abolishes the centuries-old **court dress code**, introducing the "stambouline" (frock-coat) and red *fez* (conical felt hat) in its place. The *ulama* and other clerics are permitted to retain their traditional high turbans and flowing capes.

1827 Jahangir's Muslim rebellion in **western China** is smashed by an imperial army. Jahangir is captured and sent to Beijing for execution.

Just as the **Greek War of Independence** seems doomed to failure, Britain destroys the Egyptian-Ottoman fleet off **Navarino** with French and Russian backing, severing Ibrahim Pasha's supply lines.

1830 Imitating Spanish and Portuguese attempts to establish colonies in North Africa, **France** occupies Muslim **Algeria**.

1832 Muhammad Ali of Egypt asks Constantinople to be allowed to assume the *pashalik* (governorship) of **Syria**. When Sultan Mahmud II refuses, the Egyptian dictator dispatches his son Ibrahim with an army of invasion. The Ottomans' "Triumphant Soldiers of Allah" are routed by their Egyptian prototypes, and in October Ibrahim advances into Anatolia and captures **Konya**.

Greece's newly won independence is guaranteed by a **Triple Alliance** consisting of Britain, France and Russia.

1833 Instead of advancing on Constantinople, Ibrahim Pasha is ordered home by his father.

1834 In the Caucasus, **Imam Shamil** begins a 25-year guerrilla war against Russia in the mountains of **Dagestan** and **Chechnya** (formally ceded to Moscow by Persia in 1813).

1835 In **India**, following recommendations made by Lord Macaulay, English replaces Persian (used by the Mughals) as the language of officialdom and education—to the chagrin of the Muslim elite.

THE TANZIMAT REFORMS

*B*y 1839, many in the Ottoman hierarchy were convinced that modernizing reforms were long overdue—persuaded by over a hundred years of ignominious defeat by the Austro-Hungarians and the Russians, mounting evidence of the inherent technological and political strengths of Europe's leading nations, and the example of Muhammad Ali in Egypt. It was in this context that, on November 3, the newly enthroned Abdul Mecid proclaimed the *Hatt i-serrif*, also known as the "Gulhane Decree" after the name of the pavilion by the Marmara Sea where an audience of dignitaries had been invited to hear the youthful sultan speak. Prepared by his advisers, the rescript introduced a raft of measures, including the right of all those living in the empire to the sultan's protection regardless of race or creed, the ending of "arbitrary" executions, the abolition of tax-farming among the empire's provincial administrators and the lifting of several unpopular state monopolies. Wide-ranging though such innovations were, they were insufficiently far-reaching to restore Ottoman fortunes. Further reforms were introduced over the following decades, culminating in the Constitution of 1876. Collectively, the reforms and the period of their enactment are known as *Tanzimat* ("Re-ordering"), which ended in 1877 when Abdul Hamid II reverted to the traditional despotism of the Ottoman throne.

1836 Ahmad ibn Idris, a Sufi Islamic revivalist, dies in his native Morocco. During his lifetime he has urged Muslims to pay more attention to their own reading of the Koran than to the teachings of the *ulama*, whom he criticizes for their lack of concern for ordinary believers.

1838 The first of three **Anglo-Afghan wars** is sparked when the British, fearing Russian aggrandizement in Central Asia, attempt to

Important as *Tanzimat* was, it did not really represent a cut-and-dried passage in Ottoman history. Reforms had been attempted in the 18th century, but they nearly always foundered because of the intransigence of the janissaries and the conservative *ulama*. In this respect it was Mahmud II's successful coup against the janissaries in 1826 that supplied the crucial breakthrough, even though his own reforms, introduced immediately afterwards, amounted to little more than window-dressing. Nor did Abdul Hamid II's return to absolutism signal the end of reform. Brutal and dictatorial though he was, in terms of infrastructure at least he probably did more to modernize the empire than any other 19th-century ruler. Even so, it befell Mustafa Kemal Atatürk to carry reform through to its logical conclusion once the empire itself had collapsed during World War I.

The gestation of modern Turkey was therefore somewhat protracted, and, armed with hindsight, critics have blamed *Tanzimat* for not going far enough at the time—particularly with regard to education—and also for allowing the military to continue at the heart of Turkish politics. A more balanced view, though, might applaud the ability of an essentially medieval (and partly theocratic) empire to transform itself into a democratic and generally secularist polity that is currently attempting to join the European Union.

impose direct rule on Afghanistan from India. The war lasts four years and ends in a humiliating defeat for the colonial power, although Britain eventually secures its objectives through diplomacy and subsidies given to the Durrani dynasty.

1839 Mahmud II is succeeded by his 16-year-old son **Abdul Mecid**. On November 3 the young sultan proclaims the *Hatt i-serrif* ("illustrious rescript," also known as the **"Gulhane Decree"**) before an assembly of dignitaries that includes European envoys. Although the decree is necessarily couched in terms of "restoration" rather than radical change, it inaugurates a sustained period of reform known as *Tanzimat*.

In July, the main Ottoman fleet sails to **Alexandria** and defects to Muhammad Ali, who is poised to take over the empire.

Following an incident in which a British ship is attacked by pirates operating out of Yemen in southern Arabia, Britain annexes the port city of **Aden**.

1840 Britain, France and other European powers, preferring a weak Ottoman empire to one ruled over by Muhammad Ali, put pressure on the Egyptian dictator to relinquish **Palestine**, **Syria** and **Albania**, which he governs as a result of his sons' campaigns. The three provinces return to Ottoman rule.

1846 Under pressure from the British, Sultan Abdul Mecid orders the closure of Constantinople's **slave market**. Slave markets continue elsewhere, however, and in Constantinople slaves continue to be traded privately.

1847 British-born entrepreneur **Baron Julius de Reuter**, promising modernization, wins a package of concessions from the Persian shah and his prime minister, **Hosain Khan**, which includes exclusive rights to rail and tramway development, a national bank and all mineral extraction. Although the concessions are swiftly cancelled in the wake of an uprising led by local merchants (*bazaaris*) and backed by the mullahs and the shah's own wife, less ambitious attempts by Britons to control the **Persian economy** will succeed.

1849 Muhammad Ali Pasha dies and is succeeded as ruler of Egypt by his grandson **Abbas Hilmi I Pasha**, a "reactionary" opposed to further modernizing reforms.

The Moslem quarter of a city is lonely and desolate. You go up and down, and on over shelving and hillocky paths through the narrow lanes walled in by blank, windowless dwellings; you come out upon an open space strewed with the black ruins that some late fire has left; you pass by a mountain of castaway things, the rubbish of centuries, and on it you see numbers of big, wolf-like dogs lying torpid under the sun, with limbs outstretched to the full, as if they were dead; storks, or cranes, sitting fearless upon the low roofs, look gravely down upon you; the still air that you breathe is loaded with the scent of citron, and pomegranate rinds scorched by the sun, or (as you approach the bazaar) with the dry, dead perfume of strange spices. You long for some signs of life, and tread the ground more heavily, as though you would wake the sleepers with the heel of your boot; but the foot falls noiseless upon the crumbling soil of an Eastern city, and silence follows you still. Again and again you meet turbans, and faces of men, but they have nothing for you—no welcome—no wonder—no wrath—no scorn—they look upon you as we do upon a December's fall of snow—as a "seasonable," unaccountable, uncomfortable work of God, that may have been sent for some good purpose, to be revealed hereafter.

—A.W. Kinglake, *Eothen* (1844)

1850 Sultan Abdul Mecid oversees the introduction of a Western-style **commercial code** in the empire. To administer it, "secular" (non-Shariah) courts are established.

1853 In January, **Tsar Nicholas I** tells the British envoy in St Petersburg, Sir Hamilton Seymour, that "Turkey" (by which he means the Ottoman empire) is "the sick man of Europe"—a sobriquet that becomes popular in diplomatic circles.

In July, Russian forces occupy the **"Danubian states"** (modern Romania) on the Russo-Ottoman frontier.

In September, Britain dispatches a fleet to **Constantinople** for the protection of the Ottoman empire, which declares war against Russia in October, marking the beginning of the **Crimean War**.

A government survey reveals that a majority of properties in Constantinople are owned by tax-exempt **religious trusts** (*wafd*), many set up to benefit individual families.

1854 **France** joins the Anglo-Ottoman alliance against Russia, and a coalition army is landed on the Crimean peninsula in the Black Sea to destroy Russian strongholds. Although the allies gain victories at **Balaklava** in October and **Inkerman** in November, the war continues for another two years.

Abbas Hilmi I is assassinated in Cairo, and is succeeded by his uncle **Muhammad Said Pasha**, an admirer of all things Western, who quickly grants **Ferdinand de Lesseps**, a French engineer, a concession to build a canal from **Suez** to the Red Sea—a project at first strongly opposed by Constantinople and Britain. While de Lesseps sets about raising capital on the international money markets, Muhammad Said unwisely offers him personal guarantees as well as conscripted Egyptian labor.

1855 Aggravated by punitive taxation and deprived of mining rights, Muslims in the Chinese province of **Yunnan** begin an insurrection that continues until 1873.

THE CRIMEAN WAR (1853–56)

Throughout the 19th century, a central doctrine of British foreign policy was the maintenance of a "balance of power" between Europe's leading nations, including Russia. Away from Europe, however, another vital consideration was to halt the expansion of the Russian empire in central and eastern Asia. Although the "Great Game" between Britain and Russia was mainly played out in inhospitable terrains such as Afghanistan and Tibet, in 1853 the scene shifted dramatically nearer home, when Russia began molesting the Ottoman empire's Danubian borders.

Russia's pretext was its right to protect Orthodox Christians living under Ottoman rule, especially those in the Black Sea area, enshrined in the 1774 Treaty of Kuchuk Kaynarja. But lurking in the background was a secondary dispute between Russia and France about the respective rights of Orthodox and Catholic monks living in the Palestinian Holy Land. Fearing that Russia, perennially in search of southern sea-ports in the Indian Ocean and the Mediterranean, might mount an attack on Constantinople itself, Britain and France decided to intervene.

A task force was sent to the Crimean peninsula to knock out Russia's Black Sea naval facilities—a job eventually accomplished by the surrender of Sebastopol, but only after 250,000 combatants had died, many from cholera. For some, the allied victory was scarcely worth the price, but in two important respects Crimea was a turning-point. After centuries of intermittent warfare, French and English soldiers had fought shoulder to shoulder, as they would again against Germany twice in the 20th century. More startling still was the allies' all-out defense of a Muslim empire that had humiliated Christendom in 1453. Even in the 19th century, "great power" politics did not invariably count against Islam.

As British pressure for the **abolition of slavery** grows, Sheikh Jamal of Mecca issues a *fatwa* declaring that any ban is contrary to Islamic law.

1856 Hostilities in the Crimea end in February. In March a congress of European powers meets in **Paris** and resolves to uphold the "independence" of the Ottoman empire.

1857 In January, Indian soldiers employed by the East India Company mutiny in **Calcutta** after being ordered to use the newly introduced Enfield rifle. Cartridges for the rifle are coated with a tallow containing pork and beef derivatives, offending both Muslim and Hindu troops. The mutiny is suppressed, but when its ringleaders are brought to trial at Meerut in May, popular protests spark a general revolt—called variously the **Indian Mutiny** and the **Great Indian Uprising**. Across northern India, cities and

Mutineers attacking British troops at Lucknow, India, 1857

garrisons are seized by rebels, and it will be a year before the British restore order.

In the wake of the Crimean War, Sultan Mecid issues the **Hatti Humayub** decree, granting equal rights for all religious minorities within the Ottoman empire.

1858 The revolt against British rule in India collapses in June when forces loyal to the East India Company recapture **Gwaliar**. Although Hindus and Muslims have participated in the revolt in roughly equal numbers, the British blame the Muslims, particularly since during the course of the upheavals the Mughal puppet ruler, **Bahadur Shah Zafar**, attempts to re-establish his power. Bahadur is exiled to Burma, and the **Mughal dynasty** brought to an end. The East India Company is also dissolved when India is declared a British Crown Colony in November, marking the advent of the **British Raj**.

1859 Imam Shamil's 25-year insurgency against Russia in the Caucasus ends after his fortress at **Vedeno** surrenders. Shamil himself, whose bravery captures the romantic imagination of Europe, is allowed to live in "exile" until his death in 1871.

1860 In Syria, thousands of **Maronite** (Catholic Christian) tenant farmers around Mount Lebanon are massacred by their **Druze** (Ismaili Shiite) landlords. As a civil war develops, the international community—led by France—calls for a Christian protectorate. Eventually the state of **Lebanon** is born out of this episode, although for the time being the territory continues under Ottoman rule.

Sayyid Ahmad Khan publishes *The Loyal Muhammadans of India* in an attempt to persuade the British Raj to look more favorably on India's Muslims.

1861 Abdul Mecid is succeeded as by his brother **Abdul Aziz**, who continues to modernize the Ottoman empire, but at the expense of raising unmanageable **loans** from European governments and bankers.

Bahrain in the Persian Gulf becomes a British protectorate.

1862 Muslim rebels in Yunnan briefly seize control of the Chinese province's capital, **Kunming**. A second Muslim revolt breaks out in **Gansu** province.

1863 In Egypt, Muhammad Said Pasha is succeeded by his nephew **Ismail Pasha**, who redoubles the modernization program. Under his rule **Cairo** becomes a city to rival its Mediterranean European counterparts, and hundreds of miles of **rail track** are laid. The cost of such enterprises is prohibitive, however, and Egypt's economy falls progressively under the influence of Western financiers.

THE REVOLT IN INDIA

*T*o maintain control over a territory that contained a population at least ten times greater than Britain's, the British in India had to recruit "native" soldiers, known as "sepoys." In 1857, following the introduction of the **Enfield rifle**, this expedient miscarried. The heads of its cartridges had to be bitten off before they could be fired, and this meant ingesting a grease laced with pig and cattle fat. Since British officers were adamant that no concession be made to Muslim and Hindu sensibilities, word quickly spread that the cartridges were a ploy to force Indians to convert to Christianity.

The general revolt that started in May 1857 could have been avoided, though, had it not been decided to court-martial those responsible for the earlier mutiny at **Calcutta**. Instead, India was engulfed by a spate of uprisings that lasted well into the following summer, marked by grisly massacres perpetrated by all sides. The "great revolt" was singularly uncoordinated, however; lacking a unified leadership, the rebels also suffered from inadequate supplies and inferior weaponry. In the end, the revolt was crushed by

1864 Construction of the **Suez Canal**, the most ambitious engineering feat of the 19th century, is temporarily halted when Ismail Pasha withdraws conscript labor and attempts to limit the amount of land granted to the Suez project. In the wrangles that ensue, Ismail is forced to back down and offer the **Suez Company** compensation. As Egypt slides toward bankruptcy, construction resumes.

1867 Sultan Abdul Aziz becomes the first Muslim head-of-state to visit European capitals, including **Paris**, **London** and **Brussels**. During his journey he orders modern warships for the Ottoman navy.

the sepoys themselves, the majority of whom remained loyal to the East India Company.

Without question, the principal losers were India's Muslims, made to bear the brunt of subsequent British recriminations. Following the revolt, Muslims were barred from enlisting in what became the Indian Army, and Muslim landlords had to prove they had not participated in the rebellion if they wanted to keep their property. The effect of these and other measures was to impoverish and isolate the Muslim community at a time when many leading Hindus sought to ingratiate themselves with their colonial masters. Taking a leaf from their book, Sayyid Ahmad Khan recommended Muslims adopt a similar attitude, for which he was duly given a knighthood. While some responded positively, a majority remained turned inwards in their own communities, and it was not until 1906 that a distinctive Muslim politics found its voice in India with the founding of the Muslim League under the presidency of the Agha Khan, the nominal head of the descendants of the Ismaili Assassins.

DEOBAND

*I*slam was on the defensive when what was to become the greatest madrasa (theological seminary) in the Indian subcontinent was founded in 1867 by Qasim Nanavtavi at Deoband, 150 miles north of Delhi. Muslims still suffered the stigma of blame for the revolt of 1857–58, and were as often as not shunned by Hindus glad that Mughal rule was finally over. Indeed, Nanavtavi's principal objective was simply to create a place where would-be clerics and teachers could acquire a conservative understanding of Islam for the benefit of India's ailing Muslim community. Yet Deoband became a main center for not only the religious but the political revival of Islam. In the late 19th and early 20th centuries, several of its alumni became leading activists in the struggle against British colonial rule, and later on still it helped fuel demands for an independent Muslim state once it became apparent that the days of the Raj were numbered. And even then, the importance of Deoband continued to grow. In Pakistan, new madrasas were modelled on Deoband with Deoband-trained clerics on their staff. As these proliferated, they began attracting students from neighboring Afghanistan—particularly during and after the mujahaddin *jihad* against the Soviet Union in the 1980s.

Two reasons for Deoband's success have been its emphasis on meeting the needs of ordinary Muslims and its ability to change with the times, adapting first to altered circumstances within India, and then responding to the contemporary Islamist movement. To their credit, Deobandi madrasas have often given education to the sons of the poor who might otherwise have remained illiterate. They also run special offices, known as *darul ifta,* that dispense *fatwas* (religious judgements) on every conceivable subject. Such verdicts are handwritten by *ulama* on slips of paper, like a doctor's prescription, and today they can even be procured by telephone and via the Internet.

Discontented with the title of "pasha," Ismail Pasha agrees to pay Sultan Abdul Aziz an annuity, or annual "tribute," of £350,000 in return for the title *khedive*—an ancient Persian honorific meaning "great prince."

A madrasa that will play a seminal role in Islamic revivalism in the Indian subcontinent is founded at **Deoband**.

1869 The **Suez Canal** joining the Mediterranean to the Red Sea finally opens, to international acclaim; but while the waterway drastically reduces journey times between Europe and the East, Egypt itself enjoys little of the income generated, which goes to the Suez Company.

1871 Jamal ad-Din al-Afghani, a leading Islamist ideologue, migrates to Egypt where he creates a group of reformers, among them Muhammad Abdu, who will inspire the **Muslim Brotherhood** of the 20th century.

In **China**, the Muslim rebellion in Gansu collapses after its leader, **Ma Hualong**, is captured and publicly sliced to death.

1873 The Muslim rebellion in China's Yunnan province similarly collapses when **Du Wenxiu** is captured and executed. In **Xinjiang** province Muslim insurgency continues, however, particularly among the **Uighur** people.

Ottoman forces in **Bulgaria**, attempting to suppress a revolt, perpetrate a massacre of Christians that greatly damages the Turks' reputation in the West.

1875 During a year of turmoil on the **international money markets**, the Suez Company is bankrupted and the khedive Ismail is forced to sell Britain a lease on the Canal. The equally insolvent Ottoman empire defaults on loan repayments and is forced to accept financial restructuring imposed by European bankers to protect Western interests.

As intercommunal tensions in **Bulgaria** and **Bosnia-Herzogovina** worsen, Muslims and Christians begin murdering each other.

In India, Sayyid Ahmad Khan founds the **Muhammadan Anglo-Oriental College** in Lahore as part of his campaign to encourage fellow Muslims to collaborate more fully with their colonial masters.

1876 In **Constantinople**, Sultan Abdul Aziz, held responsible for the economic decline of the Ottoman empire and criticized by the *ulama* and religious students for his profligate lifestyle, is deposed on May 30 by a diffuse group of patriots known as the **Young Ottomans** and led by the bureaucrat **Midhat Pasha**. The sultan's nephew, **Murad V**, is elevated to the throne, but in September is deposed as rumours spread that Murad has personally knifed his uncle to death. The Young Ottomans now enthrone Murad's younger brother **Abdul Hamid II**, whom Midhat Pasha persuades to promulgate a markedly **secularist constitution** on December 23. Yet although the constitution guarantees the rights of all Ottoman citizens regardless of race or creed, and although it provides for a two-house European-style parliament, the sultan retains near-despotic powers, and is still empowered to issue decrees and veto any legislation passed. Although the constitution also confirms the sultan's title as **caliph**, Islamists are bitterly critical of many of its clauses, and Abdul Hamid II becomes variously known as the "Red Sultan" and "Abdul Hamid the Damned."

As these events unfold, Russia intervenes militarily in the **Balkans** to protect Orthodox Christian communities. As the persecution of Balkan Muslims intensifies, many flee to Constantinople, putting more pressure on the city's strained resources.

1877 Sultan Abdul Hamid II dismisses (and later executes) Midhat Pasha as his grand vizier in February and begins **ruling directly**, although for cosmetic purposes parliament is convened towards the end of the year. Exiled from the capital, some Young Ottomans seek refuge in **Paris**, which becomes a focus for expatriot Turkish dissidence.

1878 In February, **Abdul Hamid** suspends parliament indefinitely. The constitution is not revoked, but nor is it applied. Over the next thirty years, the sultan introduces beneficial improvements in education and transport, but creates a **police state** through his over-reliance on domestic intelligence gathering and other security measures. Although he attempts to give his policies an Islamic gloss, his use of torture attracts widespread abhorrence.

The **Congress of Berlin** endorses Austro-Hungarian rule in the **Balkans**, excluding Bulgaria. The political influence of Muslim Slavs is dramatically reduced while that of the Catholic Croatians is enhanced.

1879 The khedive Ismail is deposed after he baulks at Anglo-French attempts to restructure the Egyptian economy. In his place his son **Tewfiq** is proclaimed khedive.

The **Second Anglo-Afghan War** begins when the British again attempt to impose direct rule over Afghanistan.

1880 The British fail to conquer Afghanistan, but their preferred Duranni candidate, **Amir Abdul Rehman**, known as the "iron amir," becomes its king. Ruling for 21 years with military and financial support from Britain, he maintains an authoritarian regime that promotes the interests of the **Pashtun people** at the expense of Afghanistan's Uzbek, Tajik and Hazara communities.

1881 Sultan Abdul Hamid II restores confidence in the Ottoman economy by instituting a **Public Debt Commission** that includes representatives from Britain, France, Germany, Belgium, Austro-Hungary and other creditor nations. The Commission oversees revenue collection and manages new **monopolies** in salt, tobacco and other commodities.

Ahmed Arabi (Ahmed bey Urubi) leads a **mutiny** among Egyptian officers opposed to both Ottoman and Anglo-French influence. The khedive Tewfiq is forced to form a new government in which Arabi assumes the post of minister of war.

In neighboring **Sudan**, a charismatic Muslim mystic, Muhammad Ahmad ibn Sayyid Abd Allah, known in the West as the **Mahdi**, proclaims a divine mission to purify Islam. Over the following four years he establishes a Sudanese empire at Egypt's expense.

Elsewhere in northern Africa, **Tunisia** is annexed by France.

1882 Dispatching troops to **Cairo**, Britain intervenes to restore its interests in Egypt. Ahmed Arabi, routed at **Tel al-Kabir**, is removed from power, and the khedive Tewfiq is "restored." In reality, Egypt becomes a **British protectorate**. The economy is stabilized, and British forces assume a leading role in combating the Mahdists in Sudan, using the opportunity to challenge the African **slave trade**.

As a result of their persecution in Russia, significant numbers of **Jews** begin emigrating to **Palestine** at a time when the concept of an autonomous Jewish homeland is beginning to be aired among the leaders of Europe's Jewish minorities.

1883 British control over Egypt is consolidated by the appointment of **Evelyn Baring** (later Lord Cromer) as "British Agent and Consul-General" in Cairo, where he remains until 1907.

1885 On January 26, the Mahdi captures the Sudanese administrative capital of **Khartoum**, massacring its garrison of British troops commanded by General Charles Gordon. The Mahdi promulgates an Islamic state in the Sudan with its capital at **Omdurman**, where he dies in June. The Mahdists, now led by Khalifa Abdullah, continue to resist both British and Egyptian attempts at suppression.

1888 The esoteric **Ahmadiyyah** sect in founded in the Punjab by **Mirza Ghulam Ahmad**; opposed to westernization, he proclaims himself to be not only the *mahdi*, but an incarnation of the Hindu god Vishnu and Jesus Christ.

1889 Abdul Hamid II issues a decree **abolishing slavery** in the Ottoman empire.

1891 To the detriment of Persian producers and consumers, Nasir ad-Din Shah grants a **tobacco monopoly** to a British company. In December a senior Shiite cleric, the *mujtahid* Mirza Hasan Shirazi, issues a *fatwa* at Najaf in Iraq condemning the sale of tobacco, and the shah is forced to withdraw the concession the following year after widespread unrest.

In northern Arabia, the ruling **Saudis** are driven out of their capital **Riyadh** by a rival clan, the Rashid of Hail.

1893 The **Durand Line**, agreed between Amir Abdul Rehmen and the British Raj, establishes the modern border between Afghanistan and what will become Pakistan. Crucially, the **Pashtun** people are divided either side of the frontier.

1895 The Ottoman authorities instigate full-scale persecutions of **Armenian Christians** after Armenian nationalists, active since the 1880s, occupy the Ottoman Bank in **Constantinople**. An estimated 20,000 Armenians are massacred.

1896 In **Persia**, Nasir ad-Din Shah is assassinated by a follower of al-Afghani.

In **Crete**, Greek Christians rebel against Ottoman Turkish rule.

In the Far East, the British proclaim a **"federation of Malay states,"** in effect a British colony.

It was the last day of Mahdism, and the greatest. They could never get near, and they refused to hold back. By now the ground before us was all white with dead men's drapery. Rifles grew red-hot; the soldiers seized them by slings and dragged them back to the reserve to change to cool ones. It was not a battle, but an execution.

—**George Warrington Steevens,**
With Kitchener to Khartoum (1898)

1897 The First Zionist Congress convenes at Basle in Switzerland. As a result, the **World Zionist Organization** is born, committed to the creation of a **Jewish state** in Ottoman-governed Palestine.

1898 After a two-year war, **Crete** is freed from Ottoman rule and unites with Greece.

On September 2, the Mahdist "revolt" in **Sudan** is crushed when a force led by Lord Kitchener defeats its army outside **Omdurman**.

JAMAL AD-DIN AL-AFGHANI (1839–97)

*W*idely regarded as the ideological father of the 20th century Islamist movement, Jamal ad- Din was almost certainly born in Iran of Shiite parentage, but having spent most of his childhood in Kabul—and because as a political activist he was dedicated to the principle that only by uniting could Islam overcome its "repression" by "imperialist" forces—he adopted the name al-Afghani ("the Afghan") to allay any Sunni misgivings.

During an extraordinary and provocative life, al-Afghani was constantly on the move, successfully seeking the patronage of Islam's various courts, and then (often as not) upsetting them by his advocacy of policies contrary to their interests. Thus, having spent five years in India, he became an adviser to the Afghan court, but was expelled in 1868. He then journeyed back to India before pitching his tent in Constantinople and, in 1871, Cairo. By 1879 he had outstayed his welcome, however, and so began the most frenetic period of his travels. These took him once again to India, to Paris, to Persia, to Uzbekistan, to London and back to Istanbul—where, pleased by al-Afghani's criticisms of the Persian shah, Abdul Hamid II granted him a pension.

During the battle, British troops are amazed by the willingness of the enemy to run at their Maxim machine guns armed with little more than sabers.

1899 In the Persian Gulf, Britain recognizes **Kuwait** as an independent state under British protection after signing a treaty with its ruler **Sheikh Mubarak**, who fears the military consequences of an extension of the Ottomans' burgeoning rail system into his territory.

But in less than a year al-Afghani was dead—killed by cancer of the jaw. He left behind a body of newspaper articles and essays that articulated nearly all the main themes that have preoccupied Muslims since. Like his contemporary radicals in China, he sought a way of exploiting the West's scientific and technological achievements without embracing Western social and moral values. To get his message across he was prepared to issue scathing attacks on Islam itself, accusing it of being inward-looking, decadent and irrational. Convinced that Islam would go under unless it adopted a more assertive stance, al-Afghani goaded his fellow Muslims with a mixture of high anger and near-mysticism. Powerful as his voice was, though, he failed to identify the means by which revival could be initiated. In Egypt, where perhaps he was at the height of his powers, avidly using the press to disseminate his views, the followers he attracted went separate ways. While Muhammad Abdul saw a revised Islamic education as the most appropriate way forward, Said Zaghlul responded by forming the distinctly nationalist Wafd party. Not until the founding of the Muslim Brotherhood, many of whose members acknowledged al-Afghani as a primary inspiration, did the sort of Islamism he argued for get properly under way.

Qassim Amin creates a furor in **Cairo** with the publication of his book *Tahir al-Mara* ("Liberation of Women"), in which he equates the backwardness of Egypt relative to Europe with the systematic repression of women. Reacting to Qassim's polemic, many Islamists adopt the **veil** as a symbol of Islamic authenticity—for all that it is not generally prescribed in the Koran.

1901 Abd-al-Aziz al-Saud, usually known as **Ibn Saud**, daringly recaptures **Riyadh** from the Rashid of Hail with only a small band of followers. Encouraged by this success, he embarks on a series of conquests in Arabia at a time of greatly diminished Ottoman power and rising Arab nationalism.

In the Maghreb, **Morocco** becomes a French protectorate after France intervenes to prop up the ruling Alawi dynasty.

Following the discovery of **oil** in Persia/Iran, the first major Middle Eastern oil concession to a Western company is made when the British **William Knox D'Arcy** concludes a sixty-year agreement with the shah. With oil increasingly replacing coal as a maritime and naval fuel, D'Arcy's success provokes a scramble for further concessions by Western interests.

1902 Ibn Saud is recognized as the **sultan of Najd** by Britain, but is unable to extend his rule eastwards because of existing British protectorates in the Persian Gulf.

1904 In April, Britain and France agree to respect each other's "interests" in **Egypt** and **Morocco**.

1905 Muhammad Abdu, a follower of al-Afghani, resigns as Egypt's *mufti*, a post he has held since 1899, and dies shortly afterwards. Less extreme in his views than his mentor, Muhammad Abdu has urged a reformed **Islamic education system** incorporating modern scientific disciplines as the best means of regenerating Islam itself. Although his ideas are resisted by conservative *ulama*, they will gain ground later in the 20th century.

In **India**, the large western province known under British rule as the **Bengal Presidency** is **partitioned** between Hindu-majority West Bengal and Muslim-majority East Bengal. While the partition will be rescinded in 1911, it sows the seeds for the eventual creation of East Pakistan, then Bangladesh.

1906 In Persia, where the absolutism of the **Qajar dynasty** has become intolerable to many, a **"constitutional revolution"** is imposed on the shah by secular "progressives." Supported by perhaps a majority of Shiite *mullahs*, the constitution provides for a national assembly, or *Majlis* ("council"), part-elected and part-appointed, to advise the shah on policy and prepare legislation.

As Britain prepares to grant limited democracy to **India**, leading Muslims found the All-India Muslim League (later known as the **Muslim League**) during a drive to secure a fairer electoral franchise for Muslims in the subcontinent.

1907 Britain and Russia intervene in **Persia** to restore **Shah Muhammad Ali's** autocracy. The 1906 constitution is revoked as the two "Great Powers" privately agree to divide Persia into their own "spheres of interest," based on the distribution of known oil-fields.

Lord Cromer resigns as consul-general in Egypt. His successor, **Sir Eldon Gorst**, pursues a less interventionist policy as Egyptian nationalism gathers strength.

1908 Amid widespread opposition to the rule of **Abdul Hamid II**—including conservative, anti-Western Islamists and pro-Western liberal secularists—a group of nationalistic officers in Salonika (Macedonia) known as the **Young Turks** and supported by Arabian rebels stage an armed mutiny that persuades the sultan to restore the 1876 constitution.

In October, exploiting the confusion in Constantinople, Austria formally incorporates **Bosnia-Herzogovina** into the Austro-Hungarian empire, while **Bulgaria** declares its independence from Ottoman rule.

In the Far East, the **Dutch** overcome the Sumatran sultanate of **Aceh** after a prolonged war during which resistance to Dutch rule has been spearheaded by Muslim "militants." Their victory provides the Dutch with a platform from which to complete their annexation of the **Indonesian archipelago**.

THE AFRICAN SLAVE TRADE

*P*erhaps the greatest social change between the time when the Koran was revealed to Muhammad and the present age is the near-total eradication of formal slavery worldwide. For its time, the Koran was enlightened. Slaves should be well-treated, it advocated, and those who professed Islam should be freed: "The man who frees a Muslim slave," Muhammad is reputed to have said, according to the *Hadith*, "Allah will free from Hell, limb for limb." But during the 19th century, the inflexibility of Islamic law, the persistence of slave-owning within Islam and the growth of a passionate anti-slavery movement in Europe created a climate in which Islam's tolerance of slavery was perceived as a symptom of moral inferiority.

Such sentiments were exacerbated by a dynamic growth in Islam's African slave trade. Throughout its history, Islam—like other civilizations—had made use of slaves. The Umayyads, the Abbasids, the Seljuks and the Ottomans all relied on slave armies to fight their wars, and concubinage was endemic. On a lesser scale, many affluent Muslim households employed slaves domestically, and the evidence is that these were generally regarded as members of an extended family. Higher up, military slaves could rise to positions of power, while a ruler's favorite concubines were similarly advantaged. But behind what until modern times was a normative system of employment lay a much darker pattern. As the Russian

1909 Following further unrest in **Constantinople**, the Young Turks march on the city. Abdul Hamid II abdicates after failing to mount a counter-coup, and **Mehmed V** is enthroned in his place as little more than a figurehead, although his retention of the caliphal title allows the Young Turks, who now dominate parliament and gov-

and Austro-Hungarian empires grew, traditional sources of slaves collapsed, and increasingly Muslims looked to Africa to make up the balance.

Africa was also relentlessly plundered for slaves by European traders supplying the American market and it has been estimated that the number of Africans enslaved by each was similar: around thirteen million individuals apiece (albeit within differing time-frames). But the proportion of males to females was exactly opposite—2:1 in the American case, but 1:2 for Islam. Whereas the principal value of Africans in America was to provide labor for cotton and tobacco plantations, among 19th-century Muslims they were used for domestic service and sex.

Worse even than the fact of enslavement was the way in which slaves were recruited. Arab and Afro-Arab slave traders like **Tippu Tip** drove deep into sub-Saharan Africa, raiding (then destroying) countless villages for young women and boys. These were then herded across the desert, either to **Libya** or to notorious slave markets such as **Zanzibar** on the east coast. As many as twenty million died en route of exhaustion, starvation and disease.

Such practices were contrary to the Koran and the Shariah, but the purchase of slaves was not. The trade diminished with the spread of European influence, and by 1914 had ceased to be of primary economic importance. Yet even today, as Amnesty International and other human rights watchdogs attest, slavery remains legally permissible in two Muslim states, **Sudan** and **Mauritania**.

ernment alike, to appear more Islamic than in fact they are. While in the years leading up to World War I they press ahead with reforms, their foreign policy provokes a series of disasters for the Ottoman Empire.

In response to lobbying by the Muslim League, an **India Councils Act** passed by the British parliament stipulates separate constituencies and generally lower franchise qualifications for Muslims wishing to vote in forthcoming elections for an "Indian" advisory council. Some Hindus, feeling that the Muslim minority has obtained an unfair advantage, mount a short-lived **terror campaign** against the British Raj, calling for full and immediate independence.

1911 Italy seizes **Libya** and the **Dodecanese** islands in the Aegean from Ottoman control. European rule over Libya contributes to the demise of the African **slave trade**.

Slaves in chains, Zanzibar

1912 In October, the first of two **Balkan Wars** begins as the Ottoman empire's remaining Greek, Serbian and Bulgarian Christian subjects fight to overthrow Muslim rule (among other objectives).

In **Indonesia**, Ahmad Dahlan founds **Muhammadiyyah**—a reformist movement that aims to bring ordinary Indonesians closer to Islamic orthodoxy by establishing local schools and charitable foundations. Although at first it eschews politics, it will become associated with Islamic-nationalist resistance to Dutch rule and later spreads to British **Malaya**.

1913 The **First Balkan War** ends in May, but the **Second** begins in June and lasts six weeks. As a consequence, the Turks lose control of 80 percent of their remaining European possessions. **Salonika** and **Thrace** are attached to Greece and **Albania** becomes an independent state.

Ibn Saud captures the Arabian province of **Hasa** from the Ottomans and begins settling unruly desert Bedouin in communities known as *ikhwan* (brotherhoods). Each *ikhwan* is both a military camp and a center for the propagation of **Wahhabism** among its members.

Against a background of mounting Arab nationalism in **Syria**, **Palestine** and **Arabia**, the Ottoman empire is threatening to disintegrate. In Constantinople, the German inspector-general of the Ottoman army, **General Liman van Sanders**, encourages anti-British feeling and begins assuring the Turks of German friendship.

1914 Following the outbreak of **World War I** in Europe, each side attempts to secure strategic advantages by strengthening its international alliances. **Egypt** is formally declared a British protectorate, and **Persia** is occupied by British and Russian troops in order to guarantee oil supplies. Britain also "demands" Ottoman neutrality, but is thwarted by Germany, which forces the Young Turks' hand by dispatching warships to the **Bosporus**.

1915 Through its Indian viceroy, the British government enters into negotiations with Ibn Saud. An understanding is reached that Britain will broadly support **Arab independence** if the Arabs rebel against their Ottoman masters.

In April, hoping to open up a new front against Germany and perhaps take the Ottoman Empire out of the war, British and other Allied troops land on the **Gallipoli peninsula** but are immediately pinned down by Turkish forces under the command of **Mustafa Kemal**, who tells his own troops: "I do not order you to attack. I order you to die."

The Turks, accusing **Christian Armenians** of supporting Russia, launch a fresh persecution that leads to over 500,000 civilian deaths.

1916 In January, Britain abandons its **Gallipoli campaign** at great cost in lives and material.

Between May and October, a secret correspondence between the British, French and Russian governments establishes the **Sykes-Picot Agreement**, partitioning a post-war Arab world between a British "sphere of interest" to the south (including Palestine) and a French "sphere of interest" to the north.

In June, an **Arab Revolt** is proclaimed by the sharif of Mecca Hussein, whose son, **Prince Faisal**, takes command of a modest Arab army. Aided by the British officer **T.E. Lawrence**, Faisal overruns Ottoman garrisons at **Mecca**, **Jeddah** and **Taifa**.

1917 On November 2, the British government signals its support for a "national home for the Jewish people" in Palestine in the form of the **Balfour Declaration**, a letter sent by Foreign Secretary James Arthur Balfour to Lord Rothschild that incurs Arab anger when it is publicized by Russia later in the month. In Palestine itself, however, Arabs rejoice when **General Allenby** enters **Jerusalem** in October at the head of a mixed Arab-British force.

1918 In the largest land battle fought outside Europe during World War I, an Allied army under Allenby destroys what remains of the Ottoman empire's army during the **Battle of Megiddo** ("Armageddon," a name used to denote a large area of land in Palestine) in September. Allenby enters **Damascus**, then **Beirut** and **Aleppo**. On October 5 the Ottomans capitulate, marking the end of the war in the Middle East as well as the Ottoman empire itself. The French strongly object to Prince Faisal's raising of an Arab flag in those cities the Allies have captured, however.

CHAPTER NINE

From World War I to the Six Day War

{1918-67 (1296-1386AH)}

The two World Wars of the first half of the 20th century brought about profound geopolitical changes. Most significantly, for a variety of reasons the European colonial powers went into decline, and with them the empires they had built. In their place there emerged two rival "superpowers," the **United States of America** and the **USSR**, the latter based on the tsarist Russian empire of earlier centuries. But the rivalry between Washington and Moscow was different in kind to the rivalries previously experienced between, say, the Dutch and the English or the British and the French. At its heart was a bitter ideological conflict: Americans believed in participatory democracy and market capitalism; Russians in collectivized people power and a command economy based on state ownership of land and industry. It was not until the collapse of the Soviet Union in 1989 that the potentially catastrophic tensions generated by the mutual fear America and Russia had of one another began to dispel.

These and other global developments greatly affected the fortunes of Islam and its constituent peoples, sometimes for the better, sometimes for the worse. While in general the 20th century witnessed a gradual political recovery—independent Muslim nations increasingly governed by at least nominally autonomous Muslim leaderships—differences over what form a Muslim society should take became exacerbated; some preferring a modern, secularized state along either American or Soviet lines in which religion was largely sidelined, others an Islamist state in which Shariah law was fully articulated.

Post-1918, the most obvious and immediate alteration to the Muslim world was the break-up of the **Ottoman empire**, and, in 1924, the demise of the caliphate—such as it was. In Anatolia itself, and in a small area west of the Bosporus, the republican and distinctly secularist state of **Turkey** was forged by Mustafa Kemal, known from 1933 as **Atatürk**, or "father of the Turks." As significantly, other, predominantly Arab states came into being in territories formerly controlled by the Ottomans, largely as a result of the Arab Revolt that the British had backed during the Great War. In Arabia itself, **Ibn Saud** was able to create the kingdom of Saudi Arabia, covering 80 percent of the peninsula, while to the north of Arabia there emerged the discrete entities of **Palestine**, **Syria**, **Transjordan** and **Iraq**. For the time being, each of these subsisted under either a British or French "mandate," and the power exercised by their rulers was circumscribed. The existence of the two European mandates also enabled the creation of two non-Muslim states that, in the second half of the 20th century, were to become focal points for Islamic militancy: **Lebanon**, originally proposed by the French to protect its indigenous Christian Maronites, who had previously survived as an embattled minority within the Ottoman province of Syria; and **Israel**, the Jewish homeland created, at the expense of Palestine, in the aftermath of World War II after several decades of campaigning by Zionists in the USA and Europe.

Thus the present-day political geography of the Near and western Middle Easts was set up. Following World War II and the disappearance of the French and British mandates, Syria, Iraq and Transjordan (soon to be called **Jordan**), each acquired full **independence**. Elsewhere in Islam, a similar tendency prevailed. In 1947 **Pakistan** became a discrete Muslim state on the back of Britain's withdrawal from India. Further east, as anti-colonial sentiment hardened, **Malaysia** and **Indonesia** also became independent; as eventually did **Morocco**, **Algeria**, **Tunisia** and **Libya** in North Africa, where, under the guidance of Colonel Nasser in the 1950s, **Egypt** also finally shook free of British tutelage—a point driven home by the **Suez Crisis** of 1956, when Britain and France were both humiliated on the world stage.

These developments restored to the Muslim world some of its damaged confidence. Yet as the century progressed, such gains looked increasingly insecure. More and more, it seemed, the USA and USSR were prepared to take over where the European powers were leaving off. In reality, Nasser's triumph over Britain and France in 1956 was achieved only because America, anxious to contain growing Soviet aid to regimes in the Middle East by appeasing Egypt, threatened sanctions against its own Western allies. Three years previously, too, Washington had intervened directly in the affairs of **Iran** (the new name for Persia), restoring the autocratic shah Muhammad Reza after an attempted republican coup.

Successive US governments adapted quickly to the principle that defending America's perceived economic and political interests justified foreign intervention. In the case of Iran in 1953, the USA's motives were twofold: to ensure a "friendly" regime in a region where Soviet influence was on the make; and to protect its access to Iranian oil fields. But now even larger oil fields were opening up in the Arabian peninsula, both in Saudi Arabia and amongst such Gulf States as Kuwait and Bahrain, and it became a mainspring of America's post-World War II Middle Eastern policy to guarantee cheap **oil supplies** for its hungry domestic market—even if that meant upholding the power of unpopular, even corrupt, "local" rulers.

In time, this kind of manipulation was to give rise to an insistent anti-Americanism, at first in the Middle East, and then more diffusely throughout Islam. But it was not just a matter of oil—the "black gold" of the modern era—that fuelled ill-feeling among Muslims. There was also the question of **Israel**. The creation of a Jewish state in Palestine was only achieved after the US government persuaded the United Nations General Assembly to vote in its favor in 1947. At the time, the reasons for creating Israel were particularly compelling. Apart from the traditional Zionist argument that the Jewish people were entitled by right to a national homeland, the suffering of Jews during the Holocaust had generated widespread sympathy for their cause. But the decision to site the new nation state in **Palestine**, where Jews still only made up a minority of the population to a majority of Muslim Arabs, was taken with only the scantest reference to Arab—or indeed Muslim—sensibilities. The new state of Israel was formally declared by **David Ben Gurion** on 14 May 1948, and almost immediately recognized by President Harry S. Truman. But tensions between Jews and Palestinians had already erupted into fierce fighting, and in the same year, under the aegis of the **Arab League**, Egypt, Iraq, Jordan and Syria dispatched their forces into Israel in an unsuccessful attempt to assert Palestinian interests.

Nineteen years later, Egypt, Syria and Jordan again conspired to destroy Israel, only to be thwarted during the **Six Day War** by perhaps the most brilliant pre-emptive military strike of modern times. Not only did Israel survive, thanks in no small measure to the superiority of its American weaponry, but it seized control of the **West Bank** and **Gaza**—two previously autonomous Palestinian enclaves—as well as Syria's **Golan Heights**. Israel's victory was comprehensive and humiliating, and was widely perceived as a body-blow not just to Arab interests, but to Islam itself. Its net effect was to legitimate an Islamist movement that, often called "**Islamic fundamentalism**" by non-Muslims, rose to world prominence in the decades following 1967.

Islam's defeat, fundamentalists argued, had come about because too few Muslims abided by true Islamic values.

Such a movement did not spring up overnight, however. In a sense it had existed throughout Islam's history. More immediately, it was nourished by the **Muslim Brotherhood**, a group founded by Hasan al-Banna in Egypt in 1928, in the first instance to encourage ordinary Muslims to live upright, godly lives, but which quickly developed a wider, anti-secularist and finally militant agenda. Critically, in the late 1950s and early 1960s, the Muslim Brotherhood was persecuted by Colonel Nasser, who executed its leaders and imprisoned hundreds of its activists. Yet it was also Nasser who, more than any other Arab leader, had provoked the disastrous Six Day War. Although he survived in power until his death in 1970, his brand of "Arab socialism," to a degree modeled on Soviet practice, came under increasing scrutiny among thinking Muslims.

1918 As the **Ottoman empire** collapses with many of its provinces occupied by British, Russian, French and Italian forces, Greek troops begin seizing Turkish possessions in the **Aegean**. Mehmed V dies and is succeeded by his son **Mehmed VI**, the last of the Ottoman sultans.

Before the year is out, **Chaim Weizmann**, leader of a Zionist commission, arrives in Palestine to begin testing the Balfour Declaration of 1917, which "favored" a "national homeland" for **Jews**, to the dismay of Prince Faisal, the military commander of the 1916 Arab Revolt, and other Arab leaders.

1919 Following a conference convened by the Allies at **Versailles** in January, in which barely any Muslim representatives participate, a series of international treaties create a radically altered world order of frontiers and nations tailored to the interests of colonial powers including Britain, France and the Netherlands. In line with the

Sykes-Picot Agreement of 1916, **Syria** and **Lebanon** are mandated to France, while **Palestine** is mandated to Britain, which also gains control of **Iraq**, added to the British Raj in India as an administrative protectorate. **Persia** (Iran) is designated a British protectorate, too, although when this is rejected by the Iranian *majilis* (assembly), Britain withdraws its troops. In addition, an entirely new entity known as **Yugoslavia** is created in the Balkans, giving Serbs dominance over Croats as well as a residual Muslim population concentrated in **Bosnia-Herzogovina**. Versailles also brings about the death of the Austro-Hungarian empire, penalized for its wartime alliance with Germany. Among Arabs especially, these provisions cause lasting resentment, as the prospect of a single Arab polity recedes. In response, **Ibn Saud** prepares to expand his influence in the Arabian peninsula, while in Palestine a group calling itself the **Black Hand** (later "Self-Sacrificers"), motivated by nationalist and religious feelings, launches terrorist attacks against increasing numbers of **Jewish settlers**.

On April 10, nearly 400 peaceful protestors campaigning against the Raj are killed by British soldiers at **Jallianwala Park** in Amritsar, India—an atrocity that fuels demands for Indian independence and inspires the Muslim **Khilafat** movement, calling for a continuation of the Islamic caliphate, now under threat in Turkey, as well as an end to British rule.

Mustafa Kemal (later known as **Atatürk**) organizes effective military resistance to Greek attempts to invade what little remains of the Ottoman empire, and in so doing begins to forge the modern republic of **Turkey**.

During the **Third Anglo–Afghan War**, Afghanistan's independence under the Durrani dynasty is reasserted.

1920 In March, **Prince Faisal** is proclaimed "king of Syria" (including **Palestine**, **Lebanon** and a new territory called **Transjordan**) by an Arab assembly convened in Damascus. In April, an international conference, sponsored by the newly created **League of Nations**

and attended by delegates from France, Britain, Italy, Greece, Belgium and Japan, meets at **San Remo** and confirms the provisions of the Sykes-Picot Agreement. An anti-British uprising in **Iraq** follows in June. In July, France, refusing to acknowledge King Faisal's authority, occupies **Damascus**.

In Arabia, **Ibn Saud** overruns **Asir** province, south of Hijaz. Shortly afterwards he proclaims himself the sultan, or king, of **Najd** (northern Arabia).

1921 In February, a military coup in **Iran** curtails the powers of Shah Ahmad, forcing him to accept government by an elected assembly.

In March, following the **Cairo Conference**, Britain offers Faisal **Iraq**. He becomes king in August, heading a civilian administration under British military protection.

1922 Egypt, a full British protectorate since 1914, is granted nominal **independence**. Britain retains control over Egypt's (and also Sudan's) defense and foreign policy, however.

Mustafa Kemal secures the abdication of Mehmed VI as sultan, although Mehmed's cousin **Abdulmecid** continues as caliph.

To appease Arab sentiment, Britain secures the exclusion of Jewish settlers from **Transjordan**.

1923 In Iran, **Reza Khan**, a middle-ranking army officer and one of the leaders of the 1921 putsch, becomes prime minister.

Atatürk abolishes the Ottoman caliphate and proclaims the **Republic of Turkey**. As its president, he embarks on a radically secularist program of modernization. **Sharif Hussein**, the Hashimite guardian of Mecca, proclaims himself caliph in succession to Mehmed VI, but in October is ousted by Ibn Saud and his Wahhabi *ikhwan* supporters.

1925 In **Syria**, Sultan al-Atrash proclaims a republic. **Lebanon** continues under French control, however, while **Palestine** remains mandated to the British.

In **Iran**, Prime Minister Reza Khan, committed to a program of radical Westernization, persuades the majilis to depose Shah Ahmad, the last of the Qajar dynasty. In October, he becomes shah, thus instituting the **Pahlavi dynasty**—which increasingly incurs the acrimony of Iran's Shiite mullahs.

1926 In January, **Medina** and **Jeddah** surrender to Ibn Saud, who proclaims himself king of Hijaz and "Protector of the Holy Cities."

France imposes a **constitution** on Lebanon that divides the country between Christian Maronites, Shiite Druze and other Muslim representative constituencies, but tips the balance of power in the Maronites' favor.

MUSTAFA KEMAL "ATATÜRK" (1881–1938)

*F*ew people have shaped a nation to the extent that Mustafa Kemal shaped the **Republic of Turkey** following the collapse of the Ottoman Empire during World War I. Born in Salonika of humble stock, he enrolled at a military academy in Constantinople and served as a cavalry officer during the **Balkan Wars**—an experience that would prove invaluable both in 1915, when he was given command of the defense of Gallipoli against the British, and in 1916, when he halted a Russian advance towards Anatolia. It was in 1918, however, that he came fully into his own.

One of the revolutionary Young Turks who had reimposed constitutional government on the sultan in 1908, he became the natural leader of a faction determined to resist the imposition of any British or American mandate on Turkey and to prevent the involuntary disbandment of its armed forces. The following year, he severed his ties with the sultanate and called for a republican **National Congress** to meet at Ankara. Despite Britain's efforts to stop it, the Congress convened, and in 1920 Mustafa Kemal was proclaimed president.

1927 In the **Treaty of Jeddah**, Britain acknowledges Ibn Saud as king of Hijaz and Najd.

In Delhi, Muhammad Ilyas founds the **Tablighi Jamaat**, ("The Society for the Propagation of the Muslim Faith"), a non-militant, non-political body designed to reinforce the faith of Sunni Muslims "tempted" by Hindu culture. In time, the movement spreads in the Islamic world, especially in those countries where Muslims form a minority. While it retains its popular devotional character, it will sometimes be used by militants to maintain contact with each other—particularly after the Tablighs transfer their headquarters to **Raiwind** in Pakistan in the 1960s.

By defeating the Greeks, who had invaded Anatolia, and by pushing the French back into Syria, he gained first the soubriquet "savior of Istanbul" and then, in 1933, the even grander title of Atatürk—"father of the Turks."

In July 1923, Turkish independence was given international recognition by the **Treaty of Lausanne**. Mustafa Kemal remained Turkey's president until his death, nurturing the emergence of the first multi-party democracy in the Muslim world—one that would become, economically and militarily, progressively identified with the West. The tone of the new state was aggressively secularist. Atatürk suppressed both the Sufi orders and the madrasas, turning the Sofia mosque into a museum, while the Shariah courts were replaced with civil courts. But the most far-reaching reforms were educational. New government schools relegated religious instruction to the margins of their curricula, and from 1928 the Roman alphabet replaced Arabic script for writing Turkish. The Turkish language itself was radically "modernized," being purged of its Arab loan-words—and therefore many of its Islamic nuances.

Kemal Atatürk, 1934

"Bung" Sukarno, campaigning against Dutch colonial rule, founds the **National Party of Indonesia**, a broad-based movement that includes communists as well as Muslims.

1928 The independence of **Transjordan** (later Jordan), previously a province of Syria, is assured by British guarantees given to its ruler, the amir—and from 1946 king—**Abdullah**, a Hashimite leader expelled from Saudi Arabia by Ibn Saud in 1925.

In Egypt, **Hasan al-Banna** founds al-*Ikhwan al-Musilimun* ("The Society of Muslim Brothers"), known as the **Muslim Brotherhood**, at Ismailiyyah in the Suez Canal Zone. Although at first the declared aims of the Brotherhood are limited to reviving the faith of workers and students, it becomes both an important political party in Egypt and a vehicle for the dissemination of an Islamist ideology in the Arab world and beyond.

1929 Attacks on the growing number of Jewish settlers in Palestine escalate following a dispute in Jerusalem about the **Western (Wailing) Wall**—regarded by Jews as part of Herod's Temple, and by Muslim Arabs as part of the Islamic haram, or sanctuary prohibited to non-believers.

In Arabia, the Bedouin *ikhwan* created by Ibn Saud revolt against him. With the help of the British army in Iraq, and using machine-guns against sabers, Ibn Saud defeats them at **Sibilla**. The *ikhwan* settlements are dismantled, and a marginally less severe form of **Wahhabism** applied in Ibn Saud's domains.

1930 Under the aegis of its French High Commissioner, the Arab republic in Syria acquires a parliamentary **constitution**.

An **Anglo-Iraq Treaty** of June 30 confirms the independence of Iraq under its ruler King Faisal I, although Britain continues to provide military "protection" which includes the policing of the **Shatt al-Arab**—the waterway at the confluence of the Tigris and Euphrates rivers giving access to Iraq's inland ports.

In December, **Muhammad Iqbal**, acting president of the Muslim League in India, calls for the creation of an autonomous Muslim homeland comprising Punjab, Sind, Baluchistan and the Northwest Frontier Province—in essence the territory of modern **Pakistan**.

In Detroit, the elusive Wallace D. Fard founds the **Nation of Islam**, the principal organization of the **Black Muslim** movement in the USA during the 20th century.

THE MUSLIM BROTHERHOOD

*W*hen Hasan al-Banna founded the Muslim Brotherhood in March 1928, he was employed by the Egyptian government as a schoolteacher. Working in the British-occupied Suez Canal Zone, he observed the lack of moral and spiritual energy among ordinary Egyptians, and became determined to bring about change.

Al-Banna was inspired by al-Afghani, by his follower Muhammad Abdu (1849–1905), and also by Rashid Rida (1865–1935), who, in his 1922 book *Al-Khalifa*, had called for a supreme Muslim leader who would have sufficient wisdom and learning to adapt the Shariah to contemporary needs. Putting the ideas of his mentors into practice, al-Banna created a mutual society that combined religious instruction with the requirements of a modern technical education, and which provided basic social welfare to its members. By 1940 the Brotherhood boasted five hundred branches, with a headquarters in Cairo since 1933. The Brotherhood's success under the double duress of "imperialist" British and "corrupt" Egyptian rule was also due to its pyramidical structure. Brothers belonged to cells, or "families," which in turn belonged to "clans" and then "battalions." At the same time, younger male members were encouraged

1931 The British prime minister Ramsay MacDonald writes to Chaim Weizmann what will become known among Arab Muslims as the "**Black Letter**," offering unambiguous support for the development of a Jewish homeland in Palestine, where Izz al-Din al-Qassam declares a *jihad* against Jewish immigrant settlers.

---

to undergo physical training, later put to militant uses, as part of their moral rearmament.

Initially the Brotherhood was not "militant"—in the sense of seeking the institution of a full Islamic state by the violent overthrow of the existing state—but as it gathered momentum as a "mass" party, it developed a militant wing, particularly in 1943 with the creation of a "Secret Apparatus" that quickly became involved in political assassinations. In 1948, the Egyptian prime minister, Mahmoud Fahmi Nuqrashi, was murdered by a Brother. In the end, though, it was failed assassination attempts against President Nasser that had the greater impact. The clampdown on the Brotherhood's activities that followed turned the Brotherhood into an internationalist body that agitated for Islamic revolution throughout the Middle East and beyond. Those who escaped Nasser's net fled to other Arab countries, while one of his detainees, Sayyid Qutb, spent his time in prison writing what would become the classic contemporary statement of Islamic "fundamentalism." While such developments were perhaps implicit in the Brotherhood's original slogan—"the Koran is our constitution"—what is striking is that Sunni Islam's leading 20th-century hardline sect was pioneered not by clerics, but by laymen.

1932 Ibn Saud, now in control of 80 percent of the Arabian peninsular, unifies his domains into a single kingdom, **Saudi Arabia**, which is formally proclaimed on September 22, with Ibn Saud its first monarch. In the same year, the discovery of sizeable **oil reservoirs** in Bahrain heralds the emergence of the Arabian peninsula as a major

THE HOUSE OF SAUD

*N*early two centuries after a small-time desert ruler, Muhammad ibn Saud, offered the fugitive sectarian Abd al-Wahhab refuge at Diriyyah, the distinctly Wahabbist Kingdom of Saudi Arabia came into being. Ever since, it has remained a bastion of Islamic conservatism—a country where, as Muhammad intended, observance of any other religion is prohibited and the strictest of the Shariah law codes is applied. Beheadings provide a regular public spectacle, women and sometimes men are stoned to death for adultery, and amputation of the hands for theft is commonplace. In the cities, the streets are patrolled by *mutawin* ("enforcers of obedience" or religious police), and an Islamic dress code that includes the obligatory wearing of the veil by women is rigorously upheld. Since the oil boom of the 1970s, tens of thousands of foreign workers have been imported into Saudi Arabia to work on oil rigs, on construction sites or as domestic servants. But though the wages can be good, few depart with happy memories—particularly if they have fallen foul of draconian prohibitions against alcohol.

Yet, among Islamic extremists especially, notably Osama bin Laden, all this is seen as a sham. The ruling elite—mostly blood relatives of the king—are presumed to enjoy luxurious and distinctly un-Muslim lifestyles within their high-walled compounds, a suggestion corroborated by the black-oil producer alongside Iran and Iraq. Standard Oil and the Texas Oil Company are among American refiners who join an international scramble for concessions.

1933 As Adolf Hitler's National Socialist Party begins persecuting Jews in **Germany**, **Jewish immigration** to Palestine further intensifies.

windowed limousines they are driven around in and the persistent allegations of embezzlement and other forms of corruption. Whereas the House of Saud has spent billions of "petro-dollars" funding *jihad* in Afghanistan, the *intifada* against Israel and mosques in Europe and America, as many billions, it is said, have been squandered on personal luxuries.

The tone was set by the founding monarch, **Abd al-Aziz ibn Saud** (1880–1953), a man of prodigious intelligence, energy—and appetites. Taking advantage of the crumbling Ottoman empire, Ibn Saud looked to Wahhabism to underwrite his conquests. His masterstroke was to settle the nomadic Bedouin in puritanical *ikhwan* settlements ("brotherhoods"). But when in 1929 he discovered their zeal could not so easily be suppressed, he concerted with the British in Iraq to crush them. Commandeering every civilian motorcar in Jeddah he could find, he drove into the desert to shoot men on camel-back with machine-guns.

Ibn Saud was also adept at outsmarting his own puritanical *ulama*. When the clerics said the radio was satanic, Ibn Saud riposted by broadcasting the Koran from Riyadh. When they said photography transgressed Islamic injunctions against the representation of humans, he persuaded them that a photograph was merely microscopic units of light and shade juxtaposed. In the meantime, he was busy fathering 269 children by seventeen wives—six more than Muhammad had allowed himself.

Ibn Saud sells the **Standard Oil Company** of California a sixty-year concession to extract oil in Saudi Arabia. Oil is also discovered in the British Gulf protectorate **Kuwait**. Not until after 1945 will the Middle East displace the USA as the world's largest oil exporter, however.

In America, Wallace D. Fard vanishes and **Elijah Muhammad** (Elijah Poole) becomes leader of the Nation of Islam.

1934 Britain guarantees the independence of **Yemen** in southern Arabia, but retains **Aden** as a colonial possession.

1936 Persia is officially renamed **Iran** on March 21.

1937 Supported by Britain, Iraq secures additional navigation rights in the **Shatt al-Arab**, previously contested by neighbouring Iran.

In Palestine, David Raziel founds **Irgun Zvai Leumi** ("The National Military Organization), a militant Zionist organization designed to inflict similar terror on Arabs as Arabs have inflicted on Jews.

1939 In May, the British government, on the brink of war with Germany and therefore anxious to promote Anglo-Arab friendship, begins back-pedaling on its commitment to a Jewish national homeland. Zionist militants respond by orchestrating a fresh **terror campaign** in Palestine in which 38 Arab civilians are killed. While **Iraq** supports Britain after Britain **declares war** on Germany on September 3, **Turkey** remains neutral.

1940 As **France** falls to Nazi Germany, the French mandates in Syria and Lebanon come under German control.

In Palestine, Abraham Stern forms a second militant Zionist group, the *Lohame Herut Israel* ("Fighters for the Freedom of Israel," better known as the **Stern Gang**), dedicated to reversing Britain's revisionist policy and challenging the policies of Jewish moderates.

In India, the Muslim League adds **East Bengal** to the territories it seeks to incorporate in a separate Muslim state once India achieves independence.

1941 In March, **Rashid Ali**, a supporter of Germany, stages a coup in **Iraq**, but is overthrown by the British, who restore the authority of King Faisal II and Prime Minister Nuri al-Said.

In June, Britain detaches Syria and Lebanon from German diplomatic influence. **Lebanese independence** is proclaimed, backed by a new constitution the following year affirming the Christian **Maronites'** marginal majority over the **Druze** and other Muslims.

British and Russian forces occupy **Iran** after it becomes apparent that Reza Shah is colluding with Germany. In September, Reza Shah is replaced by his Anglophile son **Muhammad Reza**.

In **India**, as hopes spread that Britain will concede independence once the war with Germany is concluded, the Islamist **Sayyid Abu al-Ala Mawdudi** founds the **Jamaat-i Islami**, a party dedicated to the creation of an Islamist state for India's Muslims separate from any Hindu state.

1942 In **Egypt**, where Britain's presence has been increased during the "desert war" against Germany in Libya and Tunisia, the Muslim Brotherhood establishes a clandestine group for the "defense of Islam" and begins giving **military training** to some of its members.

1943 The **Free French** under Charles de Gaulle, working with Britain and the USA to liberate France, acknowledge the independence of **Lebanon** and **Syria**.

As details of the **Jewish holocaust** in Europe are publicized in the UK and the USA, American Zionists lobby politicians in Washington for the creation of a Jewish state in Palestine.

1944 In March, Irgun Zvai Leumi, now under the direction of **Menachem Begin**, begins a bombing campaign against British targets. On March 23, the Stern Gang murders seven British policemen in Tel Aviv. In October, President Roosevelt commits himself to the creation of a "Jewish commonwealth" in Palestine. In November, the British minister resident in the Middle East, **Lord Moyne**, is assassinated by the Stern Gang in Cairo.

> Islam is different from Judaism; Islam, being a universal submission to God, has no concept of a particular Covenant or a specially chosen people. It also differs from the Christian view of the Kingdom of God in heaven and the separate kingdom of Caesar on earth. And it differs from other religions, such as Buddhism and Hinduism. Islam is a faith, a law, a way of life, a "nation" and a "state," with a system of jurisprudence that is continually evolving for the administration of this world and the satisfaction of human needs under the sovereignty of our Creator. Islam's Kingdom of God on earth, with its faith, its laws, piety, rituals, society and state, is the prelude and the means to the afterlife.
>
> —Abd-al-Rahman Azzam,
> *The Eternal Message of Muhammad* (1946)
> trans. Caesar E. Farrah

The **Arabian American Oil Company**, known as ARAMCO, a consortium of leading US oil companies, is formed to protect American oil interests in the Middle East after it is forecast that domestic oil production will be insufficient to meet the needs of the American economy.

1945 Even though World War II has turned decisively against Germany, **Turkey** joins the Axis alliance. When the war ends, the independence of Iraq, Iran, Syria, Transjordan, Lebanon and Egypt is affirmed, although in **Egypt** the British retain a military presence in the Suez Canal Zone. As the scale of the Jewish Holocaust and the need to resettle 100,000 **Jewish refugees** become apparent, Britain realigns its policy with America and renews its support for the creation of a Jewish state. Jewish terrorists continue their activities against British installations notwithstanding.

Abd al-Rahman Azzam founds the **Arab League** to foster and co-ordinate Arab interests in the Middle East, and is appointed its first secretary-general.

In **Indonesia**, occupied by Japan during the war, the nationalist leader **Sukarno** proclaims **independence** from Dutch rule on 17 August.

1946 In January, the first meetings of the **United Nations** General Assembly and Security Council are held in London. Set up to resolve international conflicts, the UN quickly attracts the membership of most Muslim-majority nations, even though some subsequent UN charters, including the **Universal Declaration of Human Rights** of 1948, are in some respects at odds with Islamic precepts.

In **India**, there is communal rioting between Hindus and Muslims as the Muslim League launches a "Direct Action to Achieve Pakistan." In August, more than 3000 are killed in **Calcutta**.

On July 22, following a British crackdown against Jewish militants, 91 are killed when Zionists blow up part of the King David Hotel in **Jerusalem**, which is being used as a British military headquarters. Despite widespread outrage, as the **Jewish Uprising** gathers momentum, British politicians begin arguing for a withdrawal from Palestine.

In October, ahead of US presidential elections, President Harry Truman puts his weight behind a plan to partition **Palestine** into Jewish and non-Jewish sectors.

The Hashimite kingdom of **Transjordan** is enlarged to include the "**West Bank**" territory of Palestine. As a result, Arab Palestinians make up half of Jordan's total population.

1947 As unrest in **Palestine** grows and it transpires that some Jewish extremists are receiving support from America, Britain refers the matter of creating a Jewish state to the United Nations. In August, the UN debates the American plan to divide non-Jordanian Palestine into two states, one Jewish and one Muslim-Arab, and on November 29 the General Assembly votes in favor of **partition** after the Jewish delegation gives assurances that non-Jews will be protected in Jewish territories. According to the provisions adopted, the Jews are to govern 55 percent of Palestine, even though they own less than 10 percent of the land and constitute less than a third of the population. In response, the Grand Mufti of Jerusalem issues a *fatwa* against Zionists. In December Jewish-Arab tensions erupt into **open warfare**. Although outnumbered, the Jews defend their settlements with clandestinely acquired Russian arms. Britain deploys its forces as peacekeepers, but when these come under fire from both sides, begins withdrawing them, thus abandoning its mandate.

INDONESIA

*W*ith its 200 million-plus inhabitants, 88 percent of whom are Muslim, Indonesia today hosts Islam's largest single population. Made up of over 13,000 islands, the nation itself was gradually forged under Dutch colonial rule from the 17th century onwards, reaching its current boundaries towards the end of the 19th century. In World War II Indonesia fell under Japanese occupation, and it was Japan's defeat that gave the nationalist politician "Bung" ("comrade") Sukarno a window of opportunity. In 1945 he proclaimed the country's independence, and successfully fought off Dutch attempts to reinstate their authority during a four-year war.

But independence brought with it problems that have bedeviled Indonesia ever since. To gain victory, Sukarno created a coalition which included nationalists, Islamists and communists, but it broke down in 1965, when Sukarno was sidelined by his deputy Suharto. To underpin his own dictatorship, Suharto, already courting the USA and attracting Muslim support,

On August 15, **India** gains **independence** from Britain and **Pakistan** comes into being, Britain having acquiesced to Muslim demands for a separate state. Based mainly on religious majorities, Pakistan consists of two territories, **West Pakistan**, including Punjab, and **East Pakistan**, comprising East Bengal and part of Assam. Although the population of East Pakistan is greater, the capital is sited at Karachi, where a government under **Muhammad Ali Jinnah** is installed.

The partition of India is attended by mass **migrations** of Hindus and Muslims between India and Pakistan in both directions, and also by extreme "communal" agitation during which half a million people die. Relations are further soured when Maharaja Hari Singh, the "princely ruler" of Muslim-majority **Jammu and Kashmir**, chooses

ordered a crackdown against communists. But when it transpired that Suharto had no great devotion to Islam, much of his subsequent reign was spent combating a rise in Islamist extremism.

Indonesia's recent history has been one of constant infighting. Christian minorities have been regularly persecuted—usually with the state turning a blind eye—and Indonesia's Chinese business community, known as *kukongs*, has also had a rough ride. Yet though the general drift seems to be towards the inculcation of stricter Islamic values among Indonesia's majority Muslim population against a backdrop of endemic corruption, that too can be misleading. An important strand in Indonesia's labyrinthine makeup is a tension between traditional or *abangan* Muslims, mixing Islam with pre-Islamic animism, and a new breed of orthodox, hardline Muslims, often primed by overseas ideologues. Today, Suharto may have gone, but his successors still play off A against B against C against A.

to join India, not Pakistan, after "Pakistani tribals" seize the state capital **Srinagar** in October.

1948 As fighting in Palestine intensifies, Jewish forces take possession of **Haifa** and **Jaffa** in April as British troops withdraw. In the same month, Zionist terrorists massacre 250 Arab civilians at **Deir Yassin**. The Arabs retaliate by murdering 77 Israeli

---

INDIA, PAKISTAN AND KASHMIR

*A*lthough the British were as responsible as anyone for bringing down the once-mighty Mughal throne, for many Muslims the prospect of Britain withdrawing from India was a mixed blessing, since that would subject them to the will of a Hindu majority. For several generations after the Great Uprising of 1857, therefore, Indian Muslim politics lacked coherence and direction. But a radical change came about in 1930 when **Muhammad Iqbal** (1873–1938) called for a separate Muslim state. This now became the ambition of Muslim activists, and culminated in the creation of **Pakistan** in 1947.

Yet the addition of a new Muslim nation to Islam has been fraught with problems. Within Pakistan itself there has been lasting disagreement over the nature of the state itself—whether it should follow the nationalist-secularist lead given by its founder, **Muhammad Ali Jinnah** (1875–1948), or become a fully Islamic state of the sort urged by **Sayeed Abu al-Ala Mawdudi** (1903–79), a utopian religious ideologue regarded by some as the equal of Sayyid Qutb. While successive regimes have alternated between these positions, two very different border problems have exacerbated unrest.

To the west of Pakistan lies **Afghanistan**, the site not only of the victorious *jihad* against the USSR in the 1980s, but of more recent Islamist movements including the Taliban and Osama bin Laden's *al-Qaeda* network. Since

doctors and nurses in Jerusalem as Britain evacuates its forces from the city. On May 14 **David Ben Gurion** proclaims the state of **Israel** inside Palestine. Almost immediately, Israel is recognized by **President Truman**, and shortly afterwards by **Joseph Stalin**, anxious that the USSR's unwanted Jews have somewhere to go.

some tribes, notably the Pashtun, straddle a notoriously uncontrollable frontier, it has been inevitable that religious and political clashes have entered Pakistan by the side door, encouraged by a phenomenal growth in "extremist" madrasas between Quetta and Peshawar.

Similar passions have fuelled conflict to the east, in Kashmir. In 1947 it was decided that the rulers of several "princely states" could decide whether to join India or Pakistan. The Hindu ruler of Kashmir and Jammu, **Maharaja Hari Singh**, chose to disregard the affinities of his Muslim-majority people and align his state with India. Since then, Muslim "separatists," their ranks recently swollen by *jihadists* returning from Afghanistan—and sometimes backed by Pakistan's armed forces—have intermittently fought to overturn Indian rule. But India refuses either to give up its legal right or to settle the dispute by calling a referendum, and in recent years the Kashmiri conflict has taken India and Pakistan to the brink of nuclear warfare. In 1971, the two nations did actually resort to arms following India's support for the Awami League of East Pakistan—which, as a result of a comprehensive Indian victory, separated from West Pakistan to become **Bangladesh**. For Pakistanis, and for some Indian Muslims (who comprise 10 percent of India's billion-odd inhabitants), it was a defeat that could be neither forgotten nor forgiven.

Ben Gurion's proclamation provokes the **First Arab–Israeli War** as Israel's neighboring Arab nations take collective action, guided by the Arab League. Egyptian, Iraqi, Syrian and Jordanian forces converge on Israel, but are repulsed. Ben Gurion capitalizes upon Israel's success by extending Israeli authority over a much larger area of Palestine than previously agreed by the UN General Assembly, so that only two fully Palestinian enclaves survive—the **West Bank** (under Jordanian administration) and the **Gaza Strip**. As a result, up to 750,000 Muslims **flee Palestine**, creating an enduring refugee problem. Some settle in the West Bank, others in Jordan itself, and in Lebanon, where, as a result, the Christian Maronites eventually cease to be a majority. The Israeli victory encourages the further immigration of Jews.

In September, UN representative **Count Bernadotte** is assassinated by Zionist terrorists, following which Ben Gurion orders the dissolution of Irgun and the Stern Gang.

As Muslim insurgency in **Kashmir** escalates, the UN Security Council passes a resolution calling for an immediate ceasefire and a **referendum** to determine the wishes of the Kashmiri people.

In December, a Muslim Brotherhood member assassinates the Egyptian prime minister **Mahmoud Fahmi Nuqrashi**.

1949 Following a ceasefire, UN peacekeepers establish a **Line of Control** in **Kashmir** on January 1. Although Muslims constitute 77 percent of Kashmir's population, they are left with less than 40 percent of its land.

The **First Arab–Israeli War** ends on February 24 when Israel and Egypt agree a ceasefire, followed by "supplementary" agreements with Syria, Iraq and Jordan. Syrian politics become destabilized as a result of what is perceived as an ignominious defeat, and Iraq dissociates itself from Britain.

Transjordan is officially renamed **Jordan** on June 2.

Hasan al-Banna, founder of the Muslim Brotherhood, is murdered with the complicity of the Egyptian government. His successor as "Supreme Guide" of the Brotherhood is the moderate **Hassan al-Hudaybi**.

1950 The United States, Britain and France reach a **Tripartite Agreement** whereby each party concedes the need to supply arms to both Israel and the Arab states in order to help achieve a "legitimate self-defense" capacity.

Following a four-year war during which it has failed to reimpose colonial rule over **Indonesia**, the Dutch government concedes Indonesian independence in August. Sukarno becomes Indonesia's first president.

As Middle Eastern **oil exports** grow, Saudi Arabia, Kuwait and other Arab oil producers seek the renegotiation of existing concessions with Western companies. Since Arab demands are generally limited to a 50 percent share of profits, the Western companies find compliance relatively pain-free.

1951 In **Iran**, against a background of mounting opposition to **oil concessions** granted by Muhammad Reza Shah, the prime minister General Razmara is assassinated by a Shiite extremist in March. As revolt against the shah spreads, in April the Iranian parliament (*majilis*) proclaims **Muhammad Musaddiq**, leader of the opposition National Front Party, prime minister. Despite international protests, Musaddiq announces the nationalization of Iran's oil reservoirs. Britain, largely dependent on Iranian oil imports, introduces **petrol rationing**.

King Abdullah of Jordan is assassinated at the al-Aqsa mosque in Jerusalem by a Palestinian youth resentful of his "pan-Arab" policies, which seem to ignore the plight of Arab Palestinians living under Israeli rule.

1952 At the instigation of the Muslim Brotherhood, civil unrest erupts in **Egypt**. On January 26, during the "**Black Saturday Riots**," British commercial interests in the capital are looted and eighteen Britons killed. On the back of these "anti-imperialist" episodes, on

23 **Gamal Abdul Nasser** stages a coup, apparently led by General Muhammad Neguib at the head of a group of "Free Officers," against the pro-British **King Farouk**, who is forced into exile. While Neguib becomes prime minister, it is Nasser who immediately implements a "revolutionary" agenda of social and agrarian reform, known as **Arab Socialism**.

In **Iran**, Muhammad Reza Shah attempts to replace Muzaddiq as prime minister with his own nominee Ahmad Qavan, but Muzaddiq is reinstated following riots in the capital **Tehran** and other cities.

GAMAL ABDUL NASSER
(1918–70)

*A*n admirer of Atatürk, Nasser was the strongman of post-colonial Egypt, and, as he habitually emphasized, was a "true" Egyptian, the son of a post office manager. After failing as a law student, he enrolled in the army, and it was while on duty in Sudan that he formed the secretive **Free Officers**, committed to getting rid of both the British and the "puppet" monarchy, and whose members included his eventual successor **Anwar Sadat**. The 1952 coup that established a "Revolutionary Command Council" was Nasser's inspiration, although his colleague Muhammad Neguib assumed visible power until 1954. In the years that followed, Nasser improvised a socialist state that developed strong ties with the USSR and cracked down hard on the Muslim Brotherhood. Yet his ambitions were scarcely limited to ruling Egypt. In *Philosophy of the Revolution*, an extraordinary book purportedly authored by Nasser and published as early as 1954, he set his sights on three major objectives: the

Turkey joins **NATO** (the North Atlantic Treaty Organization), a Western military compact designed to contain the Russian communist empire, the USSR.

The British-educated **Prince Hussein** becomes king of **Jordan** following a period of political unrest in his country.

1953 In June, **Egypt** is proclaimed a republic with Neguib as president and Nasser vice-president. In July, a series of **bombings** against American and British offices in Cairo is at first thought to be the handiwork of Islamist extremists but later exposed as the machinations of Israeli agents.

creation of a pan-Arab state; the advancement of Egypt as the controlling power of Muslim Africa as far south as Rhodesia (present-day Zimbabwe); and the eventual unification of the whole of Islam under his aegis.

In none of these was Nasser ever more than marginally successful, although his ability to outsmart both Britain and France during the Suez Crisis of 1956 made him the hero of the Middle East—a reputation he retained up to and beyond the disastrous Six Day War against Israel in 1967. Offering his resignation in the immediate aftermath of defeat, the streets of Cairo were jam-packed with adoring followers clamouring for him to stay in power—his opponents did not turn out because most of them were languishing in desert prison-camps or had fled the country. Nasser survived through a combination of charisma, cunning and a ruthless domestic intelligence network; but as soon as he was dead, the defining conflict between secularism and Islamism began to tear Egypt apart.

In **Iran**, Musaddiq is dismissed by Muhammad Reza Shah in July after soliciting Soviet aid, and the "royalist" General Zahedi is appointed prime minister in his place. Following mass riots, Zahedi is forced to take refuge in the US embassy, and the shah absconds to Rome. On August 19, however, elements of the Iranian military, supported by American and British intelligence agencies, move against Muzaddiq, and on the 22nd Muhammad Reza Shah returns to **Tehran**. Zahedi resumes office and the US government announces an "aid" package worth $45 million, more than matched by fresh concessions soon granted to American oil conglomerates.

In **Syria**, following the overthrow of the dictator Adib Shisakli, the **Baath party** (a "pan-Arab" socialist movement founded in 1947) comes to power in Damascus.

1954 Vice-President Nasser of Egypt openly offers his support for anti-British Mau-Mau rebels in **Kenya** in July. In October, following an attempt on his life, Nasser orders a mass-roundup of members of the **Muslim Brotherhood**; some are executed, others imprisoned. A few escape to Saudi Arabia, Syria, Jordan and other Muslim countries, so that Nasser's action in effect promotes the dissemination of the Brotherhood's Islamist ideology. In the same month, Britain agrees to withdraw its troops from the Suez Canal Zone within twenty months. In November, Nasser accuses President Neguib of complicity with the Muslim Brotherhood; Neguib is overthrown and Nasser becomes head of state.

In **Iran**, Muhammad Reza Shah renegotiates Britain's **oil concessions** in line with the principle of "nationalization."

A new multinational consortium is formed with the participation of American, Dutch and French companies. As a result, the USA becomes the dominant external partner in Middle Eastern oil production. Around this time, it is estimated that oil reservoirs in the Middle East account for some 75 percent of the world's total.

In **Algeria**, the secularist **FLN** (*Front de Libération Nationale*) begins an eight-year revolt against French colonial rule.

As British power wanes, **Sudan** achieves nominal independence from Egypt.

1955 As **Israel** adopts a proactive approach towards its Arab enemies, an Israeli commando force storms an Egyptian training camp in **Gaza**, killing 38. In response, Egyptian *fedayeen* ("self-sacrificers" or "suicide units") begin a campaign against Israeli military targets. As the likelihood of all-out war escalates, Israel secures a series of arms deals with the USA and other Western nations. Nasser attempts to do the same, but is forced to depend on the USSR for arms supplies.

1956 In March, King Hussein of Jordan dismisses the British-born commander-in-chief of his army, **Sir John Glubb**, in the face of burgeoning "anti-imperialist" sentiments among his subjects.

In June, the last British troops evacuate the **Suez Canal Zone**. In July Nasser provokes an international crisis by **nationalizing** the Canal, even though the Anglo-French concession on it has another twelve years to run. As **Britain** and **France** consider military action, Egypt boycotts an international conference in August convened to resolve the dispute. Fearing a wider conflagration, the US urges restraint. As negotiations stall, the French conspire with **Israel** to devise a campaign that will incapacitate Nasser's forces. On October 29 Israel occupies the **Sinai Desert**, its army advancing to within 30 miles of the Canal, and two days later Anglo-French forces attack Egyptian airfields, but these actions are condemned by the US at the United Nations early in November. On November 4 Nasser orders the Canal to be blocked with ships deliberately sunk for the purpose, and British and French paratroopers land at Port Said the following day. The **USSR** threatens to intervene, but is diverted by an uprising in Hungary. US President **Dwight Eisenhower**, meanwhile, imposes economic sanctions against Britain and France, forcing them to declare a "ceasefire," and on November 15 UN peace-keeping forces begin arriving in Egypt. Britain and France agree to withdraw their forces on December 3, and the UN peacekeep-ers enter the Canal Zone to ensure the international viability of the Canal itself.

As a result of the **Suez Crisis**, Nasser's standing in the Arab–Muslim world is greatly enhanced, while the humiliated British prime minis-ter, **Sir Anthony Eden**, is forced to resign. Israel remains in the Sinai Desert, however, and prevents the Egyptian military from developing its influence in the Gaza strip.

Morocco ceases to be a French protectorate and becomes a fully independent state ruled by **King Muhammad V**, a monarch who enjoys the support of his country's *ulama*.

1957 In January, the newly re-elected US president sets out the **Eisenhower Doctrine**, which promises military and economic aid to any nation willing to combat the spread of Soviet-backed commu-

---

In Muslim society the family will always care for its old people, its orphans, its idiots, its ne'er-do-wells and even its delinquents. In this it offers a marked contrast to the modern West, where relatives are all too often looked upon as disagreeable acquaintances and where the misfits are frequently left to their fate or thrust into public institutions. If Islam is not a welfare state, it at least produces whole welfare families where everyone is cared for whether they deserve it or not.

—Sir John Bagot Glubb,
The Great Arab Conquest (1963)

nism—an initiative that opens the way for American assistance to Egypt and other Muslim states.

With the help of the CIA and Israel's security service Mossad, Muhammad Reza Shah creates **SAVAK**, an Iranian intelligence outfit that will become a main instrument in the shah's "neo-imperialist" repression of Iranian dissidents.

As disputes about access to new **oil fields** in Arabia multiply, Saudi Arabia launches an attack against **Oman**, but this is repulsed with British assistance.

King Hussein of **Jordan** renounces protection treaties with Britain in effect since 1946, and enters into an Arab alliance with Syria, Egypt and Saudi Arabia. The USA prevents Jordan from developing links with the USSR, however.

As anti-Israeli *fedayeen* cells are established in Jordan, Iraq and Syria, **al-Fatah** (the Palestinian National Liberation Movement) is founded with Nasser's backing by Palestinian nationalists living in Cairo, among them **Yasser Arafat**.

In **Malaya**, during a hotly contested war against mainly Chinese communist insurgents, Britain agrees to grant independence to a confederation of sultanates led by **Tunku Abd al-Rahman**. In the newly created nation of **Malaysia**, Muslims make up a slender majority of the population, which includes significant numbers of Hindu Tamil Indians as well as ethnic Chinese.

1958 On February 1, Egypt and Syria declare themselves a **United Arab Republic** at Nasser's initiative, designed to counter American and British influence.

In May, unrest begins in **Lebanon** between Arab nationalists and the pro-Western Christian Maronite followers of President **Camille Chamoun**, who in July requests American aid. President Eisenhower responds by sending 10,000 marines to restore order.

In the same month, a military coup led by **Abd al-Qarim Qasim** (Karim Kassem) establishes a republican government in **Iraq** following the assassination of King Faisal II and Prime Minister Nuri al-Said. Qasim renounces Iraq's ties with Britain and proclaims its support for Egypt.

Fearing that a similar coup may occur in **Jordan**, already destabilized by clashes between Jordanians and Palestinians, King Hussein requests the help of **British troops** to safeguard his throne, which in turn prompts Nasser to visit Moscow in secret to garner Soviet support for his "Arab revolution."

Elsewhere, General Muhammad Ayub Khan, a "secularist," comes to power in **Pakistan** (and will remain in power for eleven years), and oil is discovered in **Libya**.

1959 Nasser's United Arab Republic falters after members of Syria's Baath party question the Egyptian leader's ultimate objectives. Leading cadres of the Baath party in Iraq, among them **Saddam Hussein**, are exiled after an attempt on the life of Prime Minister Qasim.

1960 Following a Saudi Arabian initiative, the Organization of Oil Producing Countries (**OPEC**) is founded in Baghdad with the aim of co-ordinating crude oil prices and protecting the interests of member states. The original members of the cartel include Saudi Arabia, Iraq, Iran, Kuwait and Venezuela.

In **Indonesia**, President Sukarno disbands the **Masjumi**, the main Islamic political party.

1961 In **Iran**, Muhammad Reza Shah launches his pro-Western "**White Revolution**," in part designed to undermine the authority of Iran's clerics.

In September, **Syria** abandons Nasser's United Arab Republic and reasserts its independence, leading Nasser to realign his foreign policy towards the West. Although diplomatic relations with

Britain are restored, Egypt continues buying arms from the USSR. At the same time Nasser brings Cairo's **al-Azhar** university under government supervision after he receives reports of the spread of Islamism among its teachers and students—a move that angers Egypt's clerics, who have long cherished al-Azhar's independence.

Kuwait renounces British protection and joins the Arab League, but when an Iraqi invasion threatens, Kuwait's ruler, **Abdullah al-Sabah**, immediately requests British military assistance.

Baqir al-Sadr, an Iraqi Shiite ayatollah, publishes *Iqtissadduna* ("Our Economy"), a blueprint for Islamic banking. This system avoids fixed-interest rates—forbidden by the Koran as usury—by offering profit-sharing "dividends" instead.

1962 Algeria's eight-year war of independence climaxes in victory for the FLN and the expulsion of the French. Under Algeria's first president, **Ben Bella**, a military regime with strong socialist leanings is established. Members of the Muslim Brotherhood and other Islamists are persecuted, and the *ulama* are denied any role in politics.

In **Yemen**, a military coup supported by Nasser and the USSR institutes a People's Democratic Republic. The toppled amir, Muhammad al-Badr, escapes to the mountains where, supported by Saudi Arabia, he forms a tribal confederacy ("**North Yemen**") that wages intermittent war against "**South Yemen**" until reunification in May 1990.

Nasser also supports, and perhaps masterminds, a coup in **Syria** that briefly imposes the authority of a pro-Egyptian military junta.

King Saud ibn Abd al-Aziz of **Saudi Arabia**, wary of Nasser's expanding influence among Arabs, promotes the creation of the **Muslim World League** in Mecca. The objectives of the League are to disseminate Wahhabism at the expense of other forms of Islam and Nasserite secularism. As Saudi oil revenues grow, the League sponsors many new mosques in various parts of the world.

In **Iran**, the ayatollah **Ruhollah Khomeini** emerges as a leading spokesmen of clerical opposition to the shah's "White Revolution."

Al-Fatah, with offices newly opened in Algiers, proclaims the legitimacy of an **armed struggle** for the "liberation" of Palestine from Israeli rule.

1963 In **Iraq**, Qarim Qasim is toppled by an army coup. **Ahmad Hasan al-Bakr**, leader of the Baath party, forms a new government.

SAYYID QUTB
(1906–66)

*T*he premier ideologue of Islamism in the 20th century, Sayyid Qutb was in part the creation of his tormentor President Nasser. An Indian Egyptian, Qutb trained as a school inspector whose sympathies lay with the nationalist and secularist Wafd party at a time when Wafd's electoral victories were regularly overruled by the British. In 1948, he was sent on a three-year course at Colorado University in Texas; his travels in America and Europe opened his eyes to the near-irredeemable "decadence" of the West, and on his return to Cairo he joined the Muslim Brotherhood. Yet what finally pushed Qutb into hardline militancy was the ten-year internment imposed by Nasser on thousands of Brothers in 1954. In prison, surrounded by fellow Brothers, Qutb wrote two books, *Fi Zilal al-Koran* ("In the Shadow of the Koran"), a scriptural commentary, and the best-selling *Maalim fi al-Tariq*, "Signposts on the Road."

In his writings, Qutb reconfigured many of the familiar elements of Islamic puritanism in a manner tailored to exploit mid-20th century anti-imperialism. Of critical importance were the concepts of the *salafi*, the original—and therefore right-minded—members of the Muslim umma; and

In Malaysia, tensions between Muslims and non-Muslims are exacerbated by the creation of a government-backed **Pan-Malayan Islamic Party**.

1964 In Saudi Arabia, King Saud abdicates in favor of his brother **Faisal ibn Abd al-Aziz al-Saud**, who attempts to assert his leadership of the Muslim world as "The Guardian of the Holy Places in Arabia."

of *jahiliyyah*, the state of infidel barbarism that preceded Muhammad's revolution. In Qutb's hands, *jahiliyyah* is expanded to include not only everything that lies outside Islam, but much of what lies inside too. Not only do secularist rulers such as Nasser merit censure, but so too do the *ulama* and other clerics for failing to preserve and enhance "true" Islamic values; *jihad* against both is justified, Qutb asserts.

The appeal of Qutb's "salafist" polemic for his contemporary Muslims, especially university students, lay in its willingness to assess other options, giving it the appearance of an all-inclusive political analysis. Ultimately, though, neither nationalism nor Marxism, democracy nor capitalism, could possibly suffice, since none had the authority of—or bore any resemblance to—the message of Allah delivered through Muhammad. Even so, Qutb's ideas might have dissipated had it not been for the Arabs' ignominious defeat at the hands of Israel in 1967. By then, Qutb himself was dead, executed in 1966 on Nasser's orders. His writings though, like the writings of Ibn Taymiyyah and al-Wahhab, lived on.

The **Palestinian Liberation Organization** (PLO), dedicated to the overthrow of Israel, is founded in Jerusalem by Ahmad Shukairy in May and endorsed by a summit of Arab leaders in Alexandria in September. Its structure includes a military wing, the **Palestinian Liberation Army** (PLA), answerable to the PLO's political authority, the **Palestine National Council**.

The world heavyweight boxing champion **Cassius Clay** joins the Nation of Islam and exchanges his "slave name" for **Muhammad Ali**, greatly raising the profile of America's black Muslims.

1965 In January al-Fatah's militant wing **al-Asifah** ("The Storm"), not wishing to be outdone by the PLA, initiates commando-style action against Israeli military installations.

On February 21 **Malcolm X**, a leading spokesman of the **Black Muslim** movement in the US, is assassinated in Harlem by members of the Nation of Islam.

Humanity today is living in a large brothel! One has only to glance at its press, films, fashion shows, beauty contests, ballrooms, wine bars, and broadcasting stations! Or observe its mad lust for naked flesh, provocative postures, and sick, suggestive statements in literature, the arts and the mass media! And add to all this, the system of usury which fuels man's voracity for money and engenders vile methods for its accumulation and investment, in addition to fraud, trickery, and blackmail dressed up in the garb of law.

—**Sayyid Qutb,**
In the Shadow of the Koran **(1966),**
cited in M. Choueiri, *Islamic Fundamentalism* **(1990)**

In **Algeria**, **Houari Boumedienne** stages a coup against Ben Bella in June and replaces him as president. Although Boumedienne (who remains in power until 1978) is also a member of the secularist FLN, he adopts a more receptive attitude toward Algeria's *ulama* and even some Muslim Brothers as a means of eroding French culture.

In September, Pakistan's army attacks Indian forces in **Kashmir** in support of Kashmir's Muslim "separatists." All-out war is only averted by UN intervention.

In **Indonesia**, Sukarno is displaced by his deputy **General Suharto** who unleashes Muslim hostility towards the country's communists. In the ensuing violence, tens of thousands of communist "sympathizers" are massacred.

1966 Nasser orders a crackdown against militant Islamists after a second attempt on his life. On August 19, **Sayyid Qutb**, the principal ideologue of the **Muslim Brotherhood**, is executed. Soon afterwards, Nasser signs a **defense pact** with Syria as he contemplates a fresh war against Israel.

In **Indonesia**, General Suharto, having used Muslims to destroy communists, begins purging Muslim extremists.

1967 Following a series of border skirmishes between the Syrian and Israeli armies early in the year, Nasser closes the **Gulf of Aqaba** to Israeli shipping and signs a mutual defense pact with

The existence of Israel is an error which must be rectified.
                    —**President al-Rahman Muhammad Arif of Iraq,**
                              radio broadcast, May 31, 1967

Jordan. On May 26 he tells the Arab Trades Union Congress that Arab states should destroy Israel—a view echoed by other Arab leaders. The **Six Day** (or **June**) **War** commences on June 5 when Israel opts for a pre-emptive strike urged by defense secretary **Moshe Dayan**. On the same day, its American-equipped air force all but destroys Egypt's Russian-supplied counterpart. During the following five days, Israeli forces occupy **East Jerusalem** (until now under Jordanian-Palestinian control), the **Gaza strip**, the **West Bank** and also the strategically important **Golan Heights** across the Syrian border. A motorized Israeli army reoccupies the **Sinai Desert** as far as the Suez Canal. In the three main areas of land fighting, Egyptian, Syrian and Jordanian armies sustain heavy losses.

The war also prompts an exodus of 200,000 Palestinian **refugees** from Israel, a majority of them resettled in camps in Jordan, but

An Israeli soldier arrests Palestinians during the Six Day War, 1967

some arriving in Lebanon. On November 22, the UN Security Council passes **Resolution 242**, calling for a "just and lasting settlement" to the Israeli-Palestinian conflict, and for the immediate withdrawal of Israeli forces from the "**occupied territories**." Israel ignores the resolution, which is also rejected by the PLO on the grounds that it makes no explicit provision for a Palestinian state.

In Damascus, Dr George Habash founds the **Marxist-Leninist Popular Front for the Liberation of Palestine** (PFLP).

In **South Yemen**, Marxist nationalists proclaim a People's Republic in the British colonial port of Aden. Not bothering to argue, Britain evacuates its garrison

CHAPTER TEN

The Resurgence of Islam

{1968–89 (1387–1409AH)}

As in 1948, the defeat of a coalition of Arab forces in June 1967 enabled Israel to expand its rule over the land that had once been Palestine. As well as seizing the strategic Golan Heights from Syria, Israeli forces occupied the West Bank, hitherto under Jordanian administration. And Jerusalem, until now partitioned between Jews and Muslims, fell under exclusive Israeli control, including the Dome of the Rock, the venue of Muhammad's *miraj* ("night flight") of 620. Although the Israeli government did not attempt to disrupt Muslim worship in Jerusalem or reclaim the Rock for the Jewish faith, it was—and remains—galling to many Muslims that one of the holiest sites in Islam should have fallen under "enemy" jurisdiction. That some Arab housing opposite the Western Wall, sacred to the Jews, was leveled by bulldozers added to their chagrin. Yet the teaching of the Koran did not admit defeat—Allah assures his followers final victory—and an important effect of the Six Day War was to unleash a progressively militant **Islamic revival**.

After the war, the Muslim Brotherhood, armed with the blistering polemics of **Sayyid Qutb**, pushed the argument that failure against Israel occurred because Islamic values had been abandoned by Arab leaders. Only in Wahhabist Saudi Arabia, which had not participated directly in the conflict, did anything like a righteous Islamic community exist. And what applied to the Muslim Arab world also applied to the larger non-Arab Muslim community.

In 1973, Egypt, Syria and Jordan attempted to confront Israel for a third time, in the "**October**" or "**Yom Kippur**" **War**. This time round, the outcome was at least inconclusive, allowing the Arabs to recover some dignity. Yet in the half-dozen years between 1967 and 1973 a different kind of tactics had emerged among Islamic "extremists." A spate of hijackings of civilian aircraft, and atrocities such as the massacre of Israeli athletes at the 1972 Munich Olympics, marked the arrival of a **terrorism** that paid no heed to national boundaries, nor the regulated international order sought by the United Nations.

The effects of this were felt most sharply in Israel, where the Israeli-Palestinian conflict steadily intensified amidst a welter of guerrilla-style operations frequently launched from neighboring **Lebanon**—where the conflict fuelled a civil war lasting from 1975 to 1990. During the course of this, French, American, UN and Syrian forces became involved, and the conflict was also noted for its spawning of several Shiite terrorist organizations, among them **Amal**, **Islamic Jihad** and **Hezbollah**, that were non-Palestinian in origin, but had as their objective the destruction of the Israeli state.

These groups were encouraged, and sometimes sponsored, by the greatest upheaval of the period, Ayatollah Khomeini's Shiite **Iranian Revolution** of 1978–79—a seismic event that suggested to Muslims everywhere that secularism could be seen off once and for all. While Khomeini's main objective was to institute a true Islamic society on earth, his principal target had been the corrupt government of Muhammad Reza Shah, of all Muslim regimes the one most intimately tied at the time to the "satanic" United States.

Other Muslim leaders took note: their dilemma was whether to contain the new tide of Islamism by accommodating some of its aspirations, or whether to suppress it altogether. Many governments tried both policies, with the result that, from **Algeria** in the West to **Indonesia** in the east, Muslim governments were confronted with varying degrees of unrest. Changing demographic patterns played their part, too: in 1975 an estimated 60 percent of Islam's total population was aged 24 or under. As a result of massively increased urbanization in many areas, an underclass suffering poverty and unemployment emerged, susceptible to the salvationist messages of ideologues operating out of mosques and schools. Most Muslim governments faced down the challenge from their militants, in fact—albeit often at great cost in lives and resources. The leading figure in this respect was Iraq's **Saddam Hussein**, who, fearing that Khomeini's revolution would spread to Shiites in his own country, where they made up a majority of the population, launched a war against Iran that lasted from 1980 to 1988.

While this was unfolding, so too was another conflict—in **Afghanistan**. The country had been occupied by Soviet forces since the same year that the Iranian shah was toppled, 1979. Ten years later, the Soviets withdrew, worn down by *mujahaddin* guerrillas operating out of Afghanistan's seemingly impregnable mountain fastnesses. The *mujahaddin* were jihadists, made up of both Afghans and non-Afghans, and drawn from all quarters of Islam. When they achieved victory in 1989, the high point of Islamic resurgence had perhaps been reached.

Yet that victory had been achieved with financial and technical support from the USSR's ideological enemy, the United States—a reminder that what happened in Islam continued to be profoundly influenced by currents in the wider world. Nor, in 1989, despite the raising of Islamic consciousness by the Muslim Brotherhood and others, was Islam itself any more unified than it was in 1968. While the Iranian Revolution and the Afghanistan war projected Islam into the headlines of the world media as never before, and while the clever manipulation of oil prices had given Saudi Arabia in particular a degree of international clout, it was clear that Islam itself was hardly about to become a superpower—any more than the cohesive umma envisioned by Muhammad was about to become a reality.

1968 In the wake of the Six Day War, in February there is a student worker uprising at **Helouan** outside Cairo, followed by similar unrest in Alexandria later in the year. Both are provoked by the **Muslim Brotherhood**, whose militant resurgence threatens to destabilize Nasser's Egypt.

In **Iraq**, the Baath party consolidates its power by launching punitive attacks against rebellious **Kurds** in the north.

The Saudi Arabian oil minister **Sheikh Yamani** insists that Saudi Arabia takes a twenty percent share in ARAMCO in addition to the percentage of oil revenues it already enjoys. Yamani is the guiding hand behind the founding of **OAPEC**, the Organization of Arab Petroleum Exporting Countries, which for a while undermines the "solidarity" achieved by **OPEC**.

Following an unsuccessful Israeli attempt to destroy an **al-Fatah** base in Jordan, al-Fatah amalgamates with the **PLO** (Palestinian Liberation Organization).

In **Malaysia**, a charismatic preacher, Ashaari Muhammad, founds the sect **Darul Arqam**. Committed to charitable works, it condemns tables, televisions and other products of "Western decadence." Its members wear black turbans and Arabian *jellabas*.

1969 In **Malaysia**, anti-Chinese protests spearheaded by an Islamist missionary movement called **Dakwah** (from the Arabic dawa, or "call to Islam") come to a head in May. The ruling **United Malay National Organization** responds by instigating positive discrimination in favor of Muslim Malays.

In October, as unrest among Palestinian refugees in **Lebanon** grows, Druze guerrillas begin attacking the mainly Maronite Lebanese Army and launching attacks against Israel.

Following a summit held at Rabat in September, the **Organization of the Islamic Conference** (OIC) is founded with a secretariat at Jeddah (Saudi Arabia) to provide a permanent forum to resolve disputes between Muslim states. Although the Conference regularly expresses solidarity with the Palestinian movement in Israel, it fails to heal rifts within Islam.

Supported by Nasser of Egypt, **Muammar al-Gaddafi** leads an army coup against King Idris and becomes president of **Libya**.

1970 A ten-day civil war erupts in **Jordan** at the end of August as the Palestinian majority, encouraged by the PLO, rise up against **King Hussein**, blamed for the loss of Palestinian territory in 1967. But the king is supported by Jordanian Islamists—who criticize the PLO for its "secularism"—and by an offer of American intervention. **Yasser Arafat**, now the leader of the PLO, brokers a ceasefire. International attention returns to Jordan when three civilian aircraft belonging to American, Swiss and British airlines are **hijacked** by Palestinian guerrillas and redirected to Amman airport. The planes are blown up and their passengers traded for the release of imprisoned terrorists, among them **Leila Khaled**, a former female student of the American University in Beirut who has participated in a failed hijacking the previous year.

Following the hijacking, the Jordanian government begins expelling Palestinian militants, most of whom resettle in southern **Lebanon**.

On September 28, Nasser dies and his deputy **Anwar Sadat** becomes president of Egypt. Although Sadat continues Nasser's secularist centralizing policies, he adopts a more conciliatory attitude toward the Muslim Brotherhood and other Islamists.

On November 19, **Hafiz al-Assad**, a secular rightist, assumes power in **Syria** after leading a successful army coup.

In **Turkey**, the opposition **Islamist Party for National Order** is founded towards the end of the year.

In **Pakistan**, Ali Bhutto succeeds to power following a December general election. His seven-year secularist-socialist government, while successfully improving Pakistan's infrastructure, generates resentment among the country's increasing number of Islamic "fundamentalists."

1971 In the Gulf, **Bahrain** and **Qatar** become fully independent from Britain. At the end of the year Bahrain joins six other Gulf states to form the **United Arab Emirates (UAE)**.

In the wake of Britain's withdrawal from the Gulf, **Iran** seizes Abu Musa and other strategically important islands, but **Iraq** reacts by preventing shipping reaching the Iranian port of Khoramshahr through the Shatt al-Arab. Iran retaliates by increasing its support for Kurdish separatists in northern Iraq.

In Iran, **Shah Muhammad Reza** stages extravagant but unpopular celebrations for "1500 years of Persian monarchy." **Ayatollah Khomeini**, in exile in Najaf, Iraq, publishes *Velayat-e Faqih: Hokumat-e Islami* ("Islamic Government Under the Guardianship of a Doctor of the Law"), a hostile critique of the shah's regime.

In December, **Pakistan** and **India** go to war following India's support for the separatist Awami League in East Pakistan and renewed Pakistani intervention in **Kashmir**. Within two weeks of fighting, Pakistan's armed forces are humiliated, and East Pakistan becomes the independent Muslim state of **Bangladesh**.

During the course of 1971, as **OPEC** militates on behalf of its member states to secure a larger share of oil profits, the price of **crude oil** doubles on world markets. In December, Colonel Gaddafi expropriates the assets of British Petroleum in **Libya**.

1972 In May, **Black September**, a terrorist group formed to "avenge" King Hussein's purge of Palestinian militants in 1970, hijacks a Belgian aircraft at Ben Gurion airport in **Israel**. On the 31st, an affiliated Japanese terrorist group called the **Red Army** massacres 24 civilians in the airport's departure lounge. In September, Black Septemberists murder eleven Israeli athletes during the **Munich Olympic Games**, deriving maximum publicity from a globally televised event. When three of the terrorists are apprehended by German police, the hijacking of another aircraft, belonging to Lufthansa, secures their release. Israel responds to its athletes' deaths by bombing Palestinian refugee camps in **south Lebanon**, where the terrorists are believed to have their bases. As Arab-Israeli tensions mount, **Egypt** and **Syria** begin preparing their armies for a co-ordinated attack against the Jewish state. Meanwhile, the **PLO** establishes its headquarters in Beirut, the Lebanese capital now under Syrian protection.

Following Libya's example, **Iraq** nationalizes its oil resources—to the detriment of Western interests.

1973 During the summer, as President Sadat further relaxes prohibitions against Islamists, a movement known as **Jamaat Islamiyyah** ("Islamic Association") becomes active in Egypt's universities and colleges, seeking to persuade students to return to the "true path" of Muhammad.

Before dawn on October 6, during the Muslim month of Ramadan and the Jewish feast of Yom Kippur, **Egypt** and **Syria** launch large-scale attacks against **Israel**, invading the Sinai desert and assaulting the Golan Heights. Iraqi and Jordanian units are also involved in what becomes known as the **October War**. Although initially the Arabs gain stunning victories, the Israeli counterattack, supported by US President Richard Nixon, comes within fifty miles of Cairo. **OPEC** imposes an embargo on oil exports to the USA, sparking a further hike in petroleum prices and a worldwide **oil crisis**. On October 24, hostilities end after the USSR threatens intervention on the Arab side and Nixon's secretary of state **Henry Kissinger** brokers a UN-backed ceasefire.

As a result of the October War, while the UN calls for the implementation of its 1967 **Resolution 242**, international efforts to achieve a "lasting peace" in Israel gain pace. Although Arab oil producers relax their embargoes, high oil prices continue, creating balance of payment problems for some smaller Western states. Conversely, new wealth flows into the Middle East, with **Saudi Arabia**, now providing 20 percent of America's domestic oil consumption, emerging as a regional power that attracts immigrant workers from Pakistan and other poorer nations. With access to seemingly limitless funds, the Muslim World League embarks on a fresh wave of **mosque-building** around the globe. In December, backed by the OIC, the **Islamic**

Development Bank is founded in Jeddah to fund projects in poorer Muslim nations with "petrodollars."

In **Afghanistan**, the Durrani king Zahir Shah is forced into exile by his cousin **Muhammad Daud Khan**, who proclaims a republic with himself as president. A left-leaning secularist, Daud cracks down on Islamists, many of whom flee to neighboring Pakistan, where they form the nucleus of the *mujahaddin* movement. Among their leaders are **Gulbuddin Hikmetyar**, **Burhanudin Rabbani** and **Ahmed Shah Masoud**.

In **Libya**, President Gaddafi announces an anti-communist, anti-imperialist, anti-capitalist (and not conspicuously Islamic) "revolution" called "**The Third Universal Theory**," which contributes to Libya's growing isolation in the years ahead.

1974 In April, members of the Islamic Liberation Party led by **Salih Siriyyah** attack a military academy outside **Cairo** in preparation for an intended coup. President Sadat tightens restrictions on Egyptian Islamists in response.

In July, **Turkey** invades **Cyprus** to prevent "**Enosis**," a union between Cyprus and Greece sought by the island's majority Greek Cypriots, and succeeds in creating a permanent Turkish Cypriot enclave in the north.

I think that if Israel did not exist, the Arab leaders would have to invent it. It is the single imaginary enemy that unifies all their people. The Moslems of the Middle East quarrel among themselves, mistrust, assassinate, plot coups, change alliances, kill each other with ferocious energy; they can agree on nothing except their nourishing hatred for the Jews of Israel.

—**Martha Gellhorn,** *The Face of War* **(1986)**

In October, Arab leaders meeting at Rabat recognize the **PLO** as the only legitimate representation of Palestinians. On November 13, PLO chairman **Yasser Arafat**'s international profile is enhanced when he addresses the UN General Assembly, calling for an autonomous Palestinian state.

Amal, a militant Shiite organization intended to reverse the marginalization of Shiites in **Lebanon**, is founded by Imam Musa al-Sadr, an exiled Iranian. In December, Israeli warplanes bomb Palestinian camps inside **Beirut** for the first time.

1975 Following negotiations orchestrated by Kissinger, **Israel** agrees to a partial withdrawal of its forces from Sinai.

From April onwards, tensions between Maronites and Muslims in **Lebanon** blow up into a full-scale **civil war**, exacerbated by the inflow of Palestinian refugees.

Tensions between **Iraq** and **Iran** are abated by the **Algiers Agreement**: Iran agrees to stop supporting Iraq's Kurdish rebels, while Iraq agrees to divide the contentious Shatt al-Arab along the **Thalweg Line**, effectively making the waterway a shared sea lane.

1976 In May, **Syria**, anticipating increased Israeli intervention against Palestinian militants, sends its troops into **Lebanon** to "restore order," effectively making the country a Syrian protectorate. The conflict between Maronites and Druze continues, however.

In **Kuwait**, Sabah al-Sabah suspends the National Assembly following popular protests about the ruling family's unwillingness to share its oil wealth.

In June, **Israeli commandos** strike "a blow against terrorism" when they rescue an aircraft hijacked by Palestinian militants at **Entebbe** airport in Uganda.

In December, **Saudi Arabia** breaks ranks with OPEC, and world oil prices—which have quadrupled since 1972—begin falling.

In the **USA**, Wallace Muhammad, leader of the **Nation of Islam** in succession to his father Elijah, renames the Black Muslim sect **The World Community of al-Islam in the West**.

1977 In an unprecedented initiative, Egypt's President Sadat negotiates directly with Israel's prime minister, **Menachem Begin**. In November, he flies to Jerusalem and offers "permanent peace" in exchange for an Israeli recognition of Palestinian statehood and withdrawal from territories occupied in 1967. Although these terms are eventually rejected by Israel, Sadat's "package," which effectively recognizes Israel's right to exist, is bitterly condemned by even moderate

LEBANON

Lebanon owes its existence to a massacre of Maronite Christians—a Roman Catholic sect dating back to the 5th century—by an Ismaili Shiite sect known as the Druze in 1860. The French intervened to create a protected area for the Maronites around Mount Lebanon, and in 1926 Lebanon emerged as a separate territory within the French mandate. In 1941 it achieved full independence, supported by a constitution that ensured a Maronite president and a Maronite majority in its legislative assembly. Even then, however, the Maronites barely represented a majority of Lebanon's population, and by 1975, following several influxes of Palestinian refugees from Israel, they had become a minority.

Until that year, Lebanon had prospered. Its capital, Beirut, was famed as an international playground where morals were lax and entertainment plentiful. But in that year the country was plunged into a devastating "civil" war that lasted fifteen years. Initially the war began as a straight fight between Maronites and Druze, who had always been rivals. But as

Muslim leaders. The **Jamaat Islamiyya** begins agitating against Sadat, and Egyptian extremist groups such as **Al-Takfir wa al-Hijira**, sometimes known as the "Society of Muslims," begin to emerge. Led by Shukri Mustafa, this latter group soon murders a senior loyalist cleric, Sheikh Dhahabi. Shukri, who has already assembled guerrilla camps in Upper (southern) Egypt, specializes in issuing *fatwas* against all Muslims who do not share his views, and forbids his followers to occupy government positions. In response, Sadat orders a further crackdown against militants and potential militants.

the war dragged on, so other groups and interests were sucked in. In 1976 Syria, a predominantly Arab nation, intervened to protect embattled Lebanese Muslims. But increasingly "Lebanese Muslims" came to include both Palestinian and non-Palestinian militant groups (such as the Iranian-backed Amal and Hezbollah) committed to the overthrow of Israel, which in turn led the Jewish state to get involved.

To begin with, the Maronites looked to Israel for support against their Muslim enemies, but gradually became divided amongst themselves as to where their real loyalties lay. Eventually, in 1990, a majority of Maronites concluded it was in their best interests to work with Syria, which now offered them protection as well, and the civil war, which had cost an estimated 150,000 lives, drew to a close. But while Beirut has returned to a sometimes uneasy peace, southern Lebanon is still used as a battleground between Israel and Islamic militants, and doubtless will continue that way for as long as the seemingly insoluble **Israeli-Palestinian conflict** lasts.

In the same month that Sadat visits Jerusalem, Israel launches air raids against refugee camps in **southern Lebanon** harboring Palestinian guerrillas, who have launched their own attacks against targets in northern Israel.

In **Pakistan**, Ali Bhutto is overthrown by an Islamist army commander, **Zia ul-Haq**, in July. During his eleven-year rule, Zia reverses

AMERICA'S BLACK MUSLIMS

*A*lthough America's millions of black slaves gained nominal freedom following the Civil War of 1861–65, they were disadvantaged politically, economically and socially for another century. While it was a Christian minister, Martin Luther King (1929–68), who eventually achieved at least partial redress by persuading President John F. Kennedy to enact beneficial civil rights laws, some African-Americans turned to a version of Islam.

As early as 1913, Timothy Drew founded a "Moorish Holy Science Temple" in Newark, its members sporting long beards and the red fez. But America's best-known Islamic sect, the Nation of Islam, was created by Wallace D. Fard, a self-proclaimed *mahdi*, and his disciple Elijah Muhammad (born Elijah Poole in 1897) in the 1930s. Committed to the creation of a separate state for blacks in North America, and boasting that its leadership had been ordained by Allah to "redeem" other colored peoples from white oppression, the Nation quickly attracted several thousand followers. It then stalled until the late 1950s, when, exploiting the anger generated by the civil rights campaign, the charismatic Malcolm X (born Malcolm Little, 1925–65) forged a powerful link between "Black Islam" and "Black Power."

the secularist policies of his predecessors and attempts to implement full **Shariah law**, including the compulsory deduction of *zakat* (Islamic alms) from personal bank accounts. Since Zia also maintains martial law, and his regime is soon perceived to be geared in favor of an elite composed of his cronies, critics question whether his efforts at Islamization are merely a pretext for the suppression of democracy.

The son of a Nebraskan Baptist minister, Malcolm X was a reformed hoodlum who openly criticized Elijah Muhammad's profligate lifestyle. In 1964 the two men clashed, and Malcolm left the Nation of Islam to form his own group, the Organization of Afro-American Unity. But less than a year later, Malcolm X was murdered by three Nation members, and it was not until the 1970s that America's Black Muslims found another leader of similar magnetism—Louis Farrakhan (born Louis Eugene Walcott in 1933). Farrakhan's method has been to incite public attention by making vitriolic attacks on Jews in particular (who were accused of injecting black babies with the HIV virus). Although in October 1995 he surprised the media by mounting a "Million Man March" on Washington, in which at least 400,000 American blacks participated, his star was already waning by September 2001.

During the course of its seventy-year existence, the Nation of Islam has seldom succeeded in establishing relations with Muslim bodies outside America, and has indeed been treated by them with some suspicion. Overtly racist in its message, and reminiscent of Baptist and other congregationalist revivalism in its style, the American Black Muslim movement is perhaps best seen as an outspoken expression of real domestic grievances.

In the USA, **Louis Farrakhan**, declaring himself a prophet, breaks away from Wallace Muhammad and re-establishes the **Nation of Islam**, attracting publicity by virulent tirades against Jews.

1978 In January, an attack on the exiled **Ayatollah Khomeini** by Iran's state-controlled media provokes widespread demonstrations in his favor. In October, Khomeini leaves Iraq for the greater safety of Paris. On December 10 and 11, Tehran and other Iranian cities are shaken by massive **protests** against Muhammad Reza Shah during celebrations held to commemorate the martyrdom of the Shiite Imam Husayn.

In March, following incursions into **Israel** from Lebanon, including an attack on a bus which kills 35 civilians, Israeli land forces advance into southern Lebanon to establish a "**buffer zone**," in the process killing up to 1000 civilians and displacing a further 200,000. Following international pressure, however, Israel withdraws, handing over its positions to **Maronite militias**.

Louis Farrakhan, leader of the Nation of Islam

In April, a group of Soviet-trained Marxist army officers seizes power in **Afghanistan**, establishing a regime that combines land reform with compulsory socialist education and harsh reprisals against its opponents. President Muhammad Daud and his family are murdered.

On September 28, a diplomatic breakthrough seems to occur when Anwar Sadat and Menachem Begin sign the **Camp David Peace Accords** brokered by US president Jimmy Carter at the presidential retreat in Maryland, where the three leaders have been holding talks. In the accords, Sadat repeats his pledge to respect Israel's pre-1967 boundaries once UN Resolution 242 has been implemented.

1979 As **Iran** descends into turmoil, Muhammad Reza Shah attempts to appease his critics by promising Islamic reforms, a ban on trade with Israel and support for a Palestinian state, but mutiny continues to spread inside his army and on January 15 he goes into voluntary exile. On February 1, **Ruhollah Khomeini** arrives in Tehran to assert control over the **Iranian Revolution** through the creation of a fifteen-man Revolutionary Council. While at first the Revolution purports to be as inclusive as possible, its religious character soon emerges as Khomeini's "secularist" allies are sidelined and the traditional authority of the Shiite *mullahs* is reinstated. A **Party of Islamic Revolution** is established before February is out, and Islamist revolutionary committees (called **komittehs**) are installed throughout the country.

> Islam is the religion of militant individuals who are committed to faith and justice. It is the religion of those who desire freedom and independence. It is the school of those who struggle against imperialism.
>
> —**Ruhollah Khomeini**, I*slam and Revolution*,
> trans. Hamid Algar (1981)

Khomeini himself leads televised Friday Prayers in Tehran, and publicly denounces America and other "satanic infidels."

Following a popular referendum, the **Islamic Republic of Iran** is set up in March, with Khomeini as its Supreme Faqih (religious authority). In August, a part-elected, part-appointed majilis (national assembly) is convened, and confirms the absolute powers vested in Khomeini. On November 4, 500 students storm the **US embassy**,

RUHOLLAH MUSAVI KHOMEINI
(1902–89)

*F*ew events of the 20th century caused greater global unease, or were more widely misreported, than the Iranian Revolution. In February 1979 there suddenly appeared on television screens worldwide the face of an elderly cleric, who had apparently seized power in Iran after a bloody coup. It seemed medieval—as did his funeral ten years later, when his coffin, surrounded by thousands of breast-beating mourners, was torn open.

In fact, Khomeini's revolution was long in the planning, and was directed against a tyrannical regime only kept afloat by the USA and Britain for the sake of Iran's oil reserves, and to prevent Soviet influence spreading. In its initial phases at least it enjoyed the support of most sections of the Iranian people, and was projected as a nationalist as well as a religious uprising.

Khomeini himself had waged an unrelenting campaign against the shah for twenty years, at first from the Faiziyah madrasa in Qum where, as a teacher, he had sufficient followers to be acclaimed an *ayatollah* ("sign of God"), or senior *mujtahid*. In 1965, following a term of imprisonment and a fresh

seizing its 66 inhabitants and creating a hostage crisis that lasts 441 days. Files found inside the embassy are used to incriminate Iranian "middle-class collaborators." Since the students have acted without Khomeini's prior approval, though, the Grand Ayatollah takes steps to curb the excesses of Islamic "anarchists."

On March 19, following the Camp David Accords, a formal peace between Egypt and Israel is declared in the **Treaty of Washington**,

attack on the shah's decision to give US servicemen based in Iran diplomatic immunity, Khomeini was forced into exile in Iraq. There he published *Velayat-e Faqih: Hokumat-e Islami* ("Islamic Government Under the Guardianship of a Doctor of the Law") in 1971, a series of lectures that, in line with **Usuli** principles, urged Iranians to adopt a wise jurisprudent as their ruler.

That wise man was, of course, Khomeini, whose sermons continued to be distributed in Iran as audio cassette tapes. He was perceived by many Shiites as the **Hidden Imam**. Astutely, Khomeini neither welcomed nor rebutted the title. Rather, he put in place a revolutionary machinery—a supreme council, a Revolutionary Guard and local committees—that owed more to Stalin and Mao Zedong than any Islamic precedent, even though the ground had been partly prepared by **Ali Shariati** (1933–77), whose writings had attempted to synthesize Islamic fundamentalism and Marx's theory of class struggle. Inevitably, a terrible purge of shahists and white-collar workers followed. But until his death Khomeini retained the allegiance of students, *bazaaris* and the poor, as well as the *mullahs*.

ending over three decades of hostilities. Displeased by Egypt's "apostasy," **Saudi Arabia** temporarily cuts oil production, causing a hike in world prices.

In April, there is a general uprising against the communist regime in **Afghanistan**. As warlordism spreads, the communists manage to retain control only in Kabul, Kandahar and some other cities.

In July, **Saddam Hussein** replaces al-Bakr as leader of the Iraqi Baath Party and becomes president of the country. He immediately eliminates his opponents, including Shiite clerics. Muhammad Baqir al-Sadr, an intimate of Ayatollah Khomeini, is incarcerated and executed the following year.

In November, as religious fervor spreads in Islam, a group of Sunni militants, led by **Juhayman al-Utayi**, a student from Riyadh University who assumes the title of *mahdi*, occupies the Grand Mosque in **Mecca**. Although the insurrection is crushed by Saudi police, King Khalid is forced to affirm that his government is run on orthodox Islamic lines and make concessions to the Saudi *ulama*.

Abu al-Ala Mawdudi, founder of the *Jamaat-i Islami* (Islamic Party) and the principal ideologue of militant revivalism in **Pakistan**, dies in the USA, where he has been seeking medical treatment.

In December, the **USSR** invades **Afghanistan** to ensure the continuance of communist rule. The existing regime is replaced by a puppet government under the presidency of **Babrak Karmal**. Widely perceived as a Russian attempt to extend their empire, the invasion dramatically reconfigures US policy in Central Asia, with the result that Islamic militants opposed to Soviet occupation, known as ***mujahaddin***, begin receiving funds from Washington channeled through Pakistan. The *mujahaddin* also receive support from **Saudi Arabia** and **China**.

1980 Bani Sadr, a leftist who temporarily enjoys Khomeini's support, is elected president of the new **Iranian Islamic Republic.** Khomeini undermines Bani Sadr, however, when he secures the closure of Tehran University pending a full Islamic "investigation" of its staff.

In April, Saddam Hussein expels all Shiites of Iranian origin from **Iraq** while providing clandestine support to **Iranian rebels** in Khuzestan. On April 30, six Iraqi-born gunmen, claiming to represent an "Arabistan" freedom movement in southwest Iran, seize the Iranian embassy in London. Five days later, British security forces storm the embassy; five of the six gunmen are killed, and all but three of their 26 hostages freed unharmed.

In July, **Pakistan**'s minority Shiites revolt against General Zia's strict Sunni administration. There are also **Shiite uprisings** in Saudi Arabia and the Gulf states. All are harshly suppressed.

On September 22, Iraq—having accused Iran of cross-border artillery bombardment—launches an all-out invasion on a 300-mile front that secures control of the **Shatt al-Arab** waterway, again the subject of dispute. The ensuing **Iran–Iraq War** lasts eight years, during which each side endeavors to destroy the other's oil wells.

On September 12, a military coup in **Turkey** ushers in a rightist dictatorship determined to suppress Islamist militants and others opposed to Turkey's Western-style secularization. A watered-down version of Islam is introduced into the state education system as a means of discouraging more radical interpretations.

In **Pakistan**, Zia ul-Haq inaugurates the **International Islamic University**, which attracts leading Wahhabis and Muslim Brothers to join its staff.

1981 In January, **Ronald Reagan** takes office as US president and secures the release of the 66 embassy staff held in **Iran** since 1979 to punish the outgoing president, Jimmy Carter, for providing support for Muhammad Reza Shah.

In Lebanon, Israel engages directly with Syrian armed forces in April after Syria builds missile batteries in the **Beqaa Valley**, threatening

Jewish settlements in Galilee. Syrian units inside Lebanon also come under fire from Maronite phalangists.

In May, Saudi Arabia, Kuwait, Oman, Qatar and the United Arab Emirates form the **Gulf Co-Operation Council**, aimed at providing mutual security in the event of an Iranian attack. The Council also pledges its support for the *jihad* against the Soviet occupation of **Afghanistan**.

In June, President BaniSadr is forced to flee **Iran** after Khomeini continues to undermine his policies. BaniSadr's supporters take to the

THE IRAN-IRAQ WAR
(1980–88)

*T*he eight-year war between Iran and Iraq claimed well over a million lives, Iran sustaining the heavier casualties. Although its immediate cause was control of the strategic **Shatt al-Arab** waterway at the point where the Tigris and Euphrates rivers converge on the Iran-Iraqi border, its ramifications were far wider than that. An important source of the conflict was a historic enmity between the Iranian-Persian peoples living east of the Euphrates, and the mainly Arab peoples living to its west. Under the Abbasids, Islam had partly overcome this rift, but with the rise of the Shiite Safavid empire in the 17th century, religion reopened old wounds. In 1979 the separateness of Persian-Iranian Islam was underscored by Ayatollah Khomeini's Iranian Revolution. That separateness, however, was scarcely clear-cut, since a large number of Twelver Shiites lived in Iraq, where Khomeini himself had taken refuge from Muhammad Reza Shah's regime. Since Khomeini had made

streets in protest, but are brutally suppressed. To bolster his position, Khomeini promotes the cult of *bassidjis* (volunteer martyrs) in the war against **Iraq**, now presented to the Iranian people through tightly controlled media as a jihad.

On June 7, Israeli warplanes bomb a factory outside **Baghdad**, claiming it is being used to develop nuclear weapons. That Israel itself has become a nuclear power is dismissed by its government as irrelevant.

On October 6, **Anwar Sadat** is assassinated during a military parade in Cairo by members of a group known simply as **Jihad**, an extreme

clear his intentions of spreading his revolution outside Iran, the potential consequences for Iraq's non-Shiite secularist Baath party government, led by **Saddam Hussein**, were considerable.

The war ended without a clear-cut victory for either side. Given the antipathy towards Iranians and Shiism among most Arab Sunnis, it is perhaps doubtful that Khomeini could have achieved his wider objectives even if Iraq had failed to oppose him. At the time, however, the need to contain Khomeini was keenly felt not just among the Arab states, but also by the USA, the USSR and other non-Muslim powers. As a result, Hussein, whose stature in the Middle East the war greatly enhanced, received support from Washington, Moscow, London and Paris, as well as from Saudi Arabia and the Gulf emirates. On their side, the Iranians had much less international support, although they were able to procure weapons from China, North Korea and even Israel—willing to help anyone who deflected Arab attention away from Palestine.

Islamist association opposed to Sadat's conciliatory policies towards Israel. Sadat's successor **Hosni Mubarak**, who assumes presidential office immediately, nevertheless affirms Sadat's policies, and orders a crackdown against Muslim extremists while seeking to improve Egypt's relations with the USA and its Western allies.

In November, the annual *hajj* to **Mecca** is disrupted when 65,000 **Iranian pilgrims** brandish portraits of Khomeini and chant anti-American slogans in the Grand Mosque. Scuffles with Saudi police lead to a pitched battle and many arrests.

In **Kuwait**, the new ruler, Jabah al-Sabah, permits National Assembly elections. To his chagrin, those elected pass laws prohibiting mixed bathing, university co-education and other activities deemed "un-Islamic."

1982 In line with the Camp David Accords, **Israel** withdraws from Sinai. Since no agreement with Syria has been reached, it continues to occupy the **Golan Heights**. Jewish "fundamentalists" begin creating settlements there.

In February, Sunni Islamists overrun Hama in northern **Syria**, hoping to spark an Islamist uprising. President Assad responds vigorously—up to ten thousand die as the "revolt" is crushed. Notwithstanding, in June Syria permits 1200 Iranian Revolutionary Guards to settle in the Baalbek area of the Beqaa valley in **Lebanon**.

On June 7, Israel launches a 75,000-man invasion of **Lebanon** named "Operation Peace for Galilee" and devised by defense minister **Ariel Sharon** to eliminate terrorist bases and Syrian army installations. Israeli ground troops advance as far as Beirut's suburbs. In early August, **West Beirut**, which contains the largest concentration of Palestinian militants, is subjected to sustained air attacks. Later that month, Israel agrees to an internationally brokered ceasefire on condition that the militants are deported from Lebanon under the supervision of UN peacekeepers. 2000 guerrillas are removed from West Beirut in September, but Israel suspects that a comparable number remain behind.

On September 16, **Bashir Gemayel**, the newly elected Maronite president of Lebanon, is assassinated by terrorists. Between September 16 and 18, two Palestinian refugee camps at **Sabra** and **Shatila** are surrounded by Israeli troops personally led by Ariel Sharon, who allows Maronite militias to move in and massacre between one and two thousand Palestinians. At the end of September, Israel begins to withdraw its forces, following domestic and international protests. As many as 20,000 Palestinians and Lebanese have been killed during the campaign, and substantial damage has been inflicted on Syria's armed forces. To protect its border, Israel agrees to fund the breakaway Maronite **South Lebanon Army** to police the "buffer" zone in the south. Syria contemplates retaliation, but President Assad instead offers direct support for the militant Shiite Amal based in the Beqaa Valley.

As these events unfold, a new militant Shiite group, **Hezbollah** ("Party of Allah"), is established in Lebanon by Iranian agents. Deliberately recruiting its membership from among poor young urbanites, Hezbollah gains a reputation as the most radical and violent of the groups opposed to Israel. It pursues a policy of **kidnapping** high-profile Westerners in Lebanon and elsewhere, partly to trade them for captured Shiite extremists, but also to exert international leverage.

Iran, having repelled Iraq's attempted invasion, launches a counterattack and captures territory around **Basra**. In Tehran, Saddam Hussein is proclaimed the "new Satan."

In **Algeria**, Mustafa Bouyali, a radical Islamist influenced by the Muslim Brotherhood, founds the **Mouvement Islamique Armé** (Armed Islamic Movement). Over the next five years, the MIA carries out frequent attacks against government installations and military posts.

1983 On April 18, the US embassy in **Beirut** is devastated by a suicidal truck bomb launched by a new terrorist group, **Islamic Jihad**, and 46 are killed. In May, the USA brokers an agreement between Israel, the Lebanese government and Syria in which Israel agrees to

It was always the same. I found a small undamaged house with a brown metal gate leading to a small courtyard. Something instinctive made me push it open. The murderers had just left. On the ground there lay a young woman. She lay on her back as if she was sunbathing in the heat and the blood running from her back was still wet. She lay, feet together, arms outspread, as if she had seen her saviour in her last moments. Her face was peaceful, eyes closed, almost like a madonna. Only the small hole in her chest and the stain across the yard told of her death.

—Robert Fisk, reporting on the massacre of Palestinians by Christian Maronites at Shatila in *The Times*, September 20, 1982

evacuate all its forces from Lebanon, and Syria agrees to pull its army units out of the Beqaa valley. Syria complies in June, handing over its installations to PLO forces led by Abu Masa. Syria also begins giving increased support to Lebanon's Druze Shiite minority. In September, the Lebanese army comes under attack from a coalition of Druze and PLO forces, but is protected by American and French armed intervention. On October 23, the headquarters of the American and French peacekeeping force in Beirut are truck-bombed by members of Hezbollah; 265 US marines and 58 French troops are killed. On November 4, Hezbollah launches a further attack on Israeli army headquarters at **Tyre**.

A branch of Islamic Jihad later known as the "**Kuwait 17**" carry out bombings in **Kuwait City**.

In **Iran**, Islamic law is fully implemented. Thieves have their hands amputated, adulterers are stoned to death and there are heavy penalties for the consumption of alcohol. The Revolutionary government also enforces a strict dress code that includes the compulsory wearing of the veil by women. Privileges are granted the families of those "martyred" fighting in the war against Iraq.

OPEC agrees to cut the price of **crude oil** and allow Saudi Arabia to produce oil in accordance with demand. As other OPEC member states follow suit, oil prices fall sharply—to the benefit of Western and other economies.

In **Malaysia**, prime minister Mahathir Mohamad coopts the popular Islamist **Anwar Ibrahim**, founder of the Malay Muslim Youth League, into his government as a means of containing Islamist criticism.

1984 International peacekeepers are withdrawn from **Lebanon** by the end of February, forcing the Lebanese government into closer ties with **Syria**. Accordingly, Amal Gemayel, Lebanese president since the assassination of his brother Bashir in 1982, rescinds a mutual defense agreement with Israel in March. In the same month, **William Buckley**, CIA "station chief" in Beirut, is abducted by terrorists. Israel continues to back the South Lebanon Army as an independent Maronite militia force, and sometimes uses its own troops to police the southern buffer zone.

In September, **Jordan** becomes the first Arab country to restore relations with **Egypt**, which has been ostracized since the Camp David Accords. Others follow suit.

In the same month, a rally of Muslim activists in Tanjung Priok, a docklands area of the Indonesian capital **Jakarta**, is violently broken up by pre-positioned army units. In the ensuing mayhem, about 300 protestors are killed—a warning by Suharto's government that Islamic extremism is not to be tolerated.

In December, **al-Azhar** university is closed down by the Egyptian government following ten days of riots by Islamist students critical of the willingness of senior *ulama* to compromise with the authorities.

In **Algeria**, President Chadli Benjedid introduces new Islamic laws in an attempt to contain the rising tide of Islamic extremism.

1985 In March, **Iran** launches a fresh offensive against **Iraq** and cuts the main Baghdad–Basra road. Iraq responds by bombing Tehran, Shiraz and other Iranian cities. But the war soon settles into stalemate as both sides dig **trench networks** reminiscent of the Western Front in World War I.

On March 8, a CIA-made **car bomb** intended to assassinate Shaikh Muhammad Hussein Fadlallah, widely believed to be the "spiritual

THE JIHAD IN AFGHANISTAN

*T*he 1973 ousting of King Zahir Shah by his socialist cousin Muhammad Daud set in motion a chain of events that plunged Afghanistan into 25 years of turmoil and presented fanatics from across Islam an unrivalled opportunity to demonstrate their commitment to militant action.

In April 1979, Daud himself was thrown out by a group of Moscow-trained communist army officers. But the regime they instituted had little relevance to the tribal traditions of Afghanistan, an inhospitable mountainous hinterland with a population of twenty million composed of many different peoples—40 percent Pashtun in the south and east, the rest Uzbeks, Tajiks, Hazaras and other lesser groups. To complicate matters, the Hazaras are Twelver Shiites with strong Iranian ties, and the country also contains Ismaili Shiites. In retrospect, the Durrani dynasty had done extraordinarily well to hold their kingdom together. Within a year the Marxist government in Kabul was falling apart: in province after province there was revolt, and

father" of Hezbollah, kills scores of innocents in **Beirut** without wounding its target.

As the number of Westerners abducted by Hezbollah and other Shiite terrorist organizations in Lebanon multiplies, President Reagan's government enters into secret negotiations with Iran to "trade arms for hostages"—an initiative that becomes known as "**Irangate**" and which later hurts Reagan's administration.

In May, against a background of terrorist incidents in **Kuwait** designed to inflame tensions between Sunnis and Shiites, a Shiite suicide bomber narrowly fails to assassinate the ruler **Jabir al-Sabah**.

the communists themselves divided into two factions, the Khalq ("masses") and the Parcham ("flag"). It seemed the USSR's plans for turning Afghanistan into a satellite had collapsed, and in December 1979 the Kremlin ordered in its troops.

Over the next decade, Afghan guerrillas fought doggedly to expel their invaders. But this was no ordinary war of national resistance. It became an international *jihad*, waged by mujahaddin, or "holy warriors," whose numbers were swelled by Arab, African, Pakistani, Muslim Chinese, even Indonesian and Filipino, volunteers. Eventually worn down, the Russians left in 1989, and a great Islamic victory was proclaimed. Yet the *mujahaddin* had only triumphed with the aid of $10 billion channeled through Pakistan, half of it supplied by Saudi Arabia, half by the USA. On another level, the outcome was a triumph for Washington: America had fought a surprisingly successful proxy war that accelerated the breakup of its ideological enemy, the Soviet Union itself.

On October 1, the Israeli air force bombs Yasser Arafat's PLO head-quarters in **Tunisia**, aided by US military intelligence. A week later, the Italian cruise liner *Achille Lauro* is hijacked by a splinter group of the Palestinian Popular Liberation Front. Arafat gains credit when the PLO persuades the hijackers to release their hostages and sur-render themselves to Egyptian authorities, but one Jewish citizen dies in the incident.

To appease Islamists, **President Mubarak** orders a series of minor concessions that include the banning of popular American television programs and the sale of alcohol on board Egyptair passenger planes.

1986 **Iran** endeavors to "internationalize" its war with **Iraq** by increasing support for **Kurdish rebels** straddling the Iraq-Turkey border and by attacking Kuwaiti shipping in the **Gulf**. When President Reagan deploys US warships to the Gulf to protect Kuwaiti and other vessels, Iran lays mines in the same waters.

Following an explosion in a **Berlin** nightclub that kills several US servicemen, and convinced that the terrorists responsible have the backing of Colonel Gaddafi, President Reagan orders an attack against **Libya** in April. American warplanes operating out of British air bases destroy Libyan naval vessels in the **Gulf of Sirte** and bomb **Tripoli**, **Benghazi** and other cities.

In May, Islamist students demonstrate against King Hussein's govern-ment at Yarmouk University in **Jordan**.

In July, Jabir al-Sabah suspends the **Kuwait National Assembly** for a second time as Islamist criticisms of his regime grow.

From October onwards, **Islamic Jihad** mounts a "terror campaign" against mainly military targets in **Israel**, attacking a group of Israeli conscripts visiting the Wailing Wall in Jerusalem.

1987 On August 1, between 300 and 400 **Iranian pilgrims** who have displayed placards denouncing the House of Saud, and who are suspected of wanting to seize the Kabbah in **Mecca**, are killed by

Saudi police. The Saudi embassy in Tehran is destroyed by a bomb shortly afterwards. King Fahd apologizes for the "shame" that the Mecca incident has brought Islam, and severely restricts the number of Iranians allowed into the Holy Cities.

In the same month, Britain and France deploy warships in the **Persian Gulf** after further Iranian attacks against American-linked commercial shipping.

In November, the USSR promotes **Muhammad Najibullah**, a security and intelligence chief, as the head of the puppet regime in Kabul following an intensification of the *mujahaddin* war against the Soviet occupation of **Afghanistan**.

In **Israel**, a Palestinian uprising which subsequently becomes known as the "**first**" *intifada* (literally "trembling" or "agitation") begins on December 7, directed against the continuing Israeli occupation of the West Bank and Gaza Strip, but also initially designed to oppose the "secularist nationalism" of **Yasser Arafat** and the PLO. As guerrilla and terrorist attacks against Israeli targets intensify, it becomes apparent that several militant Muslim groups are involved, among them Hezbollah, Islamic Jihad and a new organization linked to the Muslim Brotherhood known as **Hamas** (from the Arabic for "zeal"; its full name is *Harakat al-Muqawamah al-Islamiyyah*, "Islamic Resistance movement") and led by **Sheikh Ahmad Yassin**. Unlike its counterparts, Hamas gains the support of professionals, shopkeepers and other middle-class Palestinians living in Israel. The PLO itself is pushed to adopt a more "Islamic" profile in order to maintain its leadership of the Palestinian movement.

1988 In January, Arab ministers meeting in **Tunis** agree to give material assistance to the Palestinian intifada.

In March, Iraq deploys **chemical weapons** against Kurdish rebels backed by Iran: at the township of **Halabja**, over 4000 noncombatants are killed. In April, a UN report finds that **Iran** has also employed chemical warfare, against Iraq. After a US Navy vessel comes under

There is but one Allah and Muhammad is His Prophet. Those who become martyrs for Allah are the shaheed. The martyr smiles his way to death and death opens the door to paradise. Believers do not surrender to anyone except Allah. They may occasionally have to submit, but defeat is only a pause in the process of renewal. They are not defeated by defeat. They wait, they keep the faith, and renew their jihad until they achieve the victory that Allah promised in His bargain with the believer, specified so clearly in the Quran. Islam has always recognized the reality of war in human affairs, and set its moral and political compass.

—M.J.Akbar, *The Shade of Swords* (2002)

Iranian fire in the Gulf, American warships destroy Iran's offshore **oil terminals**. Having rejected Saddam Hussein's offers of a ceasefire for three years, Iran unconditionally accepts a UN resolution calling for an end to hostilities in July. Shortly afterwards, the US shoots down an Iranian passenger aircraft wrongly identified as a warplane, killing all 290 aboard. On August 20, Iraq agrees to a ceasefire, and the following week peace negotiations begin in Geneva.

In the same month, **Israel** conducts an effective anti-insurgency campaign against Islamic Jihad, now based in Gaza, as a result of which Hamas gains control of the *intifada*.

Earlier, in April, a **Kuwaiti airliner** is hijacked by Lebanese Shiite militants seeking the release of "Kuwait 17" members. Its passengers are held hostage on board for two weeks at Larnaca airport in **Cyprus**. Eventually they are freed, but not before two Sunni Kuwaitis have been murdered.

In May, **Iran** severs all relations with **Saudi Arabia**, which has supported Iraq, and forbids Iranians to travel on pilgrimage to Mecca.

In July, Arafat's PLO relinquishes its last base in **Beirut**. At the end of the month, King Hussein formally withdraws Jordanian responsibility for administration of the occupied **West Bank**. While the PLO swiftly moves in to fill the vacuum, the cessation of Jordan's funding for schools, hospitals and other amenities increases social unrest.

In **Pakistan**, President Zia ul-Haq is killed when what is thought to be a bomb detonates in his aircraft. Also on board are the American ambassador and General Akhtar, a leading strategist of the Islamic *jihad* against the Soviet occupation of Afghanistan. In the August elections that follow, Ali Bhutto's daughter **Benazir Bhutto** wins a clear victory at the head of her "Restoration of Democracy" party, reflecting a widespread rejection of Zia's Islamist policies.

In September, the publication in London of *The Satanic Verses*, a novel by the Indian-born writer **Salman Rushdie**, provokes protests and book-burnings by Muslims in Britain and massed riots in Pakistan and India. The book is regarded as sacrilegious on account of its portrayal of Muhammad's wives as prostitutes, among other "blasphemies."

In October, high unemployment levels in **Algeria** stimulate demonstrations against the ruling FLN. The riots are suppressed, leaving hundreds dead, and increasing popular support for radical Islamist leaders.

In November, Yasser Arafat's PLO endorses UN Resolution 242 of 1967, conceding the right of the **Israeli state** to exist. The PLO formally renounces "terrorism" as a valid instrument, but continues to condone the "use of force" to recover the Gaza Strip and West Bank. Arafat's hopes that Israel will respond with a reciprocal recognition of Palestinian statehood are unfulfilled.

On December 21, a Boeing 747 passenger airliner belonging to Pan-Am explodes over the Scottish village of **Lockerbie**, killing all 259 on board and a further eleven people on the ground. Two Libyan intelligence agents will later be tried by a Scottish court sitting in Camp Zeist, the Netherlands, but only one—**Abdel Baset al-Megrahi**—will be convicted.

1989 In January, following his announcement of the twin policies of *glasnost* ("openness") and *perestroika* ("restructuring") by President

THE ISRAELI-PALESTINIAN CONFLICT

*T*he creation of Israel in 1948 under the presidency of Chaim Weizmann triggered an immediate and lasting conflict. Palestine had formed part of the Muslim world since the 7th century, with its capital Jerusalem listed third among Islam's most holy cities. The Jews who remained there were generally left alone and accorded the right to follow their own faith. But Palestine was also the scriptural and historic homeland of the Jews, and from the late 19th century onwards, the powerful Zionist lobby—dedicated to founding a modern Jewish nation—began to make an impact.

The troubles began with the arrival of the first Jewish immigrants in the late 19th and early 20th centuries. Aware of Zionist intentions aired in **Theodore Herzl's** book *Der Judenstaat* (1896), some Palestinian Arabs reacted violently. After the Great War, however, Palestine became part of the British mandate, and under British protection the number of Jewish settlers grew. Although in 1947 they still formed barely 20 percent of the total population, after prompting from America and assurances by Jewish leaders that the rights of Muslim Arabs would be respected, the United Nations passed a resolution backing Jewish statehood that year.

The Arab response was swift. Led by Egypt, the principal Arab states went to war three times in an attempt to destroy Israel—in 1948, 1967 and

Mikhail Gorbachev, the USSR starts withdrawing its army from **Afghanistan** after a long, costly and ineffectual campaign. As it is announced in Moscow that the last Russian troops will be evacuated on February 15, Islam rejoices in the success of its *jihad*.

1973. But the net effect was merely to enlarge Israeli territory, and in 1977 President Anwar Sadat of Egypt adopted a more conciliatory tone, signaling that he was prepared to recognize Israel's right to exist. Despite Sadat's initiative, the situation inside Israel has worsened ever since. The rise of Islamic militancy, mirrored by militant Jewish sects such as **Gush Emunim** ("Community of Believers"), has generated a cycle of violence and counter-violence that now claims hundreds of civilian deaths on both sides each year.

A key episode was the launch of the first *intifada* in December 1987. The Palestinian Uprising, dedicated to creating a Palestinian state, provided an excuse for extremist anti-Israeli groups including **Islamic Jihad, Hezbollah** and **Hamas** to widen their operations. Briefly this played into the hands of **Yasser Arafat**, the leader of the PLO (Palestine Liberation Organization), who could project himself as a "moderate" during multilateral negotiations aimed at securing peace for Israelis and Palestinians alike. But as successive right-wing Israeli governments showed little inclination to recognize Palestinian autonomy, by 2001, when a second *intifada* was declared, Arafat was caught in a catch-22 which has yet to be resolved. If he repudiated the militants, he risked losing such support as he still had; but if he abandoned dialogue with the Israeli government, the "enemy" would have won.

CHAPTER ELEVEN

Islam Divided

{1989-2005 (1409-1425AH)}

The triumph of the *mujahaddin* over the USSR in **Afghanistan** was a tremendous victory, but although it boosted the confidence of Islam, it did little for its stability. Up to 40,000 non-Afghani Muslims who had fought during the great *jihad* now sought other holy wars, either in their own countries or elsewhere. As a result, militant activity escalated sharply—from **Morocco** in the west to **Indonesia** in the east. In **Egypt** and **Algeria**, there were determined efforts to replace existing more-or-less "secular" governments with revolutionary Islamist regimes. There were also Islamist uprisings in what, following the break-up of the USSR in 1989, became known as the "former Soviet republics," notably in **Uzbekistan**; and there were troubles of varying intensity in **Syria**, **Jordan**, **Iraq**, **Pakistan**, **Tunisia**, **Malaysia** and even in conservative, Wahhabist **Saudi Arabia**. In **India**, too, a Muslim minority contributed to communal violence, while in Russia, now without its empire, a full-scale Muslim separatist revolt flared up in **Chechnya** in 1994.

Islam was clearly in a state of ferment—encouraged not only by the outcome of the war in Afghanistan, but also by the example of Iran ten years before. Even in such non-Muslim Western nations as the United States, Britain and France, Islamist minority groups took action to make their voices heard. Yet in the dozen or so years following the *mujahaddin* triumph, the Islamic fundamentalists largely failed in their greater objective, which was to reform what they perceived as corrupt, ungodly societies by replacing their existing administrations with a revolution based on a literalistic understanding of the Koran and full application of Shariah law. In some—perhaps most—Muslim countries the pressure brought to bear by Islamists succeeded in influencing the policies of existing regimes, but, with two exceptions, actual regime change remained beyond the extremists' grasp.

Those two exceptions—neither of which lasted, or proved conducive to emulation elsewhere—were **Sudan** and **Afghanistan** itself. In 1989 in Sudan, Hassan al-Turabi, an army officer, staged a coup that introduced an Islamist state. Al-Turabi's government was notorious for its cruelty, however, and in 1999 was brought down after a prolonged period of civil war. In Afghanistan, the expulsion of Soviet forces induced seven years of turmoil as rival *mujahaddin* warlords battled it out to gain ascendancy, before a hitherto little-known faction made up of Pashtun tribesmen calling themselves *taliban* ("religious students") swept to power in Kabul in 1996. In power, the **Taliban** instituted a rule that subsequently became a byword for brutality and intolerance. Unwilling to admit non-Pashtuns into their ranks, they failed to exert control over the whole of Afghanistan, although it was the hospitality they extended towards the Saudi-born terrorist supremo **Osama bin Laden** and his al-Qaeda forces that led to their eventual downfall late in 2001, at the hands of an international military coalition spearheaded by the United States.

Whereas for a while at least it seemed that a fundamentalist revolution might also succeed in Egypt and Algeria, there were some Muslim states where Islamist insurgency was held firmly at bay post-1989—and others where it was simply non-apparent. Among these, the most obvious was Shiite **Iran**, where an Islamic revolution had already occurred, but where, following the death of Ayatollah Khomeini in 1989, an Islamic democracy began to emerge, promoted by the *majlis* (national assembly)—a body that had survived largely intact from pre-revolutionary days. In **Turkey**, too, a parliamentary democracy since much earlier in the century, there has been little evidence of militant Islam, although the country has experienced ethnic revolt amongst its Kurdish minority. There is also the case of **Libya**, which under the continuing and idiosyncratic stewardship of Colonel Gaddafi has remained a law unto itself.

It was not, though, only the *jihadists* returning from Afghanistan and their ideological soulmates who disturbed the fragile peace of the Muslim world. Eighteen months after the last Soviet troops pulled out of Kabul, Saddam Hussein's Iraq invaded its small but oil-rich neighbor **Kuwait**. Hussein's assault involved Islam in another great upheaval which has had far-reaching consequences. The seizure of Kuwait precipitated fears in Saudi Arabia that Hussein had embarked on a program of regional conquest, as well as widespread international alarm at the prospect of a high percentage of the world's oil supplies falling into the hands of a known tyrant. The Saudis called upon the USA, who in turn were able to forge through the United Nations a powerful multi-state coalition that easily expelled Iraqi forces during the **Gulf War**, early the following year. Yet although Hussein was badly bruised, he was scarcely out for the count. An inveterate propagandist, he was able to make political capital in at least three distinct ways. First, by declaring he would withdraw from Kuwait voluntarily if Israel withdrew its forces from occupied Palestinian territories, he aligned himself with the long-standing Muslim-Arab cause. Second, by insisting that America's sole interest lay in securing oil supplies, he undermined the credibility of the USA's self-projected image as the guarantor of international law and order. And third, by criticizing Saudi Arabia for allowing an "infidel" army to be stationed on the holy ground of Islam, which Muhammad had specifically prohibited, he cast himself in the unlikely role of true defender of the faith.

Many Muslims cared little that Iraq had been humiliated, and recognized that the oil trade benefited exporters as well as importers, even if its terms sometimes seemed unequal. But they were fired up by

Hussein's diatribe against the House of Saud. By playing host to President George Bush's soldiers, by providing him with air bases from which to strike at another Muslim nation, and by continuing to depend on the American alliance, the Saudis had committed a transgression against Islam itself—one that Osama bin Laden and other extremists were all too keen to revenge. And then of course there was the matter of the beleaguered Palestinians: since America was also Israel's principal ally, the Saudis were guilty of double treachery.

Saddam Hussein's determined efforts to create "linkage" between seemingly disparate events, combined with the accumulative frustration among fundamentalists at their own failure to effect widespread reform, set the stage, from 1992, for an unprecedented increment in terrorist activities. Many of the targets selected have been American: US embassies in Kenya and Tanzania in 1998, for example; the basement of the **World Trade Center** beforehand, in 1998; and, most devastatingly of all, the twin towers of the same complex as well as the **Pentagon** on September 11th 2001.

Since "**9/11**," as al-Qaeda's most infamous attack swiftly became known, Muslim extremists have widened their offensive still further, bombing a tourist resort in **Bali** in 2002, **Madrid** in 2003 and **London** in 2005—to name only the most celebrated incidents. Inevitably, the USA and some at least of its Western allies have responded in a variety of ways. Apart from overhauling and tightening security and intelligence systems, both domestically and internationally, the USA led the way in dismantling the **Taliban regime** in Afghanistan in an attempt to flush out Bin Laden and his associates. More controversially, in 2003 America went to war in **Iraq**, to remove Saddam Hussein and his Baath Party government, even though Saddam had long been styled "an infidel" by Bin Laden and other al-Qaeda leaders.

As American tanks rolled into Baghdad, and British tanks rolled into Basra, the world was treated to the spectacle of an improbably intimate bonding between a Republican President, **George W. Bush**, and a British Labor Prime Minister, **Tony Blair**. That both men are avowedly Christian may or may not have shaped their decision to stage another show of force in the Middle East: the containment of terrorism, the removal of a bellicose tyrant and an extension of Western-style democracy ("regime change") were the motives spoken of; and there was the unvoiced, but doubtless persuasive, need to protect Western oil supplies. Yet the problem was that none of the reasons for war, whether stated or perceived, was fully convincing, and doubts about the legitimacy of Bush's initiative have been compounded by subsequent and continuing disorder in Iraq, which has given fresh impetus to the fundamentalist *jihad*.

In one respect, however, the invasion of Iraq has been beneficial. To mount its military operation, the USA needed to know it could fully depend on Saudi Arabia and its other Arab allies in the Gulf. For this reason the Bush administration, breaking with established US foreign policy, began putting real pressure on Israel to resolve the **Israeli-Palestinian dispute**. As a result, during 2005, actual progress was made in creating a secure Palestinian state.

What happens in history is never finally predictable. For now it appears that Osama Bin Laden has sought to revive, as others before him revived, the original Muhammadan spirit of the *ghazi*, the holy warrior, often to the chagrin of his fellow Muslims. But what confronts al-Qaeda and its affiliated groups today is quite different from the enervated Persian and Byzantine empires that confronted the Prophet and his more immediate successors. The secularist underpinnings of the West, however much they may be resented by the religious-minded, of whatever faith or denomination, are a reason for its political, economic and military vitality; and within Islam itself secularism exerts a steady but powerful influence.

1989 Following the withdrawal of all Russian forces from **Afghanistan**, a socialist government headed by the "puppet" Muhammad Najibullah clings on to power in Kabul. The *mujahaddin* continue resistance, but increasingly begin fighting each other, as Afghanistan becomes prey to warlord rivalry.

On February 14, Ayatollah Khomeini issues a *fatwa* against the "Muslim apostate" **Salman Rushdie**, offering money to anyone who will kill him. Although the fatwa is condemned as un-Islamic by 48 out of 49 members of the Islamic Conference (OIC), Rushdie is forced into hiding.

In March, Islamic opponents of the FLN in Algeria form the **FIS** ("Islamic Salvation Front"), proclaimed on the 10th at the Ben Badis mosque in Algiers after President Chadli introduces a new constitution abolishing one-party rule. "Free" local and national **elections** are slated for June 1990 and December 1991.

On June 3, Ayatollah Khomeini dies of natural causes. He is succeeded as Supreme Faqih in Iran by the "revolutionary" **Ayatollah Ali Khamenei**, while the "pragmatist" **Hojjat Rafsanjani** becomes president.

In July, the Islamist army officer **Hassan al-Turabi** stages a coup against the democratically elected government of **Sudan** on the same day that the government suspends Shariah law in the hope of achieving reconciliation with Christian and other rebels in the south of the country. Enjoying limited popular support, al-Turabi imposes a "top-down" Islamic revolution, employing persecution, assassination and torture.

As casualties of the Palestinian *intifada* climb, Israeli prime minister **Yitzhak Shamir** rejects any notion of Israel condoning an autonomous Arab-Palestinian state—a position affirmed by a majority of his successors. Notwithstanding, on November 15 the PLO proclaims the state of **Palestine** with its capital in Jerusalem, invoking the UN resolutions of November 1947.

In **Turkey**, under the leadership of President Turgut Ozal, the Constitutional Council declares that democracy and Shariah law are incompatible and forbids women students to wear the veil.

In September, Israeli forces seize and imprison the Hamas leader **Sheik Ahmad Yassin** and over 200 other Palestinian "extremists." In **Lebanon**, the USA closes its Beirut embassy as warfare between Maronite militias led by General Aoun and Syrian forces escalates, complicated by factional fighting between various militant groups in the country. In November, the newly elected Lebanese president **René Muawad** is assassinated.

In October, Algerian Muslim immigrant families living in France are urged by the **Union des Organisations Islamiques de France** to adopt Islamic customs, in particular the wearing of veils by young women attending schools and colleges.

In November, Muslim Brotherhood candidates win 25 out of 80 seats in Jordan's national assembly, forcing King Hussein to appoint a handful of Islamists to his cabinet.

Abdallah Azzam, a leading Wahhabi ideologue who has promoted the Afghanistan *jihad* and acted as the principal link between Saudi Arabia and *mujahaddin* in Pakistan, is murdered in Peshawar.

In December, **Kuwait** demands exemption from oil production quotas sought by OPEC.

1990 In **Algeria**, local elections are held in January. To the dismay of the ruling FLN party, the FIS, led by **Abbassi Madani**, wins 55 percent of the vote. As a result, Shariah law is introduced in many townships.

In July, **Saddam Hussein** complains to the Arab League that Kuwait and the UAE are damaging Iraq's efforts to recuperate after its war with Iran by over-producing oil and depressing prices. Kuwait is also accused of sequestering US$2.4 billion from Iraq in 1980. For its part, Kuwait accuses Iraq of drilling for oil in Kuwaiti territory. Towards the end of the month, Iraq masses troops on the Kuwaiti border. Multilateral efforts to avert the impending crisis fail, and on August 2 Iraqi troops **invade Kuwait**, first occupying its oil-fields, then Kuwait City itself. Fearing that Hussein will drive further south into Saudi Arabia, King Fahd appeals to the United States for increased military assistance. The UN Security Council passes **Resolution 660**, repudiating Iraq's action, and a majority of Arab foreign ministers join in condemnation. Only Libya offers Hussein support. A further UN resolution imposes **economic sanctions** on Iraq as US president **George Bush**, apprehensive about the threat to Western oil supplies, works to form an **international coalition** against the Iraqi leader. On August 7, **Britain** and **France** join the coalition, which soon includes Arab and Muslim countries—among them **Saudi Arabia**, **Syria**, **Egypt** and **Turkey**. Russian president **Mikhail Gorbachev** also pledges his support. At the invitation of King Fahd, "allied" military personnel begin arriving in Saudi Arabia in large numbers. On August 12, Hussein responds by announcing that he will withdraw from Kuwait if **Israel** withdraws from the occupied Palestinian territories. When this initiative is rejected, he orders the detention of **foreign nationals** inside Iraq and Kuwait—where, by the end of November, over 700,000 Iraqi troops are stationed. In December, direct talks between Iraq and America begin, but Hussein sticks to his "principle" that Palestinian autonomy be linked to any Iraqi withdrawal from Kuwait.

In October, the Lebanese Maronite renegade General Aoun is outflanked by Syrian forces, which begin an assault on Christian **East Beirut**. Coordinating their efforts with the Lebanese government, the Syrians expel militant groups from Beirut, including the rival Shiite **Amal** and **Hezbollah**. These move to the south of the country, where they come under renewed attack from Israel. The government of Elias Hrawi, meanwhile, joins President Assad in the anti-Iraq coalition. For the first time in fifteen years, something like peace prevails in war-damaged Beirut.

Again in October, a former president of the Egyptian parliament, **Rifaat al-Mahgoub**, is assassinated in Cairo despite increased security measures against Islamic militants based mainly in city slums and the Upper Nile. To generate funds, up-country militants grow and export **hashish** (known as "Egyptian Red") and systematically extort money from the dwindling numbers of Christian Copts.

On November 6, seventy Saudi Arabian women drive cars into the center of **Riyadh** to protest against an "Islamic" prohibition against solo **women drivers**. By arguing that the Prophet's wife Aisha rode her own camel, they claim that the government is failing to uphold true Islamic law. But the protestors are subsequently dismissed from their jobs and harassed in other ways.

Following years of civil war, North and South Yemen are reunified to form a single **Yemeni republic**.

In Pakistan, **Nawaz Sharif**, president of the Muslim League and previously an associate of Zia ul-Haq, stages a military coup against Benazir Bhutto and assumes the position of prime minister for himself.

In Afghanistan, many of those whose farms and orchards have been destroyed by war begin cultivating the **opium poppy**, with the result that Afghanistan becomes, along with Myanmar, one of the world's leading sources of heroin.

In Britain, **Kalim Siddiqi**, an admirer of Ayatollah Khomeini, creates a "**Muslim Parliament**" to provide a forum for Muslim political debate.

1991 By the beginning of the year, 335,000 **US troops** are stationed in Saudi Arabia and the Gulf region. At midnight on January 15, an **ultimatum** for Iraq to withdraw from Kuwait given by the UN Security Council expires, and the **Gulf War** begins the following day when America and its allies begin **air attacks** on Iraq, targeting military, industrial and communications installations. Over the following days, television audiences worldwide view live coverage of American satellite-directed cruise missiles coursing through Baghdad. As "**Operation Desert Shield**" unfolds, Iraq launches ex-Russian "Scud" missiles against **Israel** in an attempt to force the Jewish state into the conflict and so turn it into a war between Muslims and Jews. Some of Hussein's Scuds, however, are intercepted by American "Patriot" missiles, and Israel is persuaded not to retaliate.

On January 24, the land war—"**Operation Desert Storm**"— begins when American marines capture the Kuwaiti island of **Qura**. The following day, Hussein orders the spilling of Kuwaiti **oil** into the Gulf, creating a ten-mile slick. On January 29, Iraqi forces advance into Saudi Arabia and capture **Khafgi**, but are expelled

SADDAM HUSSEIN AND THE GULF WAR

*O*n the face of it, the Gulf War was a stunning victory for international-al law and order—at least as defined by the United Nations and then-president George H.W. Bush. A task force drawn from across the world, and supported by an impressive array of nations from inside as well as outside the Middle East, was assembled in the sands of Arabia. Following an extensive bombing campaign against Iraqi military installa-tions, land forces gained their primary objective—the ejection of Iraqi forces from Kuwait—in a matter of weeks, and sustained minimal casualties.

However, in taking on Saddam Hussein, Bush confronted an inveterate propagandist. In the lead-up to "Desert Storm," as the military operation was code-named, the Iraqi leader attempted to transform his reputation— from that of a murderous bully into a potential pan-Arab leader in the mould of Nasser. Over ten years later, the Iraqi president was still in office and remained a key player in Middle Eastern politics.

within 48 hours. On February 13, Hussein protests that the US air force is bombing civilian targets in Baghdad. On February 24, the coalition's American field commander, **Norman Schwarzkopf**, moves his forces towards Kuwait and across the Saudi border into Iraq; the following day, Iraq begins withdrawing from Kuwait. As American and British troops enter, then take control of, **Kuwait City** and its airport, it is reported that over 500 **oil wells** have been set on fire by the retreating Iraqis. Having abandoned their equipment—and in some cases their uniforms—retreating Iraqi conscripts are bombed by the Americans, sustaining heavy casualties at

During the 1980s, Hussein had served Western interests well. His notorious brutality—he once shot a querulous cabinet minister mid-meeting—was conveniently overlooked, obscured by his resistance to Ayatollah Khomeini when there were widespread fears that the Iranian revolution would spread through the region. As leader of the "secularist" Baath Party, he was exactly the check sought by those opposed to extremism of any kind, and Hussein was copiously supplied with Western arms during the war with Iran. But in 1990–91 Hussein transformed himself. By aligning himself to the Palestinian cause in Israel and employing religiose rhetoric against the "satanic" West—rhetoric markedly similar to that of his old adversary, Khomeini—he became in the eyes of many Muslims the **"new Saladin."** This only worked to his advantage. As America led international economic sanctions in the face of Hussein's refusal to co-operate with UN chemical and nuclear weapons inspectors, he was able to claim—however mendaciously—that it was the US, not himself, that was causing untold suffering to the Iraqi people.

Mitla Ridge, north of Basra. Having gained his objective, President Bush orders a **ceasefire** ahead of truce negotiations. America and its allies have lost perhaps 200 combatants, Iraq anywhere between 250,000 and 600,000.

On March 3, Hussein accepts **Resolution 687** passed by the UN Security Council the previous day. The ruling al-Sabah family, having previously fled, returns to Kuwait and resumes power. On April 6, Iraq accepts a further UN Resolution calling for transparency with regard to biological and chemical weapons programs. But Hussein's refusal to cooperate with UN inspection teams in coming years will provide the USA with a pretext for continuing sanctions and enforcing "air exclusion zones" over north and south Iraq.

During the Gulf War, Saudi liberals petition King Fahd for an **elected assembly**. In May, an alternative petition is presented by "loyal" *ulama*, calling for an appointed assembly composed primarily of clerics. Fahd announces his plans for a consultative body in November, with nominated members including a mix of liberals and conservatives.

In March, a revolt against Hussein and his Baath Party begins in various parts of Iraq, particularly among the northern **Kurds** and southern **Shiites**. Hussein reacts brutally, deploying his best surviving troops. Although he succeeds against the Shiites, killing an estimated 30,000, he is unable to control Kurdish insurgency north of **Mosul**.

In May and June, the United Nations attempts to protect the Kurds by establishing militarily secure "**safe havens**," but a humanitarian catastrophe nonetheless develops when some two million people flee the region. Although Hussein appears to agree to the principle of limited Kurdish autonomy, tensions between Iraq's army and Kurdish guerrillas continue as "**Kurdistan**" fails to become an international priority. In **southern Iraq**, there is renewed Shiite insurgency in the same months, although Shiites are split between those loyal to the Iranian Revolution and those who merely want to see Hussein toppled. To flush out insurgents, Hussein begins draining Iraq's southern marshlands, displacing the indigenous **Marsh Arabs** and destroying their culture.

On May 22, **Sheik Abbas al-Mousawi** becomes leader of the pro-Iranian Shiite Hezbollah in Beirut. On the same day, the majority Christian Maronite government of **Lebanon**, having finally abandoned any sympathy for Israel, signs a **Treaty of Brotherhood, Cooperation and Coordination** with Syria. In return for offering guarantees for Syrian security, Syria recognizes Lebanese independence—viewed by Israel as an assertion of Syrian dominance. Southern Lebanon and the renegade South Lebanese Army remain within Israel's sphere of influence, however.

In the wake of the Gulf War, US secretary of state **James Baker** begins "shuttle diplomacy" to resolve the Palestinian-Israeli conflict, seen as the root of Middle Eastern volatility. On October 31, an **International Peace Conference** opens in Madrid, but grinds to a halt following disputes about protocol.

In April a coalition of non-Pashtun *mujahaddin*, led by **Ahmad Shah Masoud** (a Tajik) and **Rashid Dostum** (an Uzbek) capture Kabul in **Afghanistan**, bringing to an end the socialist government of Muhammad Najibullah, who takes refuge in the capital's UN compound. Although an Islamic government is formed with **Burhanuddin Rabbani** as its president, fighting in Afghanistan continues as the Pashtun warlord **Gulbuddin Hikmatyar** opposes the new regime and **Ismail Khan** creates a separate Shiite fiefdom in three western provinces.

In **Algeria**, anti-government demonstrations in May and June are broken up by the army. The FLN arrests Islamist leaders, believed to have provoked the unrest, although in a gesture of appeasement president **Chadli Benjedid** replaces an unpopular prime minister. In November, jihadists returning from Afghanistan decapitate a group of army conscripts at **Guenmar**. The government nonetheless orders the first round of **national elections** slated for December to proceed.

In June, following agreements between Saudi Arabia and Iran, **Iranian pilgrims** are once again allowed to participate in the annual *hajj* to Mecca.

In August, Islamic Jihad begins freeing **Western hostages** held in or near Beirut since the civil war in exchange for the release of Shiite militants held by Israel. The first two Westerners released are British journalist **John McCarthy** and American academic **Edward Tracey**, followed by the Englishman **Terry Waite** and **Thomas Sutherland**, another American, in November.

THE WAR IN BOSNIA (1992–95)

*T*he break-up of Yugoslavia from 1988 onwards was accompanied by so much violence that it seems incredible that Marshal Tito, the communist dictator who presided over Yugoslavia from the end of World War II until his death in 1980, ever held the country together. The leading protagonists were the Croats and Serbs; whereas the Croats, who were Catholic Christians, were mainly intent on creating a Croatian republic in the west, the Orthodox Christian Serbs wanted to impose their hegemony over as much of the "former" Yugoslavia as they could. Caught in the middle were the Bosnian Muslims, who made up a majority of the population of Bosnia-Herzogovina.

When the Bosnians jumped on the separatist bandwagon in 1992, the Serbs responded strongly and for three years the small Balkan province was torn apart as the Bosnian leader Alija Izetbegovic, an Islamist with connections to the Muslim Brotherhood, struggled to keep his Sarajevo government functioning. Eventually, NATO broke ranks with the UN and intervened, forcing

In **Iran**, as inflation soars and commodities become scarce, tensions between supporters of the revolutionary Ayatollah Khamenei and of the moderate centrist prime minister Rafsanjani provoke riots in **Tehran** and **Qum** in October.

In December, as the **USSR** is formally dissolved—partly as a result of its failure in Afghanistan—new Muslim-majority independent states emerge in Central Asia, including **Azerbaijan**, **Turkmenistan**, **Uzbekistan**, **Tajikistan**, **Kyrgyzstan** and **Kazakhstan**.

the Serbians back and allowing a chastened Izetbegovic to emerge the winner. Inevitably, perhaps, while it lasted the conflict attracted veteran jihadists who had fought the Russians in Afghanistan—some 4000 of them, in fact—although what impact they had has never been satisfactorily assessed. As far as the Western media were concerned, the Serbs were the villains of the piece—perpetrating, among other horrors, a massacre of 7000 Bosnian Muslims at Srebrenica in July 1995 while a Dutch UN peacekeeping force stood by. That Muslim commanders such as Naser Oric also perpetrated atrocities generated less publicity.

From a wider Islamic perspective, the salient point is that no Muslim nation became directly involved. In times gone by, the Ottomans would have pitched in gladly, since the Balkans were part of their empire. But the Ottomans' successor, Turkey, seeking greater integration with Europe, did everything it could to keep "Bosnia" at arm's length.

Towards the end of the year, **factional infighting** between the PLO, Hamas and Islamic Jihad eases Israel's security problems.

1992 In **Algeria**, Chadli Benjedid is forced out of office on January 12 by the army, following victories for the FIS during the first round of **national elections**. The second round is cancelled, a state of emergency declared and the FIS disbanded. Within a month, Islamist militants belonging to the **Groupe Islamique Armée** (GIA) and other extremist organizations launch a five-year war of terror during which an estimated 100,000 Algerians are killed.

In February, Israeli gunships kill **Sheikh Abbas al-Mousawi**, leader of Hezbollah, at his headquarters outside Beirut.

In March, following the break-up of the composite Balkan state Yugoslavia, **Bosnia-Herzegovina** proclaims its independence. Almost immediately, a three-way **civil war** erupts between majority Muslims and minority Croats and Serbs.

The extremist group **Gamaa Islamiyyah** begins terrorist operations against foreign tourists in Upper Egypt. Guided by the blind Sheik Omar Abdul Rahman, the group explicitly seeks to replace President Mubarak's "secularist" regime with an Islamic republic. On June 8, **Farag Foda**, a "loyalist" intellectual who has urged unrestrained suppression of Islamists, is murdered by its members. In November, an Islamic republic is declared in **Embaba**, a slum suburb of Cairo, but the area is "cleared" of insurgents by 10,000 Egyptian troops in December.

In September, Islamist clerics in **Saudi Arabia** issue a "**memorandum of admonition**" against King Fahd, claiming that his rule is a departure from true Islamic faith, and accusing his family—which occupies many senior positions within the kingdom—of corruption and embezzlement.

In December, Israel's prime minister **Yitzhak Rabin** orders the **deportation** of over 400 members of Hamas and Islamic Jihad to a prison camp in southern Lebanon. Many of those seized are teachers, doctors and other professionals. In the same, month the PLO leader Yasser Arafat begins "**secret**" **talks** with the Israeli government about a peace settlement.

In **India**, against a background of escalating communal tension, Hindu militants destroy the **Babri Mosque** at Ayodhya, consecrated to the memory of the first Mughal emperor, Babur.

1993 On February 26, the basement of the **New York World Trade Center** is bombed by Islamic extremists, killing six civilians and injuring a further thousand.

In July, following a campaign to restore full Shariah law in **Saudi Arabia**, spearheaded by a "Committee for the Defense of Islamic Rights," King Fahd appoints **Sheikh bin Baz** to the long-vacant post of Grand Mufti, or chief religious adviser to the throne. The Saudi government redoubles its efforts to suppress Islamist dissidents, however, including outspoken ulama.

On September 13, following months of multilateral negotiation, Israel and the PLO sign a "**declaration of principle**" working toward a "peaceful solution" of the Israeli-Palestinian conflict. The PLO itself, until now based outside Israel, is formally permitted to establish itself inside the country, and **Gaza** and **Jericho** become the first cities to be directly administered by it. A key consideration in Israel's apparent policy reversal is the hope that Yasser Arafat, now perceived as a "moderate," will furnish an effective buffer between Israel and extremist groupings, including Hamas and Islamic Jihad, that have perpetrated the *intifada* uprising.

Benazir Bhutto returns to power in Pakistan after winning a general election during which she makes conciliatory overtures to some Islamist parties. During the course of the year, the **Harakat al-Ansar** ("Partisan Movement") emerges as an effective militant party dedicated to ending Indian rule in Kashmir.

In Egypt, attacks against Western tourists spread to **Cairo**. The murders alienate many ordinary Egyptians dependent on tourism for their livelihood.

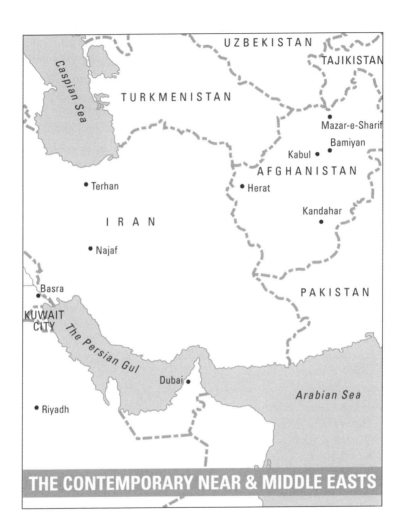

THE CONTEMPORARY NEAR & MIDDLE EASTS

In **Somalia**, eighteen US Marines on a UN peacekeeping mission are murdered by Islamic militants on October 4 and 5, following which President **Bill Clinton** orders the withdrawal of America's remaining troops. Responsibility for this and other "terrorist" incidents will be laid at the door of **Osama bin Laden**.

1994 In January, fighting between **Afghanistan**'s warlords enters a new phase when Rashid Dostum abandons his alliance with Ahmad Shah Masoud and Burhanuddin Rabbani and joins Gulbuddin Hikmatyar.

In **Israel**, thirty Palestinians are massacred at a mosque in Hebron by Jewish extremists on February 25. From April onwards, Hamas begins using **suicide bombers** against Israeli targets by way of reprisal, but the Israeli government responds by sealing off self-governing Palestinian townships and rounding up alleged militants. Notwithstanding these developments, Israel and the PLO sign the **Oslo Accords** on May 4, in line with the "declaration of principle" of the previous year. On July 24, the PLO formally accepts its responsibilities as the **Palestine National Authority**, tasked with maintaining order—including the suppression of Hamas and other extremists—in designated Palestinian areas. Opposed to any form of accommodation with Israel, militants increase the number of suicide bombings and assassinations. On November 18, Palestinian police loyal to Yasser Arafat kill sixteen Hamas members outside the Grand Mosque in **Gaza**.

In August, French police begin rounding up mainly Algerian suspected Islamic militants after five French diplomats are murdered in **Algiers**. On December 24, four Algerian terrorists—angered by France's support for Algeria's ruling military junta—hijack a French aircraft, but are killed during a rescue operation at **Marseilles**.

Also in August, Islamic militants become active in **Morocco**, attacking tourists in Marrakesh and Jews elsewhere.

In Egypt, **Naguib Mahfouz**, winner of the Nobel Prize for Literature, is murdered by a member of Gamaa Islamiyyah.

In October, a little-known Afghan faction of Pashtun Islamists called the **Taliban** ("religious students") seize 10,000 Kalashnikov assault rifles and other weapons from an arms depot belonging to Gulbuddin Hikmatyar at **Spin Baldak** near the Pakistani border. Backed by Pakistan's intelligence agencies and soon given financial aid by the CIA, on November 4 they capture Afghanistan's second-largest city, **Kandahar**, where they acquire tanks and six Soviet MiG fighter jets.

In **Malaysia**, the radical **Darul Arqam** sect, boasting 150,000 adherents, is outlawed after its leader **Ashaari Muhammad** proclaims himself a mahdi. Ashaari avoids heavy punishment by making a televised apology.

1995 An assassination attempt on the Egyptian president **Hosni Mubarak** at Addis Ababa in June is at first blamed on Gamaa Islamiyya, but is later attributed to Osama bin Laden.

On September 5, **Herat**, the largest city in western Afghanistan and a center of Shiism, falls to the Taliban. Ismail Khan flees to Iran and the protection of the Tehran government. In October, the Taliban begin their siege of the Afghan capital **Kabul**, which is defended by the Tajik warlord **Ahmad Shah Masoud**.

On November 4 **Yitzhak Rabin** is assassinated by a Jewish extremist angered by the Oslo Peace Accords.

In December, the **Dayton Accords**, brokered by the USA, bring peace to Bosnia-Herzegovina. The 4000-odd foreign jihadists who have joined the war leave the former Yugoslavian state.

During the course of 1995, under the leadership of **Shamil Bassayev**, Islamic separatists in the southern Russian province of **Chechnya** begin a revolt against the rule of Moscow. The conflict, which continues to the present, is actively supported by veteran jihadists of the war against the USSR in Afghanistan.

As civil war rages in **Algeria**, the ruling socialist regime introduces a **market economy** in a successful bid to drive a wedge between Algeria's professional classes and militants drawn from the young urban poor.

Worldwide, as the "**Islamic banking movement**" spreads, an estimated 144 Islamic banks and other financial institutions observing Koranic principles are in existence—to the despair of Western intelligence agencies endeavoring to track the flow of "terrorist" funds.

1996 In New York, **Sheikh Omar Abdul Rahman** is sentenced to life imprisonment after a court finds him guilty of involvement in the 1993 bombing of the World Trade Center.

In April, eighteen **Greek tourists**, mistaken for Jews, are murdered by Islamic extremists in a hotel in **Cairo**.

President Clinton signs an **Anti–Terrorism Act**, authorizing the freezing of assets belonging to suspected terrorists in American banks. The Act is immediately applied to accounts associated with Osama bin Laden.

On April 4, the reclusive leader of the Taliban, **Mullah Muhammad Omar**, appears in Kandahar wearing the Cloak of the Prophet to receive an oath of allegiance from his followers.

In May, a group of **French Trappist monks** are decapitated at **Tibehirine** by Algerian terrorists.

Also in May, the right-wing Likud party wins power in Israel and the "hard-liner" **Benjamin Netanyahu** becomes prime minister, leading to an expansion of **Jewish settlements** in the occupied West Bank and Golan Heights.

Following an election victory, on June 28 **Necmettin Erbakan**, leader of the Refah ("Prosperity") party, forms the first "Islamic" government in **Turkey** since the founding of the republic in 1922.

The Sudanese government, under pressure from the USA, orders the deportation of **Osama bin Laden**, who now sets up his headquarters in **Afghanistan** as a "guest" of the Taliban. On August 26, Bin Laden proclaims a *jihad* against "the American occupiers of the Holy

Places," referring to the continuing presence of US military personnel in **Saudi Arabia**—where nineteen American servicemen were
killed by terrorists at a US Air Force base at **Khobar** in June.

On September 10, the Taliban capture the strategic city of **Jalalabad**,
east of Kabul, enabling them to capture the capital itself on
September 26. After being dragged from the UN compound, the former socialist president Muhammad Najiballah is castrated, tortured
and shot. The Taliban's victory is reinforced in November, when
Nawaz Sharif returns to power in Pakistan. Ahmad Shah Masoud,
however, forms a **Northern Alliance** of surviving warlords opposed
to the Taliban, including Dostum and Rabbani. Creating a stronghold
at **Mazar-e Sharif**, the Alliance is supported by Russia, Turkey, India,
Uzbekistan, Kazakhstan, Kyrgyzstan and Tajikistan.

1997 On May 19, the Taliban capture **Mazar-e Sharif**, but four days
later their troops are massacred by an uprising in the city. The Taliban
lose 3000 men in all, and are forced to pull out.

In **Turkey**, Necmettin Erbakan's Islamic government falls on June
18—ten days short of its first anniversary—after the military put pressure on Erbakan's coalition partners to withdraw their parliamentary
support. As Turkey returns to the "secularist" fold, the path opens to
join the European Union.

In **Iran**, the "liberal" **Muhammad Khatami** becomes president
after winning a landslide national election. Controlling the *majlis*, he
embarks on a series of **reforms** that reverse many of the policies of
the Iranian Revolution. Dissociating himself from the *fatwa* issued by
Khomeini against Salman Rushdie in 1989, he seeks the "normaliza-
tion" of relations with Western governments. Ayatollah Khamenei,
however, retains much of his power, including command of the
Revolutionary Guard, and religious courts—established during the
Revolution—remain in place.

On September 28, the European Community's Commissioner for
Humanitarian Affairs, **Emma Bonino**, is arbitrarily detained, along

with 19 Western journalists, by Taliban police in **Kabul**. Although they are soon released, the episode focuses international attention on the Taliban's treatment of women. US Secretary of State **Madeleine Albright** and first lady **Hillary Clinton**, echoing the sentiments of Washington's feminist lobby, persuade President Clinton to realign US foreign policy against the Taliban regime.

On November 17, **sixty foreign tourists** are killed by members of Gamaa Islamiyyah at **Luxor** on the Upper Nile as they view the

THE TALIBAN

*W*ith the capture of Kabul in 1996, the Taliban ("religious students") became the masters of Afghanistan, instituting a regime comparable in its brutality to the Khmer Rouge in Cambodia. Yet it took several years before the outside world appreciated the full horror of Taliban methods, and their removal in 2001 only came about because Mullah Muhammad Omar, the Taliban leader, was befriended by Osama bin Laden— whose al-Qaeda terrorist organization was allowed to bed down on Afghan soil.

Internationally, the Taliban were widely welcomed when they took power, supported by Pakistan, Saudi Arabia and (indirectly) by the USA. Claiming to be above tribalism and intent on reunifying Afghanistan, they seemed to offer peace, and America noted the added attraction that several pipeline projects designed to extract oil and gas from the newly formed post-Soviet states of Central Asia might at last proceed. But with Kabul in their grasp, the Taliban projected a rather different face. It turned out that its membership was exclusively Pashtun, and no attempt was made to integrate Afghanistan's other peoples. Shiite Hazaras, Afghan Uzbeks and Tajiks were persecuted, with the result that civil war continued.

Temple of Hatsheput. Although this is the worst terrorist atrocity against tourists in Egypt to date, it is among the last. Following successful policing operations, Gamaa Islamiyyah and other fundamentalist groups in Egypt are suppressed.

During 1997, the civil war in **Algeria** attains new heights of violence. Increasingly deprived of popular support, extremists resort to slitting the throats of opponents, creating bloodbaths in **Rais**, **Messous** and other townships. Local **"patriot leagues"** are formed,

Most of the Taliban leadership had attended Deobandi madrasas in Pakistan during the anti-Russian *jihad*. From these, Mullah Omar and his companions acquired a fiercely puritanical understanding of Islam. In government, they imposed a version of **Shariah law** that included bans on such innocuous pastimes as music-making, dancing, kite-flying, chess, photography and most sports. Public floggings, amputations and death by machine-gun fire became the only public entertainment, whilst political victims were left hanging from telegraph poles in city streets. All men were forced to grow beards, all women forced to wear the all-enveloping burqa. Women were also prohibited to work outside their homes, and female education ceased.

For all this, the Taliban failed to create a functioning state. Their ministers doubled as field commanders, so government ground to a halt during their absence. Nor were they skilled at running an economy: instead of levying regular taxes, the Taliban survived by growing opium and taking kickbacks from a flourishing Central Asian contraband trade. In their bandit state, the treasury consisted of a tin trunk stuffed with hard currency beneath Mullah Omar's bed.

and the war turns decisively against the Islamists, now led by gangsters calling themselves "amirs." From the summer onwards, the government conducts an effective counter-offensive, and in September surviving rebel leaders agree to a **ceasefire**.

1998 In February, Bin Laden proclaims an "**International Islamic Front**" directed against "Jews and Crusaders." On March 8, the UN-sponsored **International Women's Day** is "dedicated" to the plight of Afghan women under Taliban rule; the Taliban respond by ordering the closure of Western aid agencies in July.

In May, as tensions escalate in **Kashmir**, Pakistan and India both test **nuclear weapons**. President Clinton persuades the two nations to step back from all-out war.

On August 7, the **US embassies** in **Nairobi** (Kenya) and **Dar-es-Salaam** (Tanzania) are destroyed by explosions caused by truck bombs. In all, 224 are killed (including 13 Americans) and 4585 are injured. The attacks are attributed to Bin Laden by American intelligence agencies, and President Clinton orders missile attacks against "**training camps**" associated with his al-Qaeda organization in Afghanistan on August 26. A factory manufacturing medical supplies at **Khartoum** in Sudan is also destroyed on the assumption—probably inaccurate—that it is used for terrorist purposes.

On August 8, the Taliban recapture the Northern Alliance stronghold at **Mazar-e Sharif**. As many as 6000 civilians, many of them Hazaras, are killed in revenge for the massacre of Taliban troops the previous year, and around 400 Hazara women are seized and taken to Kabul as concubines. The Taliban also kill eleven Iranian diplomats, almost certainly involved in supplying arms to the Alliance. **Iran** contemplates war against the Taliban, but fear of an American-backed Pakistani counter-offensive stays its hand.

In **Malaysia**, severely hit by an economic recession that is affecting the Far East, Mahathir Mohamad attempts to disgrace his popular Islamist minister **Anwar Ibrahim**, whom he accuses of sodomy and other crimes. Brought to trial, Anwar becomes the focus of widespread resentment toward Mahathir and there is rioting in **Kuala Lumpur**. It emerges that Anwar has been tortured, but Mahathir toughs it out, leaving in place many of the Islamic laws introduced by Anwar as a means of social control.

1999 In **Turkey**, during an April general election, the **Fazilet party**—in essence the reconstituted Islamist Refa party—wins less than 15 percent of the popular vote.

In Pakistan, Nawaz Sharif attempts to appease a rising tide of Islamism, fed by the conflict in Kashmir and by an unpoliced border with Afghanistan, by proposing the institution of Shariah law, but in October is overthrown by the "secularist" army commander **Pervez Musharraf**.

In **Jordan**, King Hussein is succeeded in June by his son **Abdullah II**, who signals a continuation of his father's policies by declaring his support for the PLO and imprisoning members of Hamas, Islamic Jihad and other "terrorist" organizations.

In **Algeri**a, following the restoration of democracy by the military regime, **Abdelaziz Bouteflika** is elected president. A "moderate" secularist, he calls a referendum in September to obtain the consent of the Algerian people for his policy of "national concord."

Also in September, a series of bombings in **Moscow** and elsewhere is attributed to Chechen Muslim separatists.

In December, **General Omar Hassan al-Bashir** mounts a coup against Hassan al-Turabi, bringing to an end Islamist rule in Sudan and also a protracted period of civil war.

2000 In **Israel**, following an inflammatory visit by the right-wing defense minister **Ariel Sharon** to the al-Aqsa mosque in Jerusalem, the Palestinian *intifada* resumes in September, subsequently dubbed the "Second Intifada." Islamic militants begin targeting civilian buses, restaurants, hotels and nightclubs, and the incidence of suicide bombings increases. After each attack the Israeli government makes reprisals, usually sending army units into **Nablus**, **Jericho**, **Bethlehem**, **Jenin** and other townships under the nominal control of the Palestinian National Authority, but also employing air attacks. Yasser Arafat is accused by the Israeli government of not taking effective measures against militants, and by the militants of not displaying the spirit of a revolutionary martyr.

OSAMA BIN LADEN (B. 1957) AND AL-QAEDA

*E*ver since the Six Day War in 1967, governments have dreaded the growth of international terrorism—a fear vindicated by Osama bin Laden and his al-Qaeda network, responsible not only for the September 11 attacks on New York and Washington in 2001, but for other major incidents in the preceding decade.

Osama is one of 54 children born to Muhammad bin Laden, a Yemeni bricklayer who became the chief construction contractor to the Saudi royals before being killed in a plane crash. The young Bin Laden inherited an estimated $300 million—which, supplemented by interests ranging from diamond trading in southern Africa to ostrich farming in Kenya, he has used to establish his pre-eminence in Islamic terrorist circles.

An important early influence was the Wahhabist Abdullah Azzam, the principle ideologue of the Afghan *jihad*. Traveling to Peshawar in 1982, Bin Laden became Azzam's right-hand man, channeling funds from Saudi Arabia to the *mujahaddin* while using his own money to create training camps for Arab volunteers. When the war ended, Bin Laden went looking, like others, for new Islamist opportunities. In 1990 he offered his services to King Fahd against Saddam Hussein, but was turned down—the probable origin of Bin Laden's consuming hatred for the House of Saud. He then traveled to Sudan, where he became intimate with the fundamentalist dictator al-Turabi, and it is from this time that Bin Laden emerges as a sponsor of terrorism.

On October 12, the **USS *Cole***, an American warship, is rammed by a "suicide boat" loaded with explosives while refueling at Aden in Yemen, with the loss of seventeen men. The attack is attributed to Bin Laden.

He returned to Afghanistan in 1996, having been expelled from Khartoum and stripped of his Saudi citizenship. Welcomed by the Taliban, he reconstituted his training camps and established al-Qaeda as a world-wide organization—its name, "the base," may be some sort of play on "database," since Bin Laden is known to use computers to keep tabs on those aspiring jihadists who have passed through his hands. Estimates of their numbers range from 30,000 to 100,000, and intelligence agencies suggest there are al-Qaeda cells in up to fifty countries. Exactly how such a network continues to hold together (if indeed it does) under conditions of intense surveillance is something of a mystery, although couriers assuming a variety of identities are probably as integral as a means of communication as radio, telephone, mail and the Internet—all vulnerable to undetected interception. It is, though, Bin Laden himself who holds the organization together, a quietly spoken but magnetic figure who combines a fundamentalist philosophy redolent of Ibn Tamiyyah and other Islamic ideologues with an uncanny ability to exploit the media. Following the bombing of New York, a series of carefully timed video and audio tape recordings broadcast by the Qatar-based al-Jazeera TV company kept the world on edge. When these dried up in 2002, rumors spread that Bin Laden had been killed, perhaps by the American bombardment of Tora Bora. Dead or alive, however, his self-created image is likely to endure.

2001 On January 19, the UN Security Council passes **Resolution 1333**, imposing an arms embargo and economic sanctions against the Taliban, and demanding the extradition of Osama bin Laden. On February 5, the trial opens in New York of four Arabs charged with complicity in the 1998 bombing of American embassies in Nairobi and Dar-es-Salaam.

Also in January, the hardline **Ariel Sharon** becomes prime minister of Israel at the head of the Zionist Likud party.

SEPTEMBER 11

*F*or Americans and millions worldwide, the events of the morning of September 11, 2001 were uniquely horrifying. Television coverage of the second hijacked aircraft smashing into the South Tower, images of people falling to their deaths from hundreds of feet above the ground, followed by the collapse of both the Twin Towers, created a daytime nightmare that will remain lodged in the memory.

The Muslim response was more ambiguous, however. **Muhammad Sayyid Tantawi**, the Grand Sheikh of al-Azhar university in Cairo, and **Muhammad al-Sabil**, the imam of the Grand Mosque in Mecca, were among senior Muslim clerics who swiftly added their voice to a worldwide condemnation of the attacks. Other Islamic leaders, though, were more reticent, and TV cameras caught scenes of open rejoicing among some Palestinians. In the bazaars along the Afghan-Pakistani border, too, videotapes featuring Osama bin Laden began selling like hot cakes once he had been identified as the likely perpetrator; similar videos achieved steady sales elsewhere in Islam and copies could even be found on sale in many European cities. Despite this, opinion polls conducted among Muslims outside Islam uniformly detailed a shocked and saddened reaction,

On March 10, to the dismay of archeologists and art lovers world-wide, the Taliban dynamite and shell two ancient and monumental **Buddha statues** carved out of a sandstone cliff near **Bamiyan** in central Afghanistan. Forty other Buddha images in Kabul Museum are smashed. While the Taliban cite a Koranic injunction to destroy "pagan" idols, the fact that the statues are regarded as sacred by the Hazara Shiites also enters their calculations. On

reflecting anxiety that Bin Laden had probably damaged Islam quite as much as he had damaged America. Inside Islam, majority opinion was harder to gauge, for the simple reason that most Muslim governments, operating tight controls over the media, disparage opinion polls—for all that the Koran specifically enjoins establishing a consensus.

What puzzled everyone was the profile of the hijackers. Unlike suicide bombers elsewhere, most of the nineteen were middle-class university graduates. They consumed alcohol, attended nightclubs and didn't wear beards. **Muhammad Atta**—the ground coordinator of the operation in America—was a 33-year-old Egyptian whose father was a lawyer, and who studied engineering in Cairo and Hamburg. In 1997, though, Atta "disappeared" for eighteen months; it now seems likely he attended al-Qaeda training camps in Afghanistan, before returning to Hamburg in 1998. On September 10 he flew from Florida (where he had obtained a pilot's license) to Boston, visited a Wal-Mart store and ate a pizza. Somewhere along the line Atta and his co-conspirators had been instructed in *taqiyyah* (dissimulation)—indispensable for the work they had to carry out, but for Western intelligence services and non-militant Muslims alike an ominous precedent.

August 5, eight foreign **aid workers** are placed under arrest, charged with disseminating Christianity.

On September 8, Afghanistan's Northern Alliance commander **Ahmad Shah Masoud** is murdered in the remote northeastern Panshir Valley by two Moroccan Taliban supporters masquerading as journalists.

On the morning of September 11, nineteen Muslim fanatics led by Muhammad Atta hijack four passenger airplanes in the USA. The first hits the North Tower of the **World Trade Center** in New York at 8:46am, while the second hits the South Tower at 9:03am. The third hits the **Pentagon** in Washington DC at 9:36am, and the fourth crashes into a field at **Stony Creek** in Pennsylvania at 10:06am without hitting its intended—and finally unidentified—target after its

An Afghani woman publicly shows her face for the first time in 5 years, after the Taliban defeat, 2001

passengers wrestle with its hijackers. At 9:59am, the South Tower of the WTC collapses, and the North Tower collapses at 10:26, causing over 2900 deaths (including some Muslims). A further 126 people die as a result of the strike against the Pentagon, and aboard all four aircraft a combined total of 266 passengers (the hijackers among them) and crew members are killed.

Following the identification of the suicide hijackers as Muslims—the majority of them carrying Saudi Arabian passports—on September 15 US president **George W. Bush** (son of ex-president Bush) unequivocally lays the blame for the atrocities on Osama bin Laden and his al-Qaeda network. Bush proclaims first a "crusade," then a "war," against terrorism and begins to coordinate a military offensive in **Afghanistan**, whose Taliban government is told to surrender Bin Laden or face destruction. On September 18, the UN Security Council supports Bush by reaffirming Resolution 1333. **Britain**, **France** and other NATO members (including Turkey) as well as **Canada**, **Australia** and **New Zealand**, are co-opted into an anti-terrorist coalition, which soon enjoys the backing of Russia's President **Vladimir Putin** on an understanding that no further objections will be raised to Russia's war of attrition against Muslim rebels in **Chechnya**. Simultaneously, **Uzbekistan** and **Tajikistan**, two former Soviet Muslim republics on Afghanistan's northern borders, are persuaded by promises of increased aid to allow coalition forces to use their airfields and airspace. Similar promises are made to Pakistan, whose president Pervez Musharraf has hitherto been blacklisted as a dictator.

> When the time of truth comes and zero hour arrives, then straighten out your clothes, open your chest and welcome death for the sake of Allah.
>
> —**Handwritten document found among Muhammad Atta's effects**

We calculated in advance the number of casualties from the enemy, who would be killed based on the position of the tower ... We calculated that the floors that would be hit would be three or four floors. I was the most optimistic of them all ... due to my experience in this field, I was thinking that the fire from the gas in the plane would melt the iron structure of the building and collapse the area where the plane hit and all the floors above it only. This is all that we hoped for.

—**Osama bin Laden, statement on videotape released by the Pentagon on December 13, 2001**

Faced by the possibility of an Islamist revolt, Musharraf prevaricates before finally agreeing to support the coalition. No serious attempt is made to enlist the Taliban's staunchest regional foe, **Iran**, Afghanistan's western neighbor, on the grounds that the US State Department is unwilling to declassify Iran as a "terrorist state" despite the country's steady drift towards democracy. By the end of September, small units of coalition special forces are operating inside Afghanistan.

In **Israel**, Yasser Arafat attempts to distance himself from terrorism by publicly donating some of his blood to the victims of the September 11 attacks. The *intifada* continues, however, and the Israeli government seeks to deflect criticisms of its anti-Palestinian operations by stressing that it too is fighting a "war against terrorism."

On September 29, Muslim extremists belonging to **Jiash-i Muhammad** ("Army of Muhammad") mount a suicide car bomb attack against the state assembly building in **Srinagar**, Kashmir. It is estimated that, since 1989, 30,000 have died as a result of violence in the disputed territory.

> The enemy of America is not our many Muslim friends. It is not our many Arab friends. Our enemy is a radical network of terrorists and every government that supports them. Our war on terror begins with al-Qaeda, but it does not end there. It will not end until every terrorist group of global reach has been found, stopped and defeated. Americans are asking: "Why do they hate us?" They hate what they see right here in this chamber: a democratically elected government.
>
> —President George W. Bush, addressing a joint session of the US Congress, September 20, 2001

On October 7, **air strikes** against al-Qaeda camps and Taliban targets in Afghanistan launched from American naval vessels stationed in the Indian Ocean mark the beginning of "**Operation Enduring Freedom**" (originally code-named "Infinite Justice," but changed following Muslim protests). These are coordinated with the **Northern Alliance**, whose commanders prepare to assault Taliban-held cities.

On October 9, the Kandahar-based Taliban leader Mullah Omar, now styled "**Commander of the Faithful of the Islamic Emirate of Afghanistan**" and resisting demands to hand over Bin Laden, calls for an Islamic jihad against America and its allies.

Beginning on October 12, letters containing **anthrax spores** are sent to various addresses in the USA, including government and media offices, resulting in five deaths and national panic. Although both Bin Laden and Saddam Hussein are initially blamed, no evidence for their complicity emerges.

On October 26, a former *mujahaddin* commander, **Abdul Huq**, returning to Afghanistan as an envoy of the exiled king Zahir Shah, is seized, tortured and executed by Taliban troops.

On October 28, sixteen Christians are massacred in a church at **Bahalwapur**, southern Pakistan, by Muslim terrorists.

Mazar-e Sharif falls to a Northern Alliance army led by Rashid Dostum on November 9. 700 Taliban troops trapped inside the city are massacred in revenge for previous Taliban atrocities. On the same day, the first of several **videotapes** made by Bin Laden confirming his complicity in the New York attack is aired by the Qatar-based al-Jazeera TV station. On October 11, **Herat** falls to Ismail Khan, and two days later Northern Alliance forces enter **Kabul** under their overall commander General Fahim. On November 25, a Taliban stronghold at **Kunduz** in the northeast falls. At the end of the month, over 400 Taliban prisoners stage a revolt at **Qala-i Janghi** fortress north of the capital. Most are killed by Northern Alliance troops and an American air assault. Among the 84 survivors is an American, John Walker, who is returned to America to face trial as a traitor.

On December 6, the Taliban surrender their last and most important city, **Kandahar**. Outside Afghanistan's cities, however, the country-side remains unsafe as war-bands prey on travelers. Fighting continues in the northeast, where coalition forces endeavor to flush out Bin Laden and al-Qaeda forces from the **Tora Bora** mountain range. Those troops who are captured are sent to **Camp X-Ray**, a US military detention center in Guantanamo Bay, Cuba, where they are held without being charged or brought to trial.

On December 13, five Pakistan-based Muslim extremists attack the **Indian Parliament** in Delhi with assault rifles and hand-grenades, killing seven before being shot by police. As a result of this incident, tensions in **Kashmir** worsen as India and Pakistan amass troops either side of the Line of Control.

2002 In **Afghanistan**, American, British and other forces associated with Bush's "war on terrorism" continue to hunt down Taliban and al-Qaeda fugitives, with diminishing returns. Both **Mullah Omar** and **Osama bin Laden** elude capture, although reports suggest the latter may have been wounded during an assault on Tora Bora. In the

West, some commentators continue to question the validity of pursuing a campaign that increasingly harms Afghan civilians.

On January 23, **Daniel Pearl**, an American journalist working for the *Wall Street Journal*, is abducted by Islamic militants in Karachi, Pakistan. Some weeks later, a videotape showing Pearl's execution is sent to US diplomats. In April, a British national, **Ahmad Omar** Sheikh, is found guilty of Pearl's murder by a Pakistani court and sentenced to death.

On March 31, **Yasser Arafat**, under increasing pressure from the Israeli authorities, throws in his lot with Palestinian militants by declaring his willingness to become an Islamic martyr.

On April 2, Israel launches a major offensive to clear **Ramallah**, **Nablus**, **Jenin**, **Bethlehem** and the **Gaza Strip** of "armed insurgents." On the same day, over 200 Palestinians, including thirteen suspected terrorists, take refuge in the Christian Church of the Nativity in Bethlehem, provoking a siege by Israeli forces that lasts over five weeks.

In April, following further attacks by Muslim extremists on Indian army posts in **Kashmir**, India and Pakistan increase the number of their troops along the Line of Control to 600,000 and 400,000 respectively—creating the prospect of all-out war between the two countries with the possible use of nuclear weapons. The situation is defused in June, however, when President Musharraf, bowing to pressure from Washington and risking an uprising against his regime, agrees to **suppress militants** operating out of Pakistan. India too shows restraint, despite continued attacks on its Kashmiri subjects. By July, each side has reopened its airspace to the other's civilian airlines.

In June, a *Loya Jirga* (traditional grand council of tribal and other leaders) convenes in **Kabul** to appoint a provisional government for Afghanistan. After much wrangling, **Hamid Karzai** is confirmed as interim president, a position he has held since December. The former king **Zahir Shah** returns to Kabul from exile in Rome and is given the honorific "father of the nation." Despite these moves towards a constitutional government of unity, large areas of Afghanistan remain under the control of local warlords, and bombings and assassinations perpetrated by remnant Taliban and al-Qaeda forces continue.

From June onwards, President Bush's attention shifts towards a possible full-scale military operation in **Iraq** to remove Saddam Hussein, accused by him of sponsoring terrorism and secretly pursuing chemical, biological and nuclear weapons programs. Although Bush is able to cite Hussein's success in removing United Nations weapons inspectors from Iraq in 1998 as evidence of his intentions, the president fails to enlist the support of other Western leaders, with the exception of Britain's prime minister, **Tony Blair**. Persuaded by his White House advisers not to undertake unilateral action, in September Bush begins pressing the United Nations to adopt measures to force Hussein to comply with existing UN resolutions.

The last quarter of the year sees an escalation in the number of **terrorist attacks** undertaken by groups associated with al-Qaeda, fuelling speculation that Bin Laden is still alive and active. On October 6, a French oil-tanker, the *Limburg*, is damaged by a suicide squad off the coast of Yemen. Two days later, a US marine is killed in **Kuwait**. On October 12, bombs kill up to 200 Western tourists, including 114 Australians, in the Sari nightclub on Kuta Beach on the predominantly Hindu Indonesian island of **Bali**. Indonesian police, aided by Australian, American, British and other international officials, swiftly establish that the attack is likely to have been carried out by **Jamaah Islamiyya**, a militant organization that seeks to create a single Islamic state in **Indonesia**, **Malaysia** and **Singapore**. On October 23, Chechen rebels calling themselves *mujahaddin* and sporting bandanas that have words from the Koran inscribed on them seize a theatre in **Moscow**, taking over 800 people hostage. After a three-day siege, Russian security forces storm the building. All 41 Chechen terrorists are killed, including 18 women. 128 hostages also die—some shot by the rebels, but many killed by the gas used by their would-be rescuers.

In **Turkey**, the Islamic Justice and Development Party, led by **Tayyip Erdogan**, wins victory in a general election held on November 3, prompting fears of an Islamist takeover. While Erdogan swiftly reaffirms Turkey's commitment to NATO and joining the European Union, political analysts question whether the election result accurately reflects the people's wishes under a system (originally designed to discourage Islamist groups) that disqualifies any party gaining under 10 percent of the popular vote from sitting in parliament.

On November 9, following intense American pressure, the United Nations Security Council unanimously passes **Resolution 1441**, calling for UN weapons inspectors to be allowed full and unimpeded access to all sites in Iraq including Saddam Hussein's many presidential palaces. Although Hussein agrees to let the weapons inspectors return, and an advance party led by **Hans Blix** is installed in Baghdad by the end of the month, the Resolution's terms are so strict that few doubt President Bush intends using its likely breach as a pretext for his planned invasion of Iraq.

In **Nigeria**, where the government has agreed to stage the 2002 **Miss World** beauty contest in the capital Abuja, over two hundred people are killed during three days of fighting between Muslims and Christians in the northern city of **Kaduna**, beginning on November 21. The riots are provoked by Muslims who see the event as un-Islamic and likely to promote promiscuity, and by an article in the *This Day* newspaper suggesting Muhammad would have enjoyed the pageant and "probably have chosen a wife" from among its contestants.

On November 28, fifteen are killed when the Israeli-owned Paradise Hotel outside **Mombasa** in Kenya is attacked by Muslim suicide terrorists presumed to be linked to al-Qaeda. At Mombasa airport, two rockets are fired at a departing Israeli aircraft on the same day, but miss their target.

Throughout the year, the second Palestinian *intifada* against Israel continues unabated. Frustrated by what it sees as Yasser Arafat's unwillingness (or inability) to rein in "terrorists," Israel's armed forces increasingly target buildings and complexes belonging to the Palestinian National Authority, while continuing to attack township districts where terror-

In spite of what many hasty commentators contended in its immediate aftermath, the attack on the United States was a desperate symbol of the isolation, fragmentation, and decline of the Islamist movement, not a sign of its strength and its irrepressible might. The jihadist-salafists who belonged to Bin Laden's mysterious Al Qaeda network imagined themselves as the spark that would ignite the volatile frustration of the disenchanted ones in the Muslim world and stoke a firestorm. They had no patience for the slow building of a movement that would reach out to the masses, mobilize them, and guide them on the path to power. They put their faith in example and emotion, in immediacy and violence. They believed that once the great American Satan had been made to shake on its foundations, for all to see, then a sweeping tide of jihad would overtake the modern world. This delusion bore some similarity to that of the Jihad group of Egypt who assassinated Anwar Sadat in October 1981.

—**Gilles Kepel,** *Jihad: The Trail of Political Islam*,
trans. **Anthony F. Roberts (2002)**

ists are believed to be based. Even by early August, some 2000 Palestinians and 600 Israelis have died as a result of the "uprising"—a majority of them civilians, and some of them children.

2003 Determined to remove Saddam Hussein from power in Iraq by any means, the Bush administration courts **Arab favor** by taking a tough line with Israel in the USA's quest for a resolution of the Palestinian question. Mutual distrust between Israeli prime minister Sharon and Yasser Arafat, however, impedes progress.

In March, backed by British prime minister Tony Blair, the Bush administration puts the finishing touches to its planned **invasion of Iraq**, even though invasion is vigorously opposed by France, Russia and Germany at the UN Security Council, and Hans Blix, chief of the UN weapons inspection team, says publicly he has found no evidence that Saddam is stockpiling **WMD** (weapons of mass destruction)—the declared pretext for taking action. On March 17 Bush gives Saddam an unheeded ultimatum to leave Iraq within 48 hours. In the early hours of March 20 the invasion begins with an aerial bombardment of military, governmental and Baath Party targets in Baghdad. Although precision weapons are used, there are civilian casualties, referred to by US Defense Secretary **Donald Rumsfeld** as "collateral damage." A "**coalition of the willing**," made up of 100,000 US, 45,000 British and much lesser contingents of Australian, Polish, Danish and South Korean troops, enter Iraq by its southern borders and coastline. Spain lends logistic support, but Turkey denies the coalition bases on its territory. While the Americans drive north, the British head for **Basra**, Iraq's mainly Shia second city that falls on April 6th. Saddam flees **Baghdad**, which is occupied by American forces on April 9. As a **Coalition Provisional Authority** is set up to govern Iraq, Bush declares an "end of major combat operations" on May 1. Sunnis loyal to Saddam, Shia militants and, increasingly, jihadists from outside Iraq however will make a mockery of the coalition's apparent victory over the coming weeks, months and years, and Iraq becomes a more, not less, violent country.

The Spanish capital **Madrid** is shaken by ten coordinated explosions on its commuter rail network during the morning rush hour on March 11 that leaves 198 dead and over a thousand injured. Spanish premier **José Maria Aznar** blames the Basque separatist group ETA, but it quickly becomes clear that Moroccan terrorists linked to al-Qaeda are responsible. Four days later Aznar loses a general election.

On March 26 India and Pakistan test-fire short-range ballistic missiles, stoking fears of an imminent **nuclear** exchange. Following intense diplomatic activities, on May 2 the two countries agree to restore diplomatic relations, suspended since 2002 because of tensions in **Kashmir**. By the end of November, both sides will have signed up to a ceasefire.

In June the USA and Britain, now supported by 29 other nations, establish an interim Governing Council in Iraq, headed up by **Iyad Allawi**, a Shia neurologist and suspected former CIA agent. The

THE "SECOND" GULF WAR

Given the extent to which Saddam Hussein had taunted President George H.W. Bush following the First Gulf War, it was predictable that his son **George W. Bush** should target Saddam once, by the slenderest of margins, he had been elected US President. Even though it achieved its immediate objectives with overwhelming speed, the actual invasion of Iraq was, however, arguably an act of incomparable folly. Bolstered by the strong support of British prime minister Tony Blair, but of precious few other leaders, George W. Bush failed to achieve a clear mandate from the United Nations Security Council. His pretext—that Saddam was illegally stockpiling weapons of mass destruction—was widely challenged at the time, and subsequently proved false. Worse, his argument that Saddam endorsed international terrorism was fundamentally misguided. Whatever his heinous misdemeanors as a local tyrant, Saddam the secularist was opposed to Islamic extremism, and was therefore a useful, if unattractive, adjunct in the "war against terrorism." Similarly, Bush and Blair misread "Iraq" itself, a country composed

Council's authority however is strictly limited as the USA retains the right to review and veto its decisions.

On July 22 Saddam's sons **Uday** and **Qusay** are killed by coalition forces.

In August Libya finally accepts responsibility for the downing of Pan Am Flight 103 over **Lockerbie** in 1988. The UN lifts sanctions against Libya as Libya agrees to pay $2.7 billion in compensation to

of three disparate and mutually hostile elements—Shias, Kurds and Sunnis, in descending numeric order—brought into being only by Anglo-French initiatives in the aftermath of World War I. Saddam toppled, and his Baath Party dismantled, inter-communal anarchy has followed, for all that there is a constituency of Iraqis which has welcomed the Bush-Blair program of democratization. In the British-controlled Shia south, evidence suggests that Iran supports anti-occupation insurgents. In the central "Sunni-triangle," a hardcore of vengeful Saddam loyalists are abetted by al-Qaeda operatives, crossing over the Syrian border. Shootings, suicide bombings and hostage-taking have become pandemic. By the end of 2005 well over 100,000 Iraqis had lost their lives in the wake of the invasion, compared to around 2000 US and 100 British service personnel. Yet Bush and Blair had been forewarned. Removing Saddam meant destabilizing Iraq, possibly the entire Middle East, and extending the extremists' remit. As much as intervention in Vietnam, "Iraq" has polarized American (as well as British) opinion, and tarnished the USA's pretensions to be a moral super-power.

the victims' families. Libya will also abandon its attempts to acquire nuclear weapons before the year-end.

On October 10 **Shirin Ebadi** becomes the first Muslim woman and the first Iranian to win the Nobel Prize for Peace, for work with women and children and her pro-democracy stance.

On December 13 a disheveled **Saddam Hussein** is discovered clutching a suitcase of dollars in an outside cellar at a farmhouse near his hometown of Tirkrit by American soldiers. The following day civilian administrator Paul Bremer tells a press conference in Baghdad, "Ladies and Gentlemen, we got him!" It is soon decided that Saddam will stand trial for crimes against humanity before a special court in his own country.

2004 On February 10 the French National Assembly votes to ban the wearing of the *hijab* (Islamic head scarf) at schools colleges and universities as well as other "symbols and clothing that ostentatiously show students' religious membership."

In April the USA dispatches a further 10,000 soldiers to Iraq as the security situation there worsens and national reconstruction is severely hampered. In June, following **elections** to a National Assembly in January, and after months of wrangling, a provisional Iraqi government is formed. Allawi is named prime minister. American and other coalitional forces remain in place to combat insurgents and train new Iraqi military and police forces.

On the orders of Shamil Basayev, Chechen militants take control of a school at **Beslan** in North Ossetia on September 1. Two days later the siege is ended by the intervention of Russian security forces. Among the 344 civilian dead are 186 children. President Putin continues his war of attrition against Muslim insurgents in Chechnya.

In October, *The Lancet*, a British medical journal, estimates that at least one hundred thousand Iraqis have lost their lives as a result of the previous year's invasion and its consequences.

On October 9, **Hamid Karzai** wins over 50 percent of votes cast during a presidential election held in Afghanistan following the adoption of a new constitution promulgated earlier in the year. Many of Karzai's opponents boycott the election however, and the situation in Afghanistan remains perilous as Taliban and other unruly elements plague the countryside.

On November 8 combined Iraqi and American forces launch an all-out assault on **Fallujah**, an insurgent stronghold south of Baghdad. Many civilians are killed as well as two thousand alleged rebels, and the city is leveled during the largest battle since the occupation of 2003.

On November 11 **Yasser Arafat** dies in a military hospital in Paris, where he has been airlifted with Israel's permission for the treatment of an undisclosed blood disorder. When his body is returned to **Ramallah**, tens of thousands attend his interment. But while Palestinians mourn his death, others see it as an opportunity to advance the Israeli-Palestinian peace process.

In mid-November **Margaret Hassan**, a much respected Irish aid worker who has worked for CARE International since 1991, is murdered following her abduction by insurgents on October 19. She is just one of many expatriate civilians to meet a similar fate in post-occupation Iraq, often at the hands of the al-Qaeda leader **Abu Musab al-Zarqawi** and his Jama'at al-Tawhid wal Jihad grouping.

An undersea earthquake off the northwest coast of the Indonesian island of Sumatra generates an unprecedentedly powerful *tsunami* (tidal wave) on December 26 that claims a quarter of a million lives in the Indian Ocean region. Worst affected is Sumatra itself, where over a hundred thousand Muslims die in **Aceh** province. Led by the USA, eager to prove its humanitarian values in the face of mounting criticism over its role in Iraq, the world achieves new standards of coordination and volume in the provision of emergency aid.

The Grand Central Mosque in Leeds, England, 2005

2005 Mahmoud Abbas is elected President of the Palestinian Authority on January 9. In February he meets with Israeli prime minister Sharon, President Mubarak of Egypt and King Abdullah II of Jordan at Sharm el-Sheikh to revive the **Israeli-Palestinian peace talks**. A ceasefire is brokered as Israel agrees to release nine hundred Palestinian prisoners and withdraw its troops from Palestinian towns and cities.

On February 14 in Beirut, a massive bomb detonates near the motorcade of Lebanese **Prime Minister Rafiq Hariri**, killing him and twenty others. Lebanese take to streets in massive protests, accusing Syria of Hariri's murder. Heeding a UN Security Council resolution, Syria withdraws the last of its troops from Lebanon on April 26, ending their 29-year deployment. Tension between the countries escalates in October, with Lebanese troops moving against Syrian-backed Palestinian militant bases, and the release of a UN report which implicates senior Syrian officials in Hariri's assassination.

In Iraq, a **new interim government** is formed on April 6 following elections at the end of January. **Ibrahim al-Jafaari** is chosen as Iraq's prime minister. The new authority is tasked with devising a constitution that will satisfy all three of Iraq's main constituents— Shias, Sunnis and Kurds. This however does little to assuage fears among Sunnis, who make up no more than 17 percent of the population, that theirs will be a powerless future. Inter-communal violence escalates, especially between Sunnis and Shias.

Anti-American riots erupt in **Jalalabad**, Afghanistan, on May 11 after Newsweek magazine reports systematic abuse of Taliban and other jihadists still being held at **Guantanamo Bay**.

Following elections held on June 17, **Mahmud Ahmadi-Nejad** becomes President of **Iran**, having easily defeated the moderate reformist Ali Akbar Hashemi Rafsanjani. A former Mayor of Teheran, Ahmadi-Nejad is a known hardliner who re-ignites international fears about Iran's acquisition of nuclear weapons.

A long anticipated al-Qaeda terrorist attack rocks **London** shortly before 9am on July 7 when bombs go off on three underground trains and a bus. As well as the four suicide bombers involved, fifty-two civilians are killed, and scores more injured. Worryingly for the government, it is established that three of the bombers were British citizens of Pakistani descent. On July 21 a similar attack fails when four more bombs fail to detonate on trains and buses. Britain's mainly peaceable Muslim communities experience ostracism.

King Fahd of Saudi-Arabia dies on August 1. He is succeeded by his younger brother **Abdullah bin Abdul-Aziz**, who continues Fahd's policies, especially with regard to the Saudi-American alliance.

On August 24 Israel completes the withdrawal of its forces from the **Gaza Strip** and four West Bank settlements, to the considerable dismay of Jews settled in those areas. Across Israel, there is rising discontent with Ariel Sharon's policy of conciliation toward the Palestinians.

Egyptian President **Hosni Mubarak** wins a national election on September 7. Although voting irregularities occur, and opposition leader Dr Ayman Nour contests the result, the international community welcomes Egypt's apparent return to democracy as extremist Islamic elements are perceived to recede.

The Indonesian island of **Bali** is again targeted by terrorists on October 1st, when suicide bombers detonate three bombs in tourist restaurants, killing twenty. The attacks are credited to the al-Qaeda-linked group Jamaah Islamiah.

On October 4 EU ministers meeting in Brussels agree that official talks should proceed preparatory to the admission of **Turkey** into the European Union.

On October 8 an **earthquake** measuring 7.6 on the Richter scale devastates the border area between India and Pakistan. Over the coming weeks some 50,000 are reported dead. **Kashmir** is most affected, and the two governments agree to temporarily lay aside their differences to expedite relief programs.

A new constitution prepared by the Iraqi interim government is put before voters in a **nationwide referendum** held on October 13. Overwhelmingly Shia and Kurdish provinces vote acceptance, but Iraq's predominantly Sunni provinces overwhelmingly vote rejection. As fears grow that the referendum result can only prolong division and violence, the constitution is adopted ahead of a general election called for December 15.

Saddam is finally put on trial in Baghdad on October 17. Facing a long list of charges he proclaims his innocence.

As the year draws to a close, **Western reporters** covering Iraq increasingly remain indoors in the handful of safe hotels available to them in Baghdad, preferring instead to rely upon "locals" to gather news and take photographs; and **Osama Bin Laden** remains unaccounted for, despite the biggest manhunt in history.

BOOKS

As with books about Christianity, Buddhism and other religions and their histories, there is a qualitative, insider-outsider difference between studies of Islam written by those who adhere to the faith and those who do not. Although weighted towards the latter, the following list contains works of both sorts. Wherever the title in question is in print, the UK publisher is given first, followed by the US publisher. Where a title is available in one country only, the country in question is indicated. Where a title is published by a single publisher in both territories, only the name of one publisher is given.

The Koran (Quran)

Since the 17th century, the Koran has been translated many times into English as well as other modern languages. Of the translations readily available today, two are particularly recommended: **N.J. Dawood**'s, published in the Penguin Classics series in two versions, one with and one without a parallel Arabic text (Penguin Books); and the older, "freer" translation of **Arthur J. Arberry**, now reissued in Oxford World Classics (Oxford University Press).

General history

M.J. Akbar, *The Shade of Swords: Jihad and the conflict between Islam and Christianity* (Routledge). Several recently published books have sought to characterize Islam as a religion of bloodshed: the interesting thing about this one is that it is written by a widely respected Muslim journalist. Although Akbar writes in an anecdotal and sometimes humorous manner, the underlying message is chilling.

Karen Armstrong, *The Battle for God: Fundamentalism in Judaism, Christianity and Islam* (HarperCollins; Ballantine Books). With considerable audacity, Karen Armstrong, an ex-nun, argues that extremist elements in each of the three main monotheistic faiths have created mayhem in their rivalrous quest for an "ultimate truth". While this is a gripping read, it is in places marred by an intellectual schematization that too insistently pits *logos* (reason) against *mythos* (tradition and revelation).

Karen Armstrong, *Islam: A Short History* (Phoenix Press; Modern Library Chronicles). If you are looking for a clear, punchy narrative history of Islam that can be read through on a longish plane or train journey, this is the book. That said, because of its brevity there are necessarily important aspects and episodes of Islam that are absent.

Geoffrey Barraclough (ed.), *The Times Atlas of World History* (Times Books). The sixth edition of this established historical atlas is a real help for anyone wishing to understand the spread of Islam, especially when used in conjunction with the awesome tenth edition of *The Times Atlas of the World* (Times Books).

Jonathan Bloom and Sheila Blair, *Islam: Empire of faith* (BBC Worldwide). Written to accompany a TV series of the same title, and published a short while before the terrorist attacks in September 2001, this is a culturally positive overview of Islam that hesitates to take the story beyond 1700. Even so, it can be read as a palliative to some of the shriller books that have appeared post-9/11.

John Esposito, *The Oxford History of Islam* (Oxford University Press). A scholarly, solid and ultimately "safe" account.

Cyril Glassé, *The Concise Encylopaedia of Islam* (Stacey International). The most comprehensive single-volume reference work on Islam published to date, this revised edition is compiled by an American academic who is also a practising Muslim. While it is particularly strong on Islamic theology and contains a rich treasury of quotations, it tends to shirk the more contentious international issues raised by its subject matter.

M.G.S. Hodgson, *The Venture of Islam: Conscience and History in a World Civilisation* (University of Chicago Press). Although published in 1974, Hodgson's three-volume history of Islam continues to be a useful starting point, particularly for academic students of Islamic history

Ira M. Lapidus, *A History of Islamic Societies* (Cambridge University Press). At nearly 1000 pages, this may be beyond the endurance of some, but Lapidus comes up with the goods in spectacular style, balancing a political narrative against a much-needed and wide-ranging sociological survey. If we had to recommend only one book about Islam, this would be it. A second edition has recently been published.

Andrew Wheatcroft, *Infidels: The Conflict between Christendom and Islam 638-2002* (Penguin Books). The long, long history of mutual recrimination between Muslims and Christians is here recounted by a historian who has a way with unlikely sources.

MUHAMMAD
AND THE FOUNDATIONS OF ISLAM

Karen Armstrong, *Muhammad: A Biography of the Prophet* (HarperCollins). While the ideal full-scale modern life of Muhammad has yet to be written, Karen Armstrong's biography, with its ability to breathe life into theological abstractions, fills the gap well.

Abd-al-Rahman Azzam, *The Eternal Message of Muhammad* (New English Library o/p; Mentor Books o/p). Written by the founder of the Arab League and translated by Caesar E. Farrah, this is an informed exposition of Muhammad's life, teaching and impact that wears its heart on its sleeve, but is all the more valuable because of that. Long out of print, but eminently worth tracking down.

P. Brown, *The World of Late Antiquity AD 150–750* (Harcourt Brace Jovanovich). Brown provides as good a survey as can be found of the post-Roman world into which Islam was born.

Michael Cook, *Muhammad* (Oxford University Press). A valuable addition to the Oxford Past Masters series, Cook's beautifully concise study of Muhammad is coolly analytical of its subject and the historiographic problems that surround any attempt to reconstitute his life, but also curiously responsive to what the author takes to lie at the heart of the Koranic "message."

Fred McGraw Donner, *The Early Islamic Conquests* (Princeton University Press). Covering the initial eruption of Islam into Syria and Iraq, Donner's scholarly 1981 investigation of the importance of tribal and clan allegiances among the first Arab conquerors remains seminal reading.

John Baggot Glubb, *The Great Arab Conquests* (Quartet Books UK). Published in 1963, this is a definitive military account of the first great Muslim eruption, written by a British officer who famously describes Islam as "a soldier's religion."

Albert Hourani, *A History of the Arab Peoples* (MJF Books US). Without question Hourani is the most reliable, most erudite and perhaps most elegant guide to the history of his own people— which, in large measure, he conceives also to be the history of Islam itself.

Hugh Kennedy, *The Prophet and the Age of the Caliphates* (Longman). A no-nonsense textbook that summarizes the growth of Islam from its origins through to the 11th century.

Ibn Ishaq, *The Life of Muhammad* (Oxford University Press o/p). The earliest attempt at a biography of Muhammad, Ibn Ishaq's *Sirat Rasul Allah* survives only in passages transmitted by Ibn Hashim, which are here translated by A. Guillaume.

Kanan Makiya, *The Rock: A tale of Seventh-Century Jerusalem* (Constable). Makiya's reconstruction of the events that led to Caliph Umar laying claim to a site that was already sacred to Jews and Christians, and which has remained a bone of contention ever since, is as readable as it is imaginative and non-partisan.

Annemarie Schimmel, *And Muhammad is His Messenger: The Veneration of the Prophet in Islamic Piety* (University of North Carolina Press). No other book, perhaps, examines so carefully or so well the centrality of Muhammad in Islamic culture and society.

W. Montgomery Watt, *Muhammad: Prophet and Statesman* (Oxford University Press). Although published in 1961, this remains a landmark Western biography of Muhammad, providing as it does a distillation of two previous and important books by Watt—*Muhammad at Mecca* (Oxford University Press o/p) and *Muhammad at Medina* (Oxford University Press o/p).

ISLAM IN THE MIDDLE AGES

M. Brett and E. Fentress, *The Berbers* (Blackwell). Part of Blackwell's "Peoples of Africa" series, this is the best general introduction to the development of Islam in the Maghreb.

C.W. Ernst, *The Shambhala Guide to Sufism* (Shambhala Press). Of the introductions to Sufism—the "mystic wing" of Islam—currently available, this is probably the most sympathetic and engaging.

Richard Fletcher, *Moorish Spain* (Phoenix UK). Richard Fletcher's description of the Islamic conquest of Spain, the accommodation that was reached between Muslims and Christians, and how it all went wrong is rightly regarded as a model essay in popular Hispanic studies.

Michael Haag, *The Timeline History of Egypt* (Barnes and Noble). In Haag's perspective, stretching back over 5000 years of Egyptian history, Islam is a late-comer, but its arrival is finely covered and there is a particularly useful further reading section.

C. Hillenbrand, *The Crusades: Islamic Perspectives* (Edinburgh University Press UK). Hillenbrand reviews and voices the crusades as seen from the "other" side.

Ibn Battuta, *The Travels of Ibn Battuta* (Picador; Hyperion Books). Clocking up in excess of 70,000 miles, Ibn Battuta was probably the most widely traveled human being before the advent of air travel, and his journals are rightly regarded as a classic inside and outside Islam. This translation is by Tim Mackintosh-Smith.

Ibn Khaldun, *The Muqadimmah: An Introduction to History* (Princeton University Press US). Ibn Khaldun's "Prologema," as it was known in Europe, ranks among the greatest achievements of historians anywhere and deserves to be more widely read than it is. Of the handful of translations that have been made, this by F. Rosenthal is recommended.

Bernard Lewis, *The Assassins* (Saqi Books; Basic Books). A distinguished historian of Islam paints a compelling portrait of the sect famed for its murderousness.

Robert Marshall, *Storm from the East: from Genghis Khan to Khubilai Khan* (BBC Books o/p; University of California Press). In a book that was first published to accompany a dazzling BBC television series about the Mongol invasions, Marshall exposes the devastating impact Genghis Khan and his successors wrought not just upon Islam, but almost the whole of Eurasia.

R.A. Nicholson, *Rumi: Poet and Mystic 1207–1273* (Samuel Weisler US). The Western reader is well served by this educated introduction to the life and work of al-Rumi, which contains generous extracts from his poetry in translation.

Steven Runciman, *History of the Crusades* (Cambridge University Press). Still the most elegant, as well as scholarly, introduction to the crusades. In three volumes.

Annemarie Schimmel, *Mystical Dimensions of Islam* (University of North Carolina Press). Schimmel's study of Sufism has deservedly gained a reputation as the best scholarly introduction to the subject.

J.S.Trimingham, *The Sufi Orders* (Oxford University Press). Trimingham provides the essential map to the many different Sufic associations that began sprouting in Islam from the 11th century onwards.

Justin Wintle, *The Rough Guide Chronicle: Spain* (Rough Guides). Although this Chronicle necessarily tells the story of Spain as primarily a European, and at times ardently Christian, nation, its middle sections plot the arrival, settlement and final expulsion of Spain's Muslim conquerors over a period of eight hundred years.

W. Montgomery Watt, *The Majesty That Was Islam: The Islamic world 661–1100* (Sidgwick and Jackson; Palgrave Macmillan). In common with many other Western commentators, Watt takes the view that Islam reached its apogee under the Umayyads and earlier Abbasids, at a time when European civilization was struggling to regroup.

M.J.L. Young, J.D. Latham and R.B. Serjeant, *Religion, Learning and Science in the Abbasid Period* (Cambridge University Press). Although this makes up a single volume in the *Cambridge History of Arabic Literature*, its remit is much wider, providing a balanced, scholarly assessment of Islam's claims to be the world's premier civilization—in the 10th century at least.

THE PERIOD OF THE OTTOMAN, SAFAVID AND MUGHAL EMPIRES

E. Atil, *The Age of Sultan Süleyman the Magnificent* (Washington National Art Gallery). Focusing on the splendors of Suleiman's court at Constantinople, Atil's beautifully illustrated study reveals why for a time the Ottomans were the envy of Europe.

Lesley Blanch, *The Sabres of Paradise* (John Murray o/p; Carroll & Graff). Blanch unashamedly romanticizes Sheikh Shamil's war of resistance against Russian imperialists in the Caucasus in the mid-19th century, but this is a thumping read nevertheless.

Bamber Gascoigne, *A Brief History of the Great Moghuls* (Constable Robinson UK). An abridged version of *The Great Moghuls*, now sadly out of print, this retains enough of Gascoigne's original text to make it an unusually alert guide to the multiple achievements of the earlier Mughal emperors.

Dilip Hiro, *The Timeline History of India* (Barnes and Noble). Turning to the country of his birth, this veteran analyst of Middle Eastern affairs demonstrates how the Afghan sultans and Mughal emperors impacted on Hindu culture, creating social divisions but adding to India's astonishing diversity.

Peter Hopkirk, *The Great Game* (John Murray; Kodansha International). Hopkirk's account of the tussle between Britain and Russia for control over Central Asia in the 19th century is the bedrock of any understanding about what really went on in the region.

H. Inalcik, *The Ottoman Empire: The Classical Age 1300–1600* (Phoenix Press UK). Inalcik's is a Turkish view of the Ottomans during the period of their greatness—learned, cultured and hugely absorbing.

John Keay, *The Honourable Company: A History of the East India Company* (HarperCollins). This is the standard—and very creditable—history of the principal instrument of British aggrandizement in India, which put paid to Mughal rule.

Nikki R. Keddie, *Sayyid Jamal al-Din al-Afghani* (University of California Press). Keddie supplies a useful and well-documented biography of al-Afghani, the 19th-century Muslim ideologue regarded by many as the founding father of modern Islamism.

David Morgan, *Medieval Persia 1040–1797* (Longman). Despite its title, the real subject of this clear, essential history of the country that was to become Iran is the rise and decay of the Safavid empire.

John Stoye, *The Siege of Vienna* (Birlinn UK). This classic account of the Ottomans' final attempt to drive a wedge into the heart of Europe is told with an enviable verve and a love of detail.

A. Welch, *Shah 'Abbas and the Arts of Isfahan* (Fogg Art Museum and the Asia Society US o/p). Although compiled in 1973, Welch's rounded appreciation of Shah Abbas and his remodeling of Isfahan is still a rewarding gateway into the Safavid empire at its peak.

Andrew Wheatcroft, *The Ottomans: Dissolving Images* (Penguin). Wheatcroft's is a highly readable account of the Ottomans, the empire they created in the wake of the Fall of Constantinople in 1453 and its long, painful decline. All the more annoying, therefore, that the pre-1453 Ottomans escape his attention.

ISLAM IN THE MODERN PERIOD

Leila Ahmed, *Women and Gender in Islam: Historical Roots of a Modern Debate* (Yale University Press). Widely regarded as a ground-breaking study, Leila Ahmed's 1992 book not only described the challenges facing women in contemporary Islam but helped set the stage for what is now a central issue among Islamists and conservative Muslims alike.

Peter L. Bergen, *The Holy War Inc.: Inside the Secret World of Osama bin Laden* (Weidenfeld & Nicolson; The Free Press). Bergen skillfully uncovers a dangerous alliance between religious intolerance and modern technologies.

Ahron Bregman, *Elusive Peace: How the Holy Land Defeated America* (Penguin Books). Bregman's account of mainly Bill Clinton's doomed attempts to find common ground between Yasser Arafat and Israeli leaders was written to accompany a powerful BBC television series. Spiced with interviews with all the main players.

Jason Burke, *Al-Qaeda: The True Story of Radical Islam* (I.B. Tauris). Of the many attempts to portrait the shadowy terrorist organization called al-Qaeda, Jason Burke's investigation is perhaps the most convincing.

George Crile, *My Enemy's Enemy: The extraordinary story of the largest CIA operation in history* (Atlantic Books). More than any other account so far, Crile's reveals the extent of America's ultimately catastrophic support for the mujahaddin who fought against the Soviets in Afghanistan.

Nick Fielding, *Inside al-Qaeda: Global Network of Terror* (Hurst). Focusing more on the company than its chairman, Fielding spells out just why, even if Osama bin Laden and al-Qaeda were to be taken out, they represent a phenomenon that is here to stay.

Patrick French, *Liberty or Death: India's Journey to Independence and Division* (Flamingo; Trafalgar Square). With consummate skill, Patrick French plots the demise of the British Raj in India against a rising tide of both Hindu and Muslim calls for independence, leading to the blood-stained birth of Pakistan in 1948.

Sumit Ganguly, *The Crisis in Kashmir: Portents of War, Hopes of Peace* (Cambridge University Press). By demonstrating that both Muslim militants and Indian governmental intransigence are responsible for an unrest that has lasted over fifty years, Professor Ganguly reveals why Kashmir has become a tragedy for its ordinary citizens.

Michael Griffin, *Reaping the Whirlwind* (Pluto Press). Published immediately after 9/11, Griffin's study of the Taliban and Osama bin Laden lacks depth and any great historic understanding of either Afghanistan or Islam. But if Ahmed Rashid's book clearly has the edge, Griffin's nonetheless contains a hoard of fascinating detail.

Mohamed Heikal, *Autumn of Fury: The Assassination of Sadat* (Andre Deutsch; Random House). An eminent Arab journalist gives his Western readers an array of insights into the forces that led to the murder of the Egyptian president, in the wake of his readiness to break ranks with the Arab world and negotiate directly with Israel.

Mohamed Heikal, *Illusions of Triumph: An Arab view of the Gulf War* (HarperCollins UK, o/p). As its title suggests, Heikal's book spoils the party for George H.W. Bush's 1991 victory over Saddam Hussein in 1991. Nonetheless, it is a measured account of the sort perhaps too few ensconced in the seats of Western power are prepared to read.

Dilip Hiro, *Desert Shield to Desert Storm: The Second Gulf War* (HarperCollins; Routledge). With unwavering and detailed neutrality Dilip Hiro chronicles the origins and unfolding of the Gulf War between the US-led alliance and Saddam Hussein in 1991.

Dilip Hiro, *The Longest War: The Iran-Iraq Military Conflict* (Grafton o/p; Routledge Chapman Hall). As with the previous title, Hiro proves his credentials as an impartial political analyst and observer of events with this blow-by-blow narrative of a conflict that brought Saddam Hussein face-to-face with Ayatollah Khomeini.

Dilip Hiro, *Sharing the Promised Land: An Interwoven Tale of Israelis and Palestinians* (Hodder & Stoughton; Interlink Publishing). The third volume of Hiro's "Middle Eastern" trilogy once again vindicates the virtues of its author's dispassionate, painstaking approach to tumult and upheaval.

David Holden and Richard Johns, *The House of Saud* (Sidgwick & Jackson; Holt, Rinehard & Winston). First published in 1981 when the Saudis were cresting the oil wave, Holden and Johns's revelations about the history and lifestyle of a brazenly despotic dynasty threatened to disrupt Anglo-Saudi relations.

Gilles Kepel, *Allah in the West* (Polity Press; Stanford University Press). A widely respected scholar of and commentator on Islam in the 20th century here examines the increasingly prominent presence of Islam in America, Britain and France. The translation is by Susan Milner.

Gilles Kepel, *Jihad: The Trail of Political Islam* (I.B. Tauris). Shunning the herd, Kepel argues that the eruption of Islamic terrorism since 1967 is a symptom of Islamic fundamentalism's failure to capture Muslim hearts and minds. Whether he is right or wrong remains to be seen, but more to the point his is a book of exemplary insight and sustained power, a must for anyone remotely curious about contemporary global politics. Anthony E. Roberts provides the translation.

Sayeed Rubollah Khomeini, *Islam and Revolution* (Kegan Paul International; Mizan Press). Mixing intransigence with brilliant, forceful logic, Ayatollah Khomeini gives us the reasoning behind the Iranian revolution he created. The translation is by Hamid Algar.

Michael Oren, *Six Days of War: June 1967 and the Making of the Modern Middle East* (Oxford University Press). Michael Oren rightly selects the Six Day War, when the Arabs were trounced by Israel, as the turning point in the emergence of contemporary militant Islamism.

Richard Ovendale, *The Longman Companion to The Middle East since 1914* (Longman). As its title suggests, this is a handbook to the tortuous complexities of the 20th-century Middle East with Palestine and Israel very much at its center. Facts, facts, facts, but any student should be grateful for those.

Sayyid Qutb, *Milestones* (American Trust Publications). This anonymous translation of the most widely read book by Islam's foremost 20th-century ideologue is for many the starting point of an understanding of "Islamic fundamentalism".

Ahmed Rashid, *Taliban: The Story of the Afghan Warlords* (Pan UK). First published in 2000, Rashid's updated, detailed exposure of the totalitarian practices of Afghanistan's die-hard Islamist regime became an international bestseller in the wake of 9/11, and deservedly so.

Ahmed Rashid, *Jihad: The Rise of Militant Islam in Central Asia* (Yale University Press). Capitalizing on the success of *Taliban* (see above) Ahmed Rashid produced *Jihad* in no time at all following 9/11. His revelations of a widespread Islamist movement in those former Soviet republics that have Muslim majorities are pertinent, although it is sometimes difficult to determine who is more out of control—the author or his subjects.

Malise Ruthven, *A Fury for God: The Islamist Attack on America* (Granta Books). Of the plethora of attempts to explain why 9/11 happened, Malise Ruthven's is the most impressive to date. Arguing that US policy and Islamic fundamentalism were equally to blame, Ruthven is bold enough to implicate monotheism itself as an inherently volatile project.

Malise Ruthven, *A Satanic Affair: Salman Rushdie and the Rage of Islam* (Hogarth Press; Chatto & Windus). The publication of Rushdie's *Satanic Verses* brought Islam and the secularized liberal West into cultural confrontation. Ruthven sheds invaluable light on the arguments on the Muslim side.

Ronald Segal, *Islam's Black Slaves: A History of Africa's Other Black Diaspora* (Atlantic Books; Farrar Straus and Giroux). Published in 2002, Segal's carefully researched narrative highlights one of the grimmer strands of Muslim history. But as his teasing subtitle suggests, Islam's rapaciousness towards Black Africans has scarcely been unique.

Craig Unger, *House of Bush, House of Saud: The Secret Relationship Between the World's Two Most Powerful Dynasties* (Charles Scribner & Sons). Suggesting that family honor and family advantage as well as more than a barrel of oil underlie complex political events, Unger is caviar for conspiracy theorists.

Islamic art and culture

Jonathan Bloom and Sheila Blair, *Islamic Arts* (Phaidon Press UK). A compact, well-illustrated introduction to Islamic architecture, calligraphy, textiles and ceramics.

R. Ettinghausen and O. Grabar, *The Art and Architecture of Islam 650–1250* (Penguin). One of the Pelican History of Art series, this provides a detailed and scholarly introduction to the material culture of Islam during its formative period.

Martin Frishman and Hassan-Uddin Khan (eds), *The Mosque: History, Architectural Development and Regional Diversity* (Thames & Hudson UK). The great variety of mosques that have been built around the world in Islam's 1400-year history is well captured in this comprehensive, informative and generously illustrated book.

Markus Hattstein and Peter Delius (eds), *Islam: Art and Architecture* (Könemann). This large and sumptuous volume is a comprehensive, magnificently illustrated guide to Islamic art and architecture down the ages. The historical context is always provided, and individual chapters are written by known experts. If painting and sculpture are thin on the ground, then that's because there's not a great deal to go around.

Edward W. Said, *Orientalism: Western Conceptions of the Orient* (Penguin). First published in 1978 but since republished with a new afterword, Said's critique of (mainly 19th-century) Western readings of Islam and other topics amounted to a full-scale assault on "cultural imperialism," although more recently Said himself has been criticized for overstating his case, mixing scholarship and polemic, and for remaining reticent about reciprocal misinterpretations. Nonetheless, *Orientalism* remains a landmark in the emergence of cultural relativism.

GLOSSARY

Unless otherwise stated, the terms that follow are Arabic

abd	slave; follower
al-	"the" or "of"
al-Andalus	the Islamic name for the province that contained Muslim Spain (lit. "land of the Vandals")
ahl	people
ahl adh-dhimma	protected peoples (usually Christians, Jews and Zoroastrians)
ahl al-hadith	people of the tradition—ie those who live by Islamic custom
ahl al-Kittab	lit. "People of the Book"; those mentioned in the Koran who have already received a divine revelation—ie Jews, Christians and (according to some) Zoroastrians
Alids	followers of Muhammad's cousin and son-in-law Ali ibn Talib, regarded by Shiites as the First Imam
alim	a clerical scholar (singular of *ulama*)
Allah	the god of Islam; originally an Arabic word meaning "high god"
adhan	a summons to prayer, usually issued by a *muezzin*
amir	title of a Muslim ruler: prince, commander or governor
amir al-Muminim	commander of the faithful
amir al-umara	senior amir

ansar   lit. "helpers": Muslims in Medina who received Muhammad and the *muhajirun*

ata   father (Turkic)

ayatollah   lit. "Sign of God": a senior *mujtahid*, or leading Iranian Shiite cleric (Persian)

beg (bey)   Turkic name for chieftain or military commander

bin   son (of)

bint   daughter (of)

burqa   all-enveloping dress required to be worn by some Afghan Muslim women, and made compulsory under the rule of the Taliban (1996–2002)

caliph (khalifa)   lit. "successor" (to Muhammad); a ruler of Islam who combines religious and temporal powers

dar al-Harb   lit. "abode of war"; wherever Islam is not established

dar al-Islam   lit. "abode of peace"; wherever Islam is established

dar al-Hijra   lit. "abode of exile"

dervish   a Sufi mystic (Turkic)

dhimmi   contraction of *ahl adh-dhimma*

diwan   originally the register of stipends due to warriors and prominent Muslims; later used to denote a bureaucracy

fatwa   a judgment or formal ruling based on Islamic law

faqih   a religious judge, jurist

faylasuf   a "rational" thinker or theologian whose ideas are specifically associated with Greek philosophy

fedayeen   self-sacrificers

fellahin   peasants, common people (in Egypt)

fitnah	civil war; upheaval, strife
fiqh	jurisprudence, or the study and extrapolation of Islamic laws
ghazi	a holy warrior
Hadith	the "traditions" (sometimes "sayings" or "anecdotes") of Muhammad
hajj	pilgrimage to Mecca
hanif	a true believer
haram	sanctuary
harem	women's—or, more usually, concubines'—quarters, forbidden to outsiders
Hashimites	sub-tribe of the Qaraysh to which Muhammad belonged
hijra (hegira)	Muhammad's flight from Mecca to Medina in 622; a form of exile, migration
ibn	son (of)
Ifriqiya	"Africa": name of Islamic province comprising (approximately) Libya and Tunisia
ijma	consensus; more rarely, "majority opinion"
ijtihad	independent reasoning; open-mindedness
ikhwan	brotherhood
imam	ordinarily, a prayer-leader at a mosque or stipendiary cleric; in Shiism, the Imam is the supreme religious leader
intifada	lit. "trembling" or "agitation": the Palestinian uprising in Israel
Islam	lit. "obedience"
Ismailis	a breakaway Shiite sect; also known as "Seveners"

isnad	a chain of transmission with particular reference to the preservation of *hadith*
jahiliyyah	general state of barbarism or "ignorance" in Arabia before the advent of Islam; used pejoratively to describe an un-Islamic society
jamaat	party, organization
janissary	a "new" soldier of the Ottoman empire (derived from Turkic *yen ceri*, "new troops")
jellaba	a loose-fitting over-garment of Arabian origin (usually white)
jihad	striving, struggle; holy war
jizya	a tax raised on Jews, Christians and other non-Muslims
Kabah	the holiest shrine in Islam, located in Mecca
karam	Islamic theology
khan	king or ruler (Turkic and Mongol)
Kharajites	an early sect who sought the restoration of a pure Islamic *umma*
khedive	a title meaning "great prince", adopted by the rulers of Egypt in 1867 (Persian)
Koran (Quran)	lit. "recitation": scripture revealed to Muhammad
madrasa	an Islamic school or college, often attached to a mosque
mahdi	a "guided one"; a prophet who will appear before the end of time
Maghreb	the western part of North Africa, comprising (approximately) modern Morocco and Algeria
majlis	grand council, assembly; later, parliament (Persian)
mamluk	a slave-soldier (Turkic)

mansib	in pre-Islamic Arabia, the leader of a cult or religious sect
Mecca	the holiest city in Islam, birthplace of Muhammad
Medina	the second holiest city in Islam and site of the first mosque
mihnah	inquisition
mihrab	a niche set into the wall of a mosque, indicating the *qiblah*
minaret	a tower or pillar belonging to a mosque, from the top of which a *muezzin* issues a call to prayer
minbar	the pulpit inside a mosque from which the Friday sermon is delivered by the imam
miraj	Muhammad's "night flight" of 620
mosque (masjid)	a Muslim place of worship
muezzin	one who issues a summons to prayer, usually from a minaret
muhajirun	those who followed Muhammad from Mecca to Medina
mujahaddin	religious freedom fighters
mujtahid	lit. "One fit to be followed"; a senior Shiite cleric
mufti	a Shariah expert; the religious adviser to a ruler
mullah	a learned cleric or preacher
muqallid	a follower of a *mujtahid*
Muslim	lit. "a follower" (ie of Islam)
mutawin	religious police, enforcers
muwalis	non-Arabs who have converted to Islam

Najd	the northern, arid part of Arabia
pasha	a provincial governor in the Ottoman empire (Turkish)
qadi	an Islamic judge or magistrate
Quraysh [Koresh]	the dominant tribe in Mecca at the time of Muhammad's birth, to which he belonged
qiblah	a stone or panel marking the direction in which Muslims should pray inside a mosque
qiyas	a way of interpreting the Koran by way of analogue
rashidun	the first four "rightly guided" caliphs
razzia	an Arab raid, or raiding-party
ribat	a militant religious community; the fortress in which such a community lives
salafi	the original "pure" members of the Islamic *umma*
salah	regular offering of prayers to Allah
sawm	obligatory fasting during the month of Ramadan
sayyid	a lord or chief; originally a descendant of Husayn and therefore Muhammad
shahadah	Avowal of Allah and Muhammad as His Prophet, required of all believers
shahanshah	"king of kings" (Persian)
Shariah	Islamic law based on the Koran, the *sunna* and the *hadith*
sharif [sherif	a descendant of Muhammad; noble
sheikh	a leader or nobleman (sometimes spelt *shaykh*)
Shia	from *shi'at*, meaning the "party of Ali" (see *Alids*)

Shiism	the largest of Islam's minority followings, based on the principle that Ali was the rightful successor to Muhammad
sufi	a practitioner of Sufism, or Islamic mysticism
sultan	ruler, king, emperor (originally from Aramaic *salita*, "to rule")
sunna	The customary "practices" of Muhammad and his Companions
Sunni Islam	"orthodox" or majority Islam, derived from *sunna*
sura	a chapter or section in the Koran
taifa	a party king or factional chief in al-Andalus
tanzimat	restructuring, reform during the late Ottoman period (Turkish)
tariqah	an order (sect or school) of Sufis
taqiyya	a doctrine, most often espoused by Shiites, whereby a believer may conceal his faith in order to promote Islamic ends
Twelver Shiism	the mainstream of Shia Islam, sometimes called Imamism
ulama	clerical scholars (plural of *alim*); sometimes used to denote Muslim clerics in general
umma	the community of Muslims
usul al-fiqh	sources of the law
Valide Sultana	queen mother or dowager empress during the Ottoman empire (Turkic Persian)
wafd	religious trust; charity
wakkil	In Shia Islam, an intermediary between Muslims and the Hidden Imam

Yathrib	the pre-Islamic name given to Medina
zakat	obligatory alms given to sustain the needy
zannah	"speculative" theology
Zaydis	"Fiver Shiites", a breakaway sect of "Twelver" or mainstream Shiism

INDEX

Entries in color represent feature boxes

PHOTOGRAPHY CREDITS